Bringing the Internet to School

Janet Ward Schofield

Ann Locke Davidson

Bringing the Internet to School

Lessons from an Urban District

JOSSEY-BASS
A Wiley Company
www.josseybass.co

Published by

JOSSEY-BASS
A Wiley Company
989 Market Street
San Francisco, CA 94103-1741

www.josseybass.com

Jossey-Bass books and products are available through most bookstores. To contact Jossey-Bass directly, call (888) 378-2537, fax to (800) 605-2665, or visit our website at www.josseybass.com.

Substantial discounts on bulk quantities of Jossey-Bass books are available to corporations, professional associations, and other organizations. For details and discount information, contact the special sales department at Jossey-Bass.

We at Jossey-Bass strive to use the most environmentally sensitive paper stocks available to us. Our publications are printed on acid-free recycled stock whenever possible, and our paper always meets or exceeds minimum GPO and EPA requirements.

Library of Congress Cataloging-in-Publication Data

Schofield, Janet Ward.
    Bringing the Internet to school: lessons from an urban district / Janet Ward Schofield,
      Ann Locke Davidson.—1st ed.
        p. cm.—(The Jossey-Bass education series)
      Includes bibliographical references and index.
      ISBN 0–7879–5686–4 (alk. paper)
      1. Internet in education—United States—Case studies. 2. Education—United States—
    Computer network resources—Case studies. 3. Computer-assisted instruction—
    United States—Case studies. I. Davidson, Ann Locke. II. Title. III. Series.
    LB1044.87.S34 2001
    371.33'44678—dc21   2001008231

FIRST EDITION
HB Printing 10 9 8 7 6 5 4 3 2 1

The Jossey-Bass Education Series

WITHDRAWN

Contents

For our families,
*   especially our husbands, Doug and Howard,*
*   and our children,*
*   Alanya, Heather, Emily, Jonathan, and Benjamin*
in recognition of their love and the meaning it gives to
our everyday lives

─ᴧᴧ─ Preface

Today, millions of students in the United States. and around the world can connect to the Internet from their schools. Billions of dollars have been spent to provide such access with the expectation that the information and communication resources the Internet provides will improve educational outcomes. Yet educational benefits do not flow automatically from Internet access. Attitudes and expectations; technical knowledge; classroom culture and Internet culture; and curriculum design, implementation, and follow-through all affect what teachers and students can accomplish with the Internet. In at least one critical respect, the Internet turns out to be no different from any other classroom resource. What you get out of it depends a great deal on what you put into it. Our study suggests a number of the things that students, teachers, schools, and school districts will need to attend to in order to realize existing expectations.

The five-year-long project we report on in *Bringing the Internet to School* was developed by public school and university educators to do four things: bring Internet access to numerous schools and classrooms in an urban school district, offer technical and collegial support to teachers' efforts to use the Internet in curricular activities the teachers had devised, institutionalize the use of the Internet in district classrooms, and investigate the results of these efforts. In discussing the results of this project, we focus on the problems and challenges of using the Internet in the context of the existing social organization of schools, traditional classroom structures and modes of functioning, and long-standing expectations regarding teachers' and students' classroom behavior. We also explore the problems that contrasts between the traditions and missions of those who have the Internet and those who influenced the development of the public schools created for educators who wished to use the Internet as a catalyst for change. How well educators and the school district we studied met this varied array of problems and challenges shaped the way the Internet was used in classrooms, and the form of that use clearly shaped its impact. From the findings of our study of this project, we have drawn lessons important to anyone with responsibility for the use of the Internet in the classroom.

AUDIENCE

We have written this book for anyone interested in understanding more about the use of the Internet in schools, including teachers, administrators, parents, and scholars. In addition, those interested more generically in changing education will discover many provocative ideas and findings in these chapters.

OVERVIEW OF THE CONTENTS

This book contains nine chapters and an appendix. We introduce important background in Chapter One, describing the rapid spread of the Internet in schools in the United States in recent years, the current dearth of information about the issues that schools and teachers face as they begin using this new resource, and the lack of data about the consequences of Internet use in schools. This chapter also lays out the conceptual orientation undergirding the research on which we base this book and the specific questions guiding that research. It introduces what we call the Networking for Education Testbed (NET), the large-scale Internet project that we studied, as well as the school district that undertook this project. Finally, it briefly describes the methods we used to study NET.

Teachers are often characterized as uninterested in or resistant to using computer technology in their work. Chapter Two presents evidence that teachers in the district we studied tended, on the contrary, to be very interested in gaining access to the Internet and in learning how to use it in their work. It also explores the factors that appeared to play a significant role in fostering this strong demand for Internet access.

Chapter Three discusses the implications of one of the fundamental features of Internet access: it breaches the walls between schools and the larger society in which they are embedded. Although most teachers participating in NET saw great value in connecting their students to the broader world, achieving this effectively was far from easy. This chapter examines some reasons for the generally unanticipated problems that educators encountered, including substantial differences between the organization and the culture of the schools and the Internet.

Chapter Four also deals with the ways existing norms, values, and organizational procedures in the schools shaped Internet use. Here, however, our focus remains inside the school as we explore how such things as educators' traditional understanding of the classroom as a private domain for independent professional action, their lack of familiarity with the Internet, and the fact that educators are responsible for teaching large groups of students both shaped and often limited Internet use, sometimes in quite unanticipated ways.

In Chapter Five, we consider a phenomenon of fundamental importance to making efficient and effective use of technology such as the Internet in education: the tremendous variation in the amount of Internet use at different schools, even though teachers at each participating school designed the uses they wanted for the Internet and had available to them essentially the same technical and other support services. This chapter both documents the dramatic differences that emerged in the amount and kind of Internet use at different schools and analyzes why these differences arose.

Chapters Six and Seven focus on frequent outcomes of Internet use in NET schools, looking at the classroom level and the individual level, respectively. Chapter Six argues that two broad classes of change were common in classrooms in which teachers used the Internet: (1) change in student-teacher roles and relationships and (2) change in the curriculum and the sources from which students obtained information and feedback. Chapter Seven concludes that in spite of some of the problems we discuss in earlier chapters, Internet use commonly led to potentially important changes for both teachers and students, even though not all educators or all students experienced the same kind or degree of change.

NET started as an externally funded, university-based effort whose staff of university and public school educators saw themselves as "guerillas" trying to change the educational system in their public school district. Once classrooms had begun to use the Internet under NET auspices, the challenge was to "institutionalize," that is, to establish Internet use long-term in the district. Chapter Eight explores the degree of institutionalization the district attained, first distinguishing between facets of the project that were institutionalized and those that fell by the wayside and then analyzing the reasons for these differences. As we examine the factors that led to NET's continuing impact in the district, we offer not only a description of this particular case but more general insight into the factors that may promote or undermine institutionalization of educational change efforts.

Chapter Nine, the conclusion, reflects on some of the more important findings of earlier chapters and draws a number of lessons from them about the impact that readers can expect from equipping schools with Internet access and the conditions likely to be necessary for schools to fully realize the Internet's potential to improve education. Further, it presents NET teachers' reflections on the trade-offs they would be willing to make to obtain Internet access and NET teachers' and students' reactions to the idea of losing the level of access they had obtained.

Finally, the Appendix presents a detailed discussion of our study design, data-gathering procedures, and approaches to data analysis.

ACKNOWLEDGMENTS

The study on which we based this book could not have been conducted without the cooperation and assistance of many people. Gail Futoran, Larissa Naples, and Janet Stocks, all of whom worked on this study as postdoctoral fellows, made major contributions to its conceptualization and implementation. Rebecca Eurich-Fulcer and Kelly Murphy, graduate students in social psychology and sociology respectively, also made especially valuable contributions to all phases of this work over the course of many years. Numerous other graduate students, including Helen Boyle, Mark Harrison, Judy Misko, Deena Philage, Melissa Wingert, and Kit Yassin, also contributed substantially to the work in a variety of important ways including the design of questionnaires and interviews, data gathering, and data analysis. Undergraduate students Alesha Aiken, Raelene Borochovitz, Robin Fast, Kim Jones, Sera Karinski, Michael Kelley, Thomas Koenig, Esther Malloug, Heather McCormick, Kaiyauna Parrish, Sheryl Saracena, Dawn Siciliano, Kimberly Soto, Sunita Sreedharannair, Renae Strickland, and Jennifer Voit also helped with the research in ways too varied to enumerate. Shiqi Li, Aizhen Tang, and Joel Thomas took major responsibility for analysis of much of the quantitative data on Internet account usage, and Joel Thomas also was responsible for the analysis of much of the survey data generated during the study.

The mammoth task of transcribing the thousands of pages of field notes and interviews generated by this study fell mainly on the capable shoulders of Laurie Sallows. She and Debbie Connell performed that work with remarkable patience, care, and accuracy. These two individuals, as well as Joyce Seifried, who joined the project at a later point, also did a remarkable job of organizing many parts of an extraordinarily complex data set. Debbie Connell and Joyce Seifried spent countless hours assisting in the preparation of the manuscript, and their intelligent and extraordinarily careful work saved us a great deal of time and no doubt markedly improved the quality of the end product. Thanks also to Madeline Dusseau for her assistance with similar tasks.

We would also like to express our deepest appreciation to the teachers and school librarians who let research team members become part of their everyday experiences as observers and who contributed their time so generously by participating in repeated interviews. The teachers who opened their classrooms to us day after day when all we could tell them initially was that we were trying to understand what was happening there and the role that the Internet played there deserve special acknowledgment. Only a concern about confidentiality keeps us from singling them out individually for recognition. District policymakers, central administrators, the district's technical staff, union leaders, and school principals also deserve special thanks for their cooperation with this research in spite of very busy schedules. Students in the school district we studied also made a special contribution to this work, particularly through their willingness to speak candidly and at length with us about their reactions to Internet use. Both they and their parents, whose cooperation was essential to the conduct of this research, have our thanks.

The staff of NET itself also deserves our special thanks. These individuals, as well as the project's initiators, allowed us to observe them in any and all parts of their NET-related work and responded graciously to our repeated requests for interviews and information. We deeply appreciate all they did to help us understand this very complex project, and again only a concern about confidentiality keeps us from naming them here.

Our sincere thanks also go to our families. Janet Schofield would like to express her appreciation to her mother, Sarah Ellis Ward, and her late father, William Rankin Ward, for their unfailing love and support. She would also like to thank her husband, Douglas, and her daughters, Alanya, Heather, and Emily, for enriching her life in so many ways. Ann Locke Davidson thanks her husband, Howard, and her sons, Jonathan and Benjamin, for the joy and balance they bring to her life, as well as for the ways in which they inspire her intellectual and creative spirit. She also acknowledges the important lessons her parents, Ted and Adele, and her brother, Bill, taught her about integrity, social responsibility, and tenacity.

Finally, the authors would like to thank Bob Glaser and Lauren Resnick of the Learning Research and Development Center for providing an intellectually stimulating and supportive environment that recognizes the importance of understanding how individuals learn and how educational environments can be structured to facilitate students' personal and intellectual development.

Funding for the research reported here was provided by contracts RED-9253452 and PRIME grant RED-9454715 with the National Science Foundation. Many thanks to Nora Sabelli, the program officer for this funding, for her strong interest in understanding the complexities of using the Internet effectively in schools and for her strong support and encouragement. Some of the material in this book also emerged from research conducted under contract number 42-40-94032 with the U.S. Commerce Department. In addition, grants from the Vera I. Heinz Endowment and the Buhl Foundation were essential to the successful implementation of NET. Equipment donations from SUN Microsystems's Academic Equipment Grant Program, as well as from Internet Catalyst and Apple Computers helped make possible the Internet use we studied in this research as did discounted computers from Digital Equipment Corporation and assistance from TCI of Pennsylvania. Finally, a major grant from the Spencer Foundation (number 199800209) provided essential support for data analysis and writing. However, all opinions, findings, conclusions, and recommendations found in this book are the responsibility of the authors, and no endorsement of them by the National Science Foundation, the U.S. Department of Commerce, the Spencer Foundation, the school district in which the research was conducted, or the various companies, foundations, and other organizations that made NET possible is implied or intended.

A small portion of this book has appeared previously in the place cited below. The material is reprinted with the permission of the publishers:

Schofield, J. W., Davidson, A. L., Stocks, J. E., and Futoran, G. (1997). The Internet in school: A case study of educator demand and its precursors. In S. Kiesler (Ed.), *Culture of the Internet* (pp. 361–381). Hillsdale, NJ: Erlbaum.

—◌— **The Authors**

JANET WARD SCHOFIELD is a professor of psychology and a senior scientist at the Learning Research and Development Center at the University of Pittsburgh. She is a social psychologist whose research during the last twenty-five years has explored the impact of social and technological change in educational settings. This work has led to the publication of over fifty papers and three previous books, including *Computers and Classroom Culture* and *Black and White in School: Trust, Tension or Tolerance,* which received the Gordon Allport Intergroup Relations Prize from the Society for the Psychological Study of Social Issues.

Professor Schofield received a B.A. magna cum laude in 1968 from Harvard University, where she was elected to Phi Beta Kappa. She received her M.A. and Ph.D. degrees from Harvard as well. She currently serves as a member of the National Research Council's Board on International Comparative Studies in Education as well as on its Committee on Tools and Strategies for Protecting Kids from Pornography and Their Applicability to Other Inappropriate Internet Content. She has also served as a member of the governing body of the American Psychological Association, the Council of Representatives.

ANN LOCKE DAVIDSON currently operates Educational Connections, an educational consulting firm in Portland, Oregon. She received both her Ph.D. in the design and evaluation of educational programs and her M.A. in anthropology from Stanford University in 1992. She has held research positions at both the University of Washington–Bothell and the Learning and Research and Development Center at the University of Pittsburgh. Her research focuses generally on the relationships among school and classroom features, students' construction of identity in relationship to schooling, and academic engagement. She is particularly interested in how changes in classroom practices affect students' orientations and attitudes toward learning. Her research has resulted in numerous articles as well as three books: *Making and Molding Identity in Schools: Student Narratives on Race, Gender and Academic Engagement; Adolescents' Worlds: Negotiating Family, Peers and School;* and *Renegotiating Cultural Diversity in American Schools.*

Bringing the Internet to School

CHAPTER ONE

Introduction

Schools in the United States are often characterized as highly resistant to change. They are held up as bastions of stasis and traditionalism in the midst of a society that has experienced profound and ceaseless change during the past century. Yet schools have changed dramatically in recent years in at least one area: the pervasiveness of computer technology within their walls. As little as twenty years ago, computers for student instruction were rather uncommon in most U.S. schools. But in the early 1980s, a sea change occurred and schools rushed to acquire computer technology for their classrooms. For example, between 1981 and 1987, the proportion of U.S. schools with one or more computers intended for instruction more than quintupled, from 18 percent to 95 percent (U.S. Congress, Office of Technology Assessment, 1988). In addition, the average number of computers available in schools that had them rose swiftly, increasing nearly tenfold between 1981 and 1985 ("Teachers Feel Computer Gap," 1989). Thus, computers went from being a relatively rare sight in schools during the late 1970s to appearing routinely on lists of suggested materials for schools, right alongside rulers, bulletin boards, and pencils, by the mid-1980s (Frederick, 1986; Pate, 1986). This trend continued in the 1990s; by the year 2000, the average school in the United States had one computer for every five students (Cattagni & Farris Westat, 2001). In fact, serious proposals have been made in Texas and elsewhere to replace textbooks with laptop computers, which suggests that some now see computers as absolutely central to the educational process. Just how central is made clear by the fact that more money is now spent on computer technology for U.S. schools than on books and other printed materials (Organization for Economic Co-Operation and Development, 1999).

Just as the 1980s saw computers begin to enter the schools in large numbers, the 1990s, especially the later half of that decade, saw a remarkably rapid trend toward linking these computers together, sometimes in networks within schools, sometimes in local or statewide networks, but most strikingly as part of the huge network of computer networks known as the Internet. By way of this network, schools, educators, and students have the potential to access just about any kind of material that can be stored in an electronic file. They can, for example, communicate with and work cooperatively with other individuals with Internet access by e-mail, chat, or other messaging and file transfer systems; participate in virtual reality environments; investigate scientific, literary, geographical, artistic, and historical reference materials in both text and multimedia; engage in activities from games to simulations, experiments to work sheets; and create and make widely available to others materials reflecting their interests and accomplishments through activities such as the creation of Web pages. When we speak of *Internet use,* we mean all these things and any others that students and teachers are able to dream up.

The rapidity of the Internet's arrival in schools is apparent when we consider the fact that whereas in 1994 roughly 3 percent of the country's instructional rooms had access to the Internet and its opportunities that number shot up to 77 percent by 2000 (Cattagni & Farris Westat, 2001). The rapidity of the Internet's migration into the schools is especially surprising in light of the glacial pace at which other much more basic and less expensive communication technologies, such as the telephone, have spread into classrooms.

Of course, the Internet did not arrive in schools through happenstance. Its quick spread into classrooms has been the result of many factors, including government policy, business interests, and community enthusiasm. In his State of the Union address in 1996, President

Clinton set out a policy of connecting every classroom in the country to the Internet. This policy was consistent with a slew of federal initiatives undertaken during his administration to foster such an outcome. Prominent among these was the E-rate policy, under which the Universal Service Fund subsidizes Internet connections for schools and libraries (http://www.ed.gov/Technology/eratemenu.html). The E-rate cost roughly $6 billion in its first three annual funding cycles. In addition, states and school districts across the country have begun additional major initiatives designed to link schools to the Internet.

Business interests played an important role in bringing the Internet to schools (Shade, 1999) in at least two ways. First, for many years, business leaders have been important participants in the production of widely publicized reports, such as *A Nation at Risk* (National Commission on Educational Excellence, 1983) and the *SCANS Report* (U.S. Department of Labor, 1991), that argued that technology could play a major role in solving education's problems and preparing the nation's workforce to be competitive in the increasingly global economy (Education Commission of the States, 1983). Such reports encouraged educators, policymakers, and parents to see technology as essential to effective schooling and as an engine that could power needed education reform. Second, numerous technology-based companies, including AT&T, IBM, Apple, and Pacific Bell, made schools offers designed to encourage connection to and use of the Internet that seemed too good to refuse (Lagemann & Shulman, 1999). The companies' hope was that once schools were connected to the Internet their Internet usage would yield the companies a profit.

Community enthusiasm to promote Internet use in the schools reinforced government and business efforts for the same goal. All three factors were apparent in the series of NetDays held across the United States in the mid-1990s. On NetDay in California, for example, the country's president and vice president joined more than twenty thousand volunteers, including parents and individuals representing many technology producers, in an effort to lay the more than six million feet of cable necessary to connect many of that state's schools to the Internet. More broadly, in 1996, over a quarter of a million volunteers from all around the country joined in the first NetDay to wire fifty thousand classrooms (Lagemann & Shulman, 1999). Similar efforts around the globe have helped to bring schools on-line in many other countries ranging from Finland to Singapore to Australia.

GOALS AND CONCEPTUAL
UNDERPINNINGS OF THIS BOOK

Although there is no doubt that Internet access is now commonplace in U.S. schools and that the trend toward connecting more and more individual classrooms in these schools is continuing apace, the consequences of this change are far from clear. There is considerable lack of clarity about two fundamentally important issues. First, we still do not know the actual significance for education of this change. The questions of how Internet use is likely to influence classroom structure and functioning and how it will ultimately affect students and teachers are still largely to be answered. Because of the substantial cost of providing Internet access in classrooms, understanding its impact on classrooms, educators, and students seems essential.

Second, although prior research suggests that both the nature and extent of computer use in an institution are strongly shaped by the culture and structure of that institution, we know relatively little about how the social organization of schools and the long-standing patterns of behavior within them shape use of the Internet. Yet understanding this issue is also vitally important. The ultimate value of Internet access in schools will clearly depend on the extent to which students and teachers use the Internet and on the purposes for which they use it. Thus, insight into the factors that shape schools' Internet use should suggest ways for educators to maximize the benefits and minimize the problems.

The overall goal of this book is to increase understanding of these issues by reporting the results of an intensive study of a major five-year effort, running from 1993 to 1998, to bring the Internet to the Waterford Public Schools (WPS), a large urban school district. We call this five-year effort the Networking for Education Testbed (NET). In discussing this study and the NET project, we have used pseudonyms throughout for all individuals; institutions, except for some U.S. government agencies; places; and programs in order to protect the confidentiality of those participating in this research. Similarly, we have changed individuals' titles and the names of particular departments in the district when necessary to protect confidentiality, although they still accurately reflect the general nature of each individual's or department's responsibilities.

NET was one of four large-scale Internet projects, or testbeds, that the National Science Foundation (NSF) funded in the United States.

These projects are part of a much larger number of relatively recent, large-scale efforts to use technology to improve and reform education, efforts such as the urban systemic initiatives and the Interagency Educational Research Improvement grants competition. All in all, NET procured a total of over $6 million in funding from government, foundation, and business sources. The majority of these funds came from an initial two-year grant and a subsequent three-year grant from the NSF.

NET's primary goals were to stimulate teachers in the Waterford school district to use the Internet in their work and to institutionalize Internet use in the district so that it could continue once external funds were no longer available. Specifically, the creators of NET hoped to encourage teachers at all grade levels and in all subjects to develop varied uses of the Internet in their curricula. Although project members also valued educators' use of the Internet for professional development, the emphasis was on encouraging educators to find ways to incorporate Internet use into students' everyday activities, in order to explore and demonstrate the potential of such use to improve education. The hope was that NET would function as a model for Internet activities within the nation's schools by developing approaches that other schools could successfully replicate.

NET's creators also wished to promote specific kinds of change through Internet use. The original grant proposal spoke of the need to find ways to connect teachers and students to the world outside the school and to make the tasks that students do in school less artificial and removed from their everyday lives. In addition, it spoke positively of using the Internet to facilitate active, independent student work and to enhance equity for students from diverse backgrounds. Thus, as we discuss in more detail in Chapter Six, those initiating NET expressed goals roughly in line with the view of education known as the constructivist approach, which has gained many adherents in education research circles as well as in schools (Ravitz, Becker, & Wong, 2000) in the past two decades.

In presenting findings stemming from the study of NET, this book provides the reader with a vivid research-based look at the process of introducing the Internet to schools and at the issues that can arise during this process. It also explores the consequences of such a change for classrooms, teachers, and students. However, this book is neither a how-to manual for educators desiring to use the Internet in their work nor a detailed description of the kinds of Internet projects that students can undertake in schools. Books serving each of these goals are plentiful (Cummings & Sayers, 1995; Ellsworth, 1994; Garner & Gillingham, 1996; Grey, 1999; Roberts, Blakeslee, Brown, & Lenk, 1990). Nor is this book intended as a source of ready-made recipes for successfully introducing the Internet into other school districts. The district we studied did not find a solution to all the problems that arose during NET. Moreover, there is no guarantee that the solutions that did work in the Waterford district would work elsewhere, although the fact that our findings are drawn from the study of a wide variety of schools and classrooms, a wide range of age groups, and a very diverse array of students and Internet activities should increase their value to others. Finally, consideration of the very real technical challenges inherent in the process of Internet implementation is beyond the scope of this book.

What readers will find is a close examination of the human and organizational issues and processes that shape Internet use and its consequences in the classroom. Our approach has been influenced by our prior training (one author is a social psychologist, the other an educational anthropologist) and by a theoretical perspective called the *Web model* that views computer-based systems as "social objects whose architecture and use are shaped by the social relations between influential participants, the infrastructure that supports them, and the history of commitments in the institution utilizing these systems" (Kling, 1992, p. 9). This conceptual orientation holds that "political interests, structural constraints, and participants' definitions of their situations" have major implications for how people use technology and what the consequences of such use are (Kling, 1992, p. 372).

This approach highlights the possibility that Internet use will be shaped not only by the nature of the technology itself but also by long-standing patterns of behavior and social organization within schools, the nature of the support provided to teachers and students who attempt to use the technology, and the history of computing in a particular school district. Further, this orientation suggests that anyone attempting to understand the use and impact of technology should pay close attention to the ways that access to technology influences individuals' interests and the ways they interpret its introduction in the first place. It also suggests that understanding how Internet use shapes the school environment and those in it requires attending to how such use changes aspects of the social system, such as power relations between individuals or chains of interdependence. In short, adherents of this approach do not conceptualize computers as discrete entities but as part of a social web (Kling, 1991, 1992); a tug on or alteration of one strand of the web will alter other strands and their relationships, making consideration of social as well as technical factors essential for understanding the impact of a given kind of technology on organizational processes and outcomes.

Therefore, in addition to studying such obvious issues as how Internet use affects various student outcomes, we pay considerable attention to exploring questions such as why teachers in the Waterford district chose to use or not use the Internet, why educators in some schools made much greater use of the Internet than educators in other schools, and why the school district eventually decided to institutionalize Internet use in spite of severe financial pressures and lack of compelling scientific evidence that Internet access improves the kinds of student outcomes of most salience to policymakers. We also attend closely to such issues as how Internet use can change relations between teachers and their peers as well as between teachers and students.

Existing research supports the view that simply making a given technology available to schools is not enough for schools to achieve the kinds of changes in education that many hope will follow in the wake of making such technology available (Cuban, 1986; Schofield, 1994). In the remainder of this chapter, we summarize some important findings of earlier studies of computer use in the classroom to provide a context within which readers can situate the findings that this book presents. We also introduce two major contexts that shaped Internet use in NET: that of the school district and that created by NET itself, including the individual NET schools and the project's technical design. And we briefly highlight important features of our research methodology.

COMPUTER TECHNOLOGY AND EDUCATIONAL CHANGE
What Can Schools Expect from the Internet?

The Predictions

In the tradition of the enthusiasts who have hailed the potential of other kinds of computer technology for education (Papert, 1993; Perlman, 1992; Walker, 1984), many see the Internet as having extraordinary potential for improving schools and the way they operate. For example, Carlitz (1991, p. 26) believes that the Internet "has the potential to become the foundation on which all educational programs and material are developed and distributed." Further, consistent with the widespread view that technology can bring about education reform, many see the Internet as likely to help educators achieve a variety of goals that current critics of education in the United States call for. For example, Berenfeld (1996, p. 82) argues that Internet use can bring the "real world" into the classroom. It can make schoolwork less artificial and removed from students' lives outside of school by connecting them to individuals as disparate but as potentially valuable to their education as working scientists, native speakers of languages the students are studying, and eyewitnesses to events in the students' curriculum. It also has the potential to break down barriers raised by the practice of studying each discipline in isolation. For example, it can promote interdisciplinary work by putting students in contact with individuals working on complex real-world problems that require multifaceted solutions. In addition, some have suggested that Internet access, in an instructional setting supportive of such changes, can lead teachers toward encouraging active student exploration and adopting a more interactive mode of instruction (Feldman, Konold, & Coulter, 2000). Such changes are consistent with the kinds of educational reform that many have called for over the past decade or more (Means et al., 1993).

Others predict increased collaboration between teachers as well as between schools and outside institutions. In addition, Berenfeld (1996) points out that students can use the Internet to share the products of their work with a large, geographically diverse audience outside the school, a practice many believe will increase the effort students expend on their work. Students can also use the Internet to view an extraordinary array of current information resources. Such access to the information superhighway, as the Internet was commonly called in the early 1990s, is likely to be of value to students because school library resources are both limited and dated, and textbooks are commonly dated as well.

Finally, many believe the Internet can promote equity in the country's schools through providing rich and poor schools alike with access to the same extraordinary variety of information resources and opportunities for communication (Clinton, 1996; Berenfeld, 1996). A common belief is that the Internet may foster more equitable social interactions between individuals from different backgrounds because it masks the physical markers, such as race, gender, and age, that often trigger unwarranted assumptions about the interests and capabilities of members of various social categories (Sproull & Kiesler, 1991; Riel, 1992; Zuboff, 1988).

The Realities

Yet such predictions may not be realistic. A plethora of failed reforms indicates that efforts to change schools often proceed slowly, are difficult, and frequently fail to meet their goals (Cuban, 1986; Hodas, 1996; Sarason, 1990). Despite many calls for curricular and pedagogical reform, for example, the twentieth century has seen only modest changes in classroom organization, teacher-student relationships, and instructional methods (Cuban, 1986). Reflecting on this pattern, Massachusetts Institute of Technology Professor Jerold Zacharias concluded, "It is easier to put a man on the moon than to reform public schools" (Cuban, 1986, p. 1).

Even more pertinent, studies of schools' adoption of technology have been close to unanimous in emphasizing the slowness of the process and the uncertainty of the outcome. Cuban (1986) provides a fascinating and rather sobering overview of the relationship between novel technologies and U.S. schools in the twentieth century. He demonstrates that time after time, beginning with film and continuing with radio and television, communication technologies that many hailed as having the potential to revolutionize the classroom have failed to do so. In the 1920s, for example, Thomas Edison predicted that the motion picture would soon make books obsolete (Cuban, 1986). There was similar enthusiasm for radio and television, each viewed as an improved means to bring the voices of the world's greatest leaders and best teachers into every classroom. Yet schools' use of these technologies has been far less than those outside the schools anticipated. Even more important, generally speaking, the usage that has occurred has not brought about the predicted revolutionary changes and striking improvements. Indeed, it is ironic that the radio in schools today is a contraband item that students smuggle in and use to distract themselves from classroom realities.

Likewise, many of the pre-Internet predictions that positive educational consequences would follow upon the use of computer applications in the schools have not been fully realized. Numerous scholars studying the impact of computers on what schools do and how well they do it have concluded that computers, like previous technologies, have had less impact than many had hoped (Cohen, 1987; Cuban, 1986; Hodas, 1996). For example, Cohen's analysis (1988) of computers in schools suggests that use tends to be concentrated not at the core of the educational system but at its periphery, which undercuts this technology's potential for bringing about fundamental change. Moreover, as we discuss in Chapter Five, the level of computer use that those enthusiastic about computers' potential to improve education hoped for is often much higher than the level eventually obtained (Cuban, 1986; Schofield, 1995). Although some research suggests substantial change as a result of computer use and also emphasizes that such change is likely to be evolutionary (Sandholtz & Ringstaff, 1996), the documented impact of computers in schools is still far from revolutionary.

Further, studies that have linked computer use with positive consequences have also suggested that these consequences do not necessarily stem directly from use of these machines. Rather, they often appear to stem from related factors. For example, evidence shows that the kind of structured, computer-assisted instruction (CAI) that was very popular in the 1980s, and which is still used in many districts, can have a positive effect on student achievement as commonly measured (Bangert-Drowns, Kulik, & Kulik, 1985; Hativa, 1994; Kulik, Bangert-Drowns, & Williams, 1983; Kulik & Kulik, 1991; Niemiec & Walberg, 1985; Samson, Niemiec, Weinstein, & Walberg, 1986). Applications such as intelligent tutors (Wertheimer, 1990; Mostow et al., 2000) and multimedia videodiscs can and sometimes do promote student achievement (Cognition and Technology Group at Vanderbilt, 1997; Means et al., 1993). However, changes in teachers' behaviors when using these computer applications may account for some of their apparent impact (Hativa, 1994; Schofield, 1995; Schofield, Eurich-Fulcer, & Britt, 1994).

Furthermore, intense instructional design efforts are often a crucial part of the development of software used in CAI programs, intelligent tutors, and multimedia videodiscs, and this seems to be at least partially responsible for their success (Kerr, 1996). This suggests that the particular software application educators choose can make a difference in outcomes, an observation that at one level appears obvious but that many people overlook when posing questions about the effect of computers or the effect of the Internet on education.

What Scholars Know About the
Consequences of Internet Use

To date, there has been little systematic research about the academic consequences of Internet use for precollegiate students. Indeed, as we discuss in Chapter Seven, such research is a complex and daunting task because the Internet can be used in such a broad variety of ways for such a wide range of purposes. A few studies have suggested positive outcomes for certain kinds of uses. For example, some suggest that student use of e-mail applications to communicate with others can undercut the stereotypes students have about others and broaden their horizons (Garner & Gillingham, 1996; Cummings & Sayers, 1995; Davidson & Schofield, 2002). Further, the results of teacher surveys suggest that those who often use the World Wide Web in their teaching tend to exhibit more of the pedagogical changes that many hope will stem from Internet use than do teachers who make less use of this Internet application (Becker, 1999a). To the extent that such changes in educational practice are likely to lead to improved learning for students, these findings are encouraging.

But in general, Internet use is too new in classrooms to have been studied in any depth (Windschitl, 1998), although a large number of brief reports exist in which educators detail their experiences using the Internet in schools and write about its impact, usually in quite positive terms (for example, Cahall, 1994; Donath, 1995; Christy, 1998; Curtiss & Curtiss, 1995; McCarty, 1995; Potter, 1992; Wright, 1992). Furthermore, some studies suggest that positive results require more than simply making the Internet available to students. For example, Wallace, Kupperman, Krajcik, and Soloway (2000) found that sixth-grade students tended to use Web browsers readily but naively. The students were generally successful neither at finding useful information nor at using the information they did find in a thoughtful manner. Another study points out several potential advantages in the classroom learning environment when students used the Internet but concludes that the measured learning of students in those classes was very similar to that of peers in comparison classes (Songer, 1996). Yet another major project designed to promote collaborative learning about science among students in far-flung classrooms found that teachers tended not to use the curriculum's networking features much, and it concluded, "We now believe it is critical to identify the classroom itself as the primary community of learners in which the dialogue among students takes place" (Feldman, 1999, p. 7; see also, Young, Haertel, Ringstaff, & Means, 1998). Another report based on this same work concludes, "Our thinking has evolved during [four] years of research. We are less convinced today that the Internet will provide an easy route to improved learning; we have come to believe that people-to-people connections and especially face-to-face communications play a central role in learning" (Feldman et al., 2000, p. 132).

Optimistic expectations about the Internet's ability to provide equality of educational opportunity are also not based on solid data about how Internet use works out in practice. To begin with, consider data about computer use. A number of scholars have pointed out that, far from reducing inequity in education, technology acquisition and use can reinforce it. For example, a persistent although narrowing gap exists between rich and poor districts in the prevalence and quality of the computer technology available to students, with rich districts consistently having more computer equipment and more technical and teacher support for computer use relative to the number of students they serve (Anderson & Ronnkvist, 1999; Becker & Sterling, 1987). In addition, when they do have access to computers at school, children from different backgrounds are often encouraged to use them in quite different ways, with those from more privileged backgrounds using them for more creative, less rote kinds of work (Apple, 1998; Campbell, 1984; Becker & Sterling, 1987), although this difference also appears to be waning over time (Becker & Ravitz, 1997). Finally, research suggests that, when other factors are controlled, having a computer at home has relatively little impact on the school performance of poor and minority students, although it is associated with marked positive effects on the performance of students from homes of higher socioeconomic status (Attewell & Battle, 1999).

There is no particular reason to expect patterns of Internet access and use in schools to deviate from those found for other kinds of computer applications. Indeed, existing research suggests clear parallels. For example, in spite of strong government efforts to equalize Internet access through financial subsidies of up to 90 percent of the cost of access for schools in the poorest districts, patterns of inequality persist. A survey of one thousand public schools concluded that classrooms in well-off schools were nearly twice as likely to have Internet access (74 percent to 39 percent) as those in poor schools (Mendels, 2000), and educators in well-off schools report receiving more technical and instructional support to help them use technology as well (Ronnkvist, Dexter, & Anderson, 2000). It also appears that teachers of high-achieving students are at least somewhat more likely than teachers of low-achieving students to use the Internet and to believe that it is essential to their teaching (Becker, 1999b). Moreover, students with previous experience with supportive learning partnerships energetically pursue relationships with mentors over the Internet, whereas those with fewer positive prior experiences tend not to (O'Neill & Gomez, 1998), suggesting yet another way in which Internet access may reinforce existing inequalities.

Understanding the Relation Between Internet Access and School Change

Even if some studies demonstrate that Internet access has positive consequences for some classrooms or students, there is no guarantee that it would have these results in most cases. First, Internet access does not guarantee Internet use, and it seems obvious that use must occur for there to be any realistic possibility of sustained positive outcomes. Second, because the Internet can be used in an extraordinary variety of ways, from an on-line work sheet to an unstructured tool for student communication and exploration to a mechanism for the implementation of well-planned collaborative efforts, one cannot assume that the activities for which students will use it will be part of an effective instructional plan. Third, there are no universally used, strong quality standards to help teachers differentiate well-designed Web sites from poorly designed or inaccurate ones, although resources to help educators select accurate, relevant, and usable Web sites are increasingly available. Finally, there is no reason to assume that the kinds of positive changes that often occur when teachers use CAI, artificially intelligent tutors, or well-designed multimedia videodiscs will necessarily follow from Internet use. Indeed, there is some reason to think just the contrary. For example, one of the changes that Schofield (1995) found flowing from the use of such artificially intelligent tutors was that teachers tended to increase the time they spent with weaker students because they felt confident that the tutor would be supplying the stronger students with useful instruction, allowing them to progress without necessarily needing the teacher's assistance. In the less structured and often rather chaotic world of the Internet, a teacher has no such assurance. Thus, at least some of the factors that appear to account for the achievement gains noted with other instructional uses of computing may not exist when students use the Internet.

Another issue, which we discuss in more detail in Chapter Four, is that most schools in the United States do not adequately train and support teachers to make good use of the computer technology available to them. There is little reason to expect substantially better training and support for Internet use, although growing awareness of teachers' inadequate preparation for using computer technology has led to major government programs designed to mitigate this problem. Furthermore, study after study has suggested that teachers do not feel they have the time they need to learn how to use new computer technology (Becker, 1990; Evans-Andris, 1996; Heaviside, Farris, Malitz, & Carpenter, 1995), a situation unlikely to change without significant cost or a fundamental rethinking of how to allocate teachers' time. Schools tend to allow teachers little time free from the demands of students, and they provide relatively few opportunities for teachers to engage in dialogue with their colleagues or to reflect upon their practice (Flinders, 1989; Sizer, 1985). Such school practices contribute to teachers developing "conservation strategies" (Flinders, 1989) that impede experimentation with new and complex methods and resources, including technologies.

Finally, consistent with the conceptual orientation that we described in the previous section, research suggests that the consequences of introducing any technology into ongoing organizations depend not only on the technology itself but on the context into which it is introduced. For example, introducing information technology in some work situations appears to increase productivity, but in others it decreases productivity (Attewell, 1994). Similarly, information technology reinforces existing power and authority relationships in some work situations and significantly restructures them in others (Kling, 1991). Moreover, although those deciding to spend resources on computer technology usually focus on its potential direct impact on productivity or efficiency, which in the schools would include such results as changes in student learning, such technology often has profound but slowly unfolding and unanticipated effects on the social system of the workplace, which in turn can have broad unforeseen implications for organizational functioning (Sproull & Kiesler, 1991). And virtually all the studies we cite concerning the impact of Internet use in schools emphasize the crucial importance of teachers' and students' characteristics and behavior or of the broader school context in shaping this impact. This is consistent with Walker's conclusion (1996, p. 99) that "details matter most" when trying to understand how technology influences education. It is also consistent with a long history of research on educational change that suggests that those working toward such change must be aware of the ways in which the structure and organization of educational systems influence the adoption and adaptation of innovations (Crandall & Associates, 1983; Fullan & Stiegelbauer, 1991; Gross, Giaquinta, & Bernstein, 1971; Huberman & Miles, 1984; Oettinger, 1969; Sarason, 1971; Schofield, 1982; Smith & Keith, 1971; Sussman, 1977; Van den Berg, Van Velzen, Miles, Ekholm, & Hameyer, 1986).

THE DISTRICT CONTEXT
The WPS System

Because the context in which technology is used is so important in shaping the change process and its consequences, we turn now to a description of the school district in which NET, the Internet project we studied, was conducted. Chapter Eight, which discusses the degree to which the district ultimately institutionalized Internet use, presents additional information about the district and its initial response to NET.

The WPS system is an urban district with approximately 2,900 teachers and forty thousand students. Roughly 55 percent of the district's students are African American, and a large majority of the remaining 45 percent are European American. Just under 40 percent of the students come from homes receiving public assistance, and over 60 percent are eligible for free or reduced-price lunches, which indicates a limited family income.

In spite of the fact that many of Waterford's students come from homes of relatively low socioeconomic status, which is often associated with relatively poor performance on standardized tests, the district's students, especially the younger ones, perform fairly well academically. Children in elementary school score at or very close to the national average on standardized tests of reading and mathematics skills. More than 40 percent of WPS middle school students perform above the national average on similar tests. Although fewer high school students perform as highly on these tests, almost 75 percent of

WPS high school graduates enroll in institutions of higher education. Thus, constituents of the district generally consider it to have a viable school system, and it enjoys a reasonable measure of public support.

Nonetheless, during NET's life, the WPS faced at least two significant problems that had been developing for a number of years before NET arrived on the scene. First, enrollment in the system had been declining for twenty-five years. Reflecting a concern that both European American and African American middle-class families were moving elsewhere or choosing to send their children to private schools as well as a concern about a thirty-year decline in the proportion of white students in the district's schools, school board members were immersed in a controversial redistricting proposal. This proposal, which generated heated controversy, was designed to move the district back toward neighborhood schools, the pattern that had existed before desegregation efforts started in the mid-1970s. As the district superintendent noted in a 1996 report to the community,

> The Spring of 1996 will be remembered for the unprecedented number of educational forums, public meetings and public hearings held in response to a proposal for redistricting city schools. . . . No proposal ever to come before the Board has drawn the [*sic*] level of interest and response from the community.

Second, WPS had been under severe financial pressure for more than a decade. As a result of declining property values in the region, the district's tax base had failed to keep pace with inflation, and no relief from this problem appeared likely. Coupled with sharply rising costs connected to special education, this resulted in annual budget deficits as high as $35 million during the NET years, in spite of a tax rate increase shortly before NET began. Indeed, at one point, the city council expressed a desire to audit the district's budget, implying that the district was spending money irresponsibly or that the system was corrupt. Contributing to the high cost of operating the district was a teaching force consisting predominantly of individuals with many years of experience who received higher salaries than younger individuals could command. To balance its budgets, the district had to cut staff, programs, and professional development activities and to plead for special funds from the state annually for many years. This contextual factor meant that competition for resources was fierce during NET's existence. As one district employee described it, "Every dollar has been fought over tooth and nail by everybody who has a vision that might get hold of it."

In such a situation, it is not surprising that funds for the purchase of technology were extremely limited. When NET started, the district had very little up-to-date computer equipment. In fact, a school district newsletter put out just a few months after the NET project began in 1993 said the district was at "ground zero" with regard to existing technology resources and had been in a "holding pattern" for many years due to a freeze on funds for technology purchases. It also pointed out that the computers in the district's elementary and middle schools were neither IBM- nor Macintosh-compatible and were no longer available on the market. The computers available in the district's high schools were newer, but even many of those machines were almost a decade old, which meant that they lacked the power to run many of the software applications produced in the 1990s. A consultant's report, written a year after this district self-characterization had been published, confirmed this view, saying the district "lagged behind other districts" in computer technology. District officials were often candid about the situation. As one put it, "The district is in such bad shape when it comes to technology that . . . we're talking a patient . . . near death here."

Also indicative of the district's awareness that its technology was antiquated was the fact that the district created three technology plans during NET's five-year life. Change was necessary not only because of the scarce and outdated technology in the schools but also because the district had adopted a number of computer skill standards for its graduating students; these standards were to take effect at the end of the 1990s. Similarly, the state in which the district is located was in the midst of promulgating a series of education outcome standards that included technology use standards. The first two of the district's technology plans created during NET's life, which called for spending almost $200 million and $95 million respectively, were just too expensive to gain widespread support. Even though the proposed expenditures were spread out over five or more years, they appeared too large, given that the district's entire annual budget was roughly $350 million and that there was no reason to expect the ongoing deficit to resolve itself even without the burden of major additional technology expenditures. As we discuss in Chapter Eight, toward the end of the NET project, the district ultimately adopted a third, much more modest, three-year technology plan costing $25 million and funded by a bond issue.

THE NET PROJECT

The project itself also constituted a context for the use of the Internet in the WPS district. In addition to introducing that context, we intend this section on NET to give readers an idea of the extent to which the situations of most interest to them are similar to the one studied here.

NET Structure and Staff

NET was structured as a collaboration between Fairfield University; the Waterford school district, in which Fairfield University is located; and a nearby, federally funded supercomputing center affiliated with yet another local university, which we will call Reynolds University. A high-level administrator from the school district was involved with the initial NET grant proposal as a coprincipal investigator, although a district teacher, Peter Marcus, was actually more involved in laying the groundwork for NET. In addition, the district provided some matching funds. Although the original proposal emphasized that institutionalization of Internet use within the school district was a long-term goal, most of the responsibility for implementing NET rested with people other than the district staff, a factor that eventually led to some significant conflict, as we will discuss in Chapter Eight. A university professor from Fairfield University, Don Quick, who was the primary initiator and organizer of the project, served as NET's director during the original two-year grant, and the supercomputing center was responsible for providing the required technical expertise. Responsibility for systematically studying NET was in the hands of Janet Schofield, a university professor who had recently published a book about the use of computer technology in high schools (Schofield, 1995).

The NET staff consisted of three main groups: the education staff, the technical staff, and the research staff. We discuss the first two of these groups in some detail here because they were responsible for implementing NET. Understanding their roles is important to understanding the content of this book and especially the implications of the research findings. We discuss the third group and its role in the Appendix because that group was responsible for studying NET but not for its implementation.

NET EDUCATION STAFF. The members of the NET education staff, numbering initially three and eventually four, were all experienced teachers. Although all had some experience with educational technology, their initial level of familiarity with the Internet varied greatly. The group had a variety of responsibilities. First, as we describe in Chapter Two, they provided formal and informal technical training and support and other kinds of professional development for teachers, helping educators see how they could use the Internet in their work. The education staff also brought NET and what they had learned through implementing it to the attention of educators outside the district and assisted in fundraising efforts. Second, as we describe in Chapter Eight, this group took a leadership role in working to institutionalize aspects of NET within the WPS district. As part of this effort, they were the primary liaison between NET and the school district, working with district advisory committees for various aspects of NET, maintaining a NET Web site, and publishing a NET newsletter.

In addition to carrying out these tasks, the education staff was influential in the development of many NET policies and procedures. For example, they played a crucial role in activities as diverse as crafting a policy setting forth acceptable Internet use (students and their parents were required to sign a document agreeing to this policy before students could have Internet access), designing the process through which school-based teams of educators became part of NET, crafting NET's approach to professional development activities, and deciding to what extent NET as an entity would attempt to filter the material available on the Internet.

Note that the term *NET education staff,* or *education staff,* always refers to NET staff. The terms *NET team* or *NET educators* refer to the group of teachers, school librarians, and others directly involved in NET in each NET school.

NET TECHNICAL STAFF. The NET technical staff consisted of four individuals already employed by the supercomputing center who were assigned to work part-time on NET. The specific individuals involved changed over time. As a group, they had a broad and varied set of technical skills, and they all held computer science or related degrees. They initially devoted a substantial amount of time to selecting the operating systems for the computers supplied by NET, working with educators in the NET schools to plan the wiring needed for Internet access, deciding whether a central server (a computer that manages the connection of other computers to the Internet and may also host a Web site) or school-based servers would best accomplish NET objectives, and experimenting with various kinds of connectivity at different schools. As NET progressed, they configured servers, set up and maintained computers and peripheral equipment such as printers, provided technical assistance to educators, and, as we describe in Chapter Eight, worked to build technical expertise in Internet use in the school district.

WORKING TOGETHER. Although the NET technical and education staffs had separate spheres of responsibility, they worked together very closely, and their responsibilities often overlapped. For example, NET assigned each of the schools participating in the project a pair of NET staff members, one from the education staff and one from the technical staff, who assumed special responsibility for helping teachers at that school implement proposed Internet activities. Particularly in the early stage of NET's life, there was considerable tension between members of the education and technical staffs, stemming from differences in their professional practices and routines. (For a detailed discussion of the issues that arose and how they were resolved, see Davidson, Schofield, & Stocks, 2001.) Nonetheless, over time these individuals found ways to handle such differences, and by the end of NET these problems had virtually disappeared.

School Context, Selection, and Plans

The schools that participated in NET differed in a number of ways. Moreover, each one had its own set of plans for using the Internet.

NET SCHOOLS. In all, teams of educators at twenty-nine schools—fifteen elementary schools, four middle schools, and ten high schools—formally participated in NET. These schools varied greatly in the socioeconomic status and sociocultural composition of their student bodies. So, for example, high schools participating in NET ranged from one in which 99 percent of the students were African American and 50 percent received a free or reduced-price lunch due to low family income to another in which 79 percent of the student body was European American and only 22 percent received a free or reduced-price lunch. The student bodies in the NET elementary and middle schools also varied markedly. As well, the schools varied greatly in size, the age of their physical facilities, and in their curricular emphasis.

SCHOOL SELECTION PROCESS AND COMPOSITION OF NET TEAMS. A fundamental fact shaping NET was that in spite of its substantial budget it did not have anywhere near the resources needed to bring the Internet to all the district's classrooms. Neither did it have the resources to bring all the participating schools on-line simultaneously. Thus, each year for five years, the NET staff and the project director decided how many new schools they had the resources to work with effectively. That number of new schools was then admitted to NET. In the first year, in order to get work under way promptly, NET staff chose the schools to be admitted. In all later years, a broadly constituted committee of people outside NET made the selection.

Moreover, although we refer to *NET schools*, NET did not undertake to wire entire schools or to supply all faculty at participating schools with Internet-connected computers in their classrooms. Rather, teams of educators, usually consisting of six to twelve people per school, submitted proposals for incorporating Internet use into their curricula. (We discuss this competitive procedure and the rationale for it further in Chapter Two.) It was these individuals, the *NET teams*, rather than the entire school, who received computers and who had priority with regard to receiving Internet connections and support from NET. In addition to varying in size, the NET teams also varied in composition, with some teams containing community members or the school's principal, whereas others did not. These teams also differed markedly in the extent of their members' initial familiarity with the Internet, the extent to which they included members with varying disciplinary specialties and, as we will discuss in Chapter Five, their internal dynamics. In order to provide access to as broad a cross section of individuals at each participating school as possible, NET did almost always require that a librarian be a member of each school's team. This allowed NET to place a small cluster of Internet-connected computers in the school library, where they were readily available to many more teachers and students than were typically able to use the machines placed in individual teachers' classrooms.

PLANNED INTERNET ACTIVITIES. The nature and content of the curricular projects that the selected teams proposed varied in almost every imaginable way. Some activities focused intensely on a particular discipline, whereas others were designed to support interdisciplinary curriculum units. Some proposals focused on connecting computer labs to the Internet for lab-based activities, whereas others, clearly the majority, dispersed a smaller number of computers with Internet connections throughout the classrooms of participating educators. Although educators designed most activities to enhance students' access to individuals and resources outside of the school through the Internet, others were planned to encourage students to provide information by way of the Internet to others, either within or outside the school district. Readers will find more details on the amount and kind of Internet usage that actually occurred in NET throughout the remainder of this book, especially in Chapters Two, Five, and Six.

FACILITATING INTERNET USE OUTSIDE OF NET TEAMS. Finally, although the emphasis was on providing Internet access for the NET teams selected through the annual competitions, NET's education and technical staff members tried to accommodate other educators in the district as well, in line with NET's ultimate goals of stimulating and institutionalizing productive Internet use. Thus, even though teams in only roughly one-third of the district's schools were formally selected to participate, by the time NET ended it had provided 90 percent of the schools in the district with LAN (local area networking) or dial-up access to the Internet. In addition, it had provided at least some professional development opportunities or support for teachers in most of these schools. Further, to the extent possible, the NET staff assisted those in NET schools who were not part of the formal NET teams but who were interested in using the Internet in their work. There was considerably more demand for such assistance in some schools than in others. But when members of a school's NET team could not meet this demand, the central NET staff tried to help.

Technical Design

When NET began in 1993, Internet connections in classrooms were unusual. The technical aspects of NET changed dramatically during its five-year life span as a result of two factors. The first was a planned course of technical experimentation designed to allow NET to explore alternative approaches to providing schools with Internet access and to choose those that appeared to work best. The second was the major changes that occurred in the broader technical environment as the Internet itself expanded and the hardware and software options related to Internet use proliferated and evolved. In addition, undergirding

NET's approach was the belief that the project should be as responsive as possible to educators' wishes, which also led to variation in the technical design at different schools. Because of all this, NET's technical structure was evolving and complex. However, because a general understanding of NET's technical structure is useful in determining which results of this project are likely to be pertinent to other situations, we briefly lay out here some of the more important information about NET's technical setup.

NET evolved from an initial setup with one central server to a distributed architecture in which each of the NET schools had its own server. These servers used BSD Unix, running on Pentium hardware. Several considerations in addition to cost figured heavily in the shift to decentralized servers. First, these servers provided each NET school with more Internet connections; schools with their own servers no longer had to compete with each other for Internet access, trying simultaneously to use a single server with a finite number of connections. In addition, this architecture allowed NET to transfer to the individual schools many system administration and other tasks that the technical staff would otherwise have handled centrally. This relieved some of the burden on the central resources, which grew increasingly heavy as more and more schools and educators joined NET. Of course, it also increased the burden on the school-based NET teams. The distributed architecture also facilitated local decision making about such issues as the creation of student Internet accounts and the allocation of disk space. Finally, various district and NET staff felt that providing schools with their own servers increased security. Separating the server used centrally for administrative purposes from the ones used by students lowered the risk that a student hacker could access administrative computers and files.

The Internet connections that NET provided also evolved over time. Initially, virtually all connections were through dial-up lines. As time went on, the technical staff tried various approaches to providing faster connectivity—such as local area data, or LAD, lines, Integrated Services Digital Network (ISDN), and Ethernet over cable. Ultimately, NET settled on 56K ISDN as its standard and replaced other modes with ISDN in NET schools. Classrooms were able to use both Macintosh and PC platforms when connecting to the Internet.

NET provided connection to a LAN within NET schools both for computers that it placed there and, to the extent possible, for other Internet-ready computers in these schools, although Internet access was usually provided to those participating in NET before the school's LAN was ready.

Once a school had Internet access, the project gave specific individuals within that school Internet accounts. These accounts were used for varied purposes including e-mail, accessing newsgroups and Internet Relay Chat (IRC), and storing personal files on disk space that NET provided.

In NET's early years, the education staff decided who should be given accounts. They routinely gave such accounts to NET team members. However, guided by a desire to encourage Internet use, NET staff also provided accounts to other educators in NET schools or to those who requested accounts in other district schools to which NET had provided Internet access; NET staff asked only that they make professional use of the Internet. Initially, most uses of the Internet required an account. However, over NET's life span, technical and other developments meant that a specific account was not necessary for more and more of the Internet activities that individuals engaged in at school. For example, once Internet browsers like Netscape had been developed, individuals were able to use the World Wide Web very easily without having to access their accounts, and this application became very popular with teachers and students over time. Similarly, the advent of free e-mail services provided by Internet service providers to anyone wishing such services also increased the range of activities that students and others without accounts could engage in using NET-provided Internet access. Students who wished to establish NET accounts needed a teacher's endorsement of their request, as well as parental permission. Although individual students sometimes made requests for Internet accounts, it was common for NET teachers to request individual accounts for entire classes of students. As NET schools received their own servers, the NET staff handed off the creation of accounts for individuals connected with that school to NET team members at those schools, consistent with NET's general philosophy of locating as much control and responsibility at the school level as possible.

Educators with home computers could obtain dial-up Internet access for those computers through NET as long as they had a NET account. Educators' home Internet access was a priority. During NET's first few years, the modem pools that allowed educators to connect to the Internet using their own modems and telephone lines were located at the two local universities connected with NET. Later, the WPS developed a modem pool of its own for this purpose, using phone lines already in place for administrative staff to use during the workday. In sharp contrast, students were not allowed to use their accounts to access the Internet outside of school for numerous reasons including concerns about the amount of traffic this would generate as well as about their making inappropriate use of the Internet. NET's policy was that "using someone else's network account is not acceptable." Indeed, this stricture was part of an acceptable use policy that students and their parents had to sign before students could have access. However, both teachers and students sometimes violated this policy.

METHODOLOGY

We describe in considerable detail in the Appendix the methods we used in our study. However, the way any study is conducted is of crucial importance in determining how readers should view its results. Thus, we briefly outline our approach here as well.

The two major methods of data gathering we used in this study were intensive qualitative observation and interviews. We selected a subset of five NET schools for intensive study, gathered a significant amount of data in an additional eight schools, and collected more limited information from the remaining NET schools. Furthermore, in order to understand the context in which NET functioned, we also gathered extensive data on the pertinent activities and perspectives of both the NET staff and those in the district charged with responsibilities related to NET.

All in all, over NET's five-year existence, we conducted more than one thousand hours of observation in milieus ranging from classrooms to school board meetings to teacher professional development sessions. Research staff made over 230 separate observations in over thirty-five classrooms in which the Internet was being used and observations of over one hundred meetings in which different groups of educators participating in NET drew up plans, discussed problems, and shared information about their accomplishments with their peers. We also observed over 180 meetings in which NET staff formulated plans, dealt with problems, and planned institutionalization of the NET project.

We carried out more than 400 semistructured, open-ended interviews, including over 170 interviews with teachers, over 140 with students, 47 with district administrators and policymakers, and over 50 with fourteen individuals who were part of NET (staff members, NET's director, and so on). We interviewed some individuals repeatedly, generally at one-year intervals, in order to obtain a fuller and more dynamic perspective than we could have from a single interview. Others we interviewed only once.

We supplemented observations and interviews with a wide range of other data-gathering activities. We collected a large amount of archival data, including all proposals submitted to NET's annual competitions, as well as a variety of planning documents, newsletters, and other written materials. We gathered a substantial amount of quantitative data, including NET server login data, responses to surveys of those who accessed the Internet through NET accounts, and responses to other questionnaires.

Analysis of such a large and varied data set, as described in the Appendix, was a complex and lengthy process. We analyzed each kind of data set in a manner appropriate to it, ranging from the qualitative coding of field notes to the production of descriptive and inferential statistics from the survey and questionnaire data.

An important goal of all this work was to develop an empirically based understanding both of the issues that arise when schools begin to use the Internet and of the ways educators respond to these issues. A second goal was to illuminate how Internet use is shaped by the behaviors and expectations of those in schools, ways in which Internet use can change schools, and the likely consequences of school Internet access and use. The chapters that follow offer a detailed picture of the issues, many of which are likely to arise in other districts as well, that NET staff, NET team members, students, and others had to grapple with as the Internet was introduced into their schools. The following chapters also explore the myriad ways that classroom and schoolwide contexts shape Internet usage, including the limitation of Internet use stemming from clashes between the cultures of the Internet and of the school and classroom, and the facilitation of Internet use by certain kinds of school context conditions. Other chapters illuminate many of the ways the Internet is used in classrooms as well as the impact of Internet use on outcomes as disparate as classroom roles and relationships, teachers' feelings about themselves and their work, and students' motivation. We begin our discussion of NET and its consequences with an issue that must be addressed early on in any effort at pedagogical change, building demand and support for the change among educators.

CHAPTER TWO

Building Demand and Support for Internet Use Among Educators

‑‑‑‑ The literature on school innovation is filled with depictions of teachers' ambivalent, cautious, even resistant responses to proposed reforms—whether pedagogical or technical. Studies of teachers' reactions to computer technology in particular, as well as technology in general, emphasize the uncertainty of the outcome of introducing technology into the classroom, as we discussed in Chapter One (Cohen, 1987; Cuban, 1986; Schofield, 1995). The technologies teachers have adopted tend to be simple, durable, and flexible. They also tend to reinforce teachers' current practices (Cuban, 1986; Hodas, 1996). Indeed, Cuban suggests that the most widely adopted technological innovations in the past century have been the textbook and the chalkboard. Both of these reinforce teachers' traditional practices; for example, both enable teachers to transmit predefined knowledge to large numbers of students quickly and efficiently. The chalkboard also reinforces teachers' authority because it supports them in dispensing knowledge from the front and center of the classroom. Further, teachers often express concern that use of technologies such as computers might disrupt traditional classroom practices and authority structures (Cuban, 1986; Schofield, 1995).

These as well as other findings have contributed to a sense that teachers' lack of acceptance of computer technology may make it difficult for computer use to live up to the promise that many feel it holds for improving education. Indeed, a major government report on teachers and technology devotes approximately the same number of pages in its first chapter to addressing the barriers to computer use in schools as it spends on the potential uses of computers there (U.S. Congress, Office of Technology Assessment, 1995).

Because teachers have shown a lack of enthusiasm for novel technologies in the past, it is clearly critical to consider factors that may affect their initial response to the availability of the Internet in their classrooms. Without teacher interest in using the Internet, efforts to link schools to this resource are likely to be pointless. Thus, this chapter focuses on factors that encouraged educator demand for Internet use in the Waterford Public Schools (WPS) district and especially on the positive relationship between a grassroots approach to technology implementation and teachers' interest in Internet access and use. We demonstrate that educator demand for Internet access was substantial during the Networking for Education Testbed (NET) project and contend that NET's grassroots approach to introducing technology played an important role in encouraging this demand.

A growing literature links teacher satisfaction and engagement to opportunities to participate in decisions concerning the organization and realization of their work (Bacharach, Bauer, & Conley, 1986; Corcoran, 1990; Dawson, 1985; Rosenholtz, 1987). When teachers themselves formulate and implement the strategies they will use for achieving program goals, commitment to specific reforms as well as to their work in general may increase (Hart, 1985; Talbert & McLaughlin, 1993; Rosenholtz, 1987). In practice, however, enthusiasm for reforms has typically come from school boards and administrators, who frequently fail to elicit the input and insights of teachers. In the worst-case scenario, teachers end up viewing reforms as burdens that administrators or university personnel out of touch with the daily rigors of the classroom or unsupportive of teachers impose upon them (Cuban, 1986; Grant, 1988; Hodas, 1996; Rosenholtz, 1987). In this chapter, readers will hear teachers themselves make similar points as they articulate the reasons a grassroots approach was important in encouraging teacher interest in the project and demand for the technology NET offered.

First, however, we provide a brief overview of NET's grassroots approach, which we argue played a significant role in fostering educators' interest in Internet use. We focus particularly on how NET policy and the approach that the education staff employed combined to promote educator responsibility for and control over Internet-based curriculum activities at the school level.

NET'S GRASSROOTS ORIENTATION
Historical Context and Approach

NET's grassroots orientation had a number of facets: the competitive selection process designed to encourage interested educators to apply, support for educator-developed Internet activities, voluntary professional development for educators, and encouragement of educators to solve their own technical and other problems. In addition, the characteristics and beliefs of NET staff reinforced NET's grassroots approach to introducing technology into the classroom.

Historical Context and Ongoing Approach

Although NET began its life as a funded project in January 1993, its roots reach back even further. In the late 1980s, Don Quick, a professor at Fairfield University who had become familiar with Internet capabilities through his work, became convinced that the Internet had great potential to enhance K–12 education by providing electronic access to resources outside the schools. Thus, he began to look for teachers in the WPS district, in which he lived, who shared or might come to share his vision. He met Peter Marcus, an elementary school teacher, who was also enthusiastic about the possibilities for education inherent in the Internet. Quick and Marcus began developing the activity that evolved into NET. They located other interested teachers in the district. At Quick's request, these teachers were given guest accounts for accessing the Internet through a server at Fairchild University. These educators explored the Internet primarily by dialing in by way of modems from their home computers.

Thus, from the beginning, the emphasis was on encouraging interested district educators to shape their own Internet use. We can also see this emphasis in the way schools came to participate in NET. Although NET personnel selected the schools that joined the project in its first year, in each of the subsequent years, teams of interested educators located in the district's schools applied for access through the annual competitive process (ACP). More specifically, groups of educators from the district's schools, prospective NET teams, voluntarily submitted proposals detailing how their school would use the Internet in service of their educational goals. Then, again reflecting NET's emphasis on widespread voluntary participation, a committee made up of parents, school board members, teachers, district personnel, foundation staff, and others chose among these proposals to award access to the number of schools NET could fund and support in that year. The rationale for selecting projects through a competition was twofold. First, because writing the proposals for the ACP took a substantial amount of work, NET project members felt that those submitting proposals would be truly interested in using the Internet, an important outcome as major responsibility for implementation rested with NET team members. Second, the competitive process was designed to ensure that the most promising Internet activities were funded, consistent with NET's goal of stimulating high-quality uses in order to explore the potential of the Internet in K–12 classrooms. To facilitate widespread participation in the ACP, the NET education staff provided a wide array of informational sessions and professional development opportunities so that interested teachers could develop strong proposals even if they were new to computer and Internet use.

NET was committed to having educators develop their own curriculum ideas to submit to the annual competition rather than having them implement prepackaged ideas proposed by the NET education staff or others. The education staff provided educators with resources, both physical and intellectual, that they hoped would help them figure out innovative and varied ways to use the Internet to accomplish educational goals. However, the education staff did not go the next step: specifying the details of how teachers could or should use the Internet. That was a challenge they left to teachers and other educators as they wrote their proposals. The assumption underlying this approach was that educators know best what is appropriate for their students. The education staff also strongly believed that educators would be more willing to invest time and energy in making their own ideas work in the classroom than in implementing Internet activities that others foisted on them.

Consistent with the emphasis on encouraging teachers to develop the curricular activities they believed were best suited to their situations, NET was flexible about the number of computers and Internet connections any NET team received and about the way it placed this technology in the participating schools. The goal was to customize the technology in a way that matched the needs of each team of participating educators.

Further, and again consistent with a grassroots philosophy, NET staff asked NET team members to develop their own capacities to implement their planned Internet activities once they had been selected to participate. NET provided each school with an education staff member and a technical staff member to contribute ideas, information, and support to NET teams as requested. However, these NET staffers did not go further to work out the details of implementing the activities the NET teams proposed. Instead, after an initial period of relatively intense training and support, NET staff encouraged participating educators to work by themselves and with other NET team members to further refine their ideas and serve as models for others in their schools. This approach was generally consistent not only with NET's philosophy but with the fact that the WPS district was in the midst of a major restructuring effort intended to transfer to individual schools many responsibilities that had previously been centralized.

Also reflecting NET's desire to support and develop educators' capacities, staff encouraged NET teams to take substantial responsibility for the technical functioning of their new computers. For example, each NET school, as we mentioned, was eventually given its own server. Rather than relying on an outside expert to set up accounts for new users or to back up the system, one or more NET team members from each school were trained to carry out these technical tasks. In essence, these NET team members worked as school-based systems administrators.

Finally, members of the education staff encouraged NET teams to work together to address local problems that impeded progress in using the Internet, rather than stepping in themselves as problem solvers. As we observed at one NET team meeting, for example, a member of the education staff told team members that they would have to take the lead in addressing internal issues threatening the security of their new computers:

Ms. Ianni [a teacher] spoke up [to a member of the education staff]. "Peter, we need some support. We need a secure room [for the school's computers]. We need Mrs. Martins [the principal] to understand that we don't want Girl Scouts and other people trooping in and out of here all of the time." . . . Peter said, "Well, you're better at that than I am," meaning lobbying to get a secure place. . . . "If you take leadership, we'll support you. But we don't want to take the leadership. You need to lead." Ms. Ianni said, "Oh heck!"

The explicit message in this and other such encounters was that teachers know best how to operate in their own school environments and that the NET education staff expected teachers to exercise their knowledge and skills to achieve desired changes before seeking support.

A final element reflective of NET's overall grassroots orientation was its staffing. The individuals the project hired to support educational activities all had substantial classroom experience in the district, giving them a preexisting network of friends, acquaintances, and former colleagues throughout the school system. Even the two of them who had served for a while as part of the district's central administration identified themselves as teachers, expressed pride about their tenure in the classroom, and frequently advertised their proteacher orientation. As Mark Schneider, head of the education staff, said:

> I'm a teacher. We're all teachers here. We don't have any of the bureaucratic hoo-hahs in here. We don't have any of that kind of stuff. We're all teachers. . . . In my opinion, that has been why this has been so successful. . . . I'm a member of the union for the Waterford Teachers Association. So I'm not on the side of the fence of the administration.

In the same vein, an observer at a training session reported in a field note:

> Nellie Watkins [a member of the education staff] was sitting at a computer next to a teacher and had been helping her for a while before I came upon them, and this teacher complimented Nellie very highly for her teaching skills. Actually, . . . she asked, "Are you a teacher?" and Nellie said, "Yes," and the teacher [then] said, "Well it's clear that you are, because everything that you say to me I understand—everything you tell me how to do I understand completely well." Nellie was very flattered by this. She went through . . . a brief description of all the places she's been a teacher and how much time she has spent doing it.

As is apparent from the preceding material, members of the education staff wanted educators to perceive them not as administrators, supervisors, or bureaucrats but rather as teachers working to facilitate a teacher-driven movement for change.

The Rationale for NET's Grassroots Approach

Although recognizing that the curricular applications educators proposed would not all be of even quality and that all NET teams would not progress at the same rate under this grassroots approach, the education staff believed that if teachers did not tailor their projects to their schools and take significant responsibility for maintaining the technology in their schools, Internet activities would be at risk on two levels. First, if educators did not develop technical skills themselves, they would remain dependent on NET staff and prepackaged curricular applications. This seemed likely to lead to drastic reductions in Internet use once NET ended. Second, teachers might ultimately choose to avoid using technology or curricular ideas that others brought to them (Evans-Andris, 1996). As one member of the education staff put it when explaining the rationale behind the staff's approach to teacher support:

> I'm not going to come in and make suggestions of what you should be using this for. . . . If I come in and say, "You're going to do this," it's not going to be successful. It has to be something you want, you decide is valuable, and then you carry it off, but I give you the support you need. . . . I mean, they either want to do it or they don't. And if they don't want to do it then it's best to put your energy in a place where somebody feels they do want to do something.

The NET education staff believed also that it is valuable for teachers to take control of their professional destinies as this may foster an increased sense of competence, efficacy, self-direction, and empowerment. As one education staff member said, a grassroots approach "allows you to be a professional rather than just a robot who's doing what somebody else spits out and tells you to do all the time. It allows you to use your abilities." And, added a second, "It builds self-reliance, it builds problem-solving skills, it makes people feel like they can—it builds independence." When asked to pick the most important outcome from Internet use in the classroom from a list of eight potential outcomes, two of the four education staff members reflected a particularly strong orientation toward increasing teacher empowerment by selecting this outcome: "Teachers have more control over the resources they use in teaching and how they are used, and therefore become more invested in their work." Although the two remaining education staff members ranked this outcome below potential outcomes for students, they too spoke at length about the perceived professional benefits of empowerment for their teacher-colleagues.

In summary, in its approach to eliciting participation and in its strategies for training teachers and sustaining their involvement, NET signaled allegiance to a grassroots change strategy starting with teachers rather than to a top-down strategy starting with policymakers or administrators. Consistent with this, as education staff members articulated their personal goals and values, they also revealed their preferences for this approach to change.

EVIDENCE OF EDUCATORS' DESIRE TO USE THE INTERNET

The demand for Internet access that emerged over the course of NET from WPS educators was substantial. Moreover, that demand was not just for computer hardware and software, though this motivation did play a role. Teachers who wanted access to the Internet appeared genuinely eager to explore its resources. Further, they expressed substantial interest in using the Internet in support of instruction and, as we discuss in the chapters that follow, found ways to bring this technology and the resources it offers into their classrooms. We found clear evidence of this drive to take advantage of Internet resources in teachers' response to the ACP, their willingness to use personal resources to facilitate Internet use, their use of NET Internet accounts, and their attendance at professional development programs.

Response to the ACP

The first piece of evidence supporting the conclusion that a great many teachers wanted access to the Internet is teachers' enthusiastic response to NET's ACP. Although NET staff made clear when they solicited proposals for the first year of the ACP that the project could support no more than half a dozen or so new NET teams, thirty-three separate proposals were submitted, involving about 250 school-based educators of whom approximately 170 were teachers. This level of response was almost double the education staff's predictions. It is all the more impressive because the district had no policy facilitating the preparation of proposals through practices such as formal release time from classroom responsibilities. Teachers prepared these proposals in addition to doing their regular jobs. They worked on them evenings and weekends, persuaded their principals to make time available for these efforts, or used informal but effective strategies for freeing time such as taking sick days. This pattern of widespread participation in the ACP was repeated in all subsequent years, despite the fact that proposals submitted to the later competitions required more information than the first ones had. For example, in addition to the text describing intended Internet activities (about ten pages), each later proposal had to include a letter from each team member expressing commitment to the Internet activities. The teams submitting proposals to the later ACPs were also encouraged to gather and submit letters of support from other individuals such as administrators, parents, and members of community organizations.

In order to avoid disappointing too high a proportion of the applicants and to even out the student age groups represented in NET, the project limited the second competition to middle schools. Of the nineteen eligible comprehensive and specialty middle schools in the district, ten applied to join NET. More than 120 middle school educators signed on as members of the ten proposed NET teams. The third competition was limited to district high schools, again to avoid having to turn down too high a proportion of the proposals. Of the eleven district high schools with no NET Internet access, nine submitted proposals, with roughly forty-five high school educators involved. The final year's ACP was open to all schools in the district. NET received a notable forty-two applications, involving more than 325 educators, to become one of nine new NET schools, in spite of the fact that the chance of any given proposal's being accepted was less than 20 percent.

In all, a remarkable proportion of the eligible schools applied to NET for Internet access. Over the four years that NET held the annual competitions, ninety-two educator teams, composed of 903 members, applied. Proposals came from teams at 74 percent of the district's elementary schools, 76 percent of its middle schools, and 92 percent of its high schools. Three of the district's other schools designed specifically to serve special populations (gifted or physically challenged, for example) applied as well.

Expenditure of Personal Funds to Facilitate Internet Activities

A second indicator of educators' interest in Internet activities is the large number of them who invested their own money and time in order to facilitate such activities. During the course of NET, a large number of NET team members purchased computer equipment, especially modems, for their homes with their own money. During NET's early days, the demand for information about what hardware to buy was so great that on a number of occasions NET staff seriously discussed the desirability of putting information on-line about the advantages and disadvantages of different setups to save themselves time and effort. One member of the education staff very familiar with the equipment purchases made by NET team members estimated that by the end of NET's first full academic year of operation, it had stimulated the private purchase of $100,000 worth of computer equipment by teachers. We have no way of determining how accurate this first-year estimate is. However, survey data certainly suggest that individual educators did spend a substantial amount of their own money on such equipment. The first survey, conducted at the end of NET's second academic year of operation, queried all adults with NET-sponsored Internet accounts. Roughly three-quarters of teachers and librarians responding ($N = 318$) reported having spent their own money to purchase new equipment in whole or in part to connect to the Internet from home since receiving access through NET. For those spending something, the most commonly reported amount spent was about the cost of a modem (between $100 and $250). In addition, about 30 percent of the teachers and librarians responding reported spending $1,000 or more, suggesting the purchase of a home computer. In all, teachers and librarians responding to the survey reported spending more than $115,000 of their own money since NET's beginning on equipment that would enable use of the Internet. Because only about 53 percent of adult NET account users replied to the survey, it seems reasonable to assume that actual expenditures were at least somewhat above this figure. A similar survey conducted two years later suggested a much more substantial expenditure of personal funds. Specifically, in that survey, teachers and librarians responding to this question ($N = 278$) indicated mean expenditures of just over $2,700 on computer equipment in whole or in part connected to Internet use since they had first received an account through NET. Even if no one else in the district spent anything for such purposes as a result of NET, an extremely unlikely scenario given the ubiquity of the reports about the purchase of home computers, responses to this second survey suggest that over a period of several years NET stimulated the expenditure of over $750,000 on equipment intended to facilitate educators' Internet access from home.

It is true that this period saw a substantial growth in the number of home computers in the United States generally (Hoffman & Novak, 1999) and also a tremendous growth of interest in accessing the Internet (McConnaughey & Lader, 1999). Thus, it is impossible to know exactly how much of the purchasing activity discussed here was due to NET, but educator after educator posited a direct connection in interviews, using words like those of this high school librarian: "Because of Networking for Education, that's why I bought my first computer . . . my home computer."

In addition to expending personal funds, teachers who bought new computer equipment invested time at home learning to use their equipment and to navigate the Internet, as was evident from the content of many calls that the NET education and technical staffs received regarding home use. The number of individual teachers and librarians in the district logging on to their NET accounts rose from only about 35 per month just after the first training sessions in the spring of NET's first year to between 524 and 566 per month three years later. (These numbers refer to the number of different individuals using accounts; they do not indicate how many times each user accessed an account.) On average, teachers spent more time on-line during nonschool hours than they did during school hours; further, the total login time during nonschool hours for teachers, which was typically home Internet use, increased steadily over the course of NET. As we discuss in more detail in Chapter Seven, during much, though not all, of this time educators used the Internet for a variety of professional purposes.

Demand for Access from Non-NET Schools and Teachers

Using the ACP as a means to select individuals to become involved in Internet use was consistent with NET's philosophy, which valued teachers' active desire to use the Internet in their work. However, as we discussed in Chapter One, it also came about because NET had neither the human nor the financial resources to support numerous Internet-based curriculum projects at all interested schools. One striking phenomenon that emerged was that teachers and administrators at many schools that participated in the ACP but failed to receive funding through NET continued to look for ways to finance Internet access and use. Some schools engaged in activities such as bake sales or

T-shirt sales to raise money for the equipment they needed. Others investigated alternative sources of grant support for Internet activities and succeeded in securing funding by this means. At least one school went so far as to find ways to spend money allocated for other purposes in their formal budget on computer equipment in order to gain Internet access, even at the risk of incurring later criticism for inappropriate use of funds. An observer of this strategy called it "an incredible end run . . . a revolt against the bureaucracy" in the service of bringing the Internet to students unable to get access through more orthodox channels.

It was also common for the education staff to get calls from educators asking whether they or their students could be given an account that would allow access to the Internet from a home or school computer even though they were not formally part of NET. NET staff granted such requests when feasible without noticeable additional expense when there appeared to be a sound educational purpose for the access. Reflecting this policy, the number of non-NET educators logging into NET accounts ranged from 256 to 284 per month three years into NET. This was a clear increase from the 19 to 49 such individuals logging in each month toward the end of NET's first year. Indeed, requests for accounts and for technical support from persons outside NET were a frequent topic of discussion during education staff meetings during later years. The staff did not want to disappoint or alienate interested individuals, but they were concerned about setting precedents they might not be able to maintain.

Demand for Opportunities to Increase Computer Skills

The NET education staff provided educators with a wide variety of opportunities to learn about the Internet and about computing generally. Among these opportunities were visits to NET schools by the education and technical staff in order to assist NET team members and a large number of open houses at which any interested educator could ask questions, get demonstrations, and begin to explore the Internet. A number of brief technical workshops focused on facilitating Internet use by teaching such things as file transfer protocols and how to use e-mail, the World Wide Web, or UNIX commands. Other workshops focused on such education-related topics as using the Internet productively in various subject areas. In NET's early years, the education staff generally led the workshops; as time went on, participating teachers were increasingly likely to lead them. In addition, NET provided extended courses, some substantial enough that the district gave graduate course credits to enrolled educators. Feeling strongly that home access was important, the education staff willingly assisted teachers in learning how to use modems to connect to the Internet from home and even went so far as to make house calls when necessary and feasible.

From NET's beginning, these workshops and similar professional development opportunities were consistently oversubscribed to the point that staff commonly had to set up waiting lists. To handle the high level of demand, staff also took steps such as scheduling extra sections of training sessions and limiting the number of sessions in which an individual could participate. Field notes suggest that even the education staff was surprised by the level of interest:

> Mark [Schneider] started off . . . the [education staff] meeting by saying to Peter [Marcus], who had been out of town last week, that the workshops were already mostly filled up. He commented that it was amazing because people were fighting to get into them.

Behaving in a way reportedly quite unusual in the school district, some teachers pressed to be allowed to attend an already overflowing multiday summer training workshop as unpaid observers, while others were being paid $500 by NET for their time. A later multipart training experience developed by the education staff that required a total of eighteen hours either on Mondays after school or on four successive Saturdays was oversubscribed even though no attendees received pay for their time. Finally, some curriculum-centered professional development opportunities held during NET's later years were filled before the education staff had even delivered the flyers announcing them to the schools. Educators learned of such offerings rapidly by visiting the NET Web page, and then they enrolled in them on-line. Broad interest in such opportunities, and in NET more generally, was apparent in the increasing number of visits to the NET Web site. Shortly after it was set up, it received about 260 visits per week, roughly 70 percent of which came from within the district. (This information was captured by an automated system specifically designed to record traffic.) Within eighteen months, this Web page received between twenty-six hundred and thirty-six hundred visits a week, roughly 45 percent of which came from within the district.

Demand from Novice as Well as More Experienced Computer Users

It would not be surprising to find teachers with substantial personal or prior professional experience with computers expressing interest in the Internet. For example, the individuals who volunteered to serve as leaders of the NET teams at the two high schools joining NET in its first year had substantial amounts of computer experience, including Internet experience, prior to joining NET. However, as we discuss at length in Chapter Four, substantial preexisting knowledge about computing or the Internet was the exception rather than the rule among NET team members, as it was among other teachers in the district. Even those who did have some prior experience with computing often had little or no experience with the Internet. For example, during NET's second year, we conducted a survey of teachers participating in a multisession training course for NET team members in the schools joining NET that year. A full 89 percent of the respondents ($N = 69$) indicated they had had little or no experience with the Internet prior to participating in the ACP.

We emphasize the high numbers of novice NET team members here because they are additional evidence of the extent to which NET succeeded in stimulating interest in Internet use. Most educators striving to gain access to the Internet through NET were not Internet aficionados eager to find some way to get that technology into their classrooms. Rather, they tended to be novice computer users, often with no Internet experience at all. Conversations with members of the education staff also provided many examples of these very low levels of prior experience. For example, Mark Schneider remarked:

> I have people coming in here who can't double-click a mouse. . . . During workshops I'd have to hold their hands—lift them off [the mouse] and hold them, say, "Stop!" This is the bifocal set—fifty years old, bifocals, never touched a mouse in their life.

NET team members themselves reported considerable initial anxiety at the thought of working with computers. For example, one NET team member remarked at the end of a training course, "I was a computer phobic this spring and now I love the Internet." NET team members and other school staff used phrases such as *computer phobia* and *fear of computers* repeatedly and without embarrassment to describe the reactions to computing of many educators including themselves. As one elementary school teacher put it during an interview:

Well, before I went through the NET training, I would consider myself computer illiterate. I was scared to death of computers. . . . Using the Internet is not difficult and I'm a person who never used a computer [before].

One proposal submitted to the ACP even argued that the existence of "fear of technology and . . . anxiety about integrating traditional teaching techniques with computer-assisted instruction" in prospective NET team members was a reason for accepting them into NET, on the theory that they would not be likely to change without the kind of assistance and support that NET offered.

Of course, the fact that novice computer and Internet users flocked to use the Internet through NET does not mean that NET in and of itself stimulated the interest. It is possible that the project just fulfilled a demand that other causes, such as the tremendous amount of attention the media gave to the Internet, created. However, there is evidence that NET itself stimulated such interest, just as it stimulated the purchase of home computer equipment for Internet access. An on-line survey that we sent to educators who had NET accounts in its fourth year asked, "To what extent has the existence of NET as a project influenced your interest in using the Internet for professional purposes?" The five answers to choose from ranged from "It decreased my interest a great deal" to "It increased my interest a great deal." Almost 75 percent of the teachers and 93 percent of the librarians responding ($N = 325$) selected the most extreme positive option provided, reporting that NET increased their interest in the Internet a great deal. Although such figures probably overestimate NET's impact, because it is likely that those responding to the survey were more positive about the Internet and even about NET than those who chose not to respond, the results of our observational work and interviews supported the conclusion that NET did play a role in sparking educators' interest in the Internet. For example, teachers frequently commented in interviews that NET itself contributed in a major way to sparking their interest in trying to use the Internet in their work. Illustrative of this are the comments of one NET team leader who described in an interview how she went to a NET informational open house at the request of her middle school's principal but found herself becoming sincerely interested in the Internet:

Everybody was kind of expected to go [to the informational session], but not forced to. . . . I thought, "I think . . . it's pie in the sky, but I'd

like to know about it." . . . So, I went to [the session], and that whet my
appetite. I became very interested in it, and that's where it . . . took off
from. . . . It just kind of developed from there.

Thus, although other factors may have stimulated interest in the Internet as well, it seems reasonable to conclude that for a variety of
reasons, NET not only fulfilled preexisting demand on the part of a
small number of educators who were already Internet users but also
sparked interest in the Internet among educators with little or no prior
active interest in it or in computing more generally.

EDUCATORS' PROFESSIONAL USE
OF THE INTERNET

We have argued that there was strong interest in and demand for
access to the Internet by WPS educators, and shortly we will go on to
discuss the factors that appear to lie behind this. However, it is possible that demand for Internet access might not translate into actual use,
for any number of reasons. For example, it is conceivable that some
of the response to the ACP was a reaction to pressure that principals
exerted on teachers rather than a genuine indication of teacher interest in the educational potential of the Internet; indeed, in a few cases,
principals did play a very active role in encouraging initially reluctant
teachers to write a proposal for the ACP. In such cases, one might
expect to find little or no Internet use in spite of high apparent
demand, because teachers are generally able to exercise a considerable
amount of autonomy in the classroom. Demand that does not lead to
use when hardware, software, and substantial amounts of technical
and other professional support are available, as they were in NET,
would be a phenomenon with little educational potential. Further,
teachers' Internet use may well not have much potential for improving education unless it is directed toward professional ends. For such
reasons, before discussing the origins of the WPS educators' demand
for Internet access, we briefly explore whether this demand was
accompanied by actual use.

When individuals wanted to use the Internet access provided by
NET, the first thing they had to do was get an Internet account. Not
surprisingly, at the beginning of NET, there were very few of these
accounts, and they belonged mainly to NET staff and the small num-

ber of individuals who had received accounts in earlier years as Don Quick and Peter Marcus tried to stimulate interest in the Internet among district teachers. Then, as time went on, the number of account holders rose dramatically. Indeed, throughout NET's life, the number of educators with accounts substantially exceeded the number who were officially part of the NET teams, in line with NET's philosophy of supplying accounts to educators whenever feasible. By NET's end, roughly forty-eight hundred individuals had accounts, and slightly more than one-third of these belonged to teachers. This meant that at this point roughly 1,650 of the twenty-nine hundred teachers in the district had NET accounts. However, we should point out that a great many educators with accounts were in situations that made use quite inconvenient. For example, many account holders were in non-NET schools with a small number of Internet-connected computers that were located far from their classrooms in the school's library.

Of course, as we have just discussed, having an Internet account is not the same thing as using it. To explore the robustness of the apparent demand for Internet use, we gathered information on account use. Over the first three years of NET, by way of automated monitoring of account use, we collected usage statistics from all schools that were formally part of NET. Although these data yield only extremely rough estimates of use, we present them to provide some indication of the general order of magnitude of Internet use by NET educators.

These data indicate, as does the large number of account holders, that educator use was occurring at a somewhat broader level than one would expect, given the size of school NET teams. For example, as of the third year of NET, 117 educators (104 teachers and 13 librarians) were on the NET teams at the fourteen schools then participating in NET. However, 316 educators from these fourteen schools, nearly three times the number of formal NET team members, logged on to their accounts during that year, 94 percent of them during school hours. Even during the month in the academic year with lowest use, the number of educators at these schools accessing their accounts substantially exceeded the number of NET team members (141 as compared to 117). Clearly, Internet use extended well beyond NET team members.

We found that during the NET's third academic year these NET school account users were logged in for a total of roughly 8,500 hours. Roughly 40 percent of this use was from home. However, consistent with research suggesting that home access predicts the amount of use professional educators make of the Internet (Becker, 1999b), numerous indicators showed that home use frequently involved professional purposes and was not exclusively personal. For example, in conversations with colleagues and in interviews, teachers reported exploring the Internet on their own time and finding resources relevant to realizing their curricular goals. One high school French teacher, for example, remarked of time spent on the Internet at home:

> It's been very exciting. It's inspiring to get on the Relay Chat and be able to communicate with people in France in French. It can be very motivational. . . . And if it's motivational for me, it's going to be motivational for my students as well. So I think that's been very, very exciting.

There is the possibility that the account use data overestimate educators' actual Internet use for two reasons. First, although NET strongly encouraged educators not to share their accounts with students but to set up individual student accounts for them, on occasion educators violated that policy, and students' use appeared to be educators' use because educators lent their accounts to students. Second, it is likely that many educators allowed family members to use their accounts from home, which would also inflate their apparent account use.

However, in actuality, it seems more likely that these data under- rather than overestimate educators' Internet use for several reasons. First of all, after NET's first year or two, many of the Internet applications most popular with teachers did not require logging on through an account from school computers. So, for example, 63 percent of the teachers and librarians responding ($N = 325$) to the on-line survey in NET's fourth year reported using the World Wide Web for professional purposes more frequently than any other kind of Internet application, and 71 percent of them indicated it was the Internet use they valued most highly for their work. Yet use of the World Wide Web by way of Netscape from school did not require an account, and hence it was not captured in NET account use statistics.

Second, consistent with the observation that nonaccount-based uses were quite common, teachers' self-reports of use indicated higher levels of use than did the account data. For example, in the on-line survey just mentioned, 60 percent of the teachers ($N = 94$) responding from the fourteen first-, second-, and third-year NET schools reported using the Internet between one and five hours per week for professional purposes. An additional 26 percent reported using the Internet for more than five hours per week to carry out professional tasks. Although such self-reports may exaggerate use for reasons connected both to self-selection of respondents and concerns about self-presentation, it seems clear that the account use data did miss important and popular educator uses of the Internet.

Finally, of course, we should note that in our discussion of educators' professional Internet use we have focused on their own use of the Internet for professional purposes and not their students' use of it under their supervision or direction. Yet classroom observation suggested that teachers were typically not logged into their Internet accounts when they used the Internet for instructional purposes with their students. Rather, in such cases, some or all of the teachers' students were logged in (depending on the number of students and computers in the classroom), but the teacher was not. Thus, the account use data just presented would not capture this kind of Internet use, although it was clearly something that NET encouraged and that did occur to a varying degree in all NET schools.

The data we present here suggest that teachers at NET schools did make use of Internet resources, both at home and during the school day. However, they do not say much about the extent to which such use affected educators' professional lives or their students. We will explore various aspects of these topics in Chapters Five, Six, and Seven. Here, we will just note that it did seem to have an impact. To take one example, educators from the set of all schools joining NET in its first three years clearly reported that Internet use had indeed influenced their work. Specifically, 88 percent of the 102 educators from these schools who responded to the pertinent question on the on-line survey indicated that access to the Internet had increased the variety of educational resources they used for school-related tasks; 76 percent responded that access to the Internet had changed either the content or structure of their classroom lessons; and 61 percent indicated that use of the Internet had greatly or somewhat affected the amount of work they did with others in support of school-related tasks. Again, these specific percentages may be somewhat inflated due to self-selection of the respondents or self-presentation concerns. However, because almost 90 percent of these NET team members responded to this question, it seems fair to conclude that, overall, educators believed Internet use did influence their work. In sum, it appears that the demand we discussed earlier in this chapter was real—it led to Internet use and even to reported change in educators' practice. We now turn to exploring the sources of this demand.

FACTORS CONTRIBUTING TO EDUCATORS' DEMAND FOR SCHOOL-BASED INTERNET USE

The existing literature suggests that teachers in general are unlikely to be enthusiastic about using new computer technology in their classrooms, so why did so many WPS educators go out of their way to become involved in NET? In this section, we describe six factors that played an important role in stimulating demand. No single one of these factors seemed to account fully for the educators' desire to attempt to use the Internet for curricular purposes. Rather, these factors combined in different ways in different individuals and NET teams to foster interest, as is often the case with complex social phenomena.

We begin by discussing three of the more obvious explanations for educators' strong interest in gaining Internet access through NET: the existing dearth of technology in the district, personal interest, and the belief that Internet use would enhance the curriculum and benefit students. We then discuss three additional factors that emanated from NET's grassroots change model: teachers' ability to design and define their own Internet projects, an emphasis on school-level change agents and their expertise, and NET's pronovice orientation.

The Dearth of Modern Computer Equipment

The dearth of up-to-date computers in the majority of the district's schools was one obvious factor stimulating demand to join NET. In addition to coping with outdated equipment, some schools reported difficulty getting approval for even minor technical upgrades, such as a new telephone line. This made the opportunity to get a substantial number of new computers quite appealing to many schools. In most cases, the desire for computer equipment appeared to be coupled with a sincere interest in gaining access to the Internet. However, there were also cases of what we call false demand, in which apparent interest in using the Internet was primarily a disguised desire for new computer equipment for other purposes. For example, a teacher told one member of the education staff, "The only reason I did the proposal was to get more [computer] hardware." This same staff member also remarked that one of the schools submitting a proposal to the ACP seemed to view NET as a "cash cow" that could be used to equip computer labs. Although the NET staff were generally positive about the educational possibilities of other computer applications, NET was designed to explore the Internet's potential for education. Thus, staff tended not to react positively to proposals unless they centered on Internet use for instructional purposes. However, NET's purpose did not prevent the submission of at least a few proposals that seemed designed primarily to get new computer equipment for other purposes. A field note from a meeting of a subcommittee involved in selecting second-year schools for NET offers another example:

> Mr. Galbraith [a physics teacher] began the discussion of the Crabtree proposal by saying that this proposal made him so angry and upset that he had picked a fight with his wife. He said that this proposal was just designed to get equipment for the teachers, and that the teachers did not really care about the students or how the equipment would be used to further their education. He went on to say that he was not even able to finish reading this proposal the first time he read it because it angered him so.

When it was apparent that the desire for computer hardware for purposes unrelated to Internet use (such as word processing, record keeping, and so forth) was the moving force behind a proposal, NET did not fund it. But that does not mean that the desire for up-to-date computers did not play some significant role in sparking apparent enthusiasm for the Internet and possibly increasing the response to the ACP above what it might have been had the district not had the antiquated technology base we described in Chapter One.

Of course, even though false demand may have inflated certain of the indicators we used to assess the level of demand for Internet access, educators' desire to have computers for alternative purposes is not necessarily a problem from an educational standpoint; there are many constructive uses for computers in schools (U.S. Congress, Office of Technology Assessment, 1995).

Interest in Internet Use for Personal Purposes

When NET began in 1993, use of and interest in the Internet was still concentrated primarily among individuals in universities and in the technical world. Even five years later, at NET's conclusion, general awareness and use of the Internet was nowhere near the levels it has reached today. Nevertheless, over NET's life, awareness and use of the Internet increased enormously in the general population. When we consider the extraordinarily rapid growth of the Internet during NET's life span, the pronounced attention that widely circulating magazines gave to it during that time, the heated controversies that swirled around proposals to regulate the Internet's content, and the strong marketing efforts of many suppliers of on-line services, it is not surprising that many educators appeared interested in participating in NET at least partly because they were curious about the Internet or because they hoped that they or their family members could make use of it.

This type of interest was reflected in the many personal uses educators pursued by way of their Internet connections. For example, educators reported exploring the Internet in order to find information on hobbies and interests and using e-mail to communicate with friends and relatives. In other cases, teachers wanted to learn about the Internet so that they could teach its use to their own children, who, they believed, might benefit.

That individuals start with personal motives for using the Internet does not preclude their coming to use it professionally. Indeed, Honey and Henriquez's survey (1993) of a large group of educators who use telecommunications for professional purposes found that 78 percent of these individuals reported that being personally interested was one of their initial motivations for involvement with telecommunications. In addition, a previous study suggests that a potentially effective long-term strategy for encouraging instructional use of computers is to introduce computing to teachers in a somewhat personal context—one in which teachers first learn to use computers to simplify some of the clerical and administrative work they perform (Schofield, 1995). A NET team leader argued similarly:

> I think most people initially get involved for personal reasons. . . . [Y]ou're doing your own e-mail and you're getting to explore for these things . . . like Debbie [a NET team member] does a lot of research for her [graduate school] papers that she does and so on . . . but I think

that's how you have to get people involved. You can't say, "We're going to do this for the children," because that's too big a step. . . . It has to be, "Buy into it for yourself," and then you start seeing how it's beneficial, and you start picking up on things. "Oh, I could do this with the kids!" . . . And then it spills over into what you're doing with the children.

Belief That Internet Access Will Increase Educators' Ability to Accomplish Valued Goals

Previous studies suggest that many teachers are not convinced technology will increase their effectiveness or their efficiency in meeting their classroom goals (Cuban, 1986; Schofield, 1995). One teacher captured this perspective pithily when he explained his failure to use a computer located in his room by saying, "It didn't do anything I couldn't do easier and cheaper on the blackboard" (Schofield, 1995, p. 103). In a related vein, Hodas (1996) points out that teachers often find change efforts insulting, in that insistence on reform implies that they are doing something wrong.

In striking contrast, NET team members did express strong beliefs during interviews and in their proposals that Internet access would benefit their work and their students in a variety of ways, beliefs that likely played a central role in fostering demand. Specifically, they tended to predict that access to the Internet would result in two main outcomes: it would help them enhance their curriculum, and it would benefit students in important ways. These patterns are clear in Table 2.1, which lists the goals for Internet use that educators most frequently articulated in over ninety proposals submitted to the ACP.

Curricular and Pedagogical Change

Educators commonly expressed two central hopes about curricular and pedagogical change. First, numerous teachers anticipated that Internet access would help them instigate or further efforts to make the curriculum more interdisciplinary. Second, many desired to use the Internet to enrich their existing curriculum in one or more ways. Specifically, many of the proposals indicated that they would use the Internet to provide more authentic learning experiences; for example, they described plans to place students in real-world language learning or writing contexts. In addition, many proposals saw Internet use

Goals Mentioned in Proposals Submitted to NET	Percentage
Curricular and Pedagogical Change	
Support interdisciplinary curriculum efforts	35
Enrich the existing curriculum (general)	30
Provide more authentic learning experiences	25
Provide more or better resources for learning	23
Change classroom roles and relationships	20
Support ongoing curricular change	20
Student Outcomes	
Prepare students for an increasingly technological world	43
Expand students' global awareness	37
Motivate students	33
Improve students' subject matter skills (for example, math, social studies)	33
Improve students' communication skills	30
Improve students' cognitive skills (for example, problem solving)	23
Increase tolerance and improve relations between various communities	20
Reach and enable at-risk students	19
Develop students' self-esteem	18
Other	
Enhance educators' professional development and collegiality	25
Meet district objectives and state standards	18
Provide access to technology for those without it	15

Table 2.1. Educators' Goals for Internet Use

Note: Proposals often included multiple curriculum activities, and any given curriculum activity could have more than one goal. Thus, the percentages displayed add up to well over 100.

as a way to connect students to a richer set of information resources than would otherwise be available to them. In accord with the argument we present in Chapter Three, that NET educators conceptualized the Internet as a tool that would help them carry out their ongoing work more effectively, these teachers commonly indicated that they hoped Internet access would empower them to work more effectively within the framework of their established curricula. That is, they did not see the Internet as a vehicle for initiating new and radical kinds of change. This vision of Internet use as a way to enrich existing curriculum activities is reflected in the following excerpts from, first, an ACP proposal and, second, a teacher interview:

> We will use e-mail to add an additional dimension to the students' experience with Japanese language and culture. . . .

> What we've tried to do is have it work for the curriculum. . . . [T]his particular class works systematically by vocabulary themes, so the [e-mail] exchange tried to reflect some of the themes that we were currently studying. . . . [T]hey talked about going to the movies in one exchange, they talked about marketing in one exchange, and the next exchange . . . will be a letter of introduction, but my students will talk about the automobile and driving. So it really hasn't changed the curriculum; it's rather reflected the curriculum.

A substantial number of proposals did indicate a desire to use Internet access to foster more fundamental change—for example, changed classroom roles for teachers and students or new kinds of linkages with the community surrounding the school. However, even these proposals typically saw Internet use as helping educators move along a path toward change that they were already traveling rather than changing their direction in a significant way.

In sum, educators most commonly thought of Internet access as something that would help them add desirable dimensions to a curriculum that already existed, not as something they would use to build a strikingly new curriculum or to instigate major change in their pedagogical practice. However, some did see it as a tool to facilitate somewhat more major changes that they were in the process of trying to realize.

Examination of the ACP proposals also suggests that educators quite commonly expressed the hope that Internet access might lead to enhanced professional development and collegiality for teachers. For example, in one proposal, the educators wrote that by way of their Internet connections they hoped to "enhance communication among staff members and access to resources in order to build a system for ongoing professional development." We discuss in Chapters Six and Seven the extent to which the kinds of hopes NET teams expressed in the proposals were realized.

Student Benefits

Teachers also saw Internet access as a mechanism for attaining a variety of direct benefits for their students. Indeed, four of the five goals most commonly articulated in ACP proposals refer to student outcomes. However, although educators often predicted that students would improve their academic, communicative, and cognitive skills by way of Internet activities, the most commonly mentioned goals, the development of computer skills and a global perspective, are not strictly academic ones in the traditional sense of basic subject matter learning. Consistent with this finding, when asked by questionnaire at training sessions for their "opinion about the eventual consequences of Internet access for students," educators ($N = 39$) indicated that they thought it more likely that Internet use would "result in educational experiences that [students] would not have otherwise" than that it would "enhance students' learning of traditional subject matter." Specifically, on a 5-point scale, with 1 being "very unlikely" and 5 being "very likely," the mean for the former was 4.4, roughly midway between "somewhat likely" and "very likely," whereas the mean for the latter was 3.6 between "neither likely nor unlikely" and "somewhat likely."

Educators appeared to believe that Internet use would lead to long-term benefits for students. Most commonly, educators mentioned the importance of preparing students for a changing world in which technology is likely to figure prominently. A proposal submitted to the ACP in NET's second year captured this sentiment:

> It is the goal of public education to produce citizens who are capable of success, people free of the anxiety of being ill-prepared to meet the demands of a modern workplace. In today's world, this means being computer literate and able to explore resources that are constantly expanding. . . . We must hurry to educate ourselves and our children

in the many uses and benefits of technology in education and our daily lives. It is, perhaps, the greatest gift we can give our students.

The belief that knowledge about ways to work with the Internet would have many long-term benefits for students appeared in interviews with teachers:

> I mean, the Internet is from my view, is a tool for . . . I hate to say a tool for life. It sounds like a GE commercial or something. . . . But, I mean, it's really giving individual citizens a lot of power, either to organize socially, organize politically, or to develop economically . . . so I think that, you know, learning the Internet to finish a research project in the twelfth grade is going to show up in that person's life in some way that you can't predict . . . [when] they are an adult. . . . So that's it. . . . I think it's limitless, the value, at this point, and we don't even know what it can do.

Many teachers believed also that Internet use might expand students' awareness of the world and counter their provincialism. Some were especially concerned about the consequences of students being isolated within homogeneous neighborhoods, schools, or communities. As one group of teachers expressed it in their ACP proposal:

> Waterford is composed of many ethnic communities each proud of their differences and heritages. A tradition among its citizens is to know only the area of the city in which they reside. Children with limited access to information and technology are isolated; their neighborhood becomes their "universe." It is also not safe for them to leave their neighborhoods because of the gang violence. Further limitations are placed on our students by an assignment to special education classes within their mainstream schools. . . . We must, therefore, enhance their academic world to broaden their horizons. We need to have our students prepared for inclusion in mainstream schools and society. One way to guarantee this adaptation is to provide access to the most current technology.

Another rather common theme in requests for Internet access was the hope that it would increase student motivation. As one NET team succinctly put it, "We want to motivate students to work beyond limits that middle school students normally set for themselves." The belief

and hope that Internet use would result in this outcome was pervasive. In surveys conducted after two different professional development sessions for members of NET teams just joining NET, educators
($N = 39$) expressed the strong conviction that increases in student
interest and motivation would occur in the context of Internet-based
projects. (On the 5-point scale we described earlier, the mean
responses from first- and second-year NET teachers to a question
about whether Internet use was likely to increase motivation were 4.6
and 4.1 respectively.) As one teacher put it in a written response to an
open-ended probe: "I feel it [the Internet] will motivate students who
may have difficulty in learning in a more 'traditional' setting. It will
also offer an edge or 'leg up' to those students that don't have the support." Thus, teachers saw the Internet both as a way to motivate the
general student population and as a way to motivate those who lagged
behind or were considered to be at risk.

The belief that Internet access would increase students' motivation
likely played an important role in stimulating demand for a number of
reasons. It seems reasonable to expect that students who are more interested in what they are doing may well learn more, a desirable outcome.
Also, engaged students may be easier to get along with in the classroom.
As teachers anticipated and as we discuss at length in Chapter Seven,
students did respond with great enthusiasm and increased motivation
to Internet activities. Teachers' perceptions of this and other benefits
likely played a role in sustaining their efforts in the face of technical or
other problems and in creating the positive opinions they expressed
about NET to teachers who were not yet participants. This enthusiasm,
in turn, may have indirectly encouraged demand for technology.

In short, teachers believed that Internet access could foster many
valued outcomes for their students. Although improving subject matter learning and various cognitive skills were certainly important in
many teachers' minds, other kinds of outcomes, such as improving
their ability to function effectively in an increasingly technological
world or expanding students' global awareness seemed at least as
important.

Ability to Design and Define Internet Activities

A fundamental assumption of any grassroots approach to change is
that individuals are more likely to commit themselves to implementing changes they instigate and design themselves than they are to sup-

port changes that others impose. In addition, advocates of the grass-roots approach argue, individuals may actively resist changes that they do not themselves ask for or instigate. Consistent with this idea, some have suggested that when efforts at school reform fail, it is partially because teachers view them as imperatives that administrators or university personnel out of touch with the daily life in classrooms impose on them (Cuban, 1986; Evans-Andris, 1996; Grant, 1988; Hodas, 1996).

The evidence we gathered in our research certainly indicates that NET educators strongly favored a grassroots approach to change and felt that such an approach encouraged teacher acceptance of change. For example, when asked on a survey to choose from among four options the best way to introduce Internet use into schools, more than 70 percent of the educators responding ($N = 325$) selected the option giving educators the most discretion: "Teachers should be free to develop and/or select Internet activities that are appropriate for their classrooms if they wish to." In stark contrast, only 13 percent selected the option giving teachers the least discretion: "Teachers should be required to use curriculum developed and/or selected by the school district's central support staff."

When asked to describe the benefits and drawbacks of NET's grass-roots approach to fostering Internet use, NET teachers and librarians emphasized that the grassroots approach helped promote acceptance because district educators were often wary of reforms promulgated by outside experts or by individuals high in the district bureaucracy. Specifically, a grassroots approach helped avoid negative or ambivalent responses that reflected teachers' attitudes toward the source, rather than the substance, of a given change. It also increased demand by attracting the teachers who generally avoided projects emanating from the district. As one middle school teacher, Ms. Danillo, put it:

> Well, one of the first advantages [of a grassroots approach], I think, is that you don't have resentment. I think as soon as you have things coming from the top down you see . . . resentment and resistance. This way you don't have that. You have nothing but a sense of people who buy into [the activities].

Another reason that the ability to design and define one's own Internet project encouraged demand, said teachers, is that individuals tend to be more committed to ideas and efforts that they themselves articulate and promote. As teacher Ms. Nacarato put it:

> I think the advantages are definitely you're going to get people, first of all, who are interested, and you're going to get them to continue with their interest if they're the ones who instigated it. . . . [T]hey take a vested interest, it seems to me, in this fashion—the way we came up with the original proposal. I think that if . . . [they] didn't, then when bumps came in the road people would be very willing to jump off.

As this teacher points out, having the responsibility to articulate one's own ideas may not only increase the chances that demand will emerge initially but also make it more likely that individuals will sustain their involvement through difficult challenges. An individual can easily abandon another's idea if it seems not to be working; it is more difficult to abandon one's own idea or one that has come out of collaborative conversations with colleagues. As we discuss in Chapter Five, patterns of use at NET schools demonstrated the importance of this kind of involvement. Specifically, we found that at schools where educators on NET teams exhibited a strong sense of project ownership and high levels of collaboration Internet use was higher overall.

One belief underlying educators' strong preference for the grassroots approach was that the specific needs and problems of students in one school may well be different from those of students in other schools. Educators preferred to tailor learning activities to fit the specific needs of their students rather than to adopt those developed by others for other students. Their ability to do such tailoring helped generate their interest in NET because, not surprisingly, teachers much more readily accept changes that they perceive to fill a specific need or solve a specific problem than those that do not (Daft & Becker, 1978). In interviews, educators emphasized the importance of tailoring projects to a school's perceived needs, as in these comments by an elementary school teacher and a high school librarian.

Ms. GERARD: I think a school knows its population of students better than, say, another outside organization. So we know our students best. We know what they would benefit best from. So on that level it's definitely better that the school be the one that makes decisions as to how to implement this.

Ms. IRVINE: Because this program has come from the people in this school, and serves a need that we have in this school, and really ties into the curriculum that we've developed for this school and specifically for restructuring—I see that as absolutely essential. If someone had come into our class and said, "Here's something that we want you to do on careers," everybody would have been very resistant to that. But because it's something . . . [of which] a lot of people on the faculty have said, "Yeah, this is a good idea. This is something that would be helpful to our kids. This is something I'm interested in doing with kids." I think that means that we will have success.

Thus, the opportunity to try to design projects to meet their own specific problems and needs played an important role in stimulating educator demand for Internet access. This motivation often does not exist in technology initiatives that the district undertakes, which may be perceived not only as an intrusion in the classroom but also as unlikely to help teachers meet their individual classroom goals more effectively or efficiently (Cuban, 1986; Schofield, 1995).

NET's Reliance on School-Level Change Agents

As we mentioned, prior to NET's formal initiation, Don Quick and Peter Marcus attempted to interest teachers in using Internet resources by providing them with Internet accounts. Over a number of years, this effort created a cadre of teachers interested in using the Internet in classroom environments. As a result, these educators provided strong grassroots support for NET, and many of them eventually became NET team leaders and participants at schools that they had helped to make NET schools.

These educators helped support and create demand for Internet access in at least two ways. First, they supported novice users who expressed some interest in the Internet but were uncertain about their technical skills. For example, one teacher explained:

I'm computer phobic. I always have been. I use the computer. I like the computer. But I don't trust the computer. It's going to do something. . . . [Y]ou know, that's the mind-set. . . . [However] Shelly [one of the cadre of early users] is here, and if I get in really deep over my head on the system, [there is an] advantage to knowing that that person here is a resource and Shelly will come and sit and walk me through.

Knowing that help was available, some teachers engaged in exploration that they might otherwise have avoided out of fear or lack of confidence. Indeed, when we asked in an on-line survey, "What is your primary source of support for questions about software or hardware?" the second most common answer that educators ($N = 325$) selected was other WPS teachers, with almost 22 percent of respondents selecting this answer.

Second, some of the cadre of individuals who had evidenced early interest in Internet use became what we might call second-order engineers of demand due to their efforts to introduce colleagues and others to the Internet. One of the most striking examples of this phenomenon was a NET team leader, Ms. Stewart, who was zealous in her efforts to spread interest in Internet use. By the time she had been team leader for about one year, she had met with teachers from eight departments in her high school and had plans to contact others. Working before and after school as well as during lunch and preparation periods, she held numerous forty-minute training sessions in e-mail for faculty colleagues and also for the school administrative and clerical staff. She constructed a handout summarizing login and logout procedures, which she used in training sessions and updated as necessary. She also acquired a bulletin board for posting news about the Internet and related topics and kept it updated with messages from NET staff as well as materials from a variety of other sources. She reported setting up a list of the people she had trained and also contacting them periodically by e-mail "to get them 'going' or even better to keep them hooked." Further, she reached out to parents by presenting a program on the Internet's use in school to her school's parent-teacher organization and reached out to other teachers in the district by leading them in professional development activities. Her ambition and enthusiasm for such activities, as well as some of the limits placed on them by her other responsibilities, are apparent in an e-mail message she sent, summarizing her activities over the course of that year:

> So far I have worked with about fifteen people. I have another eight clients (if I only could find the common time to do this!). I intend to have a number of about fifty people at Bogart High School who either use actively e-mail (supply them with a listserve in their field!!!) or who at least know how it works and that it is a very useful tool, available to all of us. . . . I will not be able to do this [reach all fifty people] due to lack of professional time. Important above all is the individual approach: learning on a one-to-one basis. . . . My personal reaction: I love to share knowledge. Teachers are *great* students. I wish I could do more.

Perhaps it is not surprising, given this individual's efforts, that her school was one of two schools that joined NET in its first year and then submitted a proposal to the ACP for expanding Internet access within the school building, adding additional teachers and their classrooms. Although NET did not accept this school's later proposal, this NET team leader continued to be very active.

NET's Pronovice Orientation

In accord with their emphasis on fostering teacher expertise and commitment, NET staff made concerted efforts to help classroom teachers, even the most novice computer users, become more expert. Specifically, as we mentioned, they granted requests for information, assistance, or accounts when at all possible, even when the information requested was of the most rudimentary sort and even when such requests came from educators formally outside of NET. In addition, NET staff proactively sought ways to improve educators' ability to use the Internet effectively. For example, knowing that teachers do not have a lot of free time at work during the school year and believing that time for on-line exploration and skill development is crucial for productive use of the Internet, the education staff arranged for teachers to take school computers home with them one summer. In addition, when possible, they made visits to the homes of teachers and other school staff to perform tasks like installing new modems or setting up connections to the Internet. Finally, on a day-to-day basis, NET education staff assisted teachers from non-NET schools who came to the staff work site with technical problems, as reflected in this anecdote from a member of the education staff:

> We have people who bring their computers in here—lug the whole computer in. I had a woman—I'll tell you one story. She's trying— she's the nicest woman in the world. . . . [I]n terms of her ability to understand technology, she doesn't know it, she doesn't know it at all. We send her the SLIP (Serial Line Internet Protocol) package [to facilitate remote access using a phone line and modem to the internet], but she can't install it. She takes [her computer] . . . back to Carl's Computer Store, "My computer is broken." I get a call from Carl's. They can't hook her computer up. . . . She gets her husband to bring the computer in here. . . . She had totally messed her computer up setting

it up. We fixed it all up. Me and Ian got it all set up, put her out there and—she's on the Net.

These activities took place in addition to the wide variety of formal training opportunities we described previously.

Educators involved with NET almost uniformly praised the efforts of NET staff. Teachers noted the staff's patience and readiness to help, as in this e-mail sent to the NET research group:

> If there is anywhere in your report for additional comments . . . I hope you will include this: I have never worked with a kinder, more helpful and patient group of people than those who administer Networking for Education Testbed. . . . I am a total dunce with regard to computers and working with them, but never once have I been treated with anything less than the utmost clarity, patience, and dignity by everyone involved with NET. I am in awe of how knowledgeable they are and it is heartwarming to experience how kind they are. I would like the people at the National Science Foundation to know that the project they are funding is being directed by a most capable group of professionals.

Some teachers also linked their interactions with NET staff to their own growing sense of confidence and expertise:

> It's been fantastic. All I have to do is pick up a phone and I get my answers. If I can't get the answer then, they'll send an electronic mail message and within a day or so I've got the answer. It's come to the point where I am now able, when we have one of our power failures, to go in and change scripts and codes [as] necessary. I know what to check and which area of the computer to see if when the power went out . . . the file was altered.

Though the ready welcoming of even the most neophyte computer users probably did not create educators' initial interest in Internet access, it appears to have contributed to developing and sustaining their interest and motivation. Further, this orientation may have contributed indirectly to increasing demand. Positive experiences and interactions with NET staff at professional development workshops, for example, may have eased initial anxieties and concerns among teachers who were considering submitting proposals to the ACP and among educators seeking to establish individual connections to the

Internet through NET. Further, positive word of mouth about the amount and nature of support available may well have encouraged initially hesitant educators to take the first step of attending such events.

CONCLUSIONS

A preponderance of evidence indicates that teachers manifested a great deal of interest in using the Internet as NET team members. First, roughly nine hundred district educators participated in the ACP, often spending many hours of their own time writing proposals. Once part of NET, teachers and other educators collectively spent hundreds of thousands of dollars of their own money to purchase computers and modems to gain home access to the Internet. Schools that did not compete successfully for inclusion in NET strove to obtain Internet access in other ways and funded the equipment they needed using various creative mechanisms. Teachers requested accounts allowing them to use the Internet and training to become increasingly sophisticated in its use even when they were not able to become a formal part of NET. And, finally, not only experienced computer users but also novices were eager to become involved in exploring the ways Internet resources could help them meet their educational goals. In short, NET began with a distinct advantage. A substantial proportion of the roughly twenty-nine hundred teachers in the district appeared willing and eager to explore the idea of using the Internet in their work, even without much in the way of concrete examples from peers about exactly what it would entail or what they were likely to able to accomplish.

Although not every educator who evidenced interest in the Internet was in fact deeply and personally committed to using the Internet professionally, a good many did enter NET believing that Internet use should be an integral part of education. Many teachers believed Internet use would benefit students, and these educators had fairly elaborate visions of how the ability to access resources and communicate with people around the globe would enhance students' education and future work lives. Others could see clear links between Internet use and their curricular goals. Still others were sure that Internet access was an important addition to their classrooms, even though they were as yet too inexperienced to articulate the ways in which they would use it or the exact contributions it might make.

NET's grassroots change model was important to both stimulating and sustaining teachers' demand for Internet access and training. Educators identified several aspects of this approach relevant to this result. These include the ability for teachers to define for themselves how they will use technology in school settings, an emphasis on school-level change agents and local expertise, and a pronovice orientation. Clearly, the kind of demand that NET's strategy inspired was at least partially related to other factors. For example, the priming of interest that occurred through existing school-level expertise was in turn related to the efforts preceding NET's establishment to involve teachers in exploration of Internet resources. In addition, NET's education staff was composed of individuals who, due to their employment history within the WPS, had prior relationships with teachers at many schools. Further, their ability to make novice users feel comfortable may have stemmed at least partly from their long experience within the district.

However, more than interest is necessary for teachers to incorporate Internet use into their curriculum. In addition to receiving training and support, educators must overcome barriers emanating both from features of the school and from features of the Internet itself. Moreover, it is critical to consider what encourages educators to translate interest into use and what then happens when use does occur. We turn to these issues in the following three chapters. In Chapters Three and Four, we describe the barriers that educators encountered as they began to implement their Internet projects. Then in Chapter Five, we turn to considering the things in addition to interest that enabled teachers to overcome these barriers and encouraged classroom-based Internet use.

CHAPTER THREE

School Versus Internet Culture

Implications for Communication with the Outside World

$\sim$

Schools are often quite isolated from the world that surrounds them. Owing to the way classes are arranged and scheduled, teachers have little contact during the school day with other adults—colleagues in their building, teachers at other buildings, or other working professionals (Stevenson & Nerison-Low, 1999). Indeed, Hargreaves (1993) has described isolation as the base of teachers' professional culture. In addition, considerations of safety, cost, and organizational efficiency typically keep students within their school's walls during the school day in spite of the fact that they can pursue many potentially valuable educational opportunities only elsewhere.

Research suggests that this isolation leads to several problems. First, schools—particularly those in less wealthy areas—do not provide students or teachers with access to the most current ideas and information, due to tight budgets and bureaucratic purchasing procedures that inhibit or drastically slow acquisition of up-to-date materials (Kozol, 1991). Second, students are exposed only to the views, techniques, and perspectives of their peers and the few adults around them rather then to the more varied perspectives of those in the broader community.

Third, teachers are less likely than many other professionals to exchange ideas and experiences with their colleagues; thus, they may not make improvements to their practice as readily as they might otherwise, and they may miss the opportunities to give and receive personal and professional support that those in other professions have (Huberman, 1993; Lortie, 1975; Little, 1982, 1990a).

Scholars have described computer networks as a possible antidote to the chronic isolation that plagues educational institutions, as "communications gateways" to content, resources, and colleagues (Bishop, 1991; Green & Gilbert, 1995; Owston, 1997; Viadero, 1997; Zehr, 1997). Such specific visions reflect more general views of the Internet as a revolutionary medium through which we "have the opportunity to build new kinds of communities, virtual communities, in which we participate with people from all over the world, people with whom we converse daily, people with whom we may have fairly intimate relationships but whom we may never physically meet" (Turkle, 1995, p. 10). With the Internet have come new visions of schools, with teachers and students benefiting from improved access to resources and classrooms made more vibrant through students' exposure to others' attitudes and ideas and through the opportunity for students to work with these others.

The majority of Networking for Education Testbed (NET) teachers demonstrated sincere interest in using the Internet as a vehicle to communicate with the external world. For example, as we mentioned in Chapter Two, more than one-third of the proposals educators seeking to become NET teams submitted listed among their goals use of the Internet to expand students' global awareness, and 20 percent listed the desire to increase tolerance and improve relations between various communities. In addition, roughly one-fourth of the proposals expressed a desire to reach beyond the school to help students and teachers access better resources or to involve students in more authentic learning situations. More to the point, teachers' actions indicated that they were serious about such intentions. As we discuss in Chapters Five, Six, and Seven, teachers and students frequently did use the Internet to transcend classroom borders to make connections with people and resources outside the school.

However, teachers also consistently reported that contact and communication with the outside world occurred with substantially less ease, less regularity, and less comfort than they had initially planned or envisioned.

Our focus in this chapter is on describing difficulties in initiating on-line communication from school and issues that can arise once students are on-line. First, we demonstrate that simply reaching the outside world by way of the Internet proved more challenging to achieve than educators anticipated. Second, we examine the ways in which on-line experiences could prove frustrating and even disconcerting for teachers and distracting for students. Concern about the nature of students' experiences on-line exerted a dampening effect on Internet use—leading some teachers to circumscribe students' time and activities on-line, as we discuss in some detail at the end of the chapter.

We embed our discussion of the challenges of using the Internet in schools in a broader discussion of the organizational and cultural contrasts between the Internet and the public school. Recognition of these contrasts, or mismatches, we argue, is critical to understanding the difficulties educators experienced when attempting on-line access and the dampening of enthusiasm that can occur once students make connections. We show, first, that the Internet and the public schools were created for fundamentally different purposes and by significantly different constituencies. Second, we consider the implications of such differences, illustrating how they create four types of mismatches that had significant implications for students' and teachers' use of the Internet to connect with others.

We emphasize that the impediments to on-line communication delineated in the following pages are not inevitable or insurmountable. Changing or varying the values, perceptions, and norms creating the mismatches might reduce the mismatches. For example, there was a striking mismatch between the materials educators perceived to be appropriate for students to access from school and the kinds of explicit sexual content now widely available on the Internet. If the sexually explicit content available on the Internet were to become less accessible to minors through government action or more self-policing on the part of the adult entertainment industry or if school and community attitudes about the kind of material that teens should be permitted to see were to become more liberal, this mismatch would be mitigated, at least in high schools. Yet, currently, there is an obvious and enormous mismatch between the world of the Internet and the world of the school in this regard.

CONTRASTING TRADITIONS

Today, both the public schools and the Internet are integral and given features of the national landscape. This makes it easy to forget that both are social and political creations that evolved in response to certain needs. Understanding some of the basic differences between the mission and the constituencies that drove the evolution of the Internet and those that drove the evolution of public schools lays the groundwork for understanding some of the difficulties that NET educators and students experienced once they began to conduct Internet-based curricular activities.

The Internet

Though no individual or group controls the vast communications network known as the Internet, it has been shaped by its historical connection to scientific and technological research settings and by the funding mandate that led to its development. The Internet grew largely out of a Cold War imperative to quickly develop new technical knowledge. In the 1960s, the Department of Defense Advanced Research Projects Agency (ARPA) began to disperse large sums of money to fund research relevant to ensuring national security. ARPA was especially interested in funding research into an electronic communication network that would ensure communication capabilities in the event of nuclear attack. ARPA believed also that such a network could reduce equipment costs because it could be used by ARPA-funded researchers across the country to reach the powerful computers they needed for their work. The end result of ARPA's funding and interest was ARPANET, which evolved with assistance from the National Science Foundation to become the initial backbone of the Internet in the 1980s.

ARPANET quickly acquired a technically oriented and academic constituency that extended beyond the individuals initially involved in its development. Due to both collegial links within the academic community and various technical developments, access to the network spread quickly, typically though not exclusively to those with institutional ties to the emerging discipline of computer science (King, Grinter, & Pickering, 1997). ARPA's Internet Engineering Task Force adopted a principle of open and easy network access in the belief that this would encourage the development of superior technology as more individuals contributed to the work (King et al., 1997). As a result, since early in the Internet's evolution, computers and operating systems that vary significantly in both technology and content have been connected to it.

The Public Schools

The origins of U.S. public schools reflect a very different set of concerns. The public schools were created to transmit established mainstream knowledge and values to diverse groups of children rather than to produce new forms of knowledge (Cremin, 1964). Beginning in the mid-nineteenth century, public school advocates argued that children from different cultural, economic, political, and religious backgrounds must be socialized to a common set of values in order to guard against irreconcilable conflicts arising between members of varied groups (Cremin, 1964). Although others have raised questions about the appropriateness of such goals in recent decades (Banks & Banks, 1995), they are still fundamental to the thinking of a large segment of the U.S. population about education's goals. U.S. schools have also been designed to promote the social mobility of children of diverse backgrounds. Horace Mann, the dominant figure in the early public school movement, articulated this vision when he theorized that universal education could be the "great equalizer," the "balance wheel of social machinery," a "creator of wealth unheard of" (Cremin, 1964, p. 9). Public schools, then, have long been expected to provide, at a minimum, education for citizens from all walks of life. Indeed, the idea of serving the masses lies at the core of their development.

Support for this vision of public schooling grew along with the tremendous rise in immigration as the nineteenth century progressed, with citizens organizing to lobby for public schooling in their states. By 1860, a majority of states had established school systems. Those lobbying for public schools also emphasized that citizens should retain control over these schools. From the outset, public schools have been supported by tax revenue and under local lay governance. As such, schools have been and continue to be subject to pressures from diverse constituencies, as the general public provides schools with both children and dollars. Without such support, a district will lose its legitimacy and eventually its clientele (Cuban, 1990).

In sum, whereas the Internet's initial constituency consisted of the academic elite, technical aficionados, and a government hungry for new forms of technical knowledge, the public school's most critical constituency is composed of tax-paying adults of diverse academic and social backgrounds and, especially, the parents of school-age children.

FOUR MISMATCHES AFFECTING INTERNET USE

The Internet and the public schools today reflect quite different historical missions and quite different constituencies. Whereas the Internet was created and organized around the idea of creating knowledge, public schools were organized around the idea of transmitting knowledge—both academic and cultural. The schools' historical emphasis on assimilation and enculturation also sets them apart from the Internet. Such differences, not surprisingly, have generated differences in infrastructures and other important characteristics.

In the sections that follow, we describe some of these differences, or mismatches, and discuss how they led to difficulties for NET educators as they attempted to contact the external world. The areas of mismatch involve individualization versus batch processing, change versus constancy, an emphasis on open expression versus control over content, and a toys versus tools view of technology use.

Individualization Versus Batch Processing

As the different historical circumstances leading to the creation of the Internet and the public schools suggest, the infrastructures of the public school and of the Internet are designed to support the needs of very different constituencies. In this section, we describe the implications of these different infrastructures for educators and students seeking access to the on-line world.

The backbone of today's Internet evolved in research and university settings, and today many avid users continue to access the Internet by way of servers in these environments and to access Web sites or entertainment-oriented network resources located on servers in such settings (Curtis, 1997). Web sites are also increasingly found on servers located in corporate and nonprofit environments and in individuals' homes. Because of the early decision that anyone who might contribute to building the Internet should have the opportunity to do so, even those with relatively unsophisticated computer systems can participate in developing the resources available on-line.

However, individuals in academic, research, and even many corporate environments share several work practices that distinguish their lives from those of the typical educator. First, it is often the norm that individuals can determine the manner in which they will approach particular tasks, with the result that they can juggle and shuffle priorities and activities. Second, white-collar professionals, and especially academics and researchers, tend to work on extended projects that may require coordinated but not simultaneous effort; large numbers of individuals do not typically work in the same way, on the same problem, at the same time, or in the same place. Indeed, if one has access to a computer and the relevant data, one can work in relative isolation from others, at odd hours, and in various places.

In contrast, public schools were organized to meet the simultaneous needs of large numbers of students. This led, for the sake of efficiency, to an emphasis on whole class instruction during which all individuals are presented with the same set of information in essentially the same way. Thus, traditionally schools have been organized for batch processing, a term originally used in industrial settings to refer to the simultaneous and identical treatment of large numbers of items. As McDonald (1996, p. 357) has observed, "Being in school typically means being unremittingly part of a crowd."

Specifically, influenced by democratic ideals and envisioning schools as equalizing environments, public school reformers of the 1890s argued that all children should get access in the same way to the same materials. At that time, the school-age population was increasing significantly with the arrival of Eastern European immigrants. One consequence of this burgeoning student body was the graded school, which grouped children by age and gave them a sequenced curriculum. The belief was that, by teaching all children in the same classroom in the same way at the same pace, schools could achieve greater efficiency (Tyack & Tobin, 1994), and government could curb the growing cost of public education. Although as time passed many came to see the ideal of similar schooling for all as unrealistic, and schools increasingly grouped students by ability or achievement level, the idea that schools should group students by age and teach them a sequenced curriculum remains in force today. One teacher typically engages students in whole class instruction, teaching a group of many children in a given room the same subject, in roughly the same way and at the same pace. That teacher is accountable for helping students acquire certain academic and behavioral objectives defined as appropriate to their age and ability within a set amount of time. In middle school and high school, the constraints emanating from the need to batch process students are especially marked. Here, greater numbers of students are often housed together, and content specialization dictates that a given teacher typically has face-to-face contact with a given group of students for just forty-five to fifty minutes during a set time of the day.

Significant problems occur when one tries to link individuals embedded in public school settings designed for batch processing to resources developed to support individualized work. While there are certainly servers that can handle many users simultaneously, in many instances servers hosting Web sites are configured to meet the needs of a local constituency rather than the needs of other visitors and are chosen with economic considerations in mind. Moreover, the performance of servers at the local level has traditionally been left to the locals (King et al., 1997). It is not essential for a business or university to ensure access to a Web site on a server for an entire workforce simultaneously when individuals tend to work on different projects at different times, and servers are typically accessible at all hours. Therefore, many of the servers attached to the Internet were not designed to handle access by large numbers of visitors at once, and they may malfunction or slow down considerably when subject to simultaneous demands from many users. Users may encounter busy signals as they attempt to connect to such servers from the outside. Thus, popular Web or other Internet sites may be difficult or impossible to reach during some periods of the day. Typically, Internet aficionados get around these roadblocks by trying again later, often at odd hours. But educators, constrained by the school schedule, cannot choose when their students will try to access such Web sites. When students in a classroom or lab work on many computers simultaneously, the issue is even more complex. Even if they attempt to access the Internet at a less busy time, as a group they themselves may overwhelm a given Web site or server.

In interviews, both educators and students expressed great dismay about the delays and busy signals they experienced when attempting to reach Web sites and to work as a group on servers with limited capacity. For example, students frequently mentioned this problem when asked what they liked least about using the Internet. Indeed, of the students we interviewed on this topic ($N = 37$), 22 percent spontaneously mentioned this problem. Similarly, although teachers more commonly expressed concerns about other matters such as the limited time they had to plan constructive curricular uses of the Internet, when we asked teachers (N – 64) to indicate the biggest problems impeding classroom use of the Internet, 26 percent spontaneously brought up delays, busy signals, or slow connections. Finally, as we observed classroom sessions, we saw students' attempts to work online and to access various Internet resources slowed or prevented altogether, often owing to overloads on both distant Web sites and local servers. Teachers' and students' frustrations in these various situations were readily apparent, as these two field note segments illustrate:

Kayla [a student in a middle school social studies class] chose "Web Crawler." She put in the word "Malawi," which Ms. Bigley had told her how to spell, and it wouldn't connect. . . . [T]here was some kind of message about its not being available. She tried that again and the same thing happened. Then she went to another option, which was "TravNet Malawi," and the whole computer froze. This time she couldn't move the mouse or anything. . . . At this point Kayla gave up. She just left the computer and went back to her seat.

A female student [in a high school German class] was trying to read an e-mail message, a mail message that Ms. Stewart [her teacher] wanted her to read, and she was getting very frustrated. . . . [T]he system was either working very slowly so that when she was hitting it she wasn't seeing any response or it was frozen. She was hitting keys wildly, she was huffing and puffing, and at one point she said, "The damn thing won't go down!"

Teachers explained in interviews that access difficulties were greatly exacerbated by the rigid school schedule, which predetermined the time they had available to access the Internet with students, and by their limited discretionary time during the school day. Access problems occurred even when students worked individually at a single computer while their peers did something else. However, problems were especially prevalent for students who worked in lab settings in which a number of students working at individual computers tried to use the same Web site simultaneously in order to complete a common assignment. At times, access to specific sites became virtually impossible or slowed significantly, leading to failed or significantly disrupted lessons.

Access difficulties were more than frustrating and inconvenient. They also wasted limited classroom time, prevented students from completing lessons, and created the potential for student disengagement. The following field note comes from a situation in which half of a high school French class period was consumed in failed attempts to access a specific home page on the topic of Paris. Some students never made connections:

> Ms. Hoffman noticed that everyone seemed to be sitting there waiting for something to connect, and so she asked the class, "Who is trying to load something in and waiting for something to connect?" Almost everyone raised their hand. . . . She decided that maybe it would help if they weren't all trying to connect at the same time, so she had them all stop trying to connect things. Then she tried to have one row try to connect. . . . [T]hat didn't work. . . . So then. . .she had everyone . . . get completely out of Netscape, and get back into it. Then she had a couple of people try to reconnect again. They were having a little bit better luck, although it was still slow. . . . [T]hey were at a dead stop from their curriculum plan for a good ten to fifteen minutes, just trying to get people hooked in. Several students were finally able to get back through into the resource and back into the Paris home page and start looking at monuments, but they only had a few minutes to do that, and several of them never got back in.

A similar pattern of wasted classroom time and teacher frustration is apparent in this field note from a middle school social studies class:

> [The students] got some [on-line] menus on Finnish things. . . . One [referred to] the Finnish National Gallery, and they [clicked on this option and] brought that up, but it was taking a long time to come in so they finally just stopped that and went back and chose to go to a place that was supposed to have Finnish and Swedish poetry. That one took a long time to come up too, so they stopped that. Then they went back a couple more pages and chose "Politics" from a menu of things. This didn't connect. . . . Ms. Bigley came over [to the researcher observing] and said. . . that she's had students who have spent twenty minutes . . . on the computer and not come away with any useful information, which was, in fact, what happened with these two [menu selections] today.

As these examples illustrate, when access problems occur in a lab setting, one group of students might reach a designated site and complete work, but another group might not. This not only leaves some students frustrated but also leaves the teacher with an evaluation quandary. How can he or she assess performance when some students, through no fault of their own, never had the opportunity to learn? Situations such as these left some NET team members convinced that when working with the Internet they had to plan for potential lesson failure. As one middle school teacher put it, "There's always got to be something else they can work on."

In short, the Internet, an entity initially designed to support and connect diverse individuals in varied professional settings, does not mesh readily with public school settings organized for large groups of students doing the same thing simultaneously. This proved a basic and significant impediment to electronic interaction with the outside world. Such problems can be mitigated through procedures such as downloading material from a distant server to a local one designed to handle entire classes, but this takes planning, coordination, time, and resources.

Continual Change Versus Constancy

NET EDUCATION STAFF MEMBER: [The Internet] is a weird environment. It changes more than anything I've ever seen. We've been in the business eighteen months and nothing has stayed the same for even one month.

HIGH SCHOOL SCIENCE TEACHER: I'll tell you what, even since September it's gotten to the point where it sometimes . . . just literally turns you off, because there are so many things coming out that you just don't know what to do.

Alluding to the speed with which those connected to the Internet can move across borders of time and space to new locations, people have often described the Internet as a highway. Highways, however, are generally governed by consistent and predictable navigation rules: routes from one place to another remain generally unchanged; strategies for moving along the road are familiar; and old cars often move as effectively as their newer counterparts. However, the knowledge production that leads to technical improvement that the Internet community has long prized (Davidson et al., 2001; King et al., 1997) has historically been associated with "constant, disruptive changes in the network" (King et al., 1997, p. 13). Reflecting this, rules of navigation change with astonishing frequency on the Internet. (The term *Internet time* captures the idea that a year's worth of change may take place on the Internet in just a couple of months [Hof, 1997].) Over the course of NET's five-year life, for example, Internet users moved from entirely text-based means of Internet navigation to Mosaic (the first widely used, graphically based browser) and then to the Netscape or Internet Explorer browsers. Desktop computers, servers, and modems also developed rapidly; new hardware and software enabled quicker and more efficient movement on the ever-developing Web and access to a broader array of resources, but they also required users to learn how to access and make use of additional tools in order to benefit from this change.

Whereas the Internet is a rapidly evolving entity, public school teachers are immersed in institutions known for their constancy and stability. As Tyack and Tobin (1994, p. 454) eloquently put it, "The basic grammar of schooling, like the shape of classrooms, has remained remarkably stable over the decades." Along with the persistence of age grouping and group-centered instruction, pedagogy and classroom organizational practices have remained largely unchanged over substantial periods of time. Instruction has and continues to be primarily centered on the teacher and textbook, particularly at the high school level (Cuban, 1986; Goodlad, 1984). Functioning in a context characterized by budgetary constraints, public ambivalence, and even outright hostility toward taxation, schools also tend not to replace frequently even their most basic tools, such as textbooks. Rather, a culture of durability pervades, and students and teachers commonly make do with outdated maps, textbooks, and vocational technology. Further, teachers express a preference for traditional practices that they believe to work reliably over radical pedagogical and curricular innovations (Cuban, 1986; Doyle & Ponder, 1978; Huberman, 1993; Lieberman & Miller, 1990; Lortie, 1975). Innovation requires extra time, might slow the pace of instruction, and might prove disruptive, even if it might also pay off in improved achievement or heightened student motivation. And when innovation does not pay off, as is bound to happen sometimes, students suffer the consequences, and teachers take the blame.

NET was built around groups of educators who willingly decided to make a change, to bring the Internet to their schools and classrooms. Nevertheless, NET team members experienced the constant changes associated with the Internet as a challenge and often as an inconvenience. Indeed, of the NET educators ($N = 64$) we asked to indicate the greatest problem they encountered when trying to use the Internet in their work, almost one-fifth spontaneously mentioned the constant changes they encountered there. Further, roughly half of the teachers we interviewed on the topic of experimenting with new software said they were not interested in such experimentation during the school year, especially when such software switches would require more than a minimal investment of learning time. Although teachers recognized that new software might bring improvement, they explained that they preferred not to disrupt existing learning routines, saying things like this:

> I think I would prefer my kids in research . . . to spend more time on their hands-on research than spending a couple periods a week learning new software . . . which may be excellent.

> I would prefer to use what we have and not replace it. . . . [Y]ou may replace it every two years, but if you go faster than that [students] really don't absorb it. . . . I really think there should be some time to settle.

Many others said simply that they lacked the time necessary to prepare themselves and students for significant change.

In addition to generating inconvenience and frustration for some teachers, the Internet's ethos of innovation created another kind of difficulty. First, all NET teachers grappled with keeping abreast of frequent on-line organizational and content changes. Because virtually anyone can connect to the Internet and become an information provider, resources on the Internet are highly susceptible to the whims of individuals. In addition, institutional priorities and environmental vagaries cause Web sites and resources to change, disappear, or move in accord with the desires of their creators or economic priorities. Internet resources, in short, are moving rather than predictable targets. With little discretionary time for exploring resources during the school year, teachers have little opportunity to track these changes. In extreme cases, a resource present in the morning can disappear by midday, as in the experience of one NET teacher: "I could get in in the morning, but I couldn't get in at 11:00. . . . [A]pparently that server was revamped that weekend and they . . . now have the information distributed a different way."

The rapid pace of change in Internet architecture affected access not only to specific information sites but also to whole classes of resources. For example, some language teachers in NET used Internet Relay Chat (IRC) to immerse students in real-world, instantaneous language use. However, the servers that support IRC go in and out of existence frequently. NET's technical staff initially compiled easy, menu-based access to one such server, which meant that even novice users could readily find their way to this curricular resource. However, this server then became unavailable. At that point, NET staff members expressed reluctance about investing effort in creating easy access to such a fleeting type of resource, and it was several months before they restored this capability.

Even more significant for some NET teachers, Internet resources often change in reaction to and in accord with new technical capacities. So, for example, text-based Internet sites increasingly added graphics and audio over the course of NET in response to the rapidly increasing processing and memory capacities of computers. Teachers who became part of NET early in the project's life frequently worked with computers too slow to access Web sites with many graphics at a reasonable speed. Compounding this, educators trying to broaden classroom or lab-based access to networks sometimes linked pre-NET equipment to newer systems. Most of this equipment was woefully out-of-date, not only because of the district's long moratorium on most technology purchases but also because even the most recent technology had often been purchased without the purchasers giving significant weight to future technical change. Specifically, the district in some cases bought computers with less memory or processing power than it could have in order to purchase more machines for a given expenditure, clearly a decision more responsive to batch-processing needs than to the pace of technical change.

Efforts to access on-line resources with outdated equipment created problems, especially when graphics were involved. A description from an elementary school teacher illustrates the types of frustrations and difficulties that arose:

> Well, there are actually times where the kids will go back [to the computer] and pull something up on the Web and put it in and know that

they can go back there and in about ten or fifteen minutes check on it and the search might be done. I don't know if it would be possible to get higher-powered computers. . . . I mean, it takes forever for the computer to warm up, and then just clicking on the icons to get there can take half an hour, you know? I mean, it's just very, very slow. These computers are unreal. And we don't have a lot of memory power either. For something as fabulous as the Internet, it sort of sucks up everything for the computer. So we feel like we're always reaching.

Because of the time constraints under which teachers and students typically operated, the delays created by a mismatch between the technical capabilities of the computers they were using and the capabilities needed to access a given resource efficiently proved quite frustrating. As another elementary school teacher charged with encouraging other teachers at her school to make use of Internet resources explained:

> Sometimes they try to pull stuff up, and after waiting forever, they can't finish pulling it up. . . . Now the kids usually will keep going back, but teachers I think are much more likely to say, "The heck with this. This is wasting my time. I have too many other things that I have to do," and are much less likely to go back to it.

Conversely, access to the latest and most speedy technology facilitated use. As yet another elementary school teacher put it when speaking enthusiastically about the speed associated with cable access, "It makes all the difference in the world when you're changing class and you only have forty-five minutes to have that speed. . . . It's marvelous."

In short, a tradition of rapid technical knowledge creation and the existence of an open access policy makes change the norm on the Internet. These features of the Internet clash with the desire for stability present in many public school settings and also with the funding realities that prevent continued acquisition of new equipment there. In schools, technical constancy is the rule. In numerous instances, this basic mismatch prevented or significantly impeded educators' efforts to connect with resources and individuals in the outside world.

Open Expression Versus Control over Content

So far, we have described areas of mismatch that impede classroom-based connections to the Internet. But once schools make initial connections to the outside, on-line world, what do educators and students experience as they step into that world? Images of educators and students moving with ease through a comprehensive and continually expanding library or museum archive come readily to mind. But the Internet, by virtue of its social history and ability to connect individuals readily, is quite different from a public library or museum. It is not an architectural space with contents that librarians and curators can control, organize, and rearrange. Neither is it a milieu in which professionals have selected the materials available for public use for their educational or cultural value. Rather, the Internet is a gateway to the ideas of all others who have also gained access; it is a place of democratic and social anarchy (Turkle, 1995). It provides access to things that would not be found in most public schools or libraries as well as to virtually anything a given individual with basic computer equipment decides to make available (Futoran, Schofield, & Eurich-Fulcer, 1995). In this sense, it embodies a set of values quite different from those of the school.

The anarchy of the Internet stems principally from its tradition of open access; few rules and procedures govern who gains access, and thus the Internet connects many people whose actions no one can predict or control. Perhaps because of the Internet's historical connection to academic institutions, which have traditionally valued freedom of expression, as well as the practical difficulties of controlling the material placed on the Internet, few have attempted to censor Internet materials (Krantz, 1997). As a result, the Internet is a cultural medium in which many groups, including the extreme right and the extreme left, can voice their ideas. For example, newsgroups may connect members of hate groups, make available information on bomb making and assisted suicide, and connect individuals with both mainstream and divergent sexual interests. Adult and child pornography are also accessible, both fairly readily for determined users (Mehta & Plaza, 1997). Many of the more popular on-line games incorporate violent themes and sexual fantasies. Women who visit on-line chat rooms or assert their opinions in various newsgroups risk verbal harassment, sexual advances, and even, in extreme instances, being subjected to other participants' fantasies of on-line rape (Curtis, 1997; Kantrowitz, Rosenberg, & King, 1994; Turkle, 1995).

Public schools, in contrast, "have historically been the site for identifying, containing, and civilizing that which is considered uncontrollable" (Fine, 1993, p. 76). Sex education curricula are often designed to promote abstinence, and school library committees traditionally adhere to specified procedures developed to ensure that texts, library books, and audiovisual materials will be deemed acceptable by the broad community (Futoran et al., 1995). Indeed, many school districts use an American Library Association workbook that takes educators through selection policies for written materials. Needing to retain the support of a diverse constituency, schools avoid controversial topics and often mute the voices most critical of the status quo; teachers in racially mixed schools, for example, have been known to avoid the topic of slavery for fear of causing disruptions (Schofield, 1989), and students are more likely to encounter material on Martin Luther King Jr. than on Malcolm X over the course of a public school career. Further, even though girls and women have historically experienced varied forms of sexual harassment in schools (American Association of University Women, 1993), rules and policies have been instituted to lessen this behavior. Generally, this is not the case on the Internet.

NET team members' comments indicated that they were highly sensitive to the fact that schools have historically avoided controversial topics. And all those connected with NET were well aware that an activity in which students might access material that parents or others might likely deem inappropriate carried the potential for public disapproval, as is apparent in the excerpt from an e-mail that NET staff received from a district educator:

> Considering the recent concerns of parents and politicians about sexually explicit materials being available via the Internet (not NET), I find it puzzling that NET now has three new groups of questionable value on a primary through secondary educational Internet site. The groups rec.drugs.cannabis, rec.drugs.misc, rec.drugs.psychedelic have been recently added to the NET list of newsgroups. Hopefully, this has been an oversight, but these three groups seem to me to have perhaps just a little less value than the group alt.rush-limbaugh which was removed from the NET list last year. I'm not one who advocates censorship, but recreational drug use topics don't seem appropriate for Networking for Education Testbed. Let's not give any ammunition to those who would use this type of thing against us.

Similarly, during a professional development session at a NET high school, it was readily apparent that the host school educators knew that both the public and their colleagues expected them to prevent student exposure to controversial materials. During this meeting, a teacher from a neighboring high school stumbled onto a *Penthouse* magazine picture that a student had downloaded and saved on the computer without his or her teacher's knowledge. The teachers from the host school appeared embarrassed and apologetic—expressing outrage that some students had been allowed to work in the school's computer lab unsupervised prior to the opening bell. Reflecting on the incident after the fact, a teacher from the host school commented, "Because of that [incident], I'm twice as cautious about monitoring my students, making sure they're on task. So I'm always walking and patrolling the area, making sure they're where they're supposed to be."

Teachers' definitions of inappropriate content often incorporated not just sexually explicit content but also suggestive pictures (women in negligees, for example) and other things that parents or they themselves might deem objectionable or harmful to students. For example, teachers at one high school pondered shutting down access to chat rooms on library computers because of fears about student exposure to "inappropriate language." Similarly, a teacher at an elementary school suspended conversation in a chat room when students began to discuss the personalities of other children on-line. Because the conversation was moving toward gossip, she became concerned about the feelings of the students in her charge. Still another elementary school teacher confiscated an article a student printed concerning an elementary-aged student who fell down a well. She did so out of concern about the potential effects of this article on the student's psyche: "We just didn't think it was appropriate for her to pore over this, so we took it away from her." A high school librarian suspended a student's Internet privileges permanently when he printed a fifty-page document describing how to hot-wire cars and build a variety of bombs. Teachers also said that they did not approve of students' accessing youth-oriented, popular culture resources, such as the Beavis and Butthead Web page, during school time.

During the early years of NET, the education staff implemented procedures to identify and then eliminate access to many controversial newsgroups. Along with district educators, they formed a committee that, among other things, periodically reviewed a list of available newsgroups in order to identify those to be removed. The group chose to eliminate access not only to newsgroups on topics related to sex or violence but also to those dealing with other potentially controversial topics such as religion, suicide, and abortion. In later years, however, NET discontinued this practice, partially because the university feeding newsgroups to NET began to filter out much sexually oriented material itself, partially because NET staff became extremely busy, and partially because NET staff continued to debate the merits, drawbacks, and complications associated with attempting to maintain this level of control.

In general, NET staff were not in favor of extensive access limitations or of software that filters out access to controversial materials. The reasons for this were numerous and varied. For example, unresolved disagreements among NET education staff about exactly which kinds of materials were likely to be harmful highlighted the political complexity of making decisions to block access, especially given the fact that the disagreements occurred even though members of this staff were like-minded in a great many ways. Further, some NET staff members pointed out the impracticality of such efforts—arguing that because attempts to filter material are unlikely to work perfectly, teachers have to monitor and direct student access in any event. From their perspective, filtering impinged upon teachers' professional autonomy; it might block materials they might appropriately make use of without relieving them of the need to monitor student use. A related concern was that filtering efforts are likely to lead to loss of useful information. To use a well-worn example, a filter set to block out materials containing the word *breast* because of the word's sexual connotation would also be likely to block things ranging from chicken recipes useful in home economics classes to medical sites discussing breast cancer prevention. Still another concern that derailed NET-wide solutions to the problem of inappropriate content was that the district as a whole and also many individual schools contained students of a sufficient spread in age levels that selection mechanisms designed to filter out materials inappropriate for younger students would do a disservice to older ones.

Nevertheless, the approaches that NET took in this general area do reflect the assumption that educators have a responsibility to keep students from accessing many kinds of controversial content and that they must meet this responsibility even if doing so restricts student use of the Internet. For example, as we mentioned in Chapter One, before students could get NET accounts, they and their parents were required to sign an acceptable use policy (AUP) that informed them about acceptable on-line behavior and the consequences of infractions of these behavioral rules. Further, students were required to have a specific educational purpose for using the Internet, one that a teacher endorsed as connected to their classwork. Students who wanted to familiarize themselves with the Internet, to build their technical skills, or to see what they could learn by using the Internet were generally not given accounts, in spite of the potential value of such activities. Students caught visiting sites deemed inappropriate sometimes lost their accounts, usually temporarily. Early in NET's life, losing an account meant losing Internet access for all practical purposes, including constructive ones. Later, as graphical interfaces such as Netscape developed that did not require individual accounts, the loss of an account inhibited a smaller proportion of most students' Internet use.

Members of the education staff, as the following field note illustrates, also encouraged educators to devise policies and pedagogical procedures—such as using electronic bookmarks to guide students to sites that the educators had previewed—that might prevent student exposure to controversial content:

> [At a NET team meeting, Peter Marcus] said that one of the things they had thought about when creating the acceptable use policy was that it was the responsibility of the adult in the room to monitor the student activity. Just as you don't let students come home all bloodied and beat up, in the same way, you make sure they're protected when they're on-line.

Teachers outside of NET apparently use similar strategies (McKee, 1999).

Even with tactics such as the AUP, teachers found that the anarchic and ever-changing nature of the Internet made it difficult to totally shield students from controversial material or pornography, especially those who wished to access it. For one thing, the interactions that take place on some Internet resources of use to educators are impossible to preview or control. For example, IRC allows Internet users to enter a virtual reality room and communicate in real time with others also in that room by typing messages that all users can see. Some IRC channels target speakers of languages other than English, providing excellent opportunities for English-speaking students to practice a second language. A few NET teachers attempted to make use of this

Internet function as well as some virtual reality resources such as multiuser object-oriented environments, or MOOs. However, as the following field note illustrates, describing a situation in which high school Spanish students chatted in real time with Spanish speakers, educators cannot control what other users will say to students, and they also find it difficult to control what their students say. In this instance, students approached the topic of sexuality, to the discomfort of their teacher:

> At one point, Barbara asked Mr. Lutz [the teacher], "How do you say *slave?*" [in Spanish] and Mr. Lutz told her. Barbara typed in something [in Spanish] about being a slave of love, and one of the speakers on the channel typed back, "Slave of love? Where's your whip?". . . At one point [later in the exchange], one of the lines on the screen [contained the word] . . . *"lesbianas,"* which means lesbians. . . . Mr. Lutz also saw this comment come up. And upon seeing this . . . he immediately got onto a computer [also logged into the chat room] . . . and typed in, "Careful. Don't go into any subjects that you shouldn't with my students." . . . After Mr. Lutz had typed that in, a comment from Orin [another student in the classroom] appeared that said something about Barbara being a lesbian. When Mr. Lutz saw that, he said, "Orin," in a really warning tone. And he went on to say that we need to get off of these subjects, and there's certain things that you don't say.

Even after such warnings, students in this type of on-line setting can surreptitiously persist in behaviors of which the teacher disapproves. Later in the same classroom session, for example, male students used language considered impermissible in their classroom as they signed off the system:

> [A group of boys is clustered around one screen typing a message.] I did not actually see who did the typing, but Orin signed off with the message, "Shut up, bitch." . . . They clearly were trying to hide this from Mr. Lutz, because they were clustered around the screen . . . and they were just hitting the keys really quickly so it would go off the screen as fast as possible. I was peering around to see what they were doing and caught a glimpse just as it flashed off the screen. . . . Mr. Lutz did not see this.

Reflecting NET educators' concern about such issues, this teacher later suspended use of IRC, largely owing to difficulties associated with finding what he called a "G-rated" chat room.

Yet even if educators do not allow students to access virtual reality settings, students may use other on-line tools to seek out materials traditionally not present in educational settings. Educators, especially at the high school level, reported that students could quickly learn to find illicit materials. We observed such instances, as this field note illustrates:

> [In the high school library,] the boy in the red hooded sweatshirt is very quiet. . . . He is out on the Net as well as in something called "Play-boy." As I observe, he is looking very closely at the screen. . . . [I]t appears that he's reading some text and engrossed in what he's looking at.

A high school teacher told us, "It took my ninth graders, who have not had any Internet training, one month here during home room period to learn how to get pornography . . . which amazed me." A high school librarian reflected a similar concern: "You always have hanging over your head somebody wanting to go into the word 'pornography' or something like that."

Consistent with our field observations, both teachers and students reported that purposeful violations of NET's AUP, although apparently sporadic, did occur, most frequently among middle school and high school students. For example, of the students we interviewed on this topic ($N = 54$), 33 percent in NET's early years were aware of infractions of the AUP and described the types of inappropriate access they had seen. This pattern was repeated during NET's fourth year when we asked a new group of middle and high school students ($N = 27$) to estimate the number of students whom they thought had used the Internet in ways that the school would not approve. Even though two-thirds of these students said that relatively few students (fewer than 10 percent) engaged in these activities, nearly all knew of such instances. Reports like the following, the first from a high school student and the second from a middle school student, were typical:

> I know people that look at little peep shows and stuff, you know? It's really funny to me but they [teachers and NET staff] might find it inappropriate or whatever.

> There's something called Porn Hall or something, and it has all these rips that are somewhat nasty and I know a lot of people that go on that and just to see rips and memorize them so they can use them on people.

According to some of the students we interviewed, in rare instances a technically sophisticated student would also attempt, sometimes successfully, to break into a school server or even into another person's account. Of NET middle and high school educators we interviewed about this issue ($N = 31$), 45 percent reported observing infractions of the AUP. Of those educators specifying the infractions they observed, 57 percent reported that students accessed pornography or other sexually oriented sites, and 43 percent mentioned that students accessed or used profanity on-line. For example, middle and high school students accessed Web sites distributing pornography; a group of high school boys became members of an on-line "Penis Club" and distributed pictures of women's breasts; and high school students accessed information about hate groups and bomb making.

Complicating issues of responsibility and control, students with no apparent intention to find sexually explicit or profane content did stumble upon it inadvertently on rare occasions. Even restricting Internet use to Web sites intended for school use is not necessarily a foolproof way to keep students from encountering objectionable materials, although it does so in the vast majority of cases. For example, in a notorious incident at one NET elementary school, teachers working at a Web site designated for educators and students became aware of a picture of an explicit sex scene at the bottom of the site's home page. Worse, from the teachers' perspective, the matter was brought to their attention by a concerned parent. Though the picture had apparently been placed at the Web site accidentally and was promptly removed by the Web site administrators, this incident served as a constant reminder to teachers at this school of the potential for problems. Reflecting the opinion of a teacher at this school who argued, "We have to police the Net ourselves, or else we're going to end up getting policed by someone who we don't want to police us," this school's NET team developed a set of strict guidelines limiting students' ability to work independently on-line.

The mismatch between the Internet's tradition of open expression and the public schools' tradition of presenting relatively noncontroversial material to students clearly exerted a dampening effect on

Internet activities at NET schools. Educators restricted students' time on-line and monitored them closely when they were logged on. Because it was difficult to monitor many students simultaneously and because the Internet-linked computers were often placed in the corners of a classroom, a decision to allow only closely monitored use was often in effect a decision to allow very little use.

Technology as Plaything Versus Tool

Although the Internet was initially designed as a tool to facilitate knowledge creation, for many years it has been as much a place for play as for work, a place to engage in social interaction, even a place to realize one's fantasies in virtual reality (Turkle, 1995). This latter tradition reflects in part the Internet's formative constituency, which included hackers as well as computer science undergraduate and graduate students. The social status of such individuals in U.S. high schools and colleges, argues Turkle (1984), has always been marginal. The Internet, however, has allowed members of such often-derogated communities to find similar others, to form on-line friendships, and to create virtual reality spaces conducive to play and interaction. Increasingly, with access eased by technological innovations and with growing awareness of the Internet's social and recreational potential, individuals from all walks of life are participating in such uses of the Internet, taking on character roles in virtual reality spaces and participating in a wide variety of newsgroups to discuss topics ranging from soap operas to parenting children with special needs (Baym, 1997; Mickelson, 1997; Sproull & Faraj, 1997; Turkle, 1995). In addition, the commercial potential of the Internet has fueled a rapid proliferation of entertainment- and sports-oriented Web sites. Links among Web sites and other technical capacities allow individuals to access such resources quickly from diverse locations and to jump readily from task-oriented to socially oriented or recreational sites. Thus, although the Internet was initially developed for work-related purposes, for a great many individuals it is more a place in which to pursue personal, social, and recreational interests.

Using classroom technology to support students' recreational or social interests runs counter to the norms traditionally found in educational settings. During the twentieth century, teachers adopted and used technologies such as the chalkboard and overhead projector to help them maintain social control and transmit content quickly and efficiently. At the same time, they were reticent to adopt forms of educational technology such as computers that did not give them this help (Cuban, 1986). Again, this reflects in part the nature of the public school constituency. Schooling is not voluntary, and there is no guarantee that students will feel interest in their teachers' academic agendas. Teachers may have to work hard to establish authority and negotiate for the attention of a potentially unruly population (Erickson, 1993; Powell, Farrar, & Cohen, 1985). Further, teachers are subject to substantial time pressures as they attempt to help students attain given types of knowledge in predefined periods of time. Thus, it is not surprising that in public schools technology has traditionally served as a tool to facilitate the achievement of academic goals and agendas and to maintain social control rather than as an instrument for play. Educators may view anything that weakens control, threatens teachers' authority, or distracts students from the school's learning objectives as suspect.

NET educators did indeed emphasize the importance of using the Internet as a tool to accomplish predetermined curricular goals rather than as an instrument to support play or exploration. Educators' visions of work-centered Internet use and the tensions they perceived between their agendas and what the Internet actually offers were quite apparent during interviews. For example, some educators expressed clear frustration at students' strong attraction to the entertainment and play opportunities available on the Internet, arguing also that games and other entertainment-oriented on-line resources detract from rather than contribute to student learning or that involvement in these sites ties up computers that students might better use for academic activities. Such themes are reflected in these comments from a librarian and a teacher, respectively; both from an elementary school:

I never let anybody say, "I want to play on the computer." They've learned now. You know, wrath, smoke comes out of my ears. I say, "Excuse me? . . . We don't play on the computer, you know?" To me, this invokes the idea of Nintendo games—that you don't put anything of yourself into it, all right? We think when we use the computer.

It looks like a toy, and getting beyond that—that's always a problem. "Oh, can I look at the X-Men file?" and that kind of thing—which has a place, but it's hard once you let them look at it once . . . then you've got fourteen boys standing around one machine. That's—you know, a management problem. And then you start shooing them away, and then you get hostile feelings.

A few teachers said they believed that playful exploration on the Internet could prove beneficial for students. However, most felt that such play should be done outside class time. As one high school teacher said, "There's nothing wrong with exploring, but I feel that should be done perhaps before school or after school rather than during my French class."

The data we gathered from students support educators' suspicions and concerns about the lure of alternate Internet activities. This lure seemed especially pronounced at the upper grade levels, most likely at least partly because the older students were more likely to know how to access such materials. First, of the high school students we interviewed on this topic ($N = 42$), 64 percent admitted unequivocally that they drifted away from intended educational activities during class time. Typically, students who drifted to recreational activities browsed entertainment-oriented Web sites, wrote e-mail to friends, or played games. Of the twenty-three students specifying how often this occurred, seven said they drifted from intended tasks every time they went on-line with an educational purpose, and another eight said this happened with some frequency. A high school student described this way the various pulls the outside world asserted when he worked on-line:

> Sometimes—like when we were supposed to explore countries—you know, something might come up and you just don't want to leave it. You know, you want to keep looking into it and looking into it, and then you get off-task of what you're supposed to be doing. . . . I'd say [that happens] about every time—every time.

Our field notes also show evidence of the pull of nonacademic activities, as the following excerpts illustrate:

> [In a high school Spanish class,] Chester [a student] . . . had gotten into Netscape. . . . I heard him say . . . something like, "I have to explore my sexuality." . . . A few minutes after this . . . the teacher came back

over and [looked] at Chester's screen and reprimanded Chester. . . . I heard him warn Chester in Spanish to be careful, and in English the teacher said to Chester that he could tell anywhere Chester went—that the computer kept a list of where the students were going when they were in Netscape. . . . Chester was looking at some home pages . . . that had to do with music . . . Woodstock II. Mr. Lutz [the teacher] explained to him again . . . that he can look at whatever he wants to every morning, but he's not supposed to be looking at this kind of stuff during class time. Chester was trying to argue with him and didn't want to get off this home page. . . . Chester was continuing to look at things Mr. Lutz had told him he shouldn't be spending time on and . . . Mr. Lutz came over to him and said, "Chester, I have given you clear directions on what you need to do and you haven't done it." . . . He threatened to call Chester's house tonight and talk to his parents. At that point Chester got mad. . . . He actually got up out of his seat and started to walk out of the room. . . .

[Later in the class,] Chester . . . glanced over at a . . . female student who was . . . in Netscape using search mechanisms searching for something about Jimi Hendrix. Well, Chester saw that, got mad, and pointed it out to Mr. Lutz, saying, "Oh! Look at her searching for Jimi Hendrix. And you're not calling her house." Mr. Lutz quietly told her that she wasn't supposed to be looking at that, and she got out immediately and got into something about Spain.

[In the high school library, the librarian's assistant] told Ms. Turlick [the librarian] that a boy named Charlie was caught yesterday playing games, and she said she "figured out why he always asks if Ms. Turlick is here." She said, "If you say that you're not here, he'll play games. But if you say yes, he won't play games." She said he's kind of sneaky that way.

The fact that a large study found that just over 35 percent of the top three hundred Web sites that students accessed from schools in forty-three major cities were entertainment sites suggests just how strong the lure of such sites can be (Thomas, 2000). Also indicative of students' interest in noncurricular aspects of the Internet were students' responses when we asked what they would do on-line if given complete freedom to use the Internet as they wished. Of those we interviewed ($N = 47$), 60 percent said they would use network resources for social purposes (to write to friends or family), to seek information on sports or hobbies, or to make a home page to tell others about themselves. In contrast, 26 percent said they would use the Internet for schoolwork or academically oriented activities, such as finding information about various colleges or publishing their writing on-line. One student articulated students' exploratory stance this way: "There's so much interesting stuff on there that, you know, you don't know whether you're going to get back there again, so you might as well take a look at it while you're there."

RESPONSES TO MISMATCHES OF CONTENT AND PURPOSE
Asserting Control

INTERVIEWER: If you had to give advice to other teachers about how most effectively to use the Internet in their classrooms, what would your advice be?

MS. SALVATOR: [*Laughs.*] Put the terminal behind your desk.

This middle school teacher had once been an advocate of allowing students free exploration of on-line resources. Over time, she came to an opinion we heard from a substantial proportion of the educators we interviewed. In an effort to control the on-line content that students would be exposed to as well as to foster task-oriented student behavior, teachers and librarians tried to varying degrees to assert control over the technology. For example, they implemented policies and practices designed to circumscribe students' on-line time and access in order to control the content that students explored. As we mentioned, NET limited students' Internet access privileges to school hours at least partly out of concern about the materials they might access. Similarly, NET educators often did not allow students to work unsupervised in labs or libraries or even in classrooms. As one teacher put it, "Simply, if I can't watch it I restrict access. I won't let them use it." Although such strategies limited students' access to controversial and objectionable material, they also curtailed students' opportunities to use the Internet for their schoolwork. Finally, to promote task-oriented behavior, other educators removed access to as many games as possible, created rules forbidding visits to game sites, and punished students who ignored those rules by lowering their grades or removing the student from the computer. Again, such control strategies also limited students' ability to use the Internet for legitimate work.

NET educators also attempted to assert control by implementing curricular and technological strategies that allowed them to direct students' on-line behavior. As we discuss in Chapter Six, however, educators often found it difficult or impossible to attain this goal, and in general students reported that they experienced far more autonomy during on-line activities than they did when engaged in more conventional sorts of classroom instruction. Nevertheless, some educators did implement strategies that curtailed the degree of students' autonomy, sometimes significantly. For example, a high school teacher created a personal home page with direct links to Web sites that the teacher had previewed and deemed educationally appropriate, and this educator always followed a highly structured lesson plan that left little or no room for student exploration. Others created electronic bookmarks that marked acceptable Web sites for students to visit. One librarian required students to come up with a list of search terms that she had to approve before a student could use the Internet, and another instituted a policy to check library keyboards out to students to prevent unauthorized Internet use. An elementary school teacher who worked with students in an on-line virtual reality environment limited students to areas that she had designed, feeling that there she could control her young students' interactions and protect them from others. Although such strategies decreased the probability that students would encounter objectionable material, they also tended greatly to constrain legitimate use.

Still other educators asserted control by monitoring what students did on-line, either personally or by using technical means. For example, some educators working with high school students in labs and libraries described themselves as patrolling their environments: "I roam constantly, and they know I'm always looking over their shoulders"; "I keep moving around [*laughs*], and keep moving around, and I haven't really had a problem." A smaller group of educators asserted their technical power of surveillance. Though NET technology did not allow teachers to track what students said in virtual reality spaces or e-mail, each computer recorded the various places that the student using it had traveled while on-line. Teachers reminded students of their ability to employ this technology:

It's fairly obvious when a kid is someplace where he feels he shouldn't
be when you walk around the corner and suddenly the kid starts clicking the mouse all over the place. . . . [T]hat's only been on a couple of
occasions all year. Usually what I've said is, "Gee, what's the matter?
You're closing up awfully quickly. What's going on?" And the kid said,
"Oh nothing, nothing." And I went back and viewed the history and
the kid went, "Ah! You got me!" and I said, "You know, you're not supposed to do that"; and the kid said, "Yeah." I said, "Don't let it happen
again." And the kid [said], "Fine, Mr. Galbraith," because the kid figured he was going out of here. And by handling it that way, the kids
haven't done it in here.

Less commonly, teachers tried to socialize students to monitor,
judge, and control their own behavior in relation to this novel technology. For example, one elementary school teacher explained that
although he felt that what his students might "stumble on" on-line
was not substantially different from what they might find in their corner drugstore, he tried to provide them with strategies for dealing with
it. For example, this educator and a few others asked students who did
stumble on illicit sites to alert the teacher immediately or simply to
close the Web site and move on. He explains his reaction:

My attitude about that is that they're going to stumble on these things
in life. . . . And I try and shepherd them through it. . . . There's a cigar
store in Center Town where a lot of these kids live, and the magazines
that are displayed at the front door are no better or worse than what
they're going to find on the Net.

In sum, NET educators typically tried to cope with the dangers
they perceived by asserting control. Though, as we discuss in Chapter Six, students often experienced feelings of autonomy in classrooms where they used the Internet, teachers continued to work to
maintain their traditional role as the ultimate directors of student
behavior. In fact, a good number of educators described themselves
as especially vigilant when students were working on-line as compared to when they worked in regular classroom settings. Some also
implemented various strategies designed to limit students' exploration of the Internet and thus their ability to communicate with
members of the outside world.

CONCLUSIONS

The Internet offers a new but relatively untested type of resource for schools. On-line, teachers and their students have the opportunity to enter into conversations with individuals they might otherwise never meet and to access resources previously inaccessible due to cost, location, or relative newness. The educators participating in NET appeared strongly motivated to explore ways of using the Internet to reach beyond the school's walls to enrich their instruction. They expressed this desire in the ACP proposals they prepared, and they developed and piloted curricular projects designed to connect students with real-world resources—both human and archival. However, the Internet's infrastructure, shaped by the needs and traditions of technical and academic professionals, impeded teachers' efforts to access these resources: their students sometimes encountered busy signals or endured excruciatingly slow connections to the resources of choice. To avoid losing precious instructional time through these hindrances, educators had to be ready to employ backup lesson plans. Educators also struggled at times to stay abreast of the Internet's ever-evolving resources, as they learned that these materials, unlike the "hard" materials found in their classrooms or school libraries, could be altered or removed from the Internet without notice.

Just as important, contrasts between the routines, expectations, and norms associated with the Internet and those associated with public school communities were often so extreme that on-line experiences were less comfortable for educators than they had originally envisioned. The Internet's tradition of open expression has fostered an uncensored environment radically different from what students typically encounter in school. Educators struggled to find ways to shield students from content that many of the schools' constituencies would find objectionable. Less objectionable in many ways but still of concern to teachers worried about keeping students' attention on their schoolwork are the Internet's many opportunities for play. Many of the more technically oriented individuals with whom we spoke argued that play on the Internet can lead to the acquisition of technical knowledge and is thus educationally worthwhile (Davidson et al., 2001). What many teachers observed, however, was that students were often so attracted to the recreational resources that can be found on-line that their attention was diverted from classroom work. Clearly, there are tensions between teachers' desire to keep students focused on content acceptable to much of the schools' public constituency and students' desire to enjoy the behavioral and expressive freedoms that the Internet promotes and enables. In some instances, these tensions were so worrisome or extreme that educators markedly curtailed students' on-line communication with the outside world.

Thus far, we have explored factors stemming from the clash between the infrastructure and culture of the Internet and the culture and structure of the schools that impeded students' and educators' use of the Internet. However, other barriers to students' use of the Internet may arise even before an Internet-based curricular project is implemented. In the next chapter, we change course to focus on these sorts of barriers.

CHAPTER FOUR

How School Culture and Structure Shape Internet Use

⌐ⱮⱮ⌐ M any aspects of the school environment in addition to those we discussed in Chapter Three have important implications for Internet use. In this chapter, we will discuss four such characteristics of the school environment that had important and often unanticipated or unrecognized influence on the decisions teachers made about how, when, and where they would use the Internet. They also influenced which students got to make use of the Internet in school. These four aspects of the school environment are educators' conception of the classroom as a teacher's private domain, the tradition of batch processing students, the initial lack of computer and Internet experience among educators, and educators' lack of time for activities other than classroom teaching. We explore both the manifestations of these interrelated issues and their consequences for Internet use.

THE CLASSROOM AS PRIVATE DOMAIN

Research on schools strongly suggests that teachers usually function more as autonomous individuals than as members of a professional staff of collaborating educators. Whether researchers see this tendency as a direct response to workplace conditions or as flowing from the psychological needs of the people who become teachers, they widely agree that it exists (Hargreaves, 1993; Little, 1990b). For example, Lortie's classic study (1975) contends that individualism constitutes one of the three recurrent themes that characterize teachers' outlooks on their work, concluding that the practices used in the recruitment and socialization of teachers, the system of rewards prevailing in schools, and the way schools are organized all strongly encourage such individualism.

Because educators perceive teaching as a complex and personal activity, there is no prevailing consensus that there is one right way to teach. Instead, acceptance of varying individualized teaching styles is widespread (Huberman, 1993; Lieberman & Miller, 1990). Teachers' respect for others' autonomy, combined perhaps with a desire to maintain and foster their own, leads them to take a hands-off attitude toward what occurs in their colleagues' classrooms, unless the colleagues invite them to do otherwise. As Huberman (p. 29) puts it, "noninterference with the core work of others constitutes a sign of professional respect."

Another striking feature of teachers' professional culture, and one that is consistent with autonomy, is their strong focus on the particular rooms in which they work and on the specific students in those rooms, rather than on the school or its student body generally. As Lortie observes (1975, p. 131), "Pride is not evoked by participation in school wide affairs. The classroom is the cathected forum." Similarly, McPherson (1972) notes the strong identification that the elementary school teachers she studied felt for the specific students they taught. Although this focus is hardly surprising, its strength is sometimes striking. For example, Schofield (1989) observes that middle school teachers go so far as to speak positively of problems in their school because these problems enhance the students' sense of security inside their own classrooms or can be used as negative examples, things that will not be tolerated in the classroom. McPherson (1972) reports teachers' getting into a public name-calling contest about which of their classes had the right to use a baseball field at lunchtime rather than taking a less partisan approach to the situation.

Perhaps related to teachers' strong investment of mental and emotional energy in the classroom is the sense that teachers' classrooms are private domains into which others (with the exception of the occasional supervisor or principal conducting an evaluation) should not intrude. For example, McPherson (1972) reports that even when a teacher's door stood open, her colleagues considered it wrong to enter the classroom during a class. When teachers did occasionally violate this norm, they would apologize profusely and present an excuse justifying this behavior. Teachers often resented even specialists such as music or art teachers rotating into a classroom as scheduled for invading the classroom and being "on my ground" (p. 78). Such norms protect the class from distractions but are also conducive to the development of a sense of territoriality about the classroom. Indeed, Lieberman and Miller (1990, p. 158) assert that "staking out a territory and making it one's own" is a component of the social reality of teaching.

Territoriality and Professional Autonomy in NET Classrooms

Even though teachers participating in NET had volunteered to work as members of small groups receiving Internet access within their schools, they generally exhibited the strong sense of individualism and the related heavy focus on their own particular classrooms that prior research suggests is common. For example, they often experienced activities related to the functioning of the wider school community as impositions and distractions from teachers' real work rather than as core parts of it. As a middle school teacher remarked in an interview:

> A lot of people here feel very put upon already by any number of things that we've been asked or told to do. There's committee after committee. There are documents after documents after documents that have to be filled out. There's something called an IP plan [improvement plan] and people are just feeling really really put upon.

Teachers' rather negative reaction to all-school responsibilities was due partly to the existence of responsibilities like hall duty, in which teachers performed activities that someone with less specialized knowledge and education could well have carried out. Yet teachers frequently invested considerable time and energy without complaint when unspecialized activities had a classroom focus. For example, many elementary school teachers invested substantial time and effort creating wall decorations for their rooms. Although the planning of such displays certainly drew on teachers' specialized expertise, the execution, which could be quite time-consuming, generally did not. Furthermore, negative attitudes often continued to prevail when all-school activities did require educational expertise, as shown earlier in the teacher's remark about the IP process, which was intended to help the school set goals for itself as an institution, to develop specific objectives related to those goals, and to track the attainment of these objectives.

The particularity of each classroom and the teacher's autonomy in it were apparent in the fact that although student handbooks and the like contained schoolwide rules and policies about student behavior, teachers in the district were free to promulgate and enforce their own sets of classroom rules on a wide variety of matters. In fact, teachers saw familiarizing students with the rules of their classrooms as one of the tasks that they needed to accomplish in the first weeks of school each year, something that would hardly be necessary each year in every classroom if the rules did not differ, at least to some extent, from room to room. Furthermore, teachers had considerable leeway in deciding what they would teach and how they would teach it. Although decisions about textbooks and the like were generally made at the district level, in practice teachers often made substantial use of supplementary materials and made independent decisions about classroom and homework activities. The teachers' autonomy was also apparent in the fact that, within certain limits, they also seemed to have the right to determine who would enter their classrooms.

All these facts may explain the norms we observed about not entering others' classrooms while they were teaching and a sense of territoriality on the part of some teachers similar to that noted in Lieberman and Miller's work (1990). This sense of possessiveness was so strong that one member of the education staff, himself a former teacher, characterized the physical space of classrooms as "sacred" in the teachers' view. Whether or not individual teachers actually felt a strong sense of territory, it was common for them all to follow widespread norms dictating noninterference in other's rooms, which led to a de facto hands-off policy regarding others' classrooms and the resources in them.

Consequences for Internet Use

The implications of these interrelated orientations for Internet use were numerous and sometimes quite important. Among these were higher costs and a failure to use equipment efficiently.

To begin with, these norms related to autonomy and territoriality increased costs. For example, because teachers often worked hard to obtain and then retain the particular room they wanted, moving them from one room to another based on considerations of efficiency or cost sometimes just did not seem worth the effort. To illustrate, when a NET team member in one high school refused to move to a classroom that was nearer the rooms of the other team members because she liked her classroom's location, an extra $2,000 was spent on wiring her part of the building for Internet access rather than forcing the issue and trying to make her either move or leave the NET team. There was considerable dismay later when she became one of the least active Internet users on the team in spite of the special effort to accommodate her room preference. Not only was the expensive wiring not used to any significant extent, but her attachment to the room kept others from occupying it and making use of the access point.

Similarly, computers placed in a given classroom were then seen as belonging to the teacher using that room. This tended to be a barrier to others' use of these resources. Although joint action brought the computers in, the assumption was widespread that teachers had the right to determine who would use the computers and the Internet connections located in their rooms even when a class was not in progress. After telling an interviewer about a teacher who had his computer placed in a photography darkroom that could be entered only through a storeroom at the back of his classroom, a NET team member went on to say:

> One of the problems in a lot of schools . . . [is] teachers wanting to lock this stuff [NET computers] up and hide it away, squirrel it away. . . . [These teachers] want computers that they're given access to be given only to people that they say, when they say, at the time they say, and they want total control of who has access to it. They don't want anybody else even looking at their machines.

A large majority of teachers we interviewed about this topic expressed a willingness to let other teachers have some access to the computers in their classrooms if needed. In addition, there were numerous cases in which teachers actually did enter another teacher's classroom to use the Internet connection. But there was always the sense that the teacher whose room it was had the right to grant or withhold permission. Furthermore, although most teachers said they would be willing to let other teachers have access, in reality such sharing was not the behavioral norm. Norms about the privacy of classrooms were such that teachers often felt hesitant to ask for access. As the computer coordinator in one NET school pointed out:

> The people that don't have ready access to a computer and have to step into someone else's classroom, and use it . . . are the ones that are the most reluctant to use it . . . because it is kind of a barrier. . . . They . . . feel that they have to step into somebody else's space.

The NET education staff was frequently frustrated by such norms, as indicated in a staff discussion of the idea of requiring collaboration among schools applying during the fifth-year annual competitive process (ACP):

> Peter [Marcus] and Ian [Dutton] continued to say that the point is that they [schools] would be sharing support and expertise. Mark [Schneider] raised his voice . . . and he said almost angrily and in great frustration, "Over the [one hundred] years of this school district, no one has ever shared anything!" At this, Nellie [Watkins] exclaimed and clapped her hands and said, "Yeah, exactly! That's exactly true. . . ." Mark continued, ". . . if the technology is not in your room but it's next door, . . ." and then he paused and said, "not to mention up the hill [at another school], you just don't use it."

Difficulties in Reallocating Internet Access

Unfortunately, this sense of possession persisted even when Internet connections were not used in a classroom to any noticeable extent. The sense of teacher ownership of resources located in the classroom made reallocation of computers that were woefully underused or not used at all very difficult, as indicated in a field note from a NET education staff meeting in which a heated discussion occurred about how to handle NET team members who were not using their Internet access much:

> Mark [Schneider] went on to say, "The only thing you can do is make clear they have to use it." He said . . . "I promise, coming into the fall, I will walk into their rooms and, if they are not using it, pull it out and put them where they will be used. I refuse to allow technology to be wasted because of the code that never gets mentioned, and that is 'The minute I close my door it's mine,' [so that] . . . once a teacher acquires a piece of equipment, even if they don't use it it is theirs." Peter [Marcus] said, "I don't think you can do much about Sally [a low user at

Clark]. You can't take the computer from Sally . . ." Mark replied, "We are not part of the culture there. We do not have to play by their rules."

Nevertheless, NET did play by these rules ultimately, and, to our knowledge, NET staff never took a computer from a classroom due to lack of use. In addition, NET ended up taking territoriality as a given in planning discussions. Even Mark Schneider, the proponent of clashing with school norms in order to maximize use of equipment, argued against a plan to keep a small number of spare computers handy for NET team members by housing them in classrooms and in favor of a plan to keep such computers under the control of the NET technical staff. That way, he argued, they would not become the de facto property of specific teachers but would stay available to be dispersed as needed.

The assumption that the computers that educators obtained through NET were the property of the individual members of the teams in whose rooms they were located was likely fostered by factors in addition to teachers' individualism and focus on the classroom. First, when a problem arose with a classroom-based computer, the classroom teacher generally had to solve it or to contact others to solve it. This was a disincentive for sharing because other users could inadvertently cause the problems that then had to be solved. Second, many teachers participating in NET had gone to a considerable amount of effort to bring Internet access to their classrooms, and this lent credence to the idea that they should be the ones to control the fruits of that effort.

In addition, other aspects of the school milieu reinforced the tendency not to reallocate unused computers due to territorial norms. For example, as we discussed in Chapter Two, many participating teachers felt strongly that Internet use would greatly benefit students. Hence, others might likely interpret giving up an Internet-linked computer as a sign of failure to accomplish something important for students' learning, and that might threaten the teacher's self-image. Consistent with this, Olson (1988) has observed that having a computer in the classroom can serve an important expressive function for teachers by conveying an image of modernity and progressiveness. Thus, reallocation of such a resource threatens the teacher's image in a very public way.

However, in spite of the complexity of the forces leading to the sense of Internet-linked computers as the property of specific teachers and the failure to move unused computers, the sense of individualism and the focus on the classroom as the domain in which teachers make their largest professional investment appeared to contribute especially strongly to these phenomena.

Tendency to Divide Resources Rather Than Share Them

The Waterford Public Schools (WPS) district teachers' sense of individualism and their focus on their own students and classrooms contributed strongly to the way they envisioned both Internet use and the desirable locations for Internet access. Over 60 percent of the proposals submitted to NET that specified computer location requested arrangements in which each teacher had a small number of Internet-linked computers in his or her classroom, rather than arrangements in which most computers were massed in large clusters in shared spaces such as the library or in which portable machines would allow greater flexibility of use. In contrast, only roughly 40 percent of the proposals requested Internet access for computer labs. However, about 30 percent of the proposals submitted to NET (including some of the proposals asking for classroom or lab computers) did request that some computers, usually three or four, be clustered in the school library, perhaps because the NET staff initially strongly encouraged and then later required this (as well as the participation of librarians on the NET teams). Further, three of the schools participating in the competition requested portable computers or carts to help move computers from room to room as needed. Nevertheless, the majority of the time, the emphasis was on Internet access for individual classrooms, even though financial constraints meant there would be only a few connections per class. (This is an important topic, and we will have occasion to return to it later.)

ORGANIZATIONAL STRUCTURE AND CLASSROOM PROCEDURE GEARED TOWARD BATCH PROCESSING

As we discussed in Chapter Three, for reasons of cost, efficiency, and the accomplishment of democratic ideals, U.S. public schools are organized for batch processing large numbers of students, handling them in relatively large groups and treating all in a group in roughly similar ways. This can be seen even in the way that standardized testing, which plays such an important role in the United States, is generally organized. The assumption is that all students should achieve a core set of competencies, an approach that does not encourage extensive specialization. In Chapter Three, we discussed one set of consequences that arises when the batch-processing approach meets the individualism of the Internet. Here, we discuss a related but different issue— the way that the batch processing of students influences how teachers react to the opportunity to use the Internet in their classes.

One of the clearest manifestations of the tendency to employ batch processing in U.S. classrooms is the use of whole class instruction. In fact, Goodlad's mammoth U.S. study (1984) found that lecturing and explaining, usually done in a whole class context, were the most frequent instructional activities according to teachers, students, and classroom observations.

Batch Processing in NET Classrooms

Many of the schools and classrooms participating in NET were no exception to this rule. Our observations suggest that whole class methods often predominated in NET classrooms, especially at the middle and high school levels. This should not be surprising on three counts: each teacher in these schools may deal with more than one hundred students a day; batch processing is relatively simple compared to approaches that require dividing the class into smaller groups; and this method enjoys widespread popularity among educators elsewhere. Observers noted other techniques in NET classrooms. In many elementary school classrooms, small-group activities were quite common, and such activities certainly occurred, although generally with less frequency, in NET classrooms at middle schools and high schools as well. Nonetheless, the influence of a tendency toward batch processing was often evident. For example, teachers might divide students into small groups to work on the same problem before returning to a whole class discussion rather than having each group take on a different problem or activity. Distinctly less common were situations in which children used classroom time to pursue a multitude of different activities individualized to reflect their varied interests and skills. This is not a criticism of the teachers; more individualized approaches would most likely require smaller classes and more time outside class for teacher activities such as planning and grading. Instead, our point here is that the exigencies of dealing with large numbers of children at once shape the classroom in ways that have important implications for Internet use.

Consequences for Internet Use

In classrooms characterized by batch-processing approaches to teaching and with only a few computers, student Internet use is likely to be limited and also unequally distributed among students.

LIMITED INTERNET USE. The use of whole class or group-based methods that have all children working on the same thing at the same time combined with the very common tendency to locate a small number of computers in each NET teacher's classroom limited Internet use in very clear ways. Teachers themselves recognized that having a small number of Internet-connected machines per class did not fit very well with batch-processing instructional techniques. Unfortunately, this recognition often came after the fact, as this conversation between a researcher and the leader of a middle school's NET team reveals:

> I [the researcher] stood and talked with Ms. Danillo for just a couple of minutes . . . about the constraints that exist when there is only one computer per classroom. She said that it was a problem of their own making—that when they had to write a proposal and figure out the configuration of the computers they didn't know what they were doing. She said, "We went blind." So [she said] they've made some mistakes in making their decision from the start, and they're facing the consequences of those mistakes now that they know more. They're kind of locked into it because of the wiring. . . . She doesn't think . . . that they made the right decision in doing one computer per classroom. She sees some pros to it in that it's easy for the teachers to use it for themselves in the little time they have between classes, but it's not an easy thing to use with a classroom of students.

This teacher's opinion was far from idiosyncratic. Of the NET team members responding to an open-ended question about the biggest obstacle to Internet use ($N = 64$), over 50 percent said that having a small number of computers per classroom was their most significant problem. One teacher, in reply to a similar question about the factors that would be most important in helping him use the Internet effectively with students, put it this way:

> I guess access to enough computers. I mean that would have to be the biggest factor. We can work around . . . just about everything, but having twenty students—and that's a small class—and only one computer that's hooked into the Internet is a major factor.

Interestingly, educators virtually always saw the problem to be the number of computers per classroom rather than the batch-processing approach to teaching.

It is undeniable that having a very small number of Internet-linked computers per classroom constrains students' Internet use, regardless of the instructional technique of the teacher. For example, in a class with thirty students that meets for roughly forty-five minutes a day, as is quite common in middle and high schools, the most any student could use the Internet, assuming individual and roughly equal use of one computer, is about eight minutes per week. This is not very much time, especially given the delays that students often encountered in connecting to sites and in conducting searches. Having students work in groups could increase this time markedly, although it requires students to have the ability to work together efficiently and opens the door to the possibility that one student might dominate and direct use while the others are just along for the ride. Internet use could also be increased for individual students whom educators think especially likely to profit from it, although only at the expense of other students' use, given limited classroom time and access. Teachers could also use liquid crystal display, or LCD, projectors that would allow them to display a computer screen for the entire class to see, thus involving large numbers of students at once in a whole class Internet-linked environment. NET teachers did this only infrequently, perhaps because many of them were not even aware of this technology.

In NET classrooms, the use of whole class instructional methods and other approaches that had students working in parallel on the same activity exacerbated the limits to use set by the ratio of computers to students. Such classes generally included large chunks of time during which the teacher covered material both new and fundamental enough that he or she felt all students should be paying close attention to it. Thus, the teacher devoted considerable time to activities he or she deemed to be important enough to require all students' simultaneous attention, and that time was not available for Internet use. This would not necessarily be the case in classes organized into smaller subgroups that rotated through the different learning activities designed for them, one of which involved the Internet.

Another important factor limiting Internet use when educators used whole class methods in classes with a small number of Internet access points was that the teacher was simultaneously responsible for ensuring the smooth and efficient progress of the main lesson for the bulk of the students and for assisting a smaller number of students working on the Internet when it was in use. In such cases, the teacher often had to choose between having students who encountered problems on the Internet waste time as they waited for help and putting the larger class on hold while the teacher addressed the Internet problems. One teacher described this as making her feel that she was running two classes simultaneously. Another teacher had a similar reaction:

> I feel like I have to be two places at [once], because they always have questions when they're on the computer. Always. And then I'm teaching a class, and I try to send some of them back there and then I just say, "Okay, away from the computer, because I can't come help you now."

Previous research on classroom use of other computer applications has found that whole class instruction coupled with a small number of computers raised similar obstacles (Cuban, 1986). However, these problems are exacerbated when students use the Internet. First, because many teachers are quite concerned about harmful or dangerous materials to which students might be exposed, they feel a special responsibility to monitor students' Internet activity closely. This is more difficult to do when trying to lead the whole class than it is when the teacher has small groups working on projects and is freer to circulate readily around the room. Second, because the Internet is not specifically designed for use in schools, as many of the other applications used there are, students are more likely to encounter unanticipated problems or to require help in using the application, creating more demand on the teacher's time and attention. Finally, as we discussed in Chapter Three, most teachers know from experience that students typically find sports or other entertainment-related Web sites very attractive and that many of them can access these sites very quickly. Thus, teachers have the additional concern of whether a student has drifted to such sites for recreational purposes instead of pursuing strictly educational goals as instructed. Although concern about playing rather than working is not exclusive to Internet use, it is most salient there because the Internet offers a wide range of highly attractive recreational possibilities, whereas most of the game software on school computers has at least some purported educational value.

For all these reasons, NET teachers perceived Internet use as having the potential to distract them from teaching students who were not using the Internet and to exercise that potential more strongly than did other common kinds of computer applications. This led even teachers who were very enthusiastic about the potential of the Internet to sometimes despair of using one or two Internet connections productively with students in large classes, as was apparent during a meeting of a very active NET team in an elementary school during the team's third year of work together:

> Ms. Nacarato passed out the summary of work that she had done with her students. . . . She had written, "I suggest that as a team we share and discuss ideas on ways to schedule time for students to use the computer in the classroom. I found it difficult to work with a student or group while conducting class." Ms. Fisher pointed this out to Ms. Gerard [another teacher] but didn't say anything. Ms. Gerard immediately said, "Yes . . . I think this is very important." [She then explained how she and another teacher team-teach so that while one of them is working with the majority of the students, the other one can pull certain kids out of the room to work with them on the Internet.] She said, "I really think it would be too difficult to do it otherwise." Most of the teachers murmured and laughed and Ms. Nacarato added, "Just say it's impossible."

Many NET teachers found ways to mitigate the problems associated with having a small number of classroom Internet connections available for relatively large numbers of students, often expending considerable time and effort to do so. For example, some increased the Internet time available by allowing students to use the classroom-based Internet connections before or after school, at lunchtime, or during other interstices in the school day. This constrained the teachers' use of that time because they felt at least some degree of supervision to be essential, but some teachers believed the cost to them was more than compensated for by the reward to students. Others allowed or even encouraged knowledgeable students to serve as computer and Internet helpers, thus reducing the number of problems that they were forced to handle themselves and allowing them to continue relatively unimpeded with their instruction of the larger group of students not using the Internet. Still others navigated to specific locations on the Internet before class in order to save class time and to allow students to focus on using such sites rather than on accessing them.

However, most of these tactics entailed some cost, a point we can illustrate with a practice sometimes used in elementary schools to save class time—having the teachers or librarians supervising the activity do the typing of e-mail messages that students write out by hand. Educators using this approach not only typed and sent the messages but checked for replies, printed them out on paper, and conveyed them to students. Handling young students' e-mail this way saved considerable class time because the students had such rudimentary keyboarding that it could take several minutes for them to type just one sentence. Indeed, it made possible e-mail exchanges that would otherwise have been prohibitively time-consuming.

However, this method also had some corresponding disadvantages. First, it transformed teachers and librarians into typists for at least part of the day, perhaps not the most productive use of their time given their many other responsibilities. Second, it did not allow students to develop familiarity with computers or with the process of sending and receiving e-mail, and at least some of the students involved in these exchanges appeared to have misconceptions about how e-mail actually worked, problems that using the system for themselves would most likely have rectified. Admittedly, the development of technical knowledge and skills was not highlighted in the goals many NET teams had for student Internet use, but it was certainly an additional kind of learning that occurred when students did get direct access to the Internet, even at the elementary school level (Davidson & Schofield, 2002). Third, one of the advantages of e-mail is the rapidity with which users can exchange messages. Having to go through an intermediary during both the sending and the receiving often delayed message transmission substantially. Finally, having educators type students' e-mail messages dampened the sense of openness and spontaneity that often characterizes e-mail use (Sproull & Kiesler, 1991). Some students felt inhibited in constructing their e-mail communications, even those explicitly designated as informal social communications to other students, because they knew the educator would become aware of their contents as he or she typed them into the computer, as an elementary school student noted in this interview:

> There's like some things you can't write on a computer . . . about your personal life or something. . . . I don't write those kinds of things on the computer because . . . Ms. Wolfson, she reads them, then types them up and sends them.

These student concerns were not unfounded. For example, in an e-mail exchange set up to foster communication between students of diverse racial and socioeconomic backgrounds, the supervising adult slightly reworded one student's message so that it no longer contained a direct invitation to meet and socialize, because the adult believed such a meeting might be a source of concern to the student's parents. To our knowledge, the student initiating the message never learned about the change; the student sending the message may well have interpreted the failure of the student receiving it to pick up on the invitation as lack of interest when in fact the other child did not receive the specific invitation.

The point we wish to make in this section is not that batch-processing approaches, and especially whole class instruction, obviate all or most of the potential benefits of Internet use when there are just one or two Internet-connected machines per classroom. For example, as we discuss in Chapter Seven, a substantial number of teachers reported using the Internet for professional development activities that had at least the potential to affect their classroom behavior and hence students' learning experiences. Furthermore, it was quite common for teachers to use the Internet to gather specific information, ideas, or material that they incorporated directly into their teaching, as an elementary school teacher described in an interview:

> Well, today I just finished up a unit on [the author and illustrator] Eric Carle, and so last night I was pulling up all kinds of . . . things. I got some illustrations, got a list of all his books, and all the books he illustrated. . . . It made for a better morning today because I had all these fresh ideas in my head. I had some things to show the children. . . . I printed some things out.

Rather, we intend this section to highlight the fact that the batch-processing approaches to instruction so common today limit and shape the nature and extent of students' direct use of the Internet as a learning resource in numerous potentially important ways.

UNEQUAL INTERNET USE. In addition to limiting student use of the Internet, despite the varied efforts many teachers made to increase the Internet time available, the use of whole class methods in classrooms with a small number of Internet-linked computers fostered differential patterns of use among different types of students. Occasionally, NET teachers became concerned that the fact of certain students' knowing more about the Internet and hence being able to do more than other students could with their Internet time was not consistent with the batch-processing approach. One teacher explained it this way, "Some of the teachers are trying to reduce the amount [of information] that any individual student gets [on the Internet] so that all of them get the same material." More typically, however, the batch-processing approach led to differential amounts of Internet use among students.

There were three ways in which the more advanced or better behaved students came to have disproportionate Internet access. First, the Internet was a resource that could productively fill the time of the more advanced students who finished classroom assignments ahead of their peers and who often needed less practice and review than their classmates. Because they were likely to have more free time for Internet use, they frequently ended up using it more. Second, the exigencies of trying to teach large numbers of students and simultaneously make use of limited Internet resources led to practices designed to reduce distractions caused by Internet-using students, such as allowing students skilled in Internet use more access than their less skilled peers.

Third, the combination of small numbers of Internet access points and whole class instruction increased everyone's sense that the Internet was a scarce resource. Students thus came to see Internet use as a privilege rather than as a basic resource like a textbook to which all students should have access, and this view compounded the tendency to differential use. This view was enhanced by the fact that NET teachers had made special efforts to obtain access for their students and that access was not available in most of the district's classrooms. It was also encouraged because students generally reacted very positively to chances to use the Internet, as we discuss in Chapter Seven.

Once the view of Internet access as a privilege became prevalent, it gave rise to the question of which students should be awarded this privilege. One middle school student captured his understanding of the process this way:

INTERVIEWER: Could you tell me what you know about how it's decided what kids get to use the Internet in your class and what kids don't?

TONY: Like the kids that behave and . . . get A's and B's [get to use it]. . . . The bad kids . . . sit in their chair and write.

This understanding of the linkage between behavior and Internet access developed quite early among students. One elementary school teacher described what had happened when he inquired of a group of fifth graders who were temporarily in his class why they did not know how to use computers or the Internet, given that their usual classroom had computers with Internet access:

[They said,] "Oh, we're not allowed. Well, only certain people are allowed to use it. . . . We're the bad kids, and we're not allowed." . . . We had about fifty kids in one room, and they were "the worst kids," whatever that means. And so I just said . . . "What are you interested in?" . . . It was basketball season so we searched for NBA. . . . I couldn't tear them away. And they . . . were using it in a productive way . . . in a useful way. And I'm talking about ten minutes of instruction. These kids were so eager. And we knew what their reputation is, and they are difficult, but they didn't break the machines.

We found this same understanding of Internet access in the reports of teachers and other students, and we observed it in practice in classrooms. In classes with small numbers of computers and whole class instructional methods, teachers often bestowed Internet access as a reward for desired behavior. Frequently, this meant it was granted in return for strong academic performance. However, teachers also awarded it for other kinds of desired behavior ranging from paying attention to remembering to bring in homework on time to appearing to be trustworthy. As one teacher put it:

Being [as there is] only one computer there, I use it as a reward. . . . So I think it . . . made it easier to control some . . . not control but . . . to use it as a reward for the kids who are on task and complete their work.

Educators' concerns about what students might see or do on the Internet reinforced the tendency to use access as a reward for desired academic and social behavior. Teachers believed that students who had shown by their superior academic performance that they were strongly motivated to achieve would be less likely than many of their peers to veer off into noneducational directions or to flout school rules about the kinds of Internet activities they should engage in. Similarly, students who showed a general pattern of behavior consistent with school rules were seen as more likely than their peers to obey Internet use rules. Because constant surveillance was often impractical, teachers felt most comfortable about giving such students access.

Interestingly, the teachers' power to decide which students got to use the Internet combined with the high value students placed on Internet use appeared to lead to Internet access functioning not only as a reward for desired behavior that would have occurred in any event but also as a mechanism that enhanced the teacher's control over the classroom, a result that other research also has found when access to technology use is conceptualized as a privilege (Martin, 1991). Many of the students, like Tony, the middle school student we quoted earlier, appeared to recognize a direct link between access and behavior. Moreover, in some classrooms, this link was explicit, as one high school teacher's comments on this topic illustrates:

> It's a good disciplinary tool. Like, "Okay, you're not quiet. Forget about the Internet. You're not gonna use it. We'll go back to the textbooks and we'll just go back to the transparencies and write stuff on the board."

Thus, educators used the promise of Internet access or the threat of removal of access to try to mold student behavior in various situations. This control function was clear in NET's acceptable use policy, which indicated that undesirable behavior on the Internet was sufficient reason for a student to lose Internet access. It was also highlighted by the fact that a number of teachers spontaneously characterized Internet use as "a carrot" that they used to shape student behavior. And it was not just any carrot. One teacher called it "one of the best carrots I've ever found."

EDUCATORS' INITIAL LACK OF COMPUTER AND INTERNET KNOWLEDGE

It is an established fact that, as a group, teachers in the U.S. public schools are not well prepared to employ computer technology in their teaching (Lewis et al., 1999; Willis & Mehlinger, 1996). For example, one survey found that fewer than 40 percent of the nation's teachers report that they feel well prepared to use technology for teaching (Mendels, 1999). A number of factors contribute to this situation. Many teachers belong to an age cohort that had either no exposure to computers during their years of formal education or exposure only to mainframe machines, which operate quite differently from the computers found in schools today. However, even younger teachers are often not well prepared to use computers in instruction. Teacher preparation programs do not generally require courses on instructional technology or integrate that topic into other courses. If individuals preparing to become teachers do not take such courses voluntarily, they are unlikely to be exposed to instructional technology in any depth (Willis & Mehlinger, 1996). In fact, "The universal conclusion of the literature on technology and teacher education is that teacher education, particularly preservice, is not preparing educators to work in technology enriched classrooms" (Sandholtz, Ringstaff, & Dwyer, 1997, p. 75).

Many districts around the country have responded to this situation by creating extensive in-service programs designed to prepare their teachers to use computer technology for professional purposes. Such programs are often quite useful. However, research suggests that they are often far from completely effective. One problem is that they commonly focus almost exclusively on technical skills; these are necessary for effective use of computer technology in teaching, but they do not begin to guarantee it. Too often neglected are fundamental issues such as what teachers and students might stand to gain from the use of computers, when such use is most likely to add value to teachers' efforts, and what kinds of specific applications are most likely to be useful for various institutional goals (Cuban, 1986; Schofield, 1995). Yet such issues must be addressed, for without examining these closely many teachers will have little systematic information about how and when their students would benefit from the use of computers in their classes.

Technical Inexperience Among NET Teachers

As we discussed in Chapter Two, NET team members were volunteers, most of whom evidenced eagerness to explore the Internet's possibilities either for themselves, for their students, or for both. However, like their peers across the nation, NET team members were Internet novices. In addition, again as we discussed earlier and like their peers elsewhere (Honey & Moeller, 1990), many educators participating in NET initially reported being afraid of computers and not having extensive knowledge about them.

There were, of course, some marked exceptions to this general lack of extensive computer experience. Some NET team members had built their own computers, and some had been using the Internet for a number of years in their work. In addition, it was quite common for teachers to have had a fair amount of experience with one or two specific computer applications, such as word processing. However, teachers' self-characterizations in surveys and interviews make it clear that the majority were relatively new to computing. Furthermore, even those who had some prior experience with computing often had little or no experience with the Internet. For example, when we interviewed NET team members from schools joining NET in its first two years ($N = 28$) about this topic, a full 50 percent reported that they had no experience with the Internet before becoming interested in NET. Responses to a survey of participants in a summer workshop held for teachers joining NET demonstrated the same lack of prior experience. "Last spring I had no idea of what [the] Internet even was" was a common type of comment. Indeed, when asked to describe their initial and current level of expertise in an on-line survey at the end of NET's fourth year, none of the librarians ($N = 27$) and only 5 percent of the teachers responding ($N = 296$) characterized themselves as advanced users at NET's inception. Finally, NET education staff observations were consistent with these findings. One staff member observed that it was common for teams submitting proposals to NET to include substantial numbers of individuals who had never been on-line. And another, who worked closely with the NET teams at several schools and who did a great deal of NET team member training, had this to say in an interview:

INTERVIEWER: How much experience would you say that most of the teachers who get involved have had with computers in general, and with the Internet . . . in particular before they get involved?

MS. WATKINS: I think it varied but . . . really I would say . . . very little, if any, prior involvement or knowledge.

INTERVIEWER: So you have a lot of novices on your hands?

MS. WATKINS: Oh yeah. Yeah. Yeah. A lot of novices, but it's really neat to watch their growth and just see the change in attitude. You know, we're dealing with a lot of people who have never touched a computer and who have probably vowed some time back that they never would touch a computer and these people are out there, they're doing things, and they are just so pleased and so proud.

Because the lack of computer and Internet experience was so clear, NET staff made extensive and varied efforts to provide NET team members with the training they needed. In addition, educators on some NET teams shared expertise with their colleagues, as we discuss in Chapter Five. These activities markedly enhanced educators' computer skills and knowledge about the Internet, as we discuss in Chapter Seven.

Even with this often considerable learning, NET teachers' level of expertise was often barely adequate to their responsibilities. For example, the technical staff was appalled to discover that teachers at one NET school were not using a tape backup system and were thus exposing themselves to the possibility of tremendous loss of needed materials. The teachers did not know how to perform the backup and did not have the experience that would have given them a visceral recognition of how important it was to learn to do it.

Teachers in schools joining NET in its later years were, as a group, somewhat more experienced with the Internet and with computers than those who joined in the early years. This probably reflected the considerable increase in individuals with home computers during the mid-1990s (McConnaughey, Lader, Chin, & Everette, 1998) and the dramatic expansion of the number of Internet users in the general population. In addition, and in spite of the general pattern of teacher isolation we discussed earlier, there was also some evidence of diffusion of information from members of NET teams to their colleagues in both their own and other schools. Interestingly, this often appeared to occur through informal channels such as social interactions between NET team members and their relatives or friends who also happened to be educators in the WPS district. Nonetheless, even toward the end of NET, most educators joining it still had rudimentary levels of knowledge about computing. For example, 57 percent of the teachers and librarians ($N = 54$) responding to the aforementioned on-line survey who reported having joined NET during its fourth year also characterized themselves as having joined NET as computer novices, a percentage not strikingly different from the 62 percent of teachers and librarians ($N = 34$) who joined NET in its first year who characterized themselves in the same way.

Consequences for Internet Use

The results of this generally low level of computer and Internet experience among NET team members were that teachers had some difficulty in developing effective ways to use the Internet in support of the curriculum; they sometimes hesitated to use the Internet in class at all; and they had to contend with the fact that some students knew substantially more about the technology than they did.

DIFFICULTY IN ENVISIONING CURRICULAR USES OF THE INTERNET. NET started with a very clear point of view about the role of the Internet in schools. The philosophy of those leading NET was that schools should use the Internet in the service of achieving curriculum goals and facilitating ongoing efforts at school improvement; it was not to be a schoolroom subject to be studied for its own sake. Reflecting this orientation, the proposal that originators wrote to garner funding for NET did not feature examples of how computer science classes would teach students about the Internet. Rather, it presented ways the Internet might be used in learning foreign languages, the arts, science, and mathematics.

Moreover, NET's grassroots orientation meant that the education staff encouraged and assisted teachers to gain enough knowledge about the Internet that they could develop their own ideas for integrating Internet resources into their curricula. Over time, the education staff compiled substantial lists of relevant Web sites, which they made available to teachers on the NET Web site. Furthermore, they encouraged teachers who had developed productive uses of the Internet to post their work for others to see. But both these kinds of materials were seen as resources that teachers could consult in order to develop their own ideas rather than as prepackaged curriculum units for teachers to adopt directly.

Although this approach contributed greatly to making NET appealing to a wide range of district teachers, when combined with the teachers' prevailing lack of Internet experience, it produced a significant problem. Some individuals, whom members of the education staff referred to as the visionaries, were familiar with the Internet and readily able to see how to incorporate it in their work in ways that clearly furthered their curriculum goals. For example, foreign language teachers who wanted to give students a practical use for the languages they were learning developed a set of e-mail, Internet Relay Chat, and newsgroup experiences for their students that did just this. However, a great many teachers had considerable trouble figuring out exactly how they could make good use of the Internet, partly because they knew so little about it and partly because they had little training or experience in developing curricula. Indeed, an education staff member commented that many teachers "had no more idea than the man in the moon" about how they were going to use the Internet. Thus, the need for teachers not only to learn about the Internet generally but also to have exposure to ideas and examples of how they might productively use it became apparent.

The proposals that educators submitted to NET did reflect a general awareness of the Internet as a rich source of information, with roughly 85 percent of the proposals mentioning plans to use it as an archive that teachers and students could access. This is consistent with the results of a national survey that suggest that information gathering for lesson preparation is the most common use of the Internet by teachers and that teachers have their students use the Internet more for information gathering than for any other purpose (Becker, 1999b). Furthermore, proposals also recognized the Internet's usefulness as a communication medium, with over 90 percent of them laying out at least one communication use (most typically contacting someone to get or exchange information). Nonetheless, lack of actual experience with the Internet clearly contributed to vagueness and fluidity in the plans, indicated by this note, e-mailed by one NET team member to another who had inquired about the first team member's plans several months after NET had accepted their group's proposal:

> Plans? We're not sure where to begin, as we really haven't explored yet all the possibilities of the Net. That is we're not really sure what we can do when we don't even know everything or even a significant number of the things that can be done. . . . Please keep in mind that everything is proposed, supposed, and hardly concrete.

Further, the specific curriculum activities that educators proposed often did not take full advantage of the special attributes of the Internet, such as its ability to facilitate collaborative efforts among those who are great distances apart or to provide a potentially rich and varied audience for students' work. On occasion, educators even proposed uses for which the Internet did not seem particularly well suited. For example, one proposal envisioned using the Internet to gather written histories from elderly people in the neighborhood of an elementary school for use by the students and the broader community. Although this idea had some appeal and would have enriched the resources available to the community, a number of trenchant questions were raised about it during an ACP review meeting. For example, might oral histories that community members deliver before a live student audience be more interesting and informative to students than written versions they could access over the Internet? Because the reading skills of these elementary school students were rudimentary compared to their ability to understand spoken language, might they not learn more about their community and its history from hearing someone speak about it than from receiving written messages about it? Might elderly community members, many of whom had only a grade school education and who had no computers in their homes, feel more comfortable and be more inclined to participate if they could talk directly to the students rather than having to communicate with them in writing by way of computers, with which many of them had no prior experience? Figuring out the specifics of productive uses of the Internet was not a trivial problem for participating teachers.

Compounding the impact of many teachers' lack of familiarity with the various kinds of potentially productive curriculum projects that the Internet made possible was their lack of real familiarity with the skills needed for its use. For example, some school librarians complained that teachers sent students to the library with instructions to "use the Internet," without realizing that the students needed specific search skills in order to work effectively. Students, especially younger ones, required someone to help them learn these skills and to guide them to sites providing information they could readily understand if they were to complete an Internet assignment in a reasonable amount of time. Similarly, a number of e-mail activities caused unanticipated problems owing to students' lack of keyboarding skills, as we mentioned earlier. When teachers had no prior classroom experience with students' use of e-mail and lacked extensive e-mail experience themselves, they just did not anticipate that it could take young students three or four times as long to compose messages on-line as to write them out.

Not only did coming up with ways to use the Internet effectively with students require some understanding of the opportunities the Internet provides and its requirements and constraints as an instructional tool, it required more technical knowledge than most teachers had. Throughout most of NET's life span, NET teams were expected to outline in their ACP proposals what equipment they would need and how they would deploy it. Unfortunately, teachers often did not understand much about the operational specifics of file servers and the different forms of Internet connections. Yet, these specifics frequently had substantial implications for how smoothly educators could conduct planned classroom activities. For example, we mentioned earlier that technical problems often arose when multiple users were working simultaneously. A NET staff member described a team leader as dropping "a bombshell" in letting it be known well into the project that she wanted twenty-six of her students to use the Internet in the same way at the same time. This was bound to overload the equipment at that school, which could not handle an entire class simultaneously engaged in identical work, although it could have handled this number of students if their activity had been planned to occur in a staggered or less uniform fashion.

Over time, many planned Internet activities evolved in quite unpredictable ways from their initial conceptualization as teachers learned more about the Internet's potential and also about unanticipated problems that made it difficult or impossible for them to realize their initial plans. Thus, vague, unrealistic, or less-than-optimal initial plans did not always doom NET team members to long-term lack of use of the resources they had gone to such efforts to procure or to continued unproductive use of the Internet. In many teams, individuals developed increasing expertise over time and also new and more effective plans for instructional use of the Internet. For example, one high school had unanticipated difficulty finding on-line mentors who would provide information on a variety of careers to its students, the majority of whom were not bound for college. However, once some NET team members became more familiar with the Internet, they reshaped the planned activity so that it steered students to a variety of existing databases with career information. As one teacher put it when we asked how her team's current use of the Internet compared to what she anticipated when she had joined NET a couple of years earlier:

> I couldn't have anticipated what we [are] doing. Night and day . . . because . . . I'd never seen the Internet to the extent that I have [now] seen it. I thought we would share some stories and maybe get some feedback. . . . What I see now is just incredible. . . . I couldn't have imagined it.

The major constraints on this evolution were technical choices that teachers had made earlier, when they still had little familiarity with the Internet and hence little idea of how they might most effectively use it. Specifically, NET teams had to decide right at the beginning of their participation in NET where they wanted their Internet access points placed. Lacking prior experience, team members had little concrete basis for deciding whether the access points were best clustered in labs or the library, distributed among classrooms singly or in clusters, or arranged in some combination of these plans. Once those decisions were made, the teams faced further decisions about the exact location of the computers in the library or classrooms, because the equipment NET installed typically required a physical connection between the computers and wiring used to connect them to the Internet. Furthermore, because it was much cheaper to install initially unused wiring and connection "drops" than to retrofit them later, educators had to make decisions about the desirability and likelihood of various kinds of expansion before the planned activities were under way. Therefore, teachers' initial lack of expertise in anticipating the uses that would come to be most valued continued to shape use over time, often in less than optimal ways.

HESITATION TO USE THE INTERNET IN CLASS AND TO ENCOURAGE OTHER EDUCATORS TO DO SO. One of the most obvious effects of teachers' lack of deep familiarity with the Internet was that many of them hesitated to use it as much as they would have otherwise in their classrooms. In fact, when we asked them to identify the biggest problem they encountered in trying to use the Internet in their work, almost 40 percent of the teachers we interviewed ($N = 64$) on this topic spontaneously mentioned lack of knowledge of the Internet (31 percent) or of computers in general (7 percent). Comments like these two were common:

> Until we can fly comfortably on our own, we are not ready for the children coming in.

> The teachers have to be real comfortable with it [the Internet] before they'll [use it]. . . because the kids are going to ask questions, and if the teacher's not comfortable, the teacher isn't going to know how to give the answer and [will] get very frustrated.

Obviously, it is difficult to teach efficiently and effectively when the teaching approach requires tools with which one is not familiar. This straightforward point was well illustrated in a high school classroom we observed in which the teacher was trying to show his students how to use e-mail so that they could undertake a curriculum project he and his colleagues had designed. His instructions had greatly confused the students, as their facial expressions, comments, and questions showed (the observer found them unclear also). As the teacher struggled to explain things to the class, he took a few seconds out for a whispered inquiry to the observer, asking whether she could remember his e-mail address, an action that clearly suggested a relatively low level of familiarity with e-mail.

As a result of their inexperience, even NET teachers who were quite excited about the Internet's potential for education often curtailed their use of it due to their concerns about the quality of the classroom experience they could provide to their students. Some tried to get around the problem by asking colleagues who were more knowledgeable about the Internet to trade classes from time to time. However, because trading classes often led to various kinds of inefficiencies and problems, this was not a very satisfactory or widely used solution. Furthermore, some of the more Internet-proficient teachers resented such requests; they believed that educators who wanted to use the Internet in their teaching should be willing to put in the necessary learning effort instead of imposing on others.

Finally, some kinds of Internet use raised a host of potentially important additional issues that required specialized knowledge beyond technological knowledge. When educators at one NET middle school decided to create a home page, for example, they found that in addition to needing technical knowledge they faced a number of difficult questions to which they did not know the answers. For one thing, they were not sure of the law pertaining to posting excerpts from copyrighted material on the Internet and had no knowledge of the sources (such as Rezabek, 1993; and Talab, 1986) that might have helped them answer this and other questions. Furthermore, they did not know what material by and about students they could post without parental permission and without being legally liable if an unscrupulous individual made use of the posted material to harm a student. One of the teachers involved with this activity lamented in an interview:

> [There are] so many things you have to worry about: "Can we do this?" "Is this legal?" "What about this, does this give access to the kids?" You can't take pictures of the kids and have them on there because there's legal issues around that. So all these things . . . are overwhelming. . . . I feel like I'm in the dark, running.

Indeed, faced with this complexity, educators occasionally discouraged their inexperienced peers from attempting to use the Internet with students, due to concerns both that their less experienced peers and their students might damage the equipment and that such teachers might be unable to give students appropriate guidance.

REVERSAL OF THE TRADITIONAL KNOWLEDGE DIFFERENTIAL BETWEEN TEACHERS AND STUDENTS. Teachers' lack of substantial technical knowledge not only created some difficulties as they tried to develop practical and productive uses of the Internet but also put them in an unusual situation vis-à-vis their students. Frequently, at least some of their students knew markedly more about computers and the Internet than they did, a situation not generally the case for the other subject matters they taught or the tools they used to teach them.

Teachers participating in NET were well aware of this knowledge differential. Almost 95 percent of the teachers we interviewed on this topic ($N = 48$) stated explicitly that students in general know more about computers than teachers in general do or are more comfortable with computers. Interestingly, the responses of teachers working in elementary schools were not markedly different from those working in high schools, with all but two of the twenty-one elementary school educators (88 percent) agreeing with this assessment of relative student knowledge. In answering a related question that asked these same teachers to compare their own computer knowledge with that of the students in their classrooms, the large majority (75 percent) still saw students as having the edge, in spite of the fact that educators had a substantial amount of training and support available to them through NET over and above that available to other teachers in the district. Large differences showed up between those teaching at the elementary and at the upper levels, with almost all high school and middle school teachers feeling their students knew more about computing than they did, and only a little over one-third (37 percent) of the elementary teachers feeling this way. Comments like the following from a middle school teacher suggest just how big some of the participating teachers felt the knowledge gap was:

I think that last spring I . . . had computer phobia. I was deathly afraid of them, and that was largely because of my ignorance. I've grown a great deal . . . in terms of my respect and knowledge of the computer. . . . There are actually students in this school that have a vast amount more of information and knowledge and command of computers than I do.

Students seemed to perceive the same knowledge differential. Sixty-seven percent of middle school students we interviewed ($N = 52$) reported that they sometimes knew more than their teachers about the Internet, and an additional 17 percent reported frequently knowing more about it. In sharp contrast, only 15 percent said they never knew more about it than their teachers. Results from smaller samples of high school ($N = 15$) and elementary school ($N = 28$) students followed the same general pattern with, for example, only 17 percent and 13 percent, respectively, of the students we interviewed reporting that they never knew more about the Internet than their teachers did. Although students noticed this differential, they did not seem to mind it. In fact, many seemed to take pride and pleasure in their superior knowledge, as this middle school student did:

> I think they [students] feel good [in this situation], because mostly the teacher always knows more and it sometimes feels good to know a little bit more than the teacher because it makes you feel . . . smarter and more educated.

Although all indications were that students generally reacted positively to this phenomenon, the situation was somewhat different for teachers. Classroom observations suggested that teachers' reactions to students' often superior knowledge about computing and the Internet varied markedly. The results of teacher interviews were consistent with these observations, with the majority of interviewees indicating that the reactions of their colleagues varied considerably, as the following comments from a middle school teacher suggest:

> I've seen teachers here who are very open to having students help them through [when they do not know how to accomplish something on the Internet]. I've seen other people who . . . certainly don't want to be taught this by one of their students. And I think then you have some people who are just in the middle.

Interestingly, many students also recognized this variation. For example, when we asked how teachers responded to situations in which students knew more about Internet use than their teachers, one high school student replied: "Some of them are fine [with this]; they like being ignorant at such things. Some of them [feel] ... angry that the students would know more than the teacher. And some of them just don't care."

These three different reactions appeared to have very different implications for Internet use. It was clear that some teachers reacted quite negatively when students knew more they than did, appearing to perceive this differential as a threat to their authority or to their sense of self as a teacher. For instance, when asked how his colleagues responded to knowing less than their students about the Internet, one teacher said:

> It probably would bother them. . . . [They would think] "They know more than I do," or "They could get over on me," or "I'm not the expert. . . . And that kind of diminishes me." Some people have a lot of problems with that.

Such reactions are hardly surprising. In the United States, the social structure of the classroom has traditionally been built around the complementary roles of teacher and student. An important part of the teacher's role is the exercise of authority, that is, legitimated power over the student (Bierstedt, 1970). The teacher's authority has a number of bases, but one of them is clearly his or her expertise and more specifically the gap between that expertise and the students' own (Benne, 1970). The following excerpt from an interview with a high school student suggests just how strong many students' expectations are that teachers will know more than they do:

INTERVIEWER: Let's say there's a situation where it's kind of obvious . . . that a given student knows more than a teacher does. How do the other students react to that?

DIANE: They're shocked. . . . They're amazed that the student knows more than the teacher. . . . So it's like, "Oh really, she's teaching the teacher how to do it." So they're interested and wanting to know how another student knows more than the teacher.

Any change in the classroom that undermines the teacher's image as a knowledgeable and competent individual with the ability to dispense sanctions when students act in illegitimate ways has implications not only for the teacher's sense of self but also for the functioning of the classroom. For example, some NET teachers were concerned that their lack of technical expertise would open them to disrespect and thus would increase the difficulty of maintaining control. Still others were concerned that it would undermine them by giving students an opening to behave in inappropriate ways with little fear of detection or reprisal. They were especially concerned that students with superior knowledge might cause damage to the computer equipment that the teacher would not able to accurately diagnose or repair. And their relative lack of expertise made it hard for them to distinguish between student actions that inadvertently caused problems and actions that were intended to do damage, thus creating dilemmas about how they should treat the offending student. The comments of a high school student who was unusually computer literate suggest such fears were not completely unfounded: "I guess we enjoy the idea that we can run rampant and nobody would ever know. And actually, we do run rampant and nobody ever knows it."

Teachers who saw the knowledge differential in a negative light as the likely source of challenges to image and authority reacted in numerous ways, many though not all of which diminished Internet use either directly or indirectly. Some tried to hide or downplay the disparity between their knowledge and that of their students, as the comments of one very technically proficient high school student indicate:

> I find a lot of times that our site administrator [a teacher] doesn't quite know some things about system administration that I do and is very protective of admitting that. He doesn't like to admit it to me, but he'll admit it to other teachers. So it's kind of . . . a tough spot for me to be in because I have to go to another teacher to find out if he really grasped what I [said] . . . because I'll send him some e-mail saying that something needs [to be] done on the server that is really his job. . . . [T]wo weeks later I've never gotten a reply. I'll go up to the library and speak to the librarian, and she'll say, "Oh, he came and asked me about that. I didn't know about it either."

A negative reaction to the knowledge differential tended to inhibit Internet use because it led to teachers' experiencing problems or inefficiencies with Internet use that could have been avoided or to their suffering through embarrassing situations in which their pretense became obvious. As another knowledgeable high school student explained:

The teachers who don't . . . know what they're doing [on the Internet],
. . . everybody knows that they don't know what they're doing. They
might try to act sophisticated and say, "Oh, this is what you need
to do," and I'm sitting there looking at them like, "That's not what you
do . . ." They try to act smarter than what they are.

Other teachers who reacted negatively to this differential con-
sciously decided to use the Internet less than they might have otherwise, especially at school. For example, one teacher commented that
she rarely checked her e-mail at school because she was not very good
at it, and she preferred to struggle with it in the privacy of her own
home where her tribulations would not expose her to embarrassment
in front of students and peers.

A few teachers reported that their negative reaction to the knowledge differential motivated them to find ways to enhance their
computer skills and familiarity with the Internet in ways that did
not entail student involvement. For example, teachers at one elementary school insisted that a NET staff member go around the room in
their school where much of their computer hardware was located and
put yellow Post-it™ notes with the names of the hardware on the various components of their system. A teacher at this school told the
NET staff member, "We're sick of feeling like idiots because we don't
know the names of the hardware that we're working with." Other
efforts were more substantial and included taking evening classes or
buying books or manuals for study. Such efforts at increasing their
knowledge seemed likely to ultimately increase teachers' Internet use
rather than decrease it as the other reactions to discomfort with lesser
knowledge did.

In sharp contrast to their colleagues' negative reactions, some educators' reactions to the knowledge differential ranged from a kind of
resigned acceptance to an actual welcoming of students' superior
knowledge. Two things made students' superior knowledge less threatening to teachers' sense of self and therefore eased acceptance of that
knowledge for some of them. First, an awareness that students had
grown up in a society permeated with computers and full of references
to the Internet, whereas their elders had not, made the differential
seem "natural" and "inevitable" to many teachers. Second, many noted
that a number of the most knowledgeable students had Internet access
at home, whereas many teachers did not. This also provided a clear
and relatively unthreatening rationale for the existence of the knowl-

edge differential. Although both of these understandings seemed to foster acceptance of students' greater knowledge, teachers' active welcoming of that knowledge appeared to depend on their pragmatic decision to use whatever expertise was available or on their philosophical position that such a differential was compatible with their views on teaching. We discuss these issues and the impact that acceptance of students' greater knowledge had on classroom functioning in Chapter Six.

TIME AS A SCARCE RESOURCE

Time is clearly a scarce resource in schools. A nationwide survey that asked teachers in detail about their work conditions and resources found that teachers reported shortages of time more than shortages of any other resource, including space, materials, and even such human support as direct assistance in the performance of various tasks or teaching advice and feedback (Bacharach, Bauer, & Shedd, 1986). Teachers widely perceived lack of time as a problem, both actual instructional time and time to perform such ancillary duties as planning, attending workshops, and grading. Roughly 70 percent of teachers reported that they experienced problems getting enough time for instruction itself; over 50 percent of the teachers reported constantly or frequently lacking sufficient time for activities that support instruction.

Scarcity of Time Among NET Teachers

Concern about time pressures also appeared common in the WPS district. Like their colleagues elsewhere, teachers in this district typically had relatively few extended periods during their workday when they were not scheduled to teach or to perform other structured tasks such as monitoring the lunch room or the hallways. Discretionary professional time, the time they had available free from students during work hours, was therefore generally not abundant. Furthermore, teachers had many things to do in those free moments, including planning lessons, preparing worksheets, grading papers, or just decompressing from the pressures of the classroom. As one teacher put it:

> I think people outside of public education might not realize . . . how
> little time there is to do anything. For example, in my schedule, I have

one period or forty-two minutes in the day when I'm not with students. . . . I'm supposed to be here at 8:00. Meetings start at 8:00 or
8:10, and when the meeting is over you start your classes.

Numerous school and district practices increased these time pressures for educators. For example, teachers sometimes were not sure
what classes they would be teaching until shortly before the beginning
of the school year, which meant that those who would have spent
some time over the summer preparing for their classes in order to
relieve time pressures during the school year could not do so. In addition, some of the schools participating in NET were in the midst of
restructuring efforts that consumed considerable amounts of some
teachers' discretionary time, as did a district-mandated planning
process.

For those involved with NET, several factors appeared to make lack
of time an especially pressing issue. For one thing, NET's grassroots
model of change, although popular with teachers, substantially lessened the probability that participating schools would make structural
changes to alleviate time pressures on NET participants. Because NET
was not a top-down innovation of personal interest and importance
to those in positions of power, district administrators had little reason to create policies dedicating expensive teacher time to NET or to
encourage administrators at the school level to do so. (In contrast, the
district did support substantial teacher planning time in connection
with the district-sponsored restructuring initiative, which occurred
during roughly the same time period as NET.) Thus, most NET team
members saw none or only a few of their other responsibilities light-
ened so that they could progress better with their NET tasks. Any
Internet-related work they did simply added to their workloads. Furthermore, some NET teachers worked under administrators who did
not value Internet use sufficiently to find ways to help the teachers
accomplish what they desired to. For example, in some schools, labs
with Internet connections frequently sat idle before and after school
or during lunch periods, even though many students would have chosen to use the connections at those times, because the principal did
not value students' use of the Internet enough to assign a teacher to
supervise the labs at those times.

Two other characteristics of the NET approach compounded time
pressures on NET teachers: its emphasis on having teachers develop
their own curricular applications for the Internet and its emphasis on

building school-based technical expertise. Again, the first character-istic was appealing to many teachers, but it did put much more of a burden on them than an approach that provided prepared ideas and related materials would have.

The time that NET's emphasis on the development of technical expertise in each school required of NET team members was com-pounded by the teachers' widespread initial lack of knowledge of the Internet and of computers more generally. However, even those who know how to use the Internet would find that learning to manage servers takes some time. Further, even experienced Internet users often find that seeking out resources can easily absorb tremendous amounts of time. The very richness that makes the Internet a valu-able resource can also increase the time required to find what one needs, not to mention the time spent on enticing on-line distractions. In addition, some educators and administrators in NET schools had a tendency to view teaching as the only "real" work to be done there (akin to attitudes that Evans-Andris, 1996, noted in other schools). This tendency meant that time initially set aside for technical support of NET team members sometimes ended up being devoted to higher priority concerns, making it difficult to accomplish necessary techni-cal work. The school-based systems administrator in one school, for example, complained that the school's principal constantly asked her to divert her attention to other activities. This behavior meant not only that individuals charged with specific technical responsibilities had less time in which to do them, it ultimately created problems for their Internet-using colleagues as well, because these individuals could not complete tasks that would have facilitated Internet use for them or their students.

Consequences for Internet Use

Limited Use

When we asked educators ($N = 64$) participating in NET to discuss the biggest problems they faced when trying to use the Internet, time was the barrier they mentioned most frequently, with mentions of having too few computers per classroom a close rival. Responses like this one from an elementary school teacher were common:

> Time [is the biggest problem]. Time for me to learn what to do, time
> for me to find things, time for me to figure out how to do things with

the kids, time for the kids to do things. Yeah, I would say time is the biggest problem.

Over 60 percent of all respondents in these interviews spontaneously mentioned time, with 17 percent citing problems caused by lack of in-class time to use the Internet, 25 percent mentioning problems caused by lack of out-of-class time to do things like explore Internet resources and keep up with the mass of information generated by e-mail and newsgroups, and 23 percent mentioning problems caused by both (respondents were able to mention more than one problem if they wished, although the question specifically asked about their biggest problem). Finding time in the school day into which teachers could readily fit the additional work necessary to bring their intentions for using the Internet with their students to fruition was not easy. Often, they were simply not able to find such time, and this clearly limited use, as the following excerpt from an interview with a teacher suggests:

> It takes time to learn your way around. You know, the Internet isn't easy. . . . And . . . there isn't anywhere in the schedule or in a teacher's daily routine to allow for the time that's needed, because it is a lot of time. . . . I think that's something that can be [the] . . . downfall of having all . . . these resources. Some people . . . just don't have the time to commit to learning about it and understanding it, and they just are overwhelmed by it and would rather do [their teaching] the old-fashioned way than invest the time.

The fact that the Internet is an ever-changing environment also interacted with time pressures to limit use. Web sites appear and disappear. They add and delete content. Further, the available materials expand at a remarkable pace and new Web sites specifically developed for teachers' and students' use come on-line frequently. The extra time that Internet-using teachers must invest to keep up with the changes can eventually discourage them from Internet use. Yet not keeping up can cause problems when older Web sites disappear or change.

Over the course of NET, the importance of having time set aside to enable teachers to realize their plans to use the Internet became more and more obvious, and the NET staff tried to develop mechanisms to get this time for participating educators. In its announcement requesting proposals, the first ACP (held in 1994) made no specific mention of the importance of administrative support for the NET team in terms of providing release time or related adjustments in school functioning. The second ACP held one year later required a statement of support for the NET team from the principal of any school submitting a proposal but laid out no specific requirements for the operational manifestations of that support. By the time of the fifth ACP (1996), the announcement named a specific requirement that participating schools "must be willing to contribute time for a user-administrator to support the project . . . [one who] has time, during the school day, to commit to this activity." Although this change clearly improved the situation for NET teams, even toward the end of NET time pressures remained a major factor limiting use.

NET also tried to alleviate time pressures related to teachers' need to learn about the Internet by paying participants to take training when possible, in effect lengthening teachers' formal workday or work year. Such activities were routinely oversubscribed by educators. However, because of the amount most teachers needed to learn; the rapidity of change on the Internet, which leads to the need for ongoing learning; and the limited resources available for payment for professional development activities, it was clear that much learning would have to done on a voluntary basis.

NET staff saw home Internet access as a potentially good way of building teacher expertise because it seemed plausible that many of the skills teachers would learn while accessing the Internet in the context of their personal lives would be transferable to their professional lives. Home access also allowed individuals who wished to do so to spend more time using the Internet with professional goals in mind, as many teachers did. However, even though home access appeared extremely helpful in alleviating time pressures and helping to build knowledge, it did not completely obviate time pressures as a barrier to Internet use.

A large number of NET team members devoted at least some time outside of their formal work hours to work-related Internet activities. For example, even the after-hours NET-sponsored training sessions that teachers received no remuneration for attending were routinely oversubscribed. Other teachers devoted their lunch breaks to meeting with team members or working with students who came to their classrooms to use the Internet then, or they worked at home on the Internet in the evenings to prepare for classes. However, a substantial number of teachers defined the workday fairly strictly by the hours stipulated in their union contract. One teacher who herself put in a large number of personal hours learning to use the Internet nonetheless indicated that schools could not generally expect teachers to put in large amounts of time after hours learning about the Internet for professional purposes, saying:

> You cannot expect teachers to do it on their own time. . . . Teachers will not. . . . You will find some who will, . . . but most teachers will not do that because their job description is to teach so many periods a day. They have papers to correct already anyway, and they do some professional reading.

Thus, the norms prevalent in many schools did not encourage individuals to contribute large numbers of unpaid hours to figuring out how to use the Internet effectively in their classes. Indeed, a participating teacher who was a computer hobbyist reported that he hesitated to stay as long after school working on NET activities as he wished to because such behavior was not considered appropriate at his school. The strength of such norms also was evident in a school in which the teachers involved in NET met only once in the fall and once in the spring during one of NET's early years. This team spent a good part of these two meetings fruitlessly trying to find a time when everyone could convene again. However, not once during these extended conversations did anyone even suggest meeting outside of school hours.

Teachers' lack of sufficient discretionary professional time to do all that they needed to do to enable their effective classroom use of the Internet was clearly an impediment to Internet use. However, as we indicated earlier in this chapter, NET teachers also commonly perceived lack of adequate in-class time to be a serious impediment to use. Two things appeared to be at issue here: the absolute amount of time taken by Internet activities and the lack of fit between the unpredictability of Internet access and the generally tightly scheduled school day. We discussed both these issues and their role in limiting use in Chapter Three. Here, we will just note that another factor contributing to the sense that there was not enough time for Internet-related activities was some teachers' perception that Internet use was an enrichment activity and not an important mechanism for conveying the basic curriculum or for transforming the curriculum in some desired way. This viewpoint was common in spite of the fact that NET strongly encouraged teachers to attempt to use the Internet in the service of their curricular goals, perhaps partly because the scarcity of access points combined with the delays and difficulties classes often encountered when trying to use the Internet made it impractical in many cases to build essential parts of a curriculum around Internet use. Also, as we discuss in Chapter Six, concerns about equity and about whether Internet use was the most efficient mechanism for teaching the core curriculum encouraged the view that such use was best treated as an enrichment activity.

CONCLUSIONS

In this chapter, we have discussed four preexisting conditions in the schools that appeared to shape and generally limit Internet use in important ways. The first of these, a tendency for teachers to see the classroom as a private domain for independent professional action, led to norms that treated the classroom as a teacher's personal territory and to possessiveness regarding the resources in that territory, including Internet-linked computers. It also led to a tendency to assume that access should be distributed equally across the classrooms of participating teachers. These tendencies increased the cost of access in some cases and also meant that computers were left in classrooms in which teachers made little use of the Internet.

A second condition, an emphasis on whole class instructional methods, combined with the relative scarcity of Internet access points and the tendency to distribute these points evenly across the classrooms of participating teachers, also limited Internet use substantially. Furthermore, it frequently led to inequality of use among students, with those who came to the classroom with knowledge of the Internet and those whose achievement was high or whose behavior was exemplary gaining disproportionate access (Schofield & Davidson, in press-a).

Teachers' widespread lack of extensive knowledge about computing in general and the Internet in particular also shaped and limited use. Many teachers made major strides in building their knowledge in these domains over the course of NET. Nonetheless, their limited facility and familiarity with the Internet narrowed the range of applications they were able to consider and led some teachers to limit student use due to their concern that they could not effectively teach using a tool they did not fully understand. The widespread lack of extensive technical knowledge among teachers often led to a reversal of the usual classroom situation in which the teacher knows more about the material being taught and the tools used to teach it than the students do. This reversal was sometimes apparent even at the elementary school level. Teachers' reactions to this reversal differed markedly. Some readily accepted the situation and found ways to take advantage of it, using technically knowledgeable students to build their own skills, help other students, and even perform tasks so that the teacher did not have to spend time learning how to do them. Other teachers found this role reversal uncomfortable and potentially threatening, which often led them to decrease their use of the Internet with students.

Finally, time pressures also played an important role in limiting Internet use. The NET approach itself exacerbated such pressures to some extent. However, other sources of such pressures, such as the relatively small amounts of professional discretionary time in teachers' days and the generally low level of preexisting knowledge about computers and the Internet, are not unique to NET and likely exist in many other districts attempting to institute Internet use.

Thus far, we have described and discussed a variety of impediments to Internet use. Clearly, it is especially important to consider factors that enabled educators to overcome these barriers to attain classroom use. Equally, it is critical to consider the extensiveness and types of use that educators were able to attain in NET. We turn to these topics in Chapter Five.

Achieving Internet Use

Lessons from NET Schools

A s our discussion so far makes clear, many factors came together to limit Networking for Education Testbed (NET) teachers' and students' use of the Internet in the classroom. In most cases, it was not the effectiveness or value of Internet resources in support of the curriculum that was at issue. The issue was overcoming a series of barriers that stood between teachers and students and those resources. Indeed, until such barriers are reduced, the value of Internet resources cannot be well explored.

Studies indicate that computers in schools are employed less frequently than might be expected (Anderson, 1993; Becker, 1985; Cuban, 1986; Loveless, 1996; U.S. Congress, Office of Technology Assessment, 1995; Schofield, 1995; U.S. Department of Education, 1993). For example, just 7 percent of U.S. eighth-grade math students reported frequent use of computers in their math classrooms in a 1992 international study (Anderson, 1993). Accounts of computers sitting virtually unused for long periods of time, boxed in a closet or gathering dust in a corner, are also common (Bowers, 1988; Piller, 1992; Schofield, 1995). And although more and more classrooms have Internet connections, not only do studies to date suggest that student

Internet use is relatively low but also that what use there is tends to be fairly narrow. In Becker's large-scale study (1999b) of Internet use in classrooms, for example, only one-quarter of teachers with modem-based classroom access and 30 percent of teachers with direct high-speed connections reported that they had asked students to do World Wide Web research on ten occasions or more over the course of the school year. Figures for other types of Internet use, like contacting other users through e-mail or placing student work on-line, are quite a bit lower. Becker found that just 7 percent of teachers had students use e-mail on at least three occasions during the school year, and even fewer teachers involved students in any sort of cross-classroom collaboration or Web publishing.

In Chapter Two, we demonstrated that despite educators' historical ambivalence toward technology use in schools, demand for Internet access was high among teachers of the Waterford Public Schools (WPS). We also discussed the fact that this demand translated into a growing number of NET Internet accounts over NET's five years and that teachers used their accounts on a fairly frequent basis. But in what ways did teachers use Internet resources in support of classroom instruction, and in what ways did use vary across NET schools? Our research addressed those questions, with two striking findings. Looking closely at teams of educators in a subset of NET schools, we found, first, that computers were not in the closet but were in use by teachers far more extensively in some schools than in others. Moreover, we found significant variations in student use. Teachers and librarians at some schools, as a group, made far more extensive and regular use of network resources for curricular projects and activities with students than did teachers and librarians at others.

Second, as we have been discussing, a variety of malleable and in some cases unanticipated social and organizational factors shaped this variation. That is, variation did not simply reflect differences in grade level, access to better or more equipment, or other factors such as the level of teachers' computer expertise that other studies have identified as contributing to variations in use (Becker, 1999b). Rather, high use emerged in both elementary and secondary schools. It also emerged in schools where NET teams were composed primarily of novice computer users with relatively limited access to computer resources. This chapter, then, investigates the factors that helped educators overcome barriers and attain high rates of Internet use relative to their peers. First, we look at variation in the amount of Internet use at NET schools; then we examine the different kinds of use NET teams devised; and finally we explore in considerable detail factors supporting extensive and substantive use.

VARIATION IN FREQUENCY OF INTERNET USE AMONG NET SCHOOLS

In Chapter Two, we presented data on NET teachers' overall levels of Internet account use. Behind these broad averages, however, lie some marked differences. To look at just one example, during NET's third year, the average educator working at a NET school who used a NET account was logged on to his or her personal account roughly 2.8 hours during an average month in the school year. However, at one NET school, the average was 12.1 hours per month per account-using educator, and at another it was less than ten minutes per month. Similarly, the number of educators who accessed their accounts during NET's third school year ranged from forty-five at one school to two at another, despite the fact that the NET teams at these schools were roughly similar in size.

Of course, as we discuss in Chapter Two and in the Appendix, for a variety of reasons, data on educators' account use must be considered an extremely rough estimate of their overall Internet use. Moreover, these data say little about how often educators used the Internet in support of classroom instruction, nor do they explain the variations in kinds of use. To learn more about classroom Internet use, we collected detailed data on Internet-based curricular activities implemented during NET's second, third, and fourth years at a subset of NET schools (see the Appendix for a detailed description of our choice of schools and the types of data we collected). We also collected data relevant to understanding the variations in use that we observed at these schools.

In selecting schools in which to study the issues discussed in this chapter, we limited our investigation to those that had joined NET during its first two years. This allowed us to explore use over a number of years and also avoided the potential pitfalls of basing our conclusions about the determinants of use on the study of schools only in their very earliest phases of involvement with NET, when Internet connections were still being established and teachers had not had time to have a significant amount of classroom experience with the Internet. In all, eleven schools, one of which served mainly as an office and training center for NET, joined NET during its first two years, but resource constraints made it impossible to conduct case studies at the ten that had NET teams with Internet-based curriculum activities. Therefore, we selected seven for close study of the issues we cover in this chapter: Riverdale Elementary School, Bogart High School, and Brayburn High School are the names we gave to the three first-year schools we selected; Regent Middle School, Meadowlark Elementary School, Southland Elementary School, and Clark Elementary School were the second-year schools we selected.

Of these seven schools, we chose four (Bogart, Brayburn, Southland, and Clark) because they were characterized by unusually intensive use of the Internet for instruction. At these schools, for example, NET team members collectively implemented over seventy Internet-based classroom activities, many of which required students to use the Internet regularly and intensively, during NET's second through fourth years. (The Appendix discusses our reasons for focusing on the second, third, and fourth NET years as the most informative and representative.) More than 70 percent of teachers on these NET teams carried out some sort of Internet-based curricular activity during that time period. Furthermore, at two of these schools, interest in using the Internet for professional purposes had clearly spread to teachers who were not part of the NET teams; account use data as well as data on curricular projects showed that the number of teachers making use of Internet resources was greater than the number on the original teams. Not surprisingly, then, account use during school hours at these four schools in NET's third year was markedly higher than that at any of the remaining first- and second-year schools. (Account use during school hours, or *school-time account use,* for educators and students combined at these schools ranged from 62.9 to 159 hours per month on average, compared to 31.4 hours on average at the remaining first- and second-year schools.)

The three other schools we studied with special attention to the issues covered in this chapter (Meadowlark, Riverdale, and Regent) were selected because of their relatively limited Internet use. Here, fewer educators carried out Internet-based classroom activities; we documented a total of just twenty-seven Internet activities during the three-year period from NET's second through fourth years. Further, many of these activities used the Internet in brief or irregular ways. Consistent with this finding, two of these schools evidenced extremely low rates of school-time account use for educators and students combined during NET's third year (.04 to 16.7 hours on average per month). The third attained a moderate rate of school-time account use (41.5 hours on average per month) but nevertheless, like the other two schools, was characterized by very little Internet use by many teachers. For example, just over one-third of the original NET team members at this school reported active involvement in implementing Internet-based curricular activities, and there was no evidence of Internet use spreading beyond the original NET team. Both the education staff member assigned to this school and the NET team leader there reported that it was very difficult to muster involvement and enthusiasm for Internet activities among team members.

VARIETIES OF CLASSROOM-BASED INTERNET USE

Five general types of classroom-based use occurred at the seven schools just described during NET's second, third, and fourth years. Here, we introduce these patterns and also provide an overview of the types of Internet activities that educators generally undertook. Later we move on to a consideration of the factors that encouraged Internet use and whose presence or absence helped to account for the wide variation in the amount of Internet use at different schools.

Five Patterns of Internet Use

In all, at least fifty-five educators at these schools worked individually and collaboratively to implement ninety-nine different documented classroom-based Internet activities involving several hundred students during NET's second through fourth years. These projects varied significantly in nature and scope. For example, in some instances, students worked on-line weekly or biweekly throughout the school year. In others, the Internet had only a minimal role, playing a modest part in a brief supplemental classroom project. Overall, we observed five common patterns of Internet use in NET classrooms: (1) onetime use, which gave students a brief introduction to the Internet and its resources as they carried out some relatively limited activity; (2) augmental project use, which involved students sporadically in Internet-based activities throughout the school year; (3) curriculum enhancement use, which employed the Internet briefly but quite regularly to complement students' ongoing classroom activities; (4) major project use, which involved students with the Internet and its resources for extensive amounts of time; and (5) integrated curriculum use, which made intensive Internet use a regular and important part of the curriculum. Although in practice the boundaries between these categories is sometimes blurred, they seem useful for heuristic purposes.

In the first pattern, brief onetime use, students engaged in a short assignment or project that introduced them to the Internet and some aspect of its capabilities. Activities of this sort were about 18 percent of those we documented, and they typically occurred in the early stages of Internet implementation as teachers experimented with ways of using the Internet. For example, at one high school, a social studies teacher arranged for his students to correspond on one or two occasions with a class in Leningrad in order to exchange cultural information (this project collapsed, however, along with the Soviet Union). Similarly, at an elementary school, a fifth-grade teacher interested in fostering her students' writing involved her students in an on-line project that invited them to read a draft of a children's story and provide feedback to the author. Students submitted their book reviews using e-mail and read reviews submitted by students from other schools as well. The following year, this teacher moved on to activities more directly linked to her day-to-day curriculum.

In the second pattern, augmental project use, students became involved in a supplemental project that went on for most of the school year but required activity only once or twice per month. Augmental projects made up about 19 percent of the uses we documented, and national Internet-based projects, involving students from around the country, were prominent in this category. For example, one science teacher involved 150 fifth-grade students in a national Internet program for elementary students. Students across the country planted tulip bulbs in the fall and then submitted on-line reports every two weeks from January to June about the sprouting and blooming of these tulips. Students looked at data from around the country to consider the characteristics of their own schoolyard habitat and to learn about seasonal differences in different geographic zones. In an augmental project at the middle school level, a social studies teacher involved a group of eighth-grade students in cross-cultural exchange about current events. The students selected an article from the local newspaper, wrote a reaction to it, and then placed the story and their reaction on-line. Students from other countries responded by e-mail to the article and the opinions expressed and sent articles of their own. This exchange occurred sporadically over a period of several months.

In the third common pattern, curriculum enhancement use of the Internet, teachers implemented regular, brief, and reoccurring Internet-based activities to supplement their basic curriculum. These activities, 29 percent of those we documented, exposed students repeatedly to the Internet and a variety of Internet resources. However, they did not substantially change students' daily classroom experiences, because each activity tended to enhance the existing curriculum for only a brief period. In one very common kind of curricular enhancement activity, for example, an individual or a small group of students went on-line for a brief time (usually less than twenty minutes) to gather information that would help them complete a regular daily activity or enhance a classroom discussion. For example, at one elementary school, kindergartners went on-line daily to gather information from a designated Web site about the local weather and then used this information to complete a daily weather calendar. Similarly, at the middle school level, students frequently used the Internet to collect information for an international portfolio that they worked on over the course of the school year during a homeroom period, but the Internet was only one of many sources from which these students gathered information.

In the fourth common pattern of use, major Internet-based projects, 19 percent of the uses documented involved students in a more intense and substantive way. Here, a group or class of students used the Internet for an extended period of time as an integral tool to complete a major project or to explore a major topic of interest. For example, at one elementary school, two classes of third-grade students used the Internet in producing research papers on the rainforest animals housed at a major zoo nearby. The students first used the Internet to access and download information about their particular animal from the zoo's home page. They then corresponded with adult experts at the zoo by e-mail about the animal, posing questions and including the experts' responses in their reports. Similarly, some high school students worked over a period of several weeks to create a school home page. Initially, they explored the Internet to find other school home pages to use as models. They then developed written outlines for the page, entered this text in Hypertext Markup Language (HTML), and scanned pictures and stored them in Unix directories for recall and placement on the page.

In the fifth and final pattern, intensive, integrated curriculum use, students worked with the Internet as a core part of the classroom experience, using it intensively and regularly (11 percent of the activities we documented fit in this category). Interestingly but not surprisingly, because this type of activity would tend to contribute significantly to increasing Internet use overall, ten of the eleven projects of this sort occurred at the four high-use NET schools in our subset. For example, at one high-use high school, students studying the German, French, and Spanish languages corresponded repeatedly and at length with native language speakers, forming pen-pal relationships that teachers intended to play a significant role in the students' language acquisition. They also visited their school's computer laboratory regularly to use additional Internet resources, such as newspapers and Web sites, in their chosen language. When engaging in pen-pal activities, they tended to work for the entire class period either on writing their e-mail messages or on interpreting the responses they received. In another intensive project, groups of elementary age students met weekly with their school librarian to read and respond to a variety of stories in an electronic chat environment that the librarian had created. These students also read their schoolmates' responses to these stories and replied to them, and some students published their own stories in this on-line environment. This activity was specifically designed to encourage students to learn how to write, and it constituted the primary focus of their sessions with the librarian.

Student Internet Activities

Prior studies of Internet use in schools (Becker, Ravitz, & Wong, 1999) have made the point that it is important to consider not only how much use educators and students achieve and how regularly this use occurs but also the nature of the on-line resources students use and the activities they engage in, because the Internet offers such a wide variety of choices. For analyzing Internet projects, we adopted six categories that together provided a means of characterizing the Internet activities documented in the seven schools we studied: (1) doing archival research at Web sites, (2) contacting others on-line in order to get information, (3) interacting with others on-line in order to exchange information, (4) getting sustained help on-line from an adult or other expert, (5) producing material on-line for others, and (6) acquiring technical training on-line. In many instances, a single project involved students in several of these activities.

NET educators tended to have their students make use of the Internet's archival resources relatively frequently. Of the ninety-nine

Internet-based curricular activities we documented, 46 percent required students to carry out research at some Web site. Use of this sort occurred quite often at both low- and high-use schools but relatively more often at low-use schools (67 percent of the uses at low-use schools as compared to 39 percent at high-use schools). This finding is not particularly surprising because this sort of activity is an obvious and ready way for educators to make use of Internet resources.

NET educators also took advantage of the opportunities the Internet offers for contacting individuals outside the classroom, typically through e-mail but occasionally in the context of newsgroups or on-line chat rooms. In about 40 percent of the curricular projects we documented, students used Internet resources to interact with others. Some of these interactions involved little more than students contacting others in order to gather information about a topic of interest, a use that was more typical at low-use than at high-use schools (18 percent of projects at the former compared to 6 percent at the latter). For example, students might write to an adult to ask a question about a specific topic on which the students were planning a report. However, students also contacted adult experts or mentors who provided them with regular help. Although there were an equal number of projects in which students received technical help in this manner at high- and low-use schools, activities in which students received help in academic subjects for a sustained period of time were much more prevalent at high-use schools than low-use schools (15 percent of projects at the former compared to 3 percent at the latter). Another activity somewhat more common at high-use schools than at low-use schools (17 percent compared to 11 percent) was students' use of the Internet to exchange information with peers in other parts of the country and overseas.

Finally, a good number of NET educators at these seven schools used the Internet to publish student work or information about the school. About 18 percent of the projects we documented involved Web publishing. For example, students worked with teachers to create school newsgroups or home pages, to construct personal home pages, or to publish pieces of their writing on-line. Again, a higher proportion of the projects at high-use schools used the Internet in these endeavors than did those at low-use schools (22 percent compared to 7 percent).

In sum, the students of NET educators engaged in many kinds of activities using a variety of Internet resources. However, Internet projects varied markedly in terms of the extent to which they affected students' day-to-day classroom experiences, provided students with significant and reoccurring exposure to the Internet's resources and possibilities, and functioned as an integral part of the curriculum.

Although educators at both high- and low-use schools devised a variety of uses of the Internet, educators at high-use schools tended not only to develop more Internet-based projects but also to implement intensive projects that had a recurring and substantial impact on students' school experiences, integrating the projects into the curriculum rather than appending them to it. Because of this finding, it appears especially critical to identify the factors that supported educators in providing more frequent uses of the Internet to their students.

FACTORS THAT SUPPORT EXTENSIVE INTERNET USE

To try to understand the variation in frequency and kinds of Internet use and the reasons that only some educators successfully negotiate impediments to active technology use (such as those we identified in Chapters Three and Four), we gathered a great deal of data across the seven schools (see the Appendix for details). Additional interviews with teachers at other NET schools provided further information relevant to understanding the factors that affect Internet use. Eight social and organizational factors associated with extensive Internet use emerged from analysis of these data, and we discuss them in the sections that follow. These factors include team cohesion, project ownership, collaboration, active librarian involvement, strong teacher leadership, ease of integration, discretionary professional time, and technical reliability. Table 5.1 lists them in relation to high- and low-use schools. In deciding whether to characterize a school as demonstrating each of these eight characteristics, our emphasis was on triangulation: we looked across all data sources to consider whether and to what extent different teachers, administrators, and education staff members agreed that a given high-use school had a particular characteristic.

As Table 5.1 illustrates, factors combined in different ways at different schools, and it does not appear that a school needs all eight characteristics to achieve relatively high use. However, having a predominance of these factors is clearly associated with more Internet activity. Overall, no one or two of these factors alone appears to explain the variation we observed, but in larger combinations they interact to produce and sustain relatively high levels of use.

	Team Cohesion	Project Ownership	Collaboration	Active Librarian Involvement	Strong Teacher Leadership	Ease of Integration	Discretionary Professional Time	Technical Reliability
High-Use Schools								
Bogart High School	High	High	Low	Yes	Yes	High	Moderate	Yes
Brayburn High School	Moderate	High	Moderate	Yes	No	High	Moderate	Yes
Clark Elementary School	High	High	High	No	Yes	Low	Moderate	Yes
Southland Elementary School	High	High	High	Yes	Yes	Low	Moderate	Yes
Low-Use Schools								
Meadowlark Elementary School	Low	Low	Low	Yes	No	Low	Low	Yes
Regent Middle School	Low	Low	Low	Varied[a]	No	Low	Low	Yes
Riverdale Elementary School	Low	Low	Low	No	No	Low	Low	No

Table 5.1. Social and Organizational Factors Associated with Internet Use

[a]Indicates a change in library staff.

Team Cohesion

Team cohesion refers to positive interpersonal relationships, team members' sense of being part of a special group, and regular contact among the majority of team members. With the exception of the NET team at Clark Elementary School, where an administrator was an active team member, all high-use NET teams were composed of teachers and librarians only, and at three of the four high-use schools these team members commonly described their teams in terms that suggested team cohesion, saying, for example, "It's a real warm relationship I think between the group there. . . . [I]t's real nurturing and comfortable—easy to be around." The fourth high-use school did not evidence broad team cohesion, but groups of educators did have positive interpersonal relationships and interacted with one another regularly. Educators at low-use schools, in contrast, reported infrequent to no contact among team members and a low sense of camaraderie, saying, for example, "We've never had the group together. . . . [A]s a team, there really isn't a dynamic." Our findings about the importance of team cohesion are consistent with other studies that indicate that good working relationships among teachers enhance the implementation of change efforts and promote continued use of innovative methods and materials (Berman & McLaughlin, 1978).

Team cohesion is generally beneficial, explained educators, because it helps foster social exchange about topics of common interest—in this case, Internet use. At almost all high-use schools, educators reported considerable discussion about NET-related work among all team members. "We even spend time talking about it during our lunch time," said one teacher. "Everyone is wonderful and happy in providing support to everyone else." Such discussion tended to create a sense of mutual support and gave educators access to advice, inspiration, and ideas, enhancing motivation and the acquisition of knowledge. As one educator explained, "That's our first resource, to go to one another and say, 'Are you having this?' or, 'Are you trying to find that?' or [to hear] somebody saying, 'This is a wonderful [Web] address. Try this out.'"

Even educators from schools where cohesion was low commented on the relationship between team cohesion, social support, and use. As one educator at Regent Middle School, where Internet use and the number of team meetings were both quite low, noted:

> I know that there's a lot of teachers here who have the computers
> and . . . just never touch . . . [them] because they don't know how. So

for me, not having a meeting, I can still do the things I like to do without having to ask people how to do things, whereas for other people, it's probably a drawback to them because they just see a machine sitting in the room and probably [they are] not even thinking of the Internet as on it.

Such teacher descriptions are consistent with findings from studies of teacher change, which indicate that new meanings, behaviors, skills, and beliefs are positively associated with teachers' exchanging ideas and support (Fullan & Stiegelbauer, 1991). They are also consistent with the general notion that infrastructural resources, such as access to more knowledgeable colleagues, are critical to computer acceptance and use (Kling & Scacchi, 1982).

Cohesion and the social exchange it entails also facilitate collaborative arrangements that directly support expanded Internet use. For example, after a librarian at one high-use school learned that a colleague felt frustrated because students in one of his classes had to wait substantial periods of time to use a limited number of Internet-connected computers, the librarian arranged to make library computers with Internet access available to them during this class period.

Finally, cohesion supports Internet use because it encourages educators who might otherwise suspend such use. Even at high-use schools, educators' initial level of enthusiasm for Internet use varied. But at schools with high cohesion, the less enthusiastic educators continued to be exposed to and influenced by those more involved. As one teacher explained:

There's a lot of teachers in this school very involved with the Internet, which keeps me going, because I'm one of the ones that don't know anything.... I hear them talking, and it gets me interested, and I want to keep the kids interested.

Southland Elementary exemplifies a school in which team cohesion supported use of Internet resources by a broad contingent of NET team members. Educators here consistently described positive interpersonal relationships among team members, remarking, for example: "Everybody's been very supportive of one another, and so it's been a pleasure being a part of [the group].... I think—as a faculty, we work real well together." Southland team members also had frequent and regular contact, meeting voluntarily after school monthly or bimonthly, generally for two hours or more. Team cohesion at this school facilitated social exchange, which in turn supported team members in improving their knowledge of Internet resources relevant to the curriculum. Of the eight team members at Southland, six reported minimal to no experience with any Internet application prior to joining the team. To remedy this lack, team members investigated different areas of interest. Three teachers developed significant expertise in specialized areas of the Internet, including newsgroup maintenance, virtual reality environments, and Web sites appropriate for young children; a fourth explored effective ways to make students' written work available on-line. During NET team meetings and also in less formal settings, the team members then shared their expertise with each other. For example, the librarian on the team created a virtual reality classroom oriented toward reading and writing. Subsequently, at a team meeting, she introduced all team members to this resource and its potential benefits for students. Some teachers who attended this meeting eventually developed the ability to monitor students' basic activities in this curricular resource. Similarly, a third-grade teacher who focused on Web site searches described resources appropriate for young children and the strategies she used to help her students find relevant information.

Statements from the team members confirm our observation that they learned they could rely on each other's assistance and ideas. One team member told us:

> If I have a question I know I can go to anyone, and they will try to help me as best they can; . . . there's a great deal of sharing, because there's all kinds of different levels of expertise, from those who know a lot to those who know a little, and that's worked out very nicely.

Another team member said: "I know nothing, but there are four teachers who really know a lot about the different areas on the Internet. . . . [T]hose teachers give us input when it comes to making decisions."

Cohesion also promoted cooperative arrangements and experimentation at this school. This proved helpful in keeping the less experienced or involved educators engaged in Internet activities, providing them a structured way to participate. For example, at one team meeting, teacher Ms. Fisher voiced her frustration with her ongoing struggle to use the Internet with her students as she'd planned:

> I feel like I'm so far behind I'm never going to catch up! I just can't get time to work with my students. I don't know where you guys are get-

ting the time to do this. I can't do it! I feel so far behind. I never have time in my schedule to do this! . . . I can't do it! I can't get back there!

In response, team leader Tammy Watson told Ms. Fisher that what they could do was to sit down and think together about different things she could do. As a result of the ensuing brainstorming session, Ms. Fisher became involved in a collegial effort to develop an on-line school newsgroup. In this arrangement, the NET team leader, a classroom teacher, volunteered to train small groups of students in newsgroup access and posting procedures during her planning period. Five team teachers, including Ms. Fisher, decided to excuse students from regular classroom activities for this training. They agreed to allow these students to access the newsgroup and to train fellow classmates in its use during regular class periods so that a broader group of students gained the opportunity to submit their work and ideas to the newsgroup. Thus, Ms. Fisher found a way to begin to involve her students in Internet activities, and the NET team found a solution to her problems, which, left unsolved, would most likely have curtailed Internet use in her classroom.

At schools with team cohesion, like Southland, educators also described a history of professional association among team members, fostered by things such as shared departmental or program affiliation, long common tenure at a given school, and spatial arrangements (such as open space ones in which some or all of the walls that separate classrooms are removed) that encourage interactions. For example, at Bogart High, all team teachers were members of the foreign language department, and at Southland Elementary most were Spanish-speaking educators working in that school's Spanish language magnet program. Team cohesion also appeared to be strengthened by regular team meetings, stable team membership, and active team leaders who facilitated team communication through such means as regular e-mail updates on NET-related activities. In contrast, at low-use Meadowlark Elementary School, significant staff changes after the first year of the school's involvement with NET left the original NET team with few members. The team leader suggested that this loss of team members led to declining motivation among some of the remaining team members: "The team has really shrunk down, and some people on the staff have just stopped attending meetings." This change also appeared to decrease team members' overall sense of project ownership because those who had initially invested in Internet use had departed the scene.

School-time account use was substantial at this school prior to the staff turnover but plummeted thereafter, falling from an average of fifty-eight hours per month to seventeen hours. Some of this decline was clearly due to reduced team size. However, part of it was attributable to the disheartening impact of losing team members on those who remained.

In short, in accord with ideas advanced by those who promote Web models of computing (see Chapter One; Kling & Scacchi, 1982; Kling, 1992), we find that relatively more access to a strong social infrastructure supports computer use.

Project Ownership

A broad and intense sense of ownership of the attempt to bring the Internet to their schools also distinguished teams at high-use schools from those that used Internet resources less frequently. This means that high-use team members held the conviction that their school's Internet activities were an accomplishment at least partially of their own making and a responsibility that warranted effort. We can see evidence of ownership, for example, in one educator's comment: "This is something that I really like, and that I'm interested in, and I am willing to do. And it's something I initiated." Teachers and librarians with intense manifestations of ownership did not simply participate in NET by carrying out Internet activities in their own classrooms but also eagerly pursued opportunities to shape and contribute to their school's broader Internet activities. At all high-use schools, multiple team members showed intense manifestations of ownership, and in three of these four schools 50 percent or more of the NET team members did the same. Educators at these schools were likely to make comments about Internet activities like the following:

> Everybody likes to have . . . the feeling that this is [their] project. You like to be excited about what you're doing. . . . It's not the same old . . . here we go again with somebody telling us what to do. . . . So that gets the excitement going. . . . [I]t's definitely the way to go.

In contrast, at low-use schools, ownership was either nonexistent or, when it did exist, was narrow, present in just one or two individuals.

Both intensity and breadth of perceived ownership had implications for use. First, intensity of ownership seemed to influence the amount of time and energy an individual was willing to devote to supporting his or her own Internet efforts. Thus, breadth of ownership affected the number of team members willing to devote substantial amounts of time to such work. All the high-use schools had a group of educators who devoted notable amounts of discretionary time—sometimes several hours per week—to significantly develop and expand their Internet-based curricular projects. In addition, breadth and intensity of ownership influenced the time that individuals were willing to devote to supporting team efforts. At all high-use schools, multiple educators not only carried out their own Internet activities but also volunteered for and shared duties directly related to enhancing fellow educators' use of Internet resources. Such duties included training educators not yet exposed to the Internet, organizing NET team meetings, repairing and maintaining equipment required for Internet access from their school, and seeking out resources that might further common NET team efforts.

Finally, at schools with breadth and intensity of ownership, multiple individuals (not just the team leader) highlighted the importance of Internet use to prime movers, those with the power to significantly enhance or impede Internet activities. Such communication could and did affect opportunities for Internet use. The principal at Bogart High School, for example, severely threatened Internet use when he suggested converting a computer lab into a regular classroom. The principal abandoned the suggestion when teachers on the NET team collectively mounted an immediate protest. In contrast, at Riverdale Elementary School, a low-use school, typically just one staff member communicated concerns to NET staff or others in a position to influence the school's Internet resources. This was one of the things that led NET staff to conclude that teachers at this school were less interested than others in Internet use. When discussing the schools to which they would first give the technical capability to make student Internet accounts, staff suggested placing Riverdale low on the priority list because of its team's evident low interest.

Brayburn High School exemplifies the connection between educators' perceived ownership of NET activities and Internet use. At Brayburn, where ownership was high, four NET team members donated significant amounts of time to furthering the team's activities. These manifestations of ownership increased use in a variety of ways. First, because two teachers volunteered to serve as school-based systems administrators, they affected the extent to which all team members had access to functioning equipment and a broad array of Internet resources. These two educators regularly donated substantial amounts of their own time to repair computer equipment at this school, at one point spending two hours every day after regular school hours over a period of two months on this task when some difficult problems needed to be solved. One of these same teachers also looked for innovative software programs on the Internet and downloaded those that would be beneficial to the school's network. The other drilled the holes needed to wire a room to expand access to Internet resources for his own and other teachers' students and also wrote a successful grant proposal that provided students in his class with access to additional computers.

Broad and intense levels of ownership at Brayburn also increased the number of students and teachers who received training in using Internet resources and Internet accounts. For example, a third member of Brayburn's NET team worked with another team member to introduce him and his students to Internet use. The teacher who had been mentored clearly benefited, because he began to supervise students' Internet activities on his own. In addition, the school librarian, another NET team member, held brown-bag lunch sessions for teachers and introduced several teachers not on the NET team to the Internet and its curricular possibilities. She also taught students in the classes of non-NET teachers to use the Internet for research, which resulted eventually in additional students receiving Internet accounts. Indeed, NET teachers credited her with having significantly improved the technical literacy of many students in the school's general population. Finally, the librarian developed library home pages to help students move around the Internet with ease.

Broad ownership also led several educators at Brayburn to communicate NET's importance to their work to others outside the team who controlled resources, which in turn increased the speed with which the team received access to needed resources. For example, the two user administrators and another teacher corresponded about technical and other difficulties with NET staff. The following e-mail excerpt is typical of this group's efforts to communicate the importance of Internet activities and to be specific about their needs and goals:

> We don't have enough computers in both Rooms 102 and 103 to meet the needs of the 36 research kids now working on these computers. Our deadline for submitting finished papers to the SCI competition is in two weeks. If we could get this new computer working next week it would really help us meet the deadline.

All these indicators of commitment and initiative were among the factors that led NET staff to conclude that Brayburn was an active and successful NET school. Knowing that the Brayburn teachers were trying to involve high numbers of students in Internet activities, NET staff switched a powerful server from another school to Brayburn in order to better support its Internet needs. In addition, they gave Brayburn first priority when making decisions about which schools would receive enhanced connection speed.

Two behaviors appeared to predict the degree to which teams at NET schools manifested ownership: the extent to which educators initially freely volunteered for NET team participation and the extent to which they initially shaped their own efforts to incorporate Internet use into the curriculum. At two of the three low-use schools, principals were involved in writing the annual competitive process (ACP) proposal to the point that NET teams would not have formed without their efforts, and at the third, as we described earlier, an originally enthusiastic team broke apart as the district transferred educators to other schools. An initial lack of interest could prove quite difficult to overcome. Educators at Regent Middle School, for example, first approached the NET competition with reluctance, entering largely in response to substantial encouragement from their principal, who recalled:

> I really coerced the staff to do it, because we were really tired, and we were always writing for grants and we weren't too successful in getting them, and they had given up almost. They didn't want to try anymore.

After Regent won Internet access in the ACP, no educator volunteered to serve as NET team leader or user administrator. The principal eventually approached individuals and asked them to take on these positions. They accepted with some reluctance. Understandably, these individuals did not express the same eagerness as educators at some other schools did to devote time to fulfilling such roles. No individual at this school invested discretionary time to support team activities comparable to that invested by individuals at high-use settings like Brayburn High School. As a consequence of this limited ownership, explained one NET education staff member, "There it [the equipment] is . . . collecting dust; it is sitting there, because there was no buy-in from the teacher whose room it got assigned to."

Collaboration

Collaboration refers to two or more people working together to design and carry out a project or to find a cooperative solution to a common problem. This factor is similar to cohesion in that it implies ongoing interaction among educators; it differs in that it requires joint work and problem solving rather than merely sharing social support and information. At all high-use schools, NET team members created collaborative arrangements to facilitate Internet activities. Educators at low-use schools rarely reported such arrangements. This finding is consistent with studies of teacher collegiality that find that a professional and well-organized work group contributes to enhanced instructional range and flexibility in curriculum development (Little, 1990b).

Educators' collaboration supported and enhanced Internet use in two specific ways in NET schools. First, when individual educators with diverse talents and backgrounds worked together, they were able to carry out curricular projects that would have been more difficult to achieve single-handedly. For example, at high-use Brayburn High School, a classroom teacher and the librarian combined their knowledge of varied Web resources and HTML programming to create a course teaching students how to construct a home page. At Southland Elementary, another high-use school, a writing teacher helped second- and fifth-grade students compose the stories that the school librarian then helped them post on-line in a virtual reality classroom. At Bogart High, the NET team composed of foreign language teachers collectively planned a school home page with German, Spanish, French, and English elements.

Second, collaboration helped educators devise arrangements for overcoming barriers to progress. For example, one barrier that many NET educators identified was lack of time to work with students on Internet-based activities. As we discussed in Chapter Four, NET educators typically found themselves simultaneously teaching twenty-five to thirty students and assisting a few small groups or individuals in navigating the Internet on a limited number of computers at the back of the classroom. Many found it difficult to manage this situation, particularly with elementary age students who lacked sophisticated keyboarding or reading skills, and so they used their Internet access less than they had hoped to.

Educators at Clark and Southland Elementary Schools devised two different collaborative arrangements to address this problem and increase students' time on-line. The first arrangement was structural: educators cooperated so that one teacher was free to work for an extended period on-line with a small group of students. For example, one teacher might agree to work with a larger group of students than usual, leaving the second teacher with fewer students to supervise. The second arrangement was curricular: educators designed interdisciplinary projects that involved multiple teachers. Students had relatively more time to work on-line because they worked on the same curricular activity in more than one classroom. At Clark Elementary, for example, fifth-grade educators carried out a project in which students investigated native plants from the school playground by way of on-line research. Although a science teacher initiated the project, an English teacher helped students write their reports. Students could conduct their on-line research in both classrooms. Similarly, the school's art and science teachers guided their students in extensive on-line research to support a collaborative project on bird behaviors and habitats. Again, the teachers cooperated to make sure that all students had an opportunity to participate in this research.

Preexisting collegiality between educators along with structural arrangements that promoted faculty interaction helped lay the groundwork for collaborative efforts. Collegial educators, even if not part of a cohesive team, were often aware of one another's Internet use efforts and problems. Sometimes, structural arrangements helped teachers to identify situations in which collaborative work would be mutually beneficial. For example, educators at Clark Elementary worked in an open space area. They were well aware of what others on the team were doing because of the visibility this structural arrangement afforded. As one explained:

> I think that [structure] has a lot to do with the way people were forced almost to talk about ideas. When you walked through and you saw what the kids were producing. . . . It forces people to notice what learning is going on.

The relationship we observed between collegiality and the evolution of collaborative solutions to problems is consistent with studies of other collegial teaching environments. For example, teachers immersed in settings that promote high levels of teacher collegiality along with norms of professional growth say that developing effective instructional practice becomes a top priority (McLaughlin, 1993).

Active Librarian Involvement

Librarians are not often described as critical agents in school change processes. Various widely read and cited studies concerned with change processes in secondary schools, for example, do not even mention librarians (Fullan, 1993; Fullan & Stiegelbauer, 1991). Yet, consistent with results from a major study of K–12 educators using telecommunications (Honey & Henriquez, 1993), school librarians were among the individuals who took the lead in devising and managing Internet activities at NET schools. The thirteen librarians who were members of NET teams in the first- through third-year schools, for example, logged over eleven hundred hours in their accounts during the last year that we collected data on account use. We found further that at three of the four high-use case study schools, librarians were highly involved team members who played a vital role in shaping Internet use. As an educator at Southland Elementary School put it when reflecting on the role played by the librarian there, "She is the bone in our skeleton."

Active librarians fostered and supported Internet use in a variety of ways. First, librarians introduced the Internet to students and teachers who did not have classroom access and showed them how it could help them with their work. Librarians also shared resources they found on the Internet with both NET team members and other classroom teachers. Librarians developed ways to extend teachers' Internet-based classroom projects and devised their own curricular activities. For example, some librarians offered to work on-line with students from selected classes during the school day and before or after school. Others developed teacher or student training courses. And at Southland Elementary, the librarian developed a virtual reality classroom for improving children's reading and writing skills and introduced children to this curricular setting.

The activities of the librarian at Bogart High illustrate such efforts. During the first year of Bogart's NET project, for example, this librarian logged over 560 hours on-line looking among other things for curriculum resources. She also introduced English and social studies faculty to the Internet. In the second year, she worked with the NET team leader in fundraising to acquire more technology; sent teachers information about curriculum resources on the Internet; and assisted a social studies teacher who was not a member of the original NET team with an Internet project in which students were given pen pals from another state or country, researched the place where their pen pal lived, and wrote a composition about the pen pal and where that pen pal lived. Throughout the NET years, when students and teachers came to the library to do research, the librarian directed them to the computers to investigate on-line resources. As one teacher reported, "When English teachers come here or other teachers come here to do research projects, she always pushes kids toward the computers and says, 'See if you can find something in there.'" Finally, in order to support expanded student Internet access and usage, this librarian agreed to supervise the on-line work of students who wanted an Internet account of their own in order to accomplish particular projects. Describing the overall atmosphere that this librarian fostered, a NET education staff member, Ian Dutton, commented:

> I've had teachers at Bogart . . . say to me less than a week ago that Emma Turlick, the librarian . . . is such a great person and the kids love to go in there because they know she's going to . . . give them help when they need it. . . . [One teacher said] "That's why . . . the whole library is busy all the time, and the computers in there are busy. They could put ten more in there and still be busy all the time." . . . [S]he creates an atmosphere where the students aren't afraid to go in.

Indeed, on the occasions when we visited Bogart's library unannounced, as well as during our more formal observations, the four computers in Bogart's library were virtually always all in use.

Certain features of librarians' work situation made it easier for them than for classroom teachers to support and enhance use. First, they had higher levels of access to technical resources because the NET school libraries were generally equipped with four or more machines. (Typically, classrooms had one to three computers.) Also, they tended to have more time and freedom to guide students' explorations of the Internet. Librarians are generally not expected to convey similar or identical content to large groups of students during a set block of time throughout the school day as teachers often are. Instead, they commonly encounter students as individuals or in small groups who work quite independently. As one classroom teacher noted when comparing work patterns in the library and a typical classroom: "The kids can go in there [to the library] and work by themselves, where in a classroom I think they rely more on, 'What's the teacher telling us to do?'" Another important difference is that librarians are generally expected to support individual research and investigation, and they are used to, as one teacher put it, "asking 'what if' questions and going to get the answers."

A positive attitude toward Internet use was one characteristic distinguishing highly involved librarians from those exhibiting less active Internet use. In addition, however, three of the more active librarians participating in NET were already meeting every other month for half a day as part of a school librarian network, and all three said that conversations about the Internet and its uses regularly arose in that context: "Either somebody found . . . what page is really interesting, or whatever." Thus, for librarians too, being part of a group of colleagues interested in the Internet seemed to play a part in encouraging productive use.

Strong Teacher Leadership

It is well established that active leadership within the school can galvanize and support school change efforts (Berman & McLaughlin, 1978; Fullan, 1993; Fullan & Newton, 1988; Wilson & Corcoran, 1988), and consistent with this, three of the four high-use schools had an active NET team leader. Typically, descriptions of effective school-based leaders center on the principal, as this individual frequently has the widest contact with the educators in a school and also has the power to make the administrative changes (by modifying schedules, arranging in-service training, and so forth) that can support pedagogical change efforts. However, consistent with NET's grassroots emphasis, leadership by teachers played a much more crucial role in achieving Internet use than did leadership by principals. In the three high-use schools with active leadership, highly effective teacher-leaders devised and implemented strategies that sustained and expanded use of Internet resources.

The teachers who were NET team leaders at these three schools coordinated team activities that contributed to team cohesion, publicized relevant professional development opportunities to encourage educators to become more involved, and assisted educators struggling to learn new skills. These activities promoted the other teachers' Internet use and additional project involvement. As one teacher explained when reflecting on the role the team leader at Clark Elementary School played in encouraging her Internet use:

She's the one who kept after me not to give up. . . . In fact, I don't think I would have such a desire to really use it if it wasn't for Tracy instructing me and keeping behind me and keeping me going.

These active leaders also supported use indirectly by initiating communication with prime movers in the outside world. For example, they promptly and persistently telephoned and e-mailed the NET technical and education staffs to describe technical difficulties. Some were so persistent that technical staff reportedly paid unusually prompt attention to their needs rather than suffer a flood of e-mail messages.

The work of the team leader at Bogart High School illustrates how active teacher leadership can drive and support Internet use. Team leader Ms. Stewart was extremely active: she organized and facilitated weekly NET team meetings, offered in-service activities to fellow educators, advertised professional development activities, kept in close touch with team members by e-mail, sought out resources that would further common team efforts, and volunteered to supervise the school's computer lab before school three mornings a week to give students extra Internet time. Ms. Stewart also encouraged the less active team members by offering her personal assistance, as illustrated in this report of an exchange at a team meeting:

Ms. Stewart and Mr. Roland [a fellow teacher] were getting very excited about the things they wanted to learn [at an upcoming in-service meeting]. He wants to learn how to work on the home page, and he was talking about what he knows and doesn't know, and he was throwing out words like "Pico." . . . Ms. Dickson listened to him; she started to laugh, and she made some comment like, "Pico. What is that?" She was laughing because she didn't know what it was. Ms. Dickson said to Mr. Barbera, "I'm real far behind also, so we will be together." . . . [E]arlier in the meeting he [had] commented that he was far behind and didn't know much. . . . Ms. Stewart was encouraging them and saying, "No, we'll work with you and help you and teach you."

Reflecting on the important role that this team leader played in supporting Internet activities and sustaining team motivation, Ms. Dickson exclaimed in a later interview, "I thank goodness we have a leader here in the building of the Networking for Education Testbed project who is *so* enthusiastic and is *so* dedicated that that's what keeps us all moving somewhat."

Ms. Stewart was also a tenacious and effective NET advocate, which was especially important in sustaining use at this school. Bogart's NET team faced substantial technical frustrations during their first years, including antiquated computers and an inadequate server. It is also evident from NET e-mail that technical staff was somewhat confused as to exactly what kinds of Internet activities this school had planned. As team leader, Ms. Stewart took it upon herself to correct such misperceptions and to adamantly communicate team members' technological needs and visions. For example, here is an e-mail exchange between the technical staff manager and Ms. Stewart:

TECHNICAL STAFF MANAGER: When setting up the Bogart lab, we assumed the main use would be e-mail. The current facilities, server, and PC's can adequately support this type of use. However, the current network connection and server will not adequately support 26 simultaneous menu users.

MS. STEWART: Why would we revamp the whole lab if we only wanted to do e-mail? It would not be worth the time and the money. It is also not written as such in the NSF-Grant Proposal. Plan for Bogart [this year] is as follows: 1st quarter: e-mail, weather (main menu, international and national); 2nd quarter: ctd. [continued] e-mail, newsgroups in target language; 3rd and 4th quarter: projects.

Ms. Stewart also volunteered discretionary time to e-mail regular status reports documenting technical difficulties and the general status of the school to NET's technical staff. Here, for example, is just one of her many vigorous attempts to impress team needs upon NET's technical staff:

The printing capability from e-mail and the newsgroups is vital to all students as well as all the faculty members who will use these computers as the main access route within our school. According to our proposed Action Plan for Bogart, we are looking at newsgroups as an integral part of our curriculum rather than just "surfin'" the net. . . . I am not going to mention again and again what problems this lack of printing capability has caused for e-mail.

Not surprisingly, this team leader's persistence became renowned among NET staff. Indeed, when discussing an effort to get technical staff to respond quickly to problems at Southland, a member of the education staff referred to the Southland team leader as "Molly Stewart squared." Eventually, NET staff supplied Bogart High with new equipment and worked hard to rectify this school's printing problems in spite of many other pressing demands, largely in response to Ms. Stewart's tenacious efforts.

Two factors associated with active teacher leadership were prior professional experience with the Internet and a relatively long-standing interest in the potential of the technology to improve education. Two of the three active team leaders at high-use schools, for example, had been part of the professional network of educators who worked with Don Quick and Peter Marcus to explore possible uses of the Internet in the classroom prior to NET's funding. In addition, and consistent with studies of effective leaders in successful grassroots organizations (Bettencourt, Dillman, & Wollman, 1996), team leaders at high-use schools tended to confine their roles to the leadership activities we have described in this section. They distributed responsibility for other technical and curricular NET activities among team members. For example, the NET team leader at Clark Elementary initially solved many of the NET teachers' technical problems but worked at the same time to increase their technical skills so that teachers were increasingly able to accomplish technical tasks on their own. As one teacher on that team recalls, "When we got our new printer, I said, 'How am I supposed to install this?' and she said, 'Read the directions.'"

This leadership characteristic is particularly important because leadership structures or styles that foster a sense of dependency among others can have negative effects. At Riverdale Elementary, for example, the principal appointed one teacher to be the team leader, responsible for coordinating Internet activities, helping teachers implement curricular projects, and overseeing technical problems. If this teacher had had time to fulfill these multiple roles, this assignment might have fostered Internet use at this low-use school. However, she faced a lengthy illness, had significant professional demands on her time in addition to this assignment, and also found herself overwhelmed by the school's significant technical problems. Perhaps partially in response to the fact that the principal had vested leadership responsibilities in a given individual, no other educator on the team moved forward to assist when it became apparent that the team leader could not meet all these responsibilities in a timely manner. Moreover, rather than pursue solutions on their own to problems they encountered, as was common in many other teams, teachers on the Riverdale team tended to wait for the team leader to provide the necessary technical and classroom assistance. One teacher there remarked:

> They changed their log-in procedure after our system was down, and then when we got back on, the main building knew what to do, but us that call into the main building were clueless. And Letitia [Holloway, the team leader] was out for a while, so she wasn't around to tell us how to get back in.

And another teacher at Riverdale had this to say:

> The problem is that Letitia isn't able to be free enough to do enough training on the Internet during school. I mean, she's held workshops before school and after school, but during the day it would be great to have her in the classroom teaching things briefly about keyboarding and getting into the Internet so the kids have someone sitting there with them.

In the end, teachers who experienced technical problems at Riverdale simply stopped using their computers or waited in vain for the team leader to arrive to instruct their students.

Ease of Integration

Educators are more likely to use a novel technology when it helps them perform work more easily, efficiently, and effectively than they already do (Cuban, 1986; Schofield, 1995). Making a similar point, Kling and Scacchi (1982, p. 17) write: "If one wants to predict how people will integrate computer-based systems into their organizational activities, it helps to know what people actually do and care most about when they act in organizations." As we discussed in Chapters Three and Four, a significant impediment to use in many NET schools was that having Internet access often made teachers' work more complex rather than easier. It was particularly difficult for educators who typically used whole class instructional methods to modify their practice and to simultaneously teach a classroom of students and help a smaller group navigate the Internet. But at two of the four high-use schools educators did not face this impediment. Thanks to various organizational arrangements, they were able to use the Internet to achieve existing curricular goals more effectively than before without substantially modifying their existing pedagogical practices. More- over, they could also employ the Internet to make their work and that of their most successful students more visible to the outside world. Technology added instrumental value to these teachers' daily activities, and this clearly enhanced Internet use. This finding is consistent with ideas advanced by Kling and Scacchi (1983, p. 17), who argue that technology use and acceptance increase when the technology fits nicely with "current lines of work" and "going concerns."

To provide some sense of the relationship between the ease of integrating Internet use and existing curriculum and classroom practice on the one hand and the extensiveness of Internet use on the other, we describe efforts at two high-use schools. At Bogart High School, the NET team of foreign language teachers was implementing a curriculum emphasizing active and authentic language experiences. In this context, the Internet readily functioned, as one teacher put it, as "one of the cornerstones . . . for our curriculum." Students could use their second language actively and authentically as they communicated with native language speakers through e-mail and chat rooms and as they explored Web sites produced in other countries. At the same time, the team members did not have to substantially modify their existing pedagogical practices. They had access to a lab of fifteen computers where they could take classes of students to use Internet resources, and they could transfer their experience with the use of language labs to this setting. Class size in advanced language courses was often under twenty, so teachers could simply move these students from individual desks in their classrooms to individual computers in the lab, replicating the classroom structure. The ability to reach curricular goals without substantial organizational rearrangement enhanced these teachers' use of the Internet, as shown by the fact that they used it much more with small classes, where each student could have his or her own computer, than they did with larger classes, where they found it difficult to work with pairs or small groups on the computers. Bogart High teachers were proud of the ways they found to use the Internet to enrich students' experiences, and they consequently created Web pages on which they shared curriculum ideas and lesson plans.

Brayburn High School provides another example of how ease of integration leads to higher use. Educators established the NET activities here primarily to support the work of advanced students enrolled in a special science and math program. Although whole group instruction was most common, a select group of thirty to thirty-five students also participated in a two-year research course, designing and carrying out an original laboratory investigation during the junior and senior years to submit to a prestigious national science competition. Working on the Internet gave these students greater access than they would have had otherwise to extensive and current information on their research topics, and it therefore met an existing curricular need. In addition, it gave students the opportunity to publish their final projects on-line and also to communicate with scientists about their progress and findings, which in turn allowed the school and teachers to give those in the outside world a glimpse of their most accomplished students' work.

As at Bogart, teachers at Brayburn working with advanced students did not have to alter their pedagogical practices to integrate Internet use into their classrooms as much as their NET colleagues did in traditional classrooms sparsely equipped with computers. First, even though there were fewer computers than students in Brayburn's advanced science classes, the shortfall in computers at Brayburn was much smaller than it was in a typical NET classroom because of the way educators there chose to distribute their computers and organize their instruction. Laboratory research took place during one period of the day, and thirteen working computers were available to the thirty to thirty-five advanced science students. Starting in NET's third year, these students had access to six more computers in the school library. Moreover, because the educators involved with this program taught their program-related courses at the same time, on occasion a teacher could send some students to another teacher's classroom to work. Finally, because they were working on individual projects, the students did not need simultaneous access to the Internet. They could work on other tasks while waiting for access to a computer, as in this situation, described by a program teacher: "I had four junior students doing hands-on lab research while my four senior students were on three computers . . . so access was not a problem." Equally significant, even before Internet access was available, research class instruction had never focused on the whole group. Instead, teachers worked as facilitators and coaches to support individual students in their diverse research projects. Thus, Brayburn's NET teachers were accustomed to monitoring and guiding students engaged in many different sorts of activities simultaneously.

Nevertheless, even in this relatively advantageous situation, the teachers felt that they could more easily integrate Internet use with more Internet access. And when some of these teachers sought to expand Internet use to larger classes of less advanced students, they, like other teachers in traditional classrooms, noted difficulties in meshing whole group instruction with access to just one to two computers. As one of these teachers, Mr. Waleska, commented in discussing the problems he faced when trying to use the Internet with his regular classes,

> You need a place to centralize instruction. You have to be able to teach multiple numbers of students at one time. . . . [E]very time I had to instruct students, I had students waiting. I have my mainstream students that are being shortchanged—as opposed to my [advanced] students, who had access to the machines. . . . [T]his was very unfair. And if you want to talk about discrimination, this was very discriminatory.

Thus, even at a high-use school with strongly committed teachers, it was difficult to maintain a high level of Internet use when ease of integration was not present.

Discretionary Professional Time

Few NET teachers had an abundance of discretionary professional time; however, teachers at high-use schools had relatively more of this time free from students than teachers at low-use schools did. This meant they had more time to explore Internet resources and meet as a team, activities conducive to use. Indeed, as we pointed out earlier, Becker (1990) found in a national survey that teachers reported the major impediment to computer use as lack of time to figure out how to use computers well. Moreover, an international survey (Pelgrum & Plomp, 1991) suggests that finding time to learn how to use computers and how to prepare lessons employing them is one of the major barriers to computer use in many countries.

One principal determinant of educators' discretionary professional time was the extent of their involvement in other major curricular or pedagogical change efforts. While, as previously mentioned, all WPS schools were engaged in school improvement planning efforts during NET, the teams at high-use schools were generally not engaged in actually implementing substantial change efforts during the initial years of their involvement with NET. In comparison, the teams at the two lowest-use schools were. Riverdale Elementary, for example, had recently reopened as a restructuring school just before it was selected as a NET school. That is, Riverdale faculty had agreed to participate in extensive curricular change and alternative assessment efforts and to lend their support to more than twenty other programmatic efforts at the school. Frequent meetings before and after school and other activities sapped teachers' energy and cut into the time available to develop Internet activities. As one teacher put it:

> The first few years, just trying to get a handle on the community and the kids we were teaching, and understanding how to teach in non-traditional ways, that kind of kept us going those first couple of years. And I think maybe the computers took a back burner.

Discretionary time is also affected by the extent to which scheduled meetings for any purpose dominate the school calendar. In addition, school administrators' decisions about teachers' duty periods affect it. At low-use Regent Middle School, for example, NET teachers approached the principal with the idea of having more team meetings, using time currently devoted to other school reform and content area planning efforts. The principal did not feel that teachers could give up this time and refused the request. The teachers also suggested substituting Internet-related activities for lunch and hall duty so that NET teachers could go to one another's classrooms and assist when necessary. The principal agreed to entertain these requests on a one-by-one basis but did not give NET teachers a blanket release from other duty assignments. Conversely, at high-use Clark Elementary School, the principal arranged the schedule so that the NET team leader had two extra periods for performing NET-related duties.

Technical Reliability

When computer equipment and networking resources at a school function as desired when educators need them, the school has *technical reliability*. Two principal building blocks for this are the absolute reliability of the equipment itself and access to technical expertise that enables educators to deal with problems that do arise. Almost all first- and second-year NET schools experienced moderate to significant lack of technical reliability initially. However, by NET's third year, six of the seven case study schools had attained basic technical reliability. That is, the school server and most computers in individual classrooms functioned; teachers were generally able to access the Internet or their accounts with relatively little difficulty or delay; and educators and students could generally print on-site. Such basic capabilities do not ensure Internet use, but without them use would be curtailed or nonexistent.

Five of the seven schools we discuss in this chapter achieved this level of technical reliability through reliable and appropriate equipment. The sixth school, Brayburn High, achieved reliability due to a high level of both technical expertise and dedication on the part of two teachers. Brayburn's equipment worked inconsistently, with the school's first server crashing frequently. Moreover, this server was not the same type used in other NET schools, and many of the applications developed for the standard NET servers did not function well on it. NET resolved this compatibility problem when Brayburn purchased a new server, but high rates of use at particular times of the day often overloaded the server. Computers at Brayburn also often needed repair work because teachers and students, typically inadvertently, made changes to system files that rendered these machines inoperable on the school network. Nevertheless, reliability at this school was not severely compromised because, as we mentioned earlier, the two Brayburn team members who managed the school's server addressed and resolved many problems. They restored machines damaged by teachers or students by rebuilding disk drives during their lunch periods and after school. One of them, whom the NET technical staff regarded as the most technically knowledgeable NET team member in the district, also put in place a technical strategy to get the server back on-line in less than five minutes after an overload had shut it down. If Brayburn had not had such local technical expertise, Internet use there would have been far lower. As one Brayburn educator put it, "I don't know how he [one of the technically literate teachers] does it, but if we didn't have him at this school, there wouldn't have been one-tenth of what we got."

In general, then, educators' interest in and skill with technical applications can significantly enhance a school's technical reliability, even in the face of considerable technical difficulties. Even when equipment functions well, this skill base can prove useful because it helps educators deal with day-to-day technical glitches and communicate more readily with outside technical staff. However, in order for this skill to translate into reliable equipment functioning, school personnel must find the means to free up time to put that skill to use.

Only one of the seven case study schools we discuss in this chapter, Riverdale Elementary, suffered from severe lack of technical reliability. The computers selected and purchased for this school proved quite unreliable, with a number of hard drives and motherboards requiring replacement. Basic computer breakdowns were still occurring when we last interviewed Riverdale educators, four years after the school joined NET. NET technical staff had given Riverdale a brand of server different from the brand used at most other NET schools, which meant that some NET server applications did not work or worked poorly there. Further, Riverdale had limited access to effective technical expertise, as the teacher whom the principal assigned to address these problems did not have either the time or the requisite depth and breadth of technical knowledge to solve them efficiently and effectively.

Whether a school had equipment like that found at the majority of NET schools strongly influenced the degree of technical reliability it attained and the speed with which it received technical assistance from NET. Not only were applications developed for one brand of server unreliable on other brands but technical staff reportedly directed more attention to meeting the demands of the many than the demands of the few. At Brayburn High, for example, the systems administrator noted that once the school changed to a server compatible with other NET servers, it became far easier to get good service and support. Conversely, the NET team leader at Meadowlark Elementary, a low-use school, noted, "Because we have an Apple file server [atypical for NET] it seems like we're always put further down on the [technical priorities] list." At some schools, educators had followed personal preferences and selected a mixture of IBM and Apple computers. In these instances, technical staff were often not able to get both kinds of machines to print reliably, and some educators found themselves needing to borrow colleagues' computers when printing was required—clearly not an encouragement to use.

Educators at Riverdale in particular spoke extensively about the ways persistent technical problems impeded Internet use, especially by dampening teachers' enthusiasm and project momentum. As one put it, "The glitches I think . . . pulled everybody down. And then, it's funny, because it's almost like you kind of wash your hands of it. 'Okay, it doesn't work.'" Said another, "I think that everybody has that frustration level when the equipment is down, and I think that's why it ruins a lot of attitudes. . . . I can almost say that that's what turned me off." These comments are consistent with previous findings that technical problems are a basic impediment to computer use in technology-rich classrooms (Sandholtz et al., 1997).

A third and final building block for technical reliability is the extent to which educators are able to communicate effectively with those designing the technical setup for their school. One notable example of miscommunication was that although the NET technical staff knew that teachers wanted to be able to print out materials, they also assumed that printing was far less important than broad access to the Internet and its resources (for an extended discussion of this issue, see Davidson et al., 2001). Thus, because of this assumption, printing capabilities were significantly delayed at all first-year NET schools as the technical staff concentrated instead on preparing, deploying, and fine-tuning servers and computers for accessing the Internet. Eventually, members of the education staff became aware of the failure to give printing a high priority and strongly relayed teachers' displeasure. One technical staff member expressed the staff's surprise at this turn of events: "A year into the project the education staff all of sudden just starts blowing up, 'The printing is not working,' and we didn't know why they were so upset." Poor communication and the technical staff's assumptions about printing's relative importance clearly contributed to delays in the deployment of printing capabilities to schools; they also hampered the achievement of the kind of technical reliability teachers wanted.

CONCLUSIONS

NET educators used the Internet and its resources for both professional development and student instruction. At the same time, teachers and librarians at some schools made far more regular and extensive use of these resources for classroom instruction than did educators at others. Educators at some schools were also more likely to involve their students in activities that involved sustained and time-intensive use of Internet resources and to make use of opportunities for on-line interactions and publishing.

Eight factors, most having little to do with the nature of computers or the Internet, influenced this variation. Cohesion among NET team members fostered conversation among them about Internet use. Thus, educators at cohesive schools had relatively more access to advice and ideas and relatively more exposure to enthusiastic colleagues eager to keep all team members involved.

The strength of educators' conviction that Internet-based curriculum activities were an accomplishment of the team's own making and worth investing effort in also varied across schools, and such feelings of ownership influenced the time that team members devoted to supporting Internet activities. This in turn influenced the number of students and teachers who received Internet training and the extent to which team members acted to solve technical and other problems impeding Internet use at their schools. And NET team members' collaborative arrangements, more common at high-use schools, allowed them to find ways around specific impediments to Internet use and to carry out curricular activities that would have been difficult for a single educator to implement.

The efforts of key members of NET teams also promoted Internet use. Active team leaders, for example, coordinated team activities that contributed to a sense of team cohesion; they also assisted and encouraged other educators in learning new skills. These leaders also persistently communicated team members' needs and goals to prime movers outside the team, thus helping to remove nagging impediments to progress. Active librarians introduced and promoted the Internet to students and teachers who did not have classroom access, shared resources they found on the network with classroom teachers, and devised curricular activities. Thus, both active team leaders and librarians contributed critically to shaping and strengthening their schools' support infrastructure for Internet use.

Finally, certain organizational factors enabled or constrained team members' efforts and activities. In schools where NET educators were able to use computers to help them achieve existing and highly valued curricular goals without making substantial modifications to their pedagogical practices, use occurred more readily and frequently. Thus, lower student-computer ratios and a curriculum that mapped readily to existing Internet resources often helped increase Internet use. In addition, educators at some schools had relatively more discretionary professional time to explore Internet resources and to meet and plan as a team, another factor that increased use. Finally, technical reliability, attained either through reliability of equipment and software or through ready access to local technical expertise for resolving problems quickly, also influenced the extent to which educators were able to bring students on-line consistently.

Most of these factors are malleable; they can be influenced by school leaders and policymakers. Principals and district policymakers, for example, might arrange for school technology leaders to receive training in leadership and team-building strategies. School principals might also make adjustments in school schedules where possible in order to increase the discretionary professional time available to teachers. And before funding technology efforts, policymakers might encourage cohesion among educators by explicitly asking them to define and describe ways that they will encourage and support communication among themselves.

Although many of these factors would be of value in any teaching endeavor, they may have special importance in projects involving computers and the Internet. For example, as we described in Chapter Four, teachers using the Internet are typically in unfamiliar and sometimes uncomfortable terrain. The social support offered by team cohesion and the shared knowledge arising from collaboration can be of very real and immediate emotional and practical benefit to these educators.

In addition, incorporating a new piece of technology into existing classroom practice creates organizational and logistical challenges that other kinds of change may not. Collaboration can produce solutions to problems that appear insurmountable to the individual, particularly when it links classroom teachers to individuals with relatively more flexibility in their work schedules or routines, such as school librarians.

Finally, technology use can be extremely frustrating in that computers in general and Internet access in particular are often unreliable and changing constantly. A strong sense of project ownership, the support that emanates from team cohesion, and the willingness of the team leader to step forward to seek solutions to problems can sustain educators who might otherwise become discouraged in the face of seemingly insurmountable and never-ending technical obstacles. In short, the factors that we identify here may be particularly important for achieving frequent and substantial use of technological resources like the Internet among broad groups of educators.

As this extensive and intensive Internet use occurs, however, what sorts of changes might it bring about? Chapters Six and Seven delve into this question, considering whether Internet use at NET schools led to changes in classrooms generally and how that use affected teachers and students as individuals.

CHAPTER SIX

Classroom Change Accompanying Internet Use

———~᷈᷈᷈~——

A key theme in writings about technology use in the schools in general and the Internet in particular is technology's potential for contributing to significant school reform (Bosco, 1986; Carlitz, 1991; Collins, 1990; Fabos & Young, 1999; Hunter, 1992; Means et al., 1993; Newman, 1992; Papert, 1980; Perkins, 1985; Sheingold, 1990; Viadero, 1997). As one scholar (Cohen, 1988, p. 240) notes:

> Nearly all new technologies pressed on the schools since [World War II], from paperbacks to microcomputers, have been advertised as agents that would change education by making students less dependent on teachers, and by reducing whole-class, lock-step, batch-processed teaching and learning. Americans persistently dream about the liberating effects of technical innovations.

Advocates of Internet use in the schools predict, for example, that with the proper planning and support this technology has the potential to result in "superior forms of learning" such as comprehension, reasoning, and experimentation (Means et al., 1993, pp. 1–2). They suggest also that the Internet has the potential to make learning much more individualized and enjoyable than it has been in the past

(Tapscott, 1998). Further, "classroom learning will become student-driven, interactive, experiential and collaborative—all goals long-cherished by many educators but never before attainable. Students will no longer passively receive information but will manage and synthesize it and even contribute to the infosphere" (Berenfeld, 1996, p. 83).

Networking for Education Testbed (NET) staff, especially the project director and the education staff, had similar visions. They hoped, for example, that NET would stimulate fundamental changes in schools and classrooms. On its home page, NET proclaimed its desire to support education reform and to reduce the isolation of those in the traditional classroom. This goal also featured prominently in the proposal Don Quick and others wrote to gain initial funding for NET. On many occasions, members of the education staff expressed their hope that access to the Internet would bring about changes consistent with a constructivist approach to education. As one put it:

> If we take a constructivist approach, if we nurture them [teachers], if we treat them like we do students . . . like we should be treating students, if we begin to model for them, then hopefully they will begin to take that to their classes, and you will truly get school reform. . . . The only reason I'm in NET is to do that.

For NET staff, constructivism implied changes that would increase students' opportunities to actively build and develop knowledge and reduce the time they spent passively acquiring information from teacher lectures or participating in formulaic question-and-answer sessions. The staff hoped teachers would more often adopt such practices as working as facilitators, giving students more responsibility and freedom in the classroom, and developing curricula that enabled students to create products they themselves valued, both to solve problems and to analyze the strengths and weaknesses in their knowledge base and thought processes. In keeping with this view, the education staff favored what they called "authentic" learning situations, ones in which students could apply their disciplinary knowledge in ways that let them see connections between what they were learning in the classroom and the world outside of school as well as their futures as citizens and workers.

Many of the proposals educators submitted to the annual competitive process (ACP) were quite consistent with NET's goals. Nearly 20 percent of the proposals submitted during the four years the ACP was in place (and 24 percent of those accepted) expressed educators' desire to change classroom roles and relationships so that teachers worked more as facilitators and students took a more active and direct role in their own learning. In addition, almost 25 percent expressed a desire to make learning more authentic in some way. Such orientations were revealed in statements such as these:

> Technology will make it possible for the teacher to be replaced, repositioned in the instructional scheme. Students will be increasingly self-directed.

> We want students to enter into continuing dialogue with authentic audiences in relevant problem-solving situations. An authentic audience will enhance learning.

In this chapter, we consider the extent to which NET schools realized some of these visions, describing the types of changes that occurred and their impact on classrooms and students. Our study found that Internet use did support and promote aspects of NET's constructivist agenda. At the same time, it did not fundamentally transform the look and feel of most NET classrooms, not even at schools with high rates of Internet use.

Some caveats accompany our findings. First, the data underlying this chapter come largely from the ten schools that joined NET during its first two years. These were the schools that we studied most closely and for the longest period of time. (The only other school that was formally part of NET at that time served mainly as a NET office and professional development center, and thus it is not directly pertinent to this chapter.) Although we have no reason to believe that the changes we identified apply only to these schools, we do not have the evidence necessary to assert that they occurred at schools that joined NET later.

Second, because certain classroom changes were dependent on the types of Internet activities educators undertook and the ways they organized these activities, and because NET teachers undertook many diverse curriculum projects involving Internet use, a plethora of changes would be associated with Internet use if we examined each change in each classroom. Here, we focus only on changes that occurred often, though not necessarily in every classroom, and that appeared to be linked directly to Internet use.

Finally, we do not explicitly discuss how these classroom changes evolved over time, although prior studies suggest that the ways educators use computers often do evolve over a period of years (Sand-holtz & Ringstaff, 1996). Our ability to address this issue is constrained by the limited two- to three-year period we had in which to observe NET curriculum activities in action. In addition, when evolution of use and consequent evolution of classroom impact did appear to occur, it was generally difficult to ascertain whether the passage of time in and of itself led to these changes or whether something else was responsible for them. For example, in many instances, educators not only changed their attitudes toward technology over time but also discovered opportunities for Internet-based activities that had not been available before. Therefore, the source of shift in Internet use that occurred over time could have been due to the availability of new resources rather than to a change in the educators' relationship to technology.

We turn now to describing six changes that frequently occurred with the implementation of Internet use in NET classrooms. The first group of changes we look at are (1) increased student autonomy, (2) new student roles, and (3) improved teacher-student relationships, all of which fall into the broad category of changes in classroom roles and relationships. The second group of changes we examine concerns the curriculum and the people and other resources that participated by way of the Internet in realizing the curriculum in the classroom. The changes are (1) that individuals external to the school more frequently participated in developing or assisting with curricular activities, 2) that learning experiences became available that allowed students to use or experience academic knowledge in more realistic or authentic ways, and (3) that academic resources expanded as students and teachers gained access to more up-to-date and extensive sources of information through Web sites and electronic interactions with outside experts.

CHANGES IN CLASSROOM ROLES AND RELATIONSHIPS

Both teachers and students frequently associated classroom-based Internet use with changes in classroom roles and relationships, including the three common ones we discuss here: increased student autonomy in the classroom, increased variation in the student role, and improved teacher-student relationships.

Of the students we queried on this topic ($N = 92$), more than 50 percent reported that teachers' behaviors when working with students on the Internet were different from their behaviors in other classroom situations. Similarly, of the teachers we interviewed on this topic (N = 25), more than 70 percent felt that using the Internet had influenced their roles in the classroom or their relationships with students. Moreover, these changes appear to have occurred more broadly than teachers initially anticipated or expressly desired. Specifically, the percentage of teachers who reported experiencing changes in classroom roles and relationships during interviews was much greater than the percentage of teachers who listed changes in classroom roles and relationships as a goal in their funded ACP proposal.

Increased Student Autonomy in the Classroom

A variety of data led us to the conclusion that students often experience increased autonomy when working on-line in the classroom. First, when we asked how they felt when working on the Internet as compared to doing other kinds of classroom work, students (N = 95) clearly reported increased feelings of independence. Specifically, on a scale of 1 to 5, with 5 indicating feeling "much more independent" and 1 indicating "much less independent," the mean response was 3.9, very near 4, "more independent." Students (N = 94) also said they experienced a greater sense of control over their work when working on-line as compared to working in a regular classroom (the mean was 3.8 on a similar 5-point scale). The difference between the responses of high school students and those of younger students was not statistically significant for either independence or control (F [2,92] = 1.94 and F [2,91] = 1.04, respectively).

In interviews too, students said that teachers controlled and directed student work to a much lesser degree when students worked on-line than at other times. As one high school student put it:

> It's really like [the teacher] acts different, because when he's teaching the class, it's sort of stuff we have to do—you know, assignments we have to do. But on the Internet, we have a lot more freedom to do almost whatever we want as long as we're getting the work done.

Elementary school students described similar experiences, saying, for example, "She lets us go free and see what we can learn about the Internet, and she doesn't let us go free when she's teaching the whole class." Students also described themselves as more intellectually independent when using the Internet because they were less dependent on teachers and other adults in the environment than they were at other times. As one explained, "I think it's increased how much I learn on my own, just because the motivation is there, the focus is there, and you're not dependent on somebody laying before you some information."

Teachers' self-reports, the detailed information we gathered about Internet-supported activities in NET classrooms, and our classroom observations support students' assertions that students engaged in Internet activities often worked autonomously. When we asked teachers whether they had experienced any changes in roles or relationships with implementation of Internet use, this was one of the most common responses. As one high school teacher described it:

> Once you give them the assignment, and if you give them the addresses where they are to go and get the information, they work more independently. It requires less supervision. . . . [A]s a teacher, you become more of a facilitator, I would say, because . . . well, they get a chance to explore on their own.

Of the teachers ($N = 83$) responding to a questionnaire about their Internet use in the classroom, roughly 40 percent reported, for example, that they circulate when students are working on an Internet activity and provide help only when students request it. Just 4 percent described themselves as presenting material to students working on the Internet. (An additional 24 percent said that teachers and students work collaboratively to carry out Internet activities, and about 20 percent described themselves as guiding students through these activities by way of questions and comments.) Further, in almost 60 percent of the 99 Internet activities that we tracked closely, teachers described students as commonly functioning as independent and self-directed workers.

Students' on-line activities were sometimes tightly circumscribed, when, for example, teachers sat directly beside students and directed them to a specific Web site or set of sites for the purpose of collecting information that the teacher had previewed and selected. Nonetheless, even when teachers attempted such control, they were unable to contain student activities to the same degree as they could within the structure of more conventional classroom activities. This was particularly true at the high school level, where students tended to be more advanced in their technical knowledge and could move off in new directions on-line relatively quickly and easily.

The clear perceived increase in student control and autonomy related to Internet use is especially interesting in light of the fact that teachers commonly expressed concern about the possible negative consequences of student autonomy on the Internet and implemented procedures designed to control and circumscribe students' on-line activities, as we discussed in Chapter Three. For many educators, increasing student autonomy was not a goal. For example, in at least two of the annual competitions in which teams of teachers competed to join NET, the document explaining NET specifically indicated that a shift from a teacher-centered paradigm to a partnership model in which students had more control was highly desirable. Nonetheless, the large majority of the proposals submitted to the ACP (80 percent) did not indicate that such a change was among the proposed projects' goals. Instead, as we discussed in Chapter Two, proposals tended to emphasize other goals, such as supporting interdisciplinary activities, increasing students' ability to function effectively in a world in which technology is increasingly important, and broadening students' perspectives. All of these were mentioned more frequently than increasing students' independence and control.

Several factors combined to limit teachers' ability to guide and control students during Internet activities on the one hand and to support students' ability to function relatively autonomously on the other. Students using the Internet tended to work more autonomously both because of the nature of the tasks they were engaged in and because they had no choice, given the many extra demands on their teachers in classrooms using the Internet.

FOSTERING STUDENT AUTONOMY: THREE MODES. We observed three common modes of Internet use, each of which fostered student autonomy. In the first situation, a small number of students worked on-line as the majority of classmates worked on other assignments. This was often the only practical approach available to NET teachers with a small number of computers per classroom. However, as we discussed in Chapter Four, in such situations, teachers were often very busy dealing with the larger group of students, and this undermined their ability to supervise and direct the Internet-using students. Further, computers sometimes had quirks or varying capabilities that channeled their use in different directions. For example, a computer that failed to print properly was not suitable for all Internet activities. Thus, technical constraints often made it impossible for even small numbers of students using the Internet in the same class to efficiently do the same things. With more and more individual activities, students functioned more independently because of practical limits on the time and attention their teachers could give them.

In the second situation that fostered autonomy, a group or classroom of students accessed the Internet simultaneously in a computer lab, performing different tasks, although using the same basic Internet resources. For example, a group of third graders who used a multi-user object-oriented environment (MOO) often simultaneously performed tasks ranging from reading stories, to posting responses to those stories, to composing their own stories. In such situations, teachers' time and attention were stretched thin as students posed questions and encountered problems specific to their individual activities. Thus, students had a substantial amount of autonomy because the complexity of the demands facing their teacher made it hard for the teacher to supervise any given student very closely.

In a third situation, a group or classroom of students worked at a variety of different Web sites, seeking information relevant to individual research projects or topics of interest. These students too, though working on the same basic type of Internet activity, often ended up in very different places, and their paths diverged very quickly. For example, unless teachers required all students to use the Internet as a virtual worksheet–that is, to stay at the same Web site and to collect the same information—students typically arrived at different end points and experienced different challenges along the way. In addition, as we discussed in Chapter Three, the Internet itself is structured for individual work. Technical problems often arose when teachers had large numbers of individuals try to do exactly the same thing simultaneously.

STUDENTS' TECHNICAL COMPETENCE. Another factor that strongly contributed to students' increased independence and control was that, as we discussed in Chapter Two, teachers generally were neither highly proficient computer users nor truly familiar with the Internet and all it has to offer. This situation tended to increase student independence and control because teachers commonly allowed students who were proficient Internet users to help other students use the Internet. This meant that such students were able to decide when and if they would leave their seats, talk with other students, and turn away from teacher-assigned activities—behaviors that teachers very often attempt to control otherwise. Teachers gave students this freedom not only because they wanted extra help but also in some instances because they were aware that some students were more likely to be able to solve a problem than they were. Indeed, as we will discuss in more detail in the next section of this chapter, a few high school students who were highly skilled Internet users even took on substantial responsibility for managing and maintaining their schools' servers and computers. This role gave them a striking degree of control and independence in that they had access to an important and expensive school resource that often contained various sorts of confidential information. Further, they had such access in a context in which the adults in the school were often not able to direct or closely control their behavior, because the adults lacked understanding of the technical issues. In sum, the time pressures of the classroom combined with many teachers' low levels of technical skill led to increasing independence for students, especially those with substantial technical knowledge.

TEACHERS' DESIRE FOR INCREASED STUDENT AUTHORITY. In addition to the factors that virtually compelled teachers to let students work more autonomously when using the Internet than they did at other times, we found a second and more intentional reason for the increased student independence. Some teachers, especially those working at the high school level, happily grasped the opportunity to let students work more independently due to the ready access the Internet provided for students to both information and to individuals who could contribute to their education. For example, once some teachers realized that the Internet could provide students with certain information that the teachers had previously provided, they felt less obligated to transmit this information themselves. They could place the burden for education more directly on their students, rather than, as one teacher put it, "handing . . . [information] to them on a silver platter." A foreign language teacher, for example, described how using the Internet affected his approach to vocabulary instruction in a way that increased students' control over their work:

> When we are up here [in the computer lab], I am more the facilitator and not the provider of information. Traditionally, in language classes . . . the teacher is the person who provides all the new vocabulary and

things of that nature. What I'm able to do now is just give them a few key [search] terms. They can do searches with the search engine to find articles about that topic, and then the vocabulary just starts appearing on its own. You know, they're able to find the words, and if they don't know the meaning I can provide it for them. But they're the ones who are actually looking for the words, then, instead of my giving them all the vocabulary.

Teachers also sometimes found surrogate teachers on-line who had expertise useful to the students. This often significantly reduced students' reliance on their classroom teacher for guidance and feedback. As we discuss in more detail later in this chapter, a small number of NET students became involved in projects with adults who assisted the classroom teacher by taking on relatively formal instructional roles. Individuals external to the school provided the students with challenges or asked them questions, and the classroom teacher coached them in their responses as needed.

In numerous other Internet activities, either adults or students assumed some subset of the functions typically belonging to the classroom teacher. For example, in a project coordinated at a local college, outside experts used the Internet to give groups of students at one elementary school math problems to solve. The students then used the Internet to share their solutions with and receive feedback from students in other states as well as outside experts. In yet another NET activity, elementary school students participated in an e-mail correspondence with an adult serving as a cook on an expedition to Antarctica in order to learn about that part of the world. The students determined the specific content of their questions, and they conducted this correspondence with the cook, who served as a kind of teacher for them, with a great deal of freedom. Although the degree of student autonomy in these instances was somewhat restricted because the students did not determine the general curricular topic around which the exchange centered, students subjectively experienced increased autonomy from their teachers in that they did not depend on them for feedback on their solutions or progress or for acquiring new sorts of knowledge.

STUDENT REACTIONS TO INCREASED AUTONOMY. Finally, it is important to mention that although most students were enthusiastic about opportunities for increased autonomy, some reported feelings of frustration at their teachers' increasing tendency to function as facilitators. Specifically, students reported that they were sometimes unable to get assistance from a teacher quickly because the teacher's attention was split among so many individuals. Students unable to solve problems on their own sometimes experienced extreme frustration as they waited for several minutes or even an entire classroom period for help. One teacher noted that the classroom dynamics were so different when students used the Internet that some students experienced a shock when they had to adapt to relying on peers and themselves as much as the teacher:

> The research class, if you go in and look at the Web pages from last year . . . the students specifically said, "We learned more from each other than we learned from Mr. Galbraith or Mr. Waleska," and I said, "Well, what's wrong with that?" and they said, "Well, you're the teacher. You're supposed to spend all your time right here with me!" And the point is, when you have two teachers and twenty-five kids and they're all working at the keyboards, you can't spend the whole period with every student. And if one kid knows how to do it, they show each other. . . . I will show two or three kids, because they're ready to learn it at that point, and by the time we get through the class, the rest of the class already knows this because . . . they've been teaching each other.

Nevertheless, in general, students seemed to find this independence motivating and enjoyable, as we discuss at more length in Chapter Seven.

Emergence of New Student Roles

Traditionally, students have had little role in shaping curricular materials, developing classroom activities, or teaching their peers or their teachers. When NET students engaged in Internet-supported activities, however, they frequently traded their traditionally rather passive roles for more active ones. In this section, we describe four new student roles that emerged in the context of Internet activities. Students acted more frequently as contributors and collaborators, as classroom helpers, as tutors, and as technical experts.

STUDENTS AS CONTRIBUTORS. Students, on their own initiative, took on a new role as contributors to the curriculum. For example, they sometimes identified Web sites that they thought complemented a given classroom topic and then alerted the teacher to their existence and location. One high school teacher described what happened as follows.

> Students went out and found diagrams for physics demonstrations in electrostatics, printed the demonstration, came back and said, "Can we do this? Do we have the equipment? I didn't know we could do this kind of stuff. Help me understand what is going on here." So the Internet has acted to stimulate, actually, what is going on in class.

Students also came up with ideas about the ways a teacher might have the class make use of the Internet. Though this was a less common role, one middle school teacher, Mr. Wallace, was so enamored of it that when an interviewer asked him what advice he would give to other teachers about effective classroom use of the Internet, he suggested that other teachers invite their students to act as contributors:

> I would say try to find out who in the classroom already knows how to use the Internet, and then . . . when you're doing a particular project or activity, talk to them and see what their input would be—how they would think they could best use it. Maybe they know more.

Teachers often did not have sufficient knowledge to realize their plans for Internet use efficiently. Some, like the teacher just quoted, took a pragmatic perspective on this problem and welcomed student assistance that helped them use the Internet more efficiently or effectively in their classes and thus begin to accomplish the goals they had envisioned. According to teachers, this kind of student participation in shaping classroom activities was less common in contexts not involving Internet use.

STUDENT ASSISTANTS. A second student role that commonly emerged during Internet-based instruction was that of the student assistant. In this role, rather than suggesting resources or activities, students directly assisted the teacher in solving problems in the classroom. Prototypically, this role emerged when one student helped another student who had run into a small problem while doing an Internet search. In many classrooms, students offered such help when the teacher, who could otherwise have handled the problem, was busy. We not only observed peer-to-peer assistance emerge spontaneously in many classrooms but also saw teachers encourage and legitimize this role, as the following field note from a high school classroom observation illustrates:

Emma [a student using the Internet] appeared to be still struggling with something. She was getting strange messages at the bottom of her screen about Pine Alpha and certain numbers. Star [another student], who was sitting beside her, moved over next to her to help her and began to press a bunch of keys. [Later, the teacher said] to the class, "If you need help, Star knows what she is doing. Ebony has done it too, although she is on her second letter." . . . I saw Star help a couple of girls on the end of the first row to print. A few minutes later, I saw Star move over to Emma and help her to print.

A few students took on this classroom role officially and functioned formally as peer trainers. For example, in one elementary school, a teacher well versed in using newsgroups trained a cadre of students from several classrooms to use and to post to the school newsgroup. When these students returned to their classrooms, teachers expected them to train their peers.

STUDENTS TUTORING TEACHERS. Students who functioned as tutors, the third new student role, experienced a more marked reversal of the traditional student role. These individuals actually educated their teacher in some way. As one student described it, "It was like now I was being put in their shoes and teaching them something that no one knew about. It was like I had a secret that I was telling everyone."

This role reversal occurred mostly with high school students and most commonly involved boys with advanced technical knowledge. However, students also occasionally took on tutorlike roles in subject matter areas once they had acquired a lot of information about a topic through Internet research or Internet-facilitated interactions. The latter dynamic was at work during one observation of a high school chemistry classroom:

[Mr. Jacobs, the teacher,] had gotten an e-mail message from the . . . doctor who LaToya had been working with on the research over the summer, explaining in a very brief fashion what the research was about. He was having LaToya go over this message with him sentence by sentence to explain [it] to him, because he said he didn't understand what it all meant. He had her explain certain words, like there was some kind of chemotherapy drug that she had to explain. [She also] explained the main function of the drug, which was to retard the growth of the cancer cells. It did this by cutting the DNA so that the cells could not reproduce. Mr. Jacobs also had her draw a picture of what this particular cell that she was talking about looked like.

This new student role as tutor sometimes emerged informally, often as teachers struggled to make sense of some technical step that knowledgeable students were performing on-line. However, it sometimes evolved in a planned fashion, with teachers approaching a student and asking to be trained in a technical skill, either during class or after school. For example, some students formally trained teachers in certain system administration skills and other technical matters. One teacher was describing this role when he told us:

> As far as actual software installation . . . Seth is more knowledgeable than I. So . . . he's more like the mentor to me. And he's teaching me as we go how to do the installations and so forth.

Again, we rarely saw or heard about students engaging in such tutoring in situations not involving the Internet in one way or another. Consistent with this finding, students, especially at the high school level, often said that they knew more than their teacher did about the Internet. They were far less likely to say they knew more than their teacher about a classroom subject.

STUDENTS AS TECHNICAL EXPERTS. The fourth new student role, the technical expert, emerged in the context of the school rather than the classroom. Some high school students, almost exclusively boys, functioned as school technology experts and took on substantial responsibility for managing and maintaining their school's server and its classroom computers. Sometimes, the technical functions they performed were ones that their teachers could not perform and, moreover, were not actively learning to perform. For example, when we asked what he liked most about working with the Internet in school, a student, Shelby, said:

> Well, in school, with my role as administrator and doing the maintenance work . . . I think that it's something different every day . . . something interesting. Most of my work here doesn't really deal with going through and looking for different [software] packages and installing and things like that, it's mainly just keeping the machines running. . . . Right now, we have a problem. Three of these machines will not take Ethernet cards for the network, and there's no solid answer why.

FACTORS THAT LED TO NEW STUDENT ROLES. Three basic factors, often functioning in combination, led to the emergence of these four new roles for students. The first and most important was, as we described in Chapter Four, teachers' relative lack of familiarity with computers generally and the Internet in particular. Although some students' greater technical knowledge created discomfort for some teachers and discouraged Internet use in some classrooms, other teachers accepted this knowledge differential and decided to make constructive use of it.

Second, once on-line, students, especially those of high school age, could act autonomously to increase their knowledge in many areas. With so much technical information readily available on the Internet, a determined student could readily acquire more technical knowledge than teachers had. And whereas students in traditional classrooms often face barriers to acquiring advanced knowledge in standard disciplinary areas because they lack access to well-endowed libraries and to disciplinary experts, with Internet connections they can begin to make their way around these barriers and grow in their knowledge of these disciplines as well.

Third, some teachers embraced such role development because it fit with their existing teaching philosophy. They sometimes expressed this philosophy in terms that reflected current theory in the field of education, and sometimes they put it in more down-to-earth words. But the underlying idea was that students and teachers learning from each other is a desirable model for classroom functioning because this reciprocal relationship has beneficial consequences above and beyond the usefulness of any specific piece of information that they might share. So, for example, some teachers felt these new roles were important in fostering students' self-esteem. Some said that reversal of the usual knowledge disparity combined with teachers' willingness to learn from students reinforced to students the importance of learning throughout life. Others felt that this disparity encouraged desirable student independence. And, finally, some felt that these experiences helped students realize that they themselves have the power to discover and share knowledge. Representing this latter perspective, for example, one teacher asserted: "I think it's great, because I think it's nice to be able to learn something from the kids. You know, I think it's important that they see that, 'Hey, I might know this. I can teach you something.'"

According to students and teachers, in addition to providing benefits to students, the new sorts of give-and-take occurring between teachers and students helped improve relationships between them. For example, these two high school students speak positively about being treated as equals rather than as children and of enjoying the sense of responsibility and knowledge this treatment implies.

LaToya: There's a lot of teachers that are cautious when it comes to using the Internet and computers in general. They're like, "Well, I don't want to break it. I don't want to touch it." So . . . it makes us feel empowered, but . . . it also makes you have a certain responsibility and feel a little older, because you can share knowledge with someone who's way older than you. So it's a nice experience.

Shamara: When I was . . . on the Internet . . . the computer froze, and [the teacher] did not know what was going on, so we had to tell her. And she didn't know how to print . . . and I guess got nervous or something, so we just had to show her. . . . She was . . . surprised.

Interviewer: . . . Did she treat you differently?

Shamara: Yeah. . . . She like treated [us] like we was equal, not one is adult and one is a child.

Interviewer: And how did that make you feel?

Shamara: Good . . . like finally somebody's treating me like I'm the same as them, not a little kid.

Some students also described receiving respect and admiration from their peers in response to their demonstrations of technical knowledge. As one put it, "It's a different kind of respect. It's more . . . like a . . . formal respect as opposed to like a buddy respect or . . . a *compadre*-type respect."

PROBLEMS FOR TECHNICALLY KNOWLEDGEABLE STUDENTS. However, three problems sometimes developed when students took on significant responsibilities for technology use. First, the especially skilled students sometimes spent so much time helping others that they had little time left to devote to work of their own. As Malcolm, a high school student, related:

> Me and this other kid named Darryl, we basically took it upon ourselves, and we got real good, so we ended up showing . . . we ended up teaching the kids how to do it. Not that we . . . well, I mean, even though Galbraith and Waleska were running around showing people how to do stuff, we were basically the ones that they were interacting with, showing them how to do stuff and showing them how to put it on. And meanwhile, me and him, our home pages weren't kind of thriving because during the class, we were too busy running around helping everyone else . . . to get work done ourselves.

In short, it was not only teachers who experienced pulls on their time and attention when students used the Internet for classroom projects; students with significant levels of expertise experienced this phenomenon as well.

Second, students who assumed the role of technical expert felt that because of their knowledge they sometimes faced unfair suspicion when something went wrong with a classroom computer or a server. As one recalled, "They didn't . . . exactly accuse me, but they were kind of hinting that maybe I did it to their computer, because I know so much." In addition, some of these students said they experienced criticism and even loss of their accounts for behaviors they did not feel warranted such reactions. The disputed behaviors varied from case to case but often involved activities that students felt they were entitled to undertake given their responsibilities but that teachers felt they should not have done. For example, a teacher might criticize a student for having looked in certain files that the teacher felt the student should not have looked at but that the student felt he or she was entitled to inspect as the school's systems administrator. Although such disputes led to the loss of Internet access for a small number of students, teachers were hesitant to impose this sanction because they then lost that student's valuable help.

The third problem was that the work students undertook as technical experts or helpers often increased the already existing gap between their technical knowledge and that of their peers. Students who served as helpers or technical experts typically entered the classroom with more technical expertise than their classmates did. They tended to have computers in their homes and to use them frequently. That gap in expertise only increased as they learned even more by assisting others. Moreover, students in general were quite aware that their peers with computers at home were often more technically competent and that it was these students who had special roles. Although most teachers and students seemed to appreciate the contribution of these technically knowledgeable students, a few did express concern about their relatively higher levels of school-based Internet access and use compared to other students.

IMPLICATIONS OF NEW STUDENT ROLES FOR TEACHERS' AUTHORITY. Looking at the results of the development of these new student roles, we concluded that despite the generally positive reactions of the teachers and students involved, there was no global change in the traditional structure of the student-teacher relationship, though there were occasional instances when students reported such change. Perhaps this was because both students and teachers typically felt that it was natural for young people to know more about computing than their elders and that teachers still had more knowledge in general than students did. One technically skilled high school student, who also stated that he did not know more than his teachers in traditional subject matters, described the situation this way:

TOD: I've sort of grown up . . . knowing that adults usually would know less than I would with computers and stuff.

INTERVIEWER: Does it change your relationship with the teachers . . . ?

TOD: Not really. I mean, when we sit down and we're working about computer stuff it does, but like whenever we're passing in the hall . . . they're the teacher. They're still my superior while I'm in school. . . . [W]hile we were working on the computers, then it reverses.

Nevertheless, even though students and teachers typically returned to their routine roles and behavior during traditional activities, students who experienced interactions in which they assisted teachers were often left with feelings of competence and increased responsibility.

Improved Teacher-Student Relationships

A third major change related to Internet use, one that students and teachers emphasized, has to do with the quality of day-to-day interactions between teachers and their students. Many said that during Internet activities such relationships improved, often becoming warmer and less adversarial. So, students reported, teachers acted happier, treated the class more "nicely," and tended to yell less. Reflecting the themes emerging in interviews, students ($N = 92$) given a questionnaire asking them to compare how friendly their teachers seemed when students were working on Internet activities and how friendly these same teachers seemed at other times in the classroom responded that their teachers were more friendly when students used the Internet. Elementary school students, whose mean response on a 5-point scale on which 4 represented "more friendly" was 4.1, were especially likely to report this change ($F [2,89] = 5.36, p (\leq.01)$). Indeed, of those students, 73 percent indicated that their teacher seemed more or much more friendly when students were using the Internet. However, many students at the middle and the high school levels also found that teachers were somewhat friendlier in this situation, with means of 3.5 and 3.3, respectively, on the 5-point scale. Only a very small percentage of any age group reported that teachers were less or much less friendly when using the Internet. Similarly, and consistent with student reports, many teachers reported that Internet use positively affected their relationships with students. A comment from Ms. Ebert, a NET team member at Southland Elementary School, illustrates this perspective:

> You're much closer to the kids you've worked with on the Net, because you get to do them in a small group. And not only that, when they start commenting about stories, or when they have e-mail with somebody, you start learning how they feel as people. . . . [I]t makes them like . . . they're more of a little human being, and you're more of a real human being to them.

This change in the affective quality of student-teacher relationships is especially interesting because, although it seemed widespread, it did not appear to be at all planned. When we coded the goals for Internet use commonly mentioned in the ACP proposals, not a single one of the eighteen categories we developed reflected a desire to improve student-teacher relationships, because potential NET teams so infrequently mentioned that goal. Furthermore, interviews with teachers about what they hoped to accomplish with the Internet and how they would judge success also suggested that they rarely, if ever, sought this outcome.

Change in the quality of student-teacher relationships appeared to be related to five factors. First, as teachers worked more often in a facilitating role and as students worked more often in small groups or independently on the Internet, teachers and students typically had more private and personal interactions during Internet use than at other times. This gave teachers an opportunity to tailor conversations to the individual students, connecting more directly with them on both academic matters and topics of personal interest to them. In this environment, teachers could begin to communicate more effectively with those students who tend not to speak up in large-group situations, as an elementary school teacher, Ms. Gerard, observed:

I mean, I always try to listen to them, but . . . it seems that they're more willing to say things and tell their little stories when it's a smaller group. It's more intimate. Maybe it's more comfortable for them for whatever reason. . . . For instance, Derrik[,] you may notice, is very quiet. He doesn't tend to be a real talker, and he's very quiet in class. He'll raise his hand and answer questions, but in working with him on the Internet, we have . . . I've heard things about his parents and his trips that I don't think I would have heard in a large group.

In short, removed from the public spotlight of the classroom, students spoke up more readily, and teachers saw them more distinctly and individually. Perhaps in this sort of environment, students also felt more comfortable interacting with their teachers because they did not need to worry as much about what their peers might think about those interactions. For example, one is not so likely to be accused of being teacher's pet when other students are not direct witnesses to one's conversations with a teacher. Further, when students did drift from their intended task on-line in small groups or as individuals, teachers could encourage them privately and without embarrassing them to focus and be more productive; teachers did not have to raise their voices to get the attention of a small group or to chastise individuals in front of the entire class. Therefore, even when individuals deviated from the teacher's agenda while using the Internet, there was generally no need for a public contest of wills.

Second, some teachers at the middle or high school level reported that classroom Internet use led them to develop a more multifaceted and appreciative view of the potential of some of their students, including those who had previously not impressed them. This occurred when students displayed talent using the Internet that had not been apparent in specific classroom subject areas. The remarks of two high school teachers, Mr. Jacobs and Ms. Hoffman, illustrate this finding:

It's surprised me that it's not necessarily the better students that want to use the Internet . . . much to my surprise. Kids that I wouldn't think were academically gifted are gifted on the Internet and . . . surprise me by what they've been able to do.

Well, it enabled me to see some of my students in a different light. Some who were very capable in language skills were quite uncomfortable with the computer. And on the other hand, those who struggled with language may have had an opportunity to really shine because they were more comfortable with the Internet than they were with their language.

When such students, or others, were able to help their teachers in a variety of ways, a more reciprocal relationship developed between them that appeared to help build positive bonds. As one high school teacher, Ms. Richardson, put it, reflecting on the positive aspects of students' high levels of technical knowledge:

> It breaks down barriers there for both of us, because they know so much more than I do, sometimes, and other times, I can help them along. So, it puts you on the same level. You're both learners. It's not like they're looking to you to give all the answers, and I think it really helps to achieve a nice bridge in learning. You just, you feel comfortable together, or frustrated together, as well.

In short, when working on Internet activities, some students revealed unexpected, surprising, or very useful talent, a phenomenon that often affected teachers' attitudes and behaviors toward those students in ways the students found rewarding.

Of course, this opportunity to learn about the other could operate in both directions. A third factor that contributed to improving relationships is that some students also came to know and appreciate their teachers better as individuals due to Internet-related interactions. During encounters with individual students or small groups of students working on Internet projects, teachers revealed more personal feelings, perspectives, or vulnerabilities than they did in whole class situations. Also, teachers' uncertainties and difficulties when dealing with technology were often quite apparent. They may have looked more human to students in these circumstances—like individuals also struggling with the task of learning. An elementary school student, for example, was observed empathizing with her teacher when the teacher encountered a problem with moving e-mail from one file to another:

> The room was incredibly loud at this moment, and suddenly in the midst of it, Ms. Ebert exclaimed, "Oh, this is not my day!" Danielle turned sharply towards Mike and said, "Don't yell! She's having a hard time. She might erase everything." Ms. Ebert was kneeling on the floor with her elbows on the table that the computers were sitting on, and she hung her head and ran her fingers through her hair. It turned out

she had erased, or she believed that she had erased, all of the letters that she had highlighted instead of moving them. She said a couple of times, "I just can't believe this. I can't believe this." Danielle began to pat her back soothingly, as if to reassure her.

In addition to letting students learn more about a teacher and see that teacher as an individual who also experiences frustration with learning, moments like these can build camaraderie in two ways. First, students can identify a point of similarity between themselves and the adult. Second, as students help teachers, they can develop a more reciprocal relationship that builds bonds between them.

A fourth reason that relationships between students and teachers were warmer and less adversarial when students engaged in Internet activities is that teachers often did not have to exert the same sorts of control strategies that they felt compelled to use in the regular classroom. As we discuss in Chapter Seven, students generally enjoyed working on-line more than working in the typical classroom situation. Because of this enjoyment, teachers said, students working on-line acted more interested and were less disruptive, decreasing the pressure on teachers to exert external controls on them. Teachers also reported that some students were decidedly easier to get along with when they were performing Internet activities, as a high school science teacher found:

> I have noticed probably about three or four students that didn't impress me very much in class but when they got access to the network they just became totally different people. They actually became more humane, and they were willing to speak in normal sentences; they were polite . . . mainly because they needed information for the computer system that they weren't going to get if they were going to continue acting the way they were. And it just sort of helped. . . . [A]bout three or four or five kids just really blossomed, because all of a sudden there's something that they really want to learn, and they can have an intelligent conversation with the teacher . . . on something that they're really interested in.

When students engage in work readily, teachers have more time and energy for positive and individual interactions with them. In addition, seeing students respond positively to schoolwork is likely to lead to a positive reaction in teachers, which may account for students' observations that their teachers appeared generally more positive and happy when students were engaged in on-line activities than they did at other times. A high school teacher who was not a NET educator but who became interested in using the Internet in her work as a result of observing NET team members argued that Internet use gave some teachers "a renewed sense of what they're here for and how they can relate to kids." She went on to link teachers' positive reactions to students' behavior with the following words, "You suddenly learn that if kids are gonna respond to something in this manner and you're good at it, then you're gonna have a better time with the kids."

Fifth and finally, a few teachers asserted that having to learn something that they had no prior experience with and were even somewhat afraid of reminded them of what being a student could be like and made them more patient or empathetic with their own students.

CHANGES IN CURRICULUM, PEOPLE, AND RESOURCES

In this section, we move from changes in classroom roles and relationships to changes in delivering the curriculum. Access to the Internet provides students with educational opportunities not typically present in the traditional classroom with any regularity. In NET classrooms, this Internet contact with the outside world had a variety of consequences—for the classrooms generally, for the curriculum, for individual students, and for individual teachers. In Chapter Seven, we will discuss consequences of this contact for teachers and individual students. In the sections that follow, we focus on consequences of contact with the outside world for the curriculum. First, we look at the increased contact students had with people outside the school and the exchange of ideas, experiences, and information this fostered. Then, we describe two specific curricular changes that occurred relatively frequently—more authentic uses of subject matter knowledge than are available in the traditional classroom (including publishing online) and access to more timely, extensive, and sometimes unusual educational resources.

Increased Contact with Those Outside the School

Although, as we discussed in Chapters Three and Four, teachers did not connect to the external world with as much ease and regularity as they had initially envisioned, most did take advantage of the Internet to make such connections in their classes. For example, we collected detailed data on the ninety-nine Internet activities that NET team members implemented at the four high-use and three low-use sites described in Chapter Five. Just under 45 percent of these activities emphasized archival research of some sort: students went to a Web site or newsgroup to collect information about a topic of interest. Almost 40 percent emphasized student interaction with others outside of the school. In these types of activities, students contacted individuals online for the purpose of getting or exchanging information of some sort to improve their academic skills (for example, writing to foreign language pen pals), or in the context of a mentorship relationship (for example, high school students wrote to an adult who helped them with a long-term science project). Finally, roughly 18 percent of these activities emphasized students placing their work on-line—that is, they engaged in Web-based publishing.

Consistent with these data, both students and teachers indicated that after the Internet arrived, they had contact from school with individuals in the outside world more frequently than they had prior to the Internet's arrival. For example, when educators responded to a survey ($N = 325$) asking them to describe how use of the Internet had affected the amount of contact they had with outsiders in carrying out school-related tasks, 67 percent indicated that Internet use had greatly or somewhat increased such contact. Similarly, when we surveyed students about how often they had used the Internet at school to make contact with people outside the school district, among the elementary school students surveyed ($N = 27$), roughly 30 percent responded that they had done so "frequently" or "very frequently," and an additional 15 percent reported having done so "sometimes." Responses ($N = 26$) were similar at the high school level.

More Authentic Contexts for Learning

Many scholars advocate placing learners in situations where they use or experience disciplinary knowledge in more realistic or authentic ways than they do in traditional classrooms (Bereiter & Scardamalia, 1987; Collins, Brown, & Newman, 1989; Smith, Snir, & Grosslight, 1992), and numerous NET team members wished to achieve this goal, as we discussed in Chapter Two. However, realizing this vision can prove difficult. One consequence of Internet access for the curriculum is that it enabled many teachers to come closer to this goal. In comparison to what they could do in a traditional classroom, students accessing the Internet used or experienced knowledge more as disciplinary experts might, and they also applied their disciplinary knowledge in ways closer to real-world practice. Such changes emerged in a wide variety of subject areas and across grade levels. Almost one-third of the ninety-nine Internet projects we documented in detail involved students in learning experiences with one or both of these characteristics.

We first look more closely at the finding that Internet access often allowed teachers to place students in learning situations in which they experienced academic disciplines in more authentic ways than they had previously. Most academic disciplines have characteristic ways of working with and applying knowledge, including certain patterns of social interaction that facilitate experts' disciplinary knowledge acquisition, production, and use (Collins et al., 1989). NET teachers in a variety of subject areas found ways to use the Internet to further the extent to which students experienced such patterns of interaction. One subject in which this very commonly occurred was language arts. Writers typically do not write for only one person but rather receive, react to, and respond to critical feedback from a variety of sources as they work on a piece of writing. Even after a work is published, writers continue to experience feedback of various sorts. In most language arts classrooms, students typically have a very limited audience for their writing—their teacher and in some classrooms their immediate classmates (Applebee, Auden, & Leer, 1981). With the Internet, many teachers were able for the first time to connect students to a broader audience as these young writers published their pieces in school home pages, newsgroups, and other Web environments. In many classrooms, students who participated in such activities received responses to their work from an audience beyond the classroom. As one student noted:

> It just gets out all over the city, and lots of people can look at it if they go to that Web site. Whereas if you make it a piece of paper only the people that want can get it, whereas anyone in the world can basically look at it on the Net. . . . [I]t's not just like a closed-in audience.

Similar sorts of change also occurred in other subject areas. For example, expert mathematicians sometimes engage in scholarly discourse with colleagues throughout the nation or the world about a mathematical problem, presenting possible solutions and commenting on the merits and drawbacks of each other's proposed solutions. Using the Internet, young students experienced some aspects of this process as they worked to solve a difficult mathematical problem on paper and then shared their work with peers in other parts of the country on-line. They then had opportunities to respond to each other's solutions. Similarly, scientists increasingly work in teams and draw their conclusions about natural or social phenomena from analyses of data that numerous individuals collect in a systematic and coordinated way. In several activities that NET team members carried out, students contributed data they had collected as a class about some phenomenon to a large database containing contributions from students around the country. They then had opportunities to work with the data that they and others collected to draw conclusions about the phenomenon they were studying. Finally, one very common way of working in the scientific community involves placing less experienced scientists in apprenticelike relationships with scientists more senior and more knowledgeable than themselves. In NET classrooms at both the high school and the middle school levels, students contacted scientists to seek help with and advice about extensive projects they were preparing for a regional competition. In some instances, these contacts evolved to the point that adult scientists actively mentored students, helping them plan and design their investigations and interpret their results.

In addition to allowing students to interact with others in ways characteristic of disciplinary experts, access to the Internet enabled students to work in ways that approached real-world applications of disciplinary knowledge. The most striking examples of this occurred in foreign language classrooms, both for native English speakers learning a second language and for immigrant children seeking to acquire English as a second language. At the high school level, as we described earlier, for example, foreign language students composed and sent e-mail correspondence to native speakers overseas and responded to e-mail from these peers as well. Some students engaged in real-time foreign language conversations by visiting on-line chat rooms. Prior to this experience, these language learners had had very few opportunities to apply their language skills in interactions with native speakers. During these interactions, students encountered native speakers using slang, employing a variety of dialects, and making cultural allusions that students did not encounter in their textbooks. Students also sometimes vividly experienced the miscommunication that arises from imprecise use of a foreign language. As one teacher observed,

"One of the good things that I like is that most of the pen pals will actually write back and say, 'I assume you meant *this* when you wrote *this.*'" Both foreign language teachers and students vigorously asserted that learning a second language to succeed on a classroom test is not the same as learning it to communicate in real-world contexts.

Although these curricular changes certainly occurred, they were relatively difficult to sustain. Authentic projects, unless brief, typically depended on the sustained interest and continued goodwill of individuals in the external world with whom the students interacted. Usually, teachers used the Internet to locate the adults with whom students could work, often by posting information in newsgroups or mailing lists. In some instances, however, individuals or organizations who initially expressed interest eventually decided not to become involved. For example, educators at one NET school proposed e-mail-based mentorships between African American high school students in an honors science and math program and employees in a technology-oriented corporation. Though the school had a special relationship with the corporation and the potential mentors were interested, the corporation did not want its internal network connected to the Internet due to concerns about industrial security. In other instances, individuals who had agreed to donate their time did not always remain interested in supporting the students, particularly as the growth of the Internet brought with it increasing requests for such help. As one high school teacher explained, "The people that we were counting on previously just slipped by the wayside, and probably because they have gotten so doggone busy that it's ridiculous, you know?" Faced with such problems, educators had to change their plans in significant and sometimes undesirable ways. For example, unable to find pen pals who were native speakers of a foreign language, one NET teacher had students develop pen pal relationships with U.S.-born foreign language students, who were no more advanced and in some instances less advanced than her students.

In sum, in many instances, teachers were able to use the Internet to add interactive or communicative elements that expanded students' experience of a subject area and made it more authentic. Of course, the Internet did not transform classrooms into writing salons or research laboratories. However, it did expose students to experiences they would not have had otherwise in the fields they were studying. At the same time, teachers often found it difficult to sustain these activities for long periods of time because they were so dependent on the goodwill and commitment of those outside of the school. Therefore, in many instances, these curricular changes proved relatively fragile and transitory.

Access to More Timely and Extensive Educational Resources

Making students' experiences of academic disciplines more real was only part of the Internet's effect on the curriculum. When we interviewed teachers ($N = 45$) about the effect that access to the Internet had had on the way they taught or organized the classroom, one of the most common responses they gave (38 percent) was that it had enriched the existing curriculum by giving students and teachers access to more educational resources. Similarly, more than 85 percent of the educators ($N = 325$) responding to a survey in NET's fourth year indicated that access to the Internet had greatly increased the variety of educational resources they used in carrying out school-related tasks. Under 15 percent reported that Internet access had not changed the resources they used in their teaching. No one reported that use of the Internet had decreased available resources. Finally, when asked to indicate what they felt was the most important impact of Internet use on students, these teachers' most popular response (26 percent), which they selected from among fourteen possible choices, was "access to better resources." The only other response option that was anywhere near this one in popularity was "motivate students," which 22 percent of teachers selected.

Teachers took advantage of Internet resources in myriad ways. For example, several teachers reported that when a student asked questions about a topic of study then under way, the teacher would invite the student to carry out a relevant on-line search. In addition, many teachers called on Internet resources for visual as well as textual information for their classes. Although access to additional resources played out in the classroom in these and many other ways, in this section we focus on two basic but broadly important results of the variety of increased resources that we observed at NET schools. First, teachers were able to make their curriculum more current. Second, teachers were able to compensate for their schools' resource deficits.

We turn first to the issue of timeliness. One challenge teachers face is providing their students with access to up-to-date information about issues and events. Such current information is especially critical for social studies teachers because political systems are often in flux. But staying up-to-date also proved a challenge for foreign language teachers who wanted students to learn about the countries that spoke the language they were learning and for science teachers teaching in areas of rapid scientific progress.

Teachers in these content areas often bemoaned the fact that their textbooks and the resources in their school libraries were woefully out of date. Indeed, one asserted that the encyclopedia in her school's library was published well before she had even been born. They also spoke enthusiastically about how the Internet gave them convenient access to up-to-date resources. As one said, for example:

> It keeps me up-to-date.... [A] lot of times you find a lot of pertinent and current information on things. Times change—especially in biology ... every ten years they can ... rewrite the whole textbook.

Internet access to current resources (including such authentic resources as on-line foreign language newspapers) helped language teachers at one high school achieve a curricular goal they had long sought but found difficult to attain. They had revamped their foreign language curriculum so that it revolved around thematic units dealing with current events. With textbooks going quickly out of date and foreign language newspapers not readily available in the school library, it would have been difficult for them to reach the full potential of this curricular vision without Internet access. Their students too recognized that they were able to gain more up-to-date and therefore often more accurate information on-line. As one student recounted:

> [In Spanish,] we had to basically do a research project, and it was about different Spanish cultures and different countries. And I learned a lot about the type of dress and different customs and things like that ... basically through Internet use. And it was more updated than it was in the book, because the books were real old. And it was just telling how certain cities—that in the book ... were still [presented as] these ancient cities—how they had modernized and caught up with the times and the different things they had.

This student not only gained access to more current information but also learned something about learning, that dated information can leave a reader with a mistaken impression of places, people, and events.

Another characteristic of the information traditionally available in schools is its relatively narrow scope. NET teachers noted, for example, that their libraries not only offered little information about potentially interesting research topics but that this information was often located in just one book. That limited the types of assignments teachers could design, especially when students' homes were located in communities with limited or no public library resources, limiting students entirely to using in-school resources. For example, it limited assignments requiring students to provide different perspectives on the same material, because the sharing of one copy of a book often caused logistical problems. Moreover, teachers could fuel and foster students' interest in many curricular topics only so far before running out of resources and information to share from the text or the library. Finally, the few resources that were available in the school on a particular topic might not always be appropriate or engaging for some portion of the school population.

Access to the Internet helped NET team members address these resource deficits. First, teachers could use the Internet to access pertinent information not otherwise available in the school and print it to share with students, or they could help students reach these Web sites during class time. Second, teachers told us that Internet use especially enhanced access to the types of information not generally found in school libraries, such as databases. Third and finally, teachers could access more varied types of information. For example, they might find ways to connect students to individuals who could supply eyewitness reports about a topic of current interest or to access a variety of graphic or multimedia resources.

In addition to providing richer educational experiences overall, access to a broader set of resources had another consequence. Teachers felt that it gave them more opportunities to find resources appropriate for and engaging to a wide variety of students. For example, one teacher of hearing-impaired elementary school students emphasized the important role that on-line resources had come to play in her interactions with them:

> Our children, . . . being hearing-impaired and language-impaired, if they open a dictionary or open an encyclopedia, they're gonna see, maybe a picture and then a lot of text. And the text is not written at any level that they can read. Whereas on the Internet, if I'm sitting right with them and they see this beautiful picture that comes up and they see pictures and different things, they can go deeper and deeper. . . . I've had them say, "Can we go back and look for something more on this?" or . . . for example . . . one student was doing something on Native

Americans for her geography/history class. She had to do a poster of the state of New Mexico and she wanted to do a map of the Native American tribes and where they were located—the reservations in New Mexico. She found information on the one tribe and then it just led down further into their crafts, their history, their religion, and so forth, and she just went off on a tangent about that. "Well, I didn't know about this. I wanna learn this." . . . [T]hat opened her eyes, and she wanted to change her poster a little bit, explore a little bit differently.

As this teacher suggests, an increase in the variety of resources present in an educational environment may generate students' interest in and enthusiasm for a curricular topic.

Of course, the plethora of on-line information presented classroom challenges as well as benefits. First, as we discussed in Chapter Three, factors that make the Internet rich in resources can also make it difficult to incorporate into daily classroom life. There are so many links between Web sites, for example, that students working independently easily get off track, either purposely or without really thinking about what they are doing. Web sites pertaining to entertainment, especially sports, television programs, and popular music, exerted a very strong pull, and teachers were often not aware that particular students were straying from the assignment at a given moment because the teachers were occupied with others.

Second, students sometimes find it difficult to process the sheer amount of information they encounter. Indeed, one librarian asserted that access to the Internet at her school had changed an information deficit to an information overload. Moreover, although an increasing number of Web sites are organized specifically for educational purposes, much of the material available on the Internet has not been prepared with students' level of background knowledge and reading ability in mind. Thus, materials relevant to a topic under study might not be usable because they do not mesh well with students' reading levels and their degree of related knowledge. Even students with advanced reading skills sometimes found it difficult to sift through the masses of information they acquired about a topic of interest to select accurate and pertinent information. This in turn meant that teachers often needed to work very closely with students as they used the Internet, particularly at the earlier grade levels.

Third, although archival information is often easy to obtain on-line, other sorts of information, such as eyewitness descriptions of an event or experience, often are not. As we have pointed out, outsiders who could provide help and information sometimes reject project goals or simply lack interest in the students or in a proposed project. As this elementary school teacher makes clear in an interview, visions for on-line projects were often more rosy than the reality teachers encountered:

Ms. FAIRFAX: The reason that we use video so often in a people study is because . . . there's this immediate link. Now you're seeing . . . you're there. It's the closest we can get. And I think the Internet has that same capacity in order to have people touch people in a global world. And what better way to know the Masai than to be able to communicate with one? I mean, it would be great if we could bring them in the room [*laughs*], but that's maybe not a possibility. So to be able to communicate on the Internet is wonderful.

INTERVIEWER: Do you do that with them though?

Ms. FAIRFAX: We've tried and we've tried and that did not come to fruition. The addresses, the people . . . we weren't getting things back, they weren't getting there. We had gotten a few different addresses of different colleges where they would be interested in this, so we thought we were writing to them, we weren't getting things back, and things weren't . . . [i]t just fizzled out. And then it became so frustrating . . . [we said] "Forget it. Let's go with the old post office."

In still other instances, outsiders might reject the goal of the teacher or school outright. For example, in one elementary school, a teacher wanted her students to correspond with a Native American group. However, group members felt that the teacher simply wanted her students to be able to say they had written to Native Americans. The group did not want to participate unless members were allowed to shape the curricular activity more than the teacher wanted, and consequently the teacher abandoned the project.

Finally, as we mentioned in Chapter Three, Internet resources are much less circumscribed than other resources normally found in schools. Some Internet sources present a balanced picture; others are blatantly biased; and still others are subtly biased. Also, they may contain errors. Although textbooks and other sources traditionally used in schools may contain factual errors or bias, they are not as prone to blatant falsehoods and very strong biases as are many materials on the Internet, where anyone can say anything he or she desires, no matter how utterly outrageous or false. In one sense, educators can view this array of materials as an educational opportunity. Teachers can draw examples from it to alert students to the importance of reading critically. As one teacher commented, "You're finding a lot of conflicting information. . . . [I]t's very interesting, and I think that in itself [it] could be an entire core curriculum about misinformation, and tone, and the way words are used." There were certainly instances when students found such conflicting information, and it generated classroom discussions about textual veracity that likely would not have occurred otherwise. Yet many NET teachers, used to teaching materials whose content they can accept as accurate, did not have the inclination or even the necessary background to discuss ways in which students might read more critically. As one high school teacher put it, with some frustration:

> That's a difficult item to handle because how do I assess whether it's truth or not? It's like any piece of material that you pick up from a book. You have to evaluate the source—where it came from—and we're not at that level yet in evaluating sources.

To cope with this situation, some teachers selected sets of Web sites they felt were accurate and appropriate for their students and guided students to those sites; others ignored the situation. This left many students unprepared to deal in a sophisticated way with judging the truth and reliability of the materials they discovered on the Internet and hence posed a potentially significant problem, particularly because many teachers reported that students exhibited a distinct tendency to believe the information they found on-line.

In short, there were many challenges associated with bringing information from the outside world into the classroom through on-line resources. However, both teachers and students generally expressed the view that the benefits of expanded access to information were worth the trade-offs and challenges they encountered. Up-to-date and more in-depth information about topics of interest helped to enrich curricula previously limited by the few and usually older resources available in the local school library.

CONCLUSIONS

This chapter describes a number of classroom changes that occurred with the introduction of the Internet. Some of these changes were very much in accord with goals embraced by NET staff and articulated by a subset of NET team members in their proposals. These changes include enriching the curriculum by providing more authentic class-room activities and access to a broader array of educational resources. Though we do not argue that Internet use will necessarily bring changes of this sort, it appears that when teachers desire such changes the Internet facilitates their ability to achieve them. Indeed, use of the Internet in NET classrooms in some cases resulted in more intensive change than teachers initially envisioned. For example, teachers who desired a broader array of resources in the classroom were sometimes dismayed by just how broad an array of material it made available. Furthermore, some teachers who initially favored increased student independence felt themselves losing more control over student activities than they had initially envisioned or desired; Internet use brought about more radical manifestations of student autonomy in the classroom than they would have put into place on their own (Schofield & Davidson, in press-b).

Internet use was also associated with some changes that specific NET teachers or staff did not initially envision. For example, educators who did not set out to increase student independence often found it emerging nonetheless when their classes used the Internet, a potentially important finding because increased perceptions of control on students' part may contribute to increased student motivation (Ames, 1990; Schofield, 1995) as well as students' positive attitudes toward school (Henderson & Dweck, 1990). Another unanticipated change was the emergence of new student roles in the classroom as students functioned as contributors, tutors, and so forth. Although some proposals submitted to the ACP did mention some students functioning as trainers for other students, no proposal anticipated that teachers and students would experience the more extreme sorts of role reversal that we described in this chapter. Rather, references in these proposals to changed roles and relationships virtually always referred to having teachers move toward the role of facilitator of students' work and sometimes to having students work somewhat more autonomously. Nor did teachers appear to fully anticipate the full ramifications of the gap in technological knowledge that separated them from some of their students. Because many teachers in the United States have relatively little experience with technology and many teacher preparation programs still do not emphasize the use of technology in the classroom, this pattern may well emerge in other schools.

Another change that educators did not generally anticipate was the extent to which Internet use would be associated with improved relationships between teachers and students. Students and teachers seemed to work more easily and harmoniously together during many Internet-based activities. Even though teachers did anticipate that students would enjoy the Internet and hoped that they might pay more attention in response, the fact that Internet use helped students and teachers better understand and appreciate one another as individuals and revealed hidden strengths and abilities in some students came as a pleasant surprise. Further, this change is likely to do more than just make school experiences more pleasant for students. Research has demonstrated that the nature of interpersonal relationships between teachers and students influences students' motivation toward and interest in school as well as in particular classes, with more positive relationships leading to increased interest in school as well as positive academic motivation and achievement (Midgley, Feldlauger, & Eccles, 1989; Wentzel & Wigfield, 1998; Wentzel, 1998). In turn, interest in school generally or in particular classes helps to explain students' subsequent academic performance (Wentzel, 1998). Scholars have also related teacher-student relationships to students' feeling that they fit in and belong at their school, which in turn helps to predict students' academic achievement (Roeser, Midgley, & Urdan, 1996). In addition, at-risk students from a variety of backgrounds tend to speak particularly ardently about the importance of connecting meaningfully with teachers who explicitly demonstrate interest in students as individuals (Davidson, 1999; Wehlage & Rutter, 1986).

It is important to emphasize that the changes that we have described did not transform classroom life to the extent that some advocates for the use of the Internet have publicly hoped. However, consistent with prior research (Becker, 1999a), our study certainly suggests that Internet use helps people who want to move pedagogy in constructivist directions to do so. For example, there is no doubt that it helped many teachers to provide students with more authentic contexts for learning and to allow students to function more independently. In addition, it may prod others in that direction, because individuals who want to use the Internet will need to adapt to its influence both on the complexity of the teachers' work and on social relationships in the classroom. Moreover, Internet use was associated with a variety of outcomes for teachers and students beyond those affecting everyday life in the classroom. We turn to this topic in the next chapter.

CHAPTER SEVEN

Teacher and Student Outcomes Related to Internet Use

T he changes that Internet use made in classroom roles and relationships as well as in the curricula to which students were exposed were extremely important because they directly and significantly influenced students' educational experiences. In this chapter, we discuss a closely related set of outcomes, many of which also have clear implications for classroom functioning—outcomes for teachers and students as individuals.

As in Chapter Six, we are not asserting that Internet access automatically results in the outcomes we discuss. None of these outcomes is automatic or universal because none of them occurred for every teacher and student in the classrooms with Internet access that we studied. Neither do we claim that providing Internet access is necessarily the best or the least expensive way to foster such outcomes. One can imagine many potentially effective ways to foster most of the outcomes we discuss that do not involve Internet access. Additionally, such outcomes may well not occur as soon as schools provide access. As we explained in Chapter Four, Internet use in Networking for Education Testbed (NET) schools appeared to evolve, especially among teachers initially inexperienced in using the Internet in the classroom, and it is only logical to expect that different kinds of outcomes might occur at different points in time, consistent with earlier studies of other computer applications in classrooms (Sandholtz et al., 1997). Also, different teachers made use of the Internet in very different ways and for very different purposes, and it is again logical to expect that the consequences of e-mail exchanges between NET students and their peers in this nation and overseas would not be the same as the consequences of using the Internet to access archival resources or to facilitate teachers' discussions with colleagues about professional issues.

Finally, we do not have the kind of data on outcomes that policymakers and others often desire when considering education policy decisions involving school and classroom innovations. For example, we do not have data that would allow us to compare the standardized test scores of students in classrooms with Internet access and those of their peers in control classrooms taught by the same teacher. Neither have we done intensive and replicable analysis of students' written products to see, for example, whether the writing skills of those with Internet access improve more than the skills of their peers over the course of the school year. We did not obtain such data for many reasons. First, the continuing evolution of Internet use in many NET classrooms made it difficult if not impossible to set up studies yielding these kinds of data in the context of this research. Second, there was a significant danger of drawing inappropriate conclusions about achievement change due to Internet use if we studied such change too early during that use. It is a truism in the organizational change literature that one should expect dips in performance after introducing new approaches to work, even when the innovation is likely ultimately to be productive. In addition, some research suggests that it takes teachers three or more years to make really productive use of new computer resources (Hadley & Sheingold, 1993; Honey, 1994; Sheingold, 1990; Stearns, David, Hanson, Ringstaff, & Schneider, 1991). Thus, only a small subset of the schools that participated in the five-year NET project was on-line long enough to warrant such studies, especially because it took roughly a year after schools joined NET to provide them with the wiring and equipment necessary for Internet access. Third and very important, studies of this sort must use a specific hypothesis to guide the selection of pre- and postmeasures. But when researchers know little about the topic, as is certainly the case with regard to the Internet's impact on students and teachers, any hypothesis is likely to guide one to a set of measures that miss unexpected impacts, both positive and negative. Qualitative approaches that can pick up such outcomes have a major advantage (Singleton, Straits, & Straits, 1993). Finally, as we discussed in Chapter Two, the majority of the curriculum activities NET educators devised were not set up with the goal of improving students' achievement in specific subject areas such as increasing students' reading skills or improving their writing; goals like preparing students for an increasingly technological world and decreasing provincialism were equally or even more common.

In spite of all these caveats, we believe that our study did yield useful information about the possible outcomes of Internet use in schools. In the rest of this chapter, we discuss the outcomes that we observed or that students and teachers commonly reported. As in Chapter Six, we do not discuss every single outcome that appeared to stem from Internet use in NET; rather, we focus on those that seemed to occur commonly and that appeared to have significance for individuals or their schools. Finally, because individuals who have gone to the effort of participating in a competition to bring the Internet to their classrooms might easily inadvertently overestimate its impact, we tried to be especially careful to triangulate different kinds of data to ensure that educators' reports of outcomes were supported by other independent evidence, such as interviews with students, observational data, and the like. We achieved such triangulation most readily in analyzing student outcomes, because teachers were more likely to have information on student outcomes than vice versa. However, even in the case of teacher outcomes, it was often possible to obtain triangulated data from other sources, such as our field notes or interviews with principals.

TEACHER OUTCOMES

We look first at five major outcomes of Internet use for NET teachers. Compared to their previous practice and experience, they communicated more with others about professional matters, engaged in more professional development activities, increased their knowledge of computing and the Internet, took on more professional roles outside the classroom, and experienced more pride and enthusiasm about their work.

Increased Work-Related
Communication with Others

Isolation from colleagues in one's own school and in other schools is a long-standing condition of teachers in the United States (Lieberman & Miller, 1990; Lortie, 1975; U.S. Department of Education, 1999). Such isolation is generally problematic because it prevents or at least greatly constricts the flow of information, ideas, and even emotional support that helps other professionals perform effectively. Reducing isolation was one of the four educational opportunities the original NET grant proposal argued that Internet access could provide.

NET appears to have been quite successful in reducing teachers' isolation, in spite of the many barriers to communication with the outside world that we discussed in Chapter Three. Access to the Internet did appear to facilitate connections between schools and the world outside. In Chapter Six, we focused on the ways this change affected the amount and kind of information available to those in classrooms and the implications of this change for classroom functioning. Here, we focus on the impact of this change on teachers' work-related communication with others. It appears that Internet access did markedly increase such interaction. For example, of the educators we interviewed on this topic ($N = 24$), almost three-quarters indicated that Internet access had increased their interaction with others; they spontaneously mentioned with roughly equal frequency increased interaction with teachers in their own school (25 percent), teachers in their district but outside their school (21 percent), and educators outside the district (21 percent). This communication was apparent to observers by one of its results—educators frequently circulated materials they had obtained from others to NET team colleagues or used such material in their classes.

Although a few teachers mentioned that Internet access had increased the amount they communicated with parents or even with certain students, most emphasized their increased interaction with other educators. Teachers often specifically noted that this increased interaction fostered group cohesion or reduced their isolation, as did Ms. O'Malley, an elementary schoolteacher:

> It's certainly increased my connection to people. . . . I tend otherwise to be a sort of isolated person. I kind of just stay to myself. So it's kind of forced me a bit out of my shell. Without a doubt, it has made me feel more in touch with people.

Not all teachers reported feeling isolated before attaining Internet access. For example, in discussing their situation before joining NET, teachers at two of the high-use schools we discussed in Chapter Five made comments like, "We're a pretty tight group," and "At Bogart, we have conquered that sense of isolation." Yet even these teachers and their peers generally spoke positively of the increase in professional interaction they experienced as a result of Internet use.

Because educators reported increases in interaction with colleagues at both their own and other schools and because the causes, purposes, and consequences of these two changes were far from identical, we discuss each in turn.

INCREASED INTERACTION WITH COLLEAGUES IN THE SCHOOL. Internet access facilitated communication within schools in a number of observable ways. At the most basic level, it helped educators overcome barriers to communication caused by schedule conflicts or a school's physical layout. Teachers used e-mail to reach colleagues whom they might not have been able to find without expending significant time and effort. They also used e-mail distribution lists for quick and convenient sharing of information with a relatively large group of in-school colleagues. For example, one teacher at a high school sent an e-mail message to all the teachers in a program that required students to write research papers in order to notify them that students could purchase such papers over the Internet. He even listed the topics closely aligned with the program's curriculum on which he had readily discovered papers for sale so that his colleagues could avoid having students write on these topics or take other measures to increase the chances that the papers handed in would be the students' own work. Obviously, he could have spread this information by mouth or by placing printed notices in his colleagues' mailboxes in the main office. However, he found e-mail quicker and easier, and using a distribution list of the program teachers ensured that he would leave no one out of the loop inadvertently, as he might have done if he had decided to mention this personally to his colleagues when he got the chance.

The ease of transmitting information over the Internet clearly contributed to increasing communication among educators in the same school. However, this was far from the only cause. The fact that NET required teams of educators to submit proposals and that it encouraged multidisciplinary and interdisciplinary work also played a big role in fostering communication and interaction among the members of most teams. Although some teams engaged in a great deal more collaboration than others and some were teams virtually in name only, the mere requirement of a team structure was conducive to increased communication. Team members had to collaborate to decide what each one would commit to in the proposal they submitted to the annual competitive process (ACP) and to figure out how to distribute the NET resources flowing to the team. Unless the interaction necessary to achieve these purposes came at the expense of other communication with colleagues, which it did not appear to, it added to the existing collegial interaction. Furthermore, where conditions were conducive to it, collaboration often continued well beyond the writing of the proposal, as we discussed in Chapter Five.

The fact that a great many NET educators were new to computing in general and to using the Internet in particular meant that Internet access led, rather ironically, to more frequent face-to-face communication among them. Small groups of educators in many schools often conferred in person about either technical issues or educational uses of the Internet. Having committed themselves to a major new effort without in most cases having enough personal knowledge to carry it off gave them a strong impetus to communicate with each other. Interestingly, the norm of autonomy, of not asking for help or giving it, mentioned in Chapter Four, seemed somewhat less strong with regard to Internet use than it was in other work-related areas, as the comments of one elementary school principal we interviewed during her school's third year in NET suggest:

> [NET] . . . has made a number of them [teachers] more accessible to each other. . . . The talk in the teachers' room, the talk in the office here related to . . . computers. . . . "Well, mine doesn't work that way. What am I doing wrong?" "Well, try this. I'll come over to your house and help you out if you need some help. ". . . Whereas they might be less willing to ask about a teaching strategy, . . . they don't seem to be as hesitant to talk about . . . something related to computers.

Indeed, perhaps because Internet use was a rapidly developing, cutting-edge area not covered in most teachers' training, many educators seemed relatively relaxed about admitting ignorance of it to their peers. Acknowledging a need to learn about the Internet and working with others in order to fill this need did not seem to be threatening to their sense of themselves as professionals. Rather than seeing it as a sign of incompetence, educators often took an acknowledged lack of Internet knowledge as an indication of willingness to expend extra effort to master a new tool that many other teachers had no idea how to use.

Although increased interaction with colleagues was common, some individuals appeared much more willing than others to seek out help from or to provide help to their colleagues. Thus, the increased communication that often occurred in connection with such help typically occurred within team subgroups rather than across an entire team, as the comments of Ms. Hoffman, a veteran high school teacher suggest:

> I would say that for those of us using the Internet, it helped build a bond because we did help one another and for those who were more expert at using the Internet and HTML [Hypertext Markup Language] there was more a sense of [camaraderie] because of helping one another. And there were those who were rather closed about it . . . who . . . because of their own time investment and their own expertise were not willing to share. . . . There were those who were willing to share what they learned and those who were not willing to share.

It was not clear whether educators' sharing of information and ideas that they needed to learn to use computers and the Internet more generally led to communication about other work-related topics between these same colleagues, a potentially important outcome. During our study, we saw relatively little evidence that this occurred on a broad scale. Indeed, a principal who had observed increased interaction on the topic of Internet use among his teachers specifically noted that he did not think this increase had spread to other kinds of professional interaction by his school's third year in NET. However, teachers did report that at least in some cases talk about the Internet seemed to be the basis for the development of closer personal relations or a sense of camaraderie, saying, for example:

> These guys . . . they'll come over and talk to me and talk about . . . wiring the room, and getting on-line. . . . I think it opens things up when other people find out that you have an account or that you know a little bit. They want to come and talk to you all the time. . . . Some of these guys . . . we have nothing in common but that. [But] you start to realize you have other things in common and, yeah, it just breaks down a lot of barriers. It's really nice.

It is certainly possible that such enhanced personal relations would be conducive to greater professional communication on other topics as well, although this increased communication would not necessarily follow, given teachers' norms regarding autonomy.

INCREASED INTERACTION WITH COLLEAGUES OUTSIDE THE SCHOOL. Internet access also appeared to increase communication between NET educators and their peers outside their schools. In fact, among the educators responding to an on-line survey ($N = 325$), 67 percent reported "greatly" or "somewhat" increased contact with outsiders. Fewer than 1 percent reported that such contact decreased.

Work-related communication with outside colleagues had numerous purposes. Educators communicated with those in other schools in the district for specific information on those schools or to learn more about district policies, through informal as well as formal channels. Communication with colleagues both inside and outside the district had purposes ranging from setting up joint curriculum projects, to sharing technical expertise, to maintaining relationships, and even to arranging for others to pick up materials at a conference for a teacher who was unable to attend.

Although most of the increased work-related communication with outsiders was between educators, teachers also occasionally used the Internet to communicate with other people for a wide range of professional purposes. For example, one teacher e-mailed parents on the spot in front of her class when a disciplinary problem arose, indicating that she felt such prompt action and the threat of it in the future strengthened her ability to maintain the classroom decorum she desired. Other teachers used e-mail to contact scientists, physicians, and others about the possibility of serving as mentors for students.

Increased Opportunities for Engagement in Professional Development Activities

One major purpose of the increased communication with those inside and outside the school was *professional development*, a term we use broadly to refer to educators' efforts to expand knowledge and skills relevant to performing their work, either as they currently approach it or as they wish to learn to approach it. Consistent with this are the results of a survey of over five hundred U.S. teachers who use telecommunications in their work. These teachers reported using the Internet more frequently for professional development than they used it with their students in classrooms (Honey & Henriquez, 1993).

Much of NET educators' communication with those outside the school district related to various professional issues and as such could be considered a form of professional development. For example, such communication not infrequently took the form of participation in newsgroups or e-mail discussion groups dealing with pedagogical issues or with specific subject areas. Although much of this interaction was informal and sporadic, Internet access also encouraged formal and quite intensive professional development activities. For example, a small number of teachers enrolled in on-line graduate courses in their subject areas.

Another very common use of the Internet that could be considered a kind of professional development was exploring Web sites to get specific information or ideas for planning or enriching lessons. This activity appeared to be common not only among NET educators but also among a national sample of teachers (Becker, 1999b). One new elementary schoolteacher, Mr. Stern, who found this kind of Internet use extremely helpful, described his experience this way:

> I'm a first-year teacher. . . . I could not have pulled this off this year if I hadn't had experience on the Net and knew how to make use of it. Some of the best lesson ideas I've come up with have been [from] sitting late at night at home poking around looking for ideas, and not necessarily on teacher pages, but just . . . looking for resources, exploring for picture prompts, looking for ideas, looking for literature. . . . In my mind, I've been very successful in here. If I hadn't had that access . . . I [might] very well have been a failure in here.

Veteran teachers as well found the Internet very useful in locating information they used in their classes, as illustrated by the comments of Mr. Waleska, who had taught for more than two decades:

> [Internet access] made information available to me that I would have never taken the time or had the energy to find in a library or correspond with another human being about, which was available to me instantly. I mean, I found stuff out that I can't believe I found out.

Another major kind of professional development that occurred in NET was the development of Internet and other technical skills. Work-related communication with people both inside and outside the school frequently concerned the development of such skills or the solution of technical problems. For example, in just one nine-month period during NET's fourth year, teachers initiated a total of 376 e-mail interchanges, some of them quite extended, with NET staff at the e-mail address that staff had set up to help teachers with technical problems. Such interchanges covered a broad range of topics but most commonly involved Internet applications, achieving and maintaining Internet access, and networking software.

Educators' degrees of involvement with Internet-mediated professional development activities varied tremendously from individual to individual, and the specific activities they engaged in varied widely. Further, the quality of their experiences varied, as would likely be the case with professional development activities not related to the Internet as well. Thus, it is hard to make a generalization about the impact of participation in such activities. However, some teachers certainly felt such activities had a major impact on them. "My whole view as an educator, of education per se, has changed," said Mr. Sandburg, an elementary school teacher, "because I feel much more in touch with educators at large because I'm subscribing to list serves [e-mail discussion groups]." Even though such sweeping claims were not the norm, we should not dismiss their importance for the individuals who made them.

When asked to estimate the percentage of district teachers who would use the Internet one or more hours per week for professional development if they had access to it in their classrooms, educators responding to an on-line survey ($N = 309$) gave a mean estimate of 53 percent, very similar to the 58 percent of educators who predicted that district teachers would use the Internet regularly for student instruction if it were available to them. Some individuals argued that the Internet was conducive to engaging in professional development activities because obtaining help from those at a distance did not threaten educators' image in their everyday workplaces as much as obtaining similar help closer to home might. Others pointed to the convenience of on-line professional development, which does not require commuting and can take place whenever convenient. Still others mentioned that the vast array of information and assistance available through the Internet far outweighed the resources that a single school or even a district could possibly provide. More than 80 percent of the teachers and librarians ($N = 322$) responding to another question on this survey indicated that the time they themselves had spent on professional development activities on the Internet was either somewhat or extremely productive, which may also have contributed to their relatively high estimate of their colleagues' potential use of the Internet for this purpose.

Increased Knowledge of Computing and the Internet

As we discussed in Chapter Four, NET teachers' initial knowledge about computing generally and the Internet in particular was, with some notable exceptions, rudimentary. Generally speaking, their level of knowledge increased substantially over the course of NET's five-year life, although again there were some exceptions. For example, among the educators replying to a survey in the project's fourth year ($N = 323$), two-thirds reported that they were novices at the project's inception. Roughly 70 percent indicated that they had progressed to an intermediate level of knowledge, and another 15 percent reported having developed advanced skills. Only 15 percent said they remained novices. Although respondents to an on-line survey were quite likely to be more sophisticated Internet users than their peers who did not respond, there were many other clear indications of development over time. For example, when NET staff moved the file servers that were initially located centrally to participating schools, it meant that each school had to have at least one person with enough knowledge to function as the systems administrator and to perform various basic technical functions independently. Eventually, each of the participating schools was able to find or develop this capacity, though this clearly would not have been possible at NET's inception.

Further suggesting substantial technical learning, among the teachers ($N = 43$) whom we interviewed during their first year with NET and asked to indicate what they believed to be their greatest NET-related accomplishment, 60 percent mentioned an achievement relating to growing technical comfort or competence. This excerpt from an interview with a first-year NET team member in an elementary school exemplifies the kinds of change these teachers reported:

INTERVIEWER: As you think back over your experiences using the Internet since last spring, what would you say your biggest accomplishments have been?

Ms. MILLER: Well, I don't know if I would call it an accomplishment but being so comfortable with it now. Before . . . I had an account, but

I could never remember my password. I could never remember what I was supposed to do. I would have big problems with it, and I couldn't figure out whom I was going to write to anyway if I [*laughs*] . . . and now it's just being able to subscribe to some of these lists and start to communicate with people. . . . I've come a long way on doing that. . . . I think my biggest accomplishment is being able to get in there . . . and [be] comfortable and use it on a daily basis now . . . to the point that I can't imagine not having it.

Of the teachers ($N = 42$) we interviewed in their second year with NET, a smaller but still substantial 38 percent also said that changes in their technical competence and their comfort using computers were their premier accomplishment. A larger proportion of teachers in their second year with NET mentioned curricular or student outcomes (36 percent versus 19 percent, respectively).

Such changes in computer-related attitudes and skills were important because they helped teachers overcome a strong barrier to use and allowed them to begin to explore ways in which the Internet could serve them and their students. Further, such exploration often led to an increase in technical knowledge, which in turn led to even more exploration and additional growth in technical skills.

Some of the NET teachers' increase in comfort with the Internet and in their knowledge of how to use it arose out of formal professional development activities such as enrolling in Internet courses offered at local universities or over the Internet. However, undertaking this kind of major formal learning experience was relatively rare, as we mentioned earlier. Furthermore, the individuals who engaged in such activities tended to have at least a moderate amount of technical knowledge already. Much more commonly, NET educators' increased knowledge about computing and the Internet appeared to stem from other experiences.

One way educators acquired these important experiences was through the wide variety of professional development activities that NET staff developed. A large number of NET teachers participated in these activities. For example, NET staff offered an eighteen-hour course on weekends and evenings during the school year that was substantial enough that the district allowed teachers graduate credit for it. Although this course called for a considerable investment of time and energy and was offered at a time when only eleven schools were formally participating in NET, over ninety educators enrolled in it.

Inspection of records and our interviews with the education staff suggested that by NET's fourth year the education and technical staffs had provided at least some technical training to educators at over 80 percent of the schools in the district and that they had provided relatively intensive training (from five to ten instructional sessions) for NET teachers at eighteen of the twenty schools accepted into NET at that time. In addition, during that year, the NET staff provided technical support on an average of at least once a week to someone at nineteen of these NET schools and provided occasional support to the one other NET school.

Of course, the mere fact that educators received training and support is not conclusive evidence that learning occurred. However, a number of factors suggest that it did. First, as we described in Chapter Two, although educators were not paid for participating in most of these activities and generally did not receive any other sort of compensation for attending them, interest in these professional development activities was very high. Typically, NET's professional development activities were oversubscribed, with many individuals desiring to participate having to be turned away. This suggests that teachers found these experiences instructive enough that they were willing to give up their free time on afternoons, evenings, and weekends. Second, attendance at such sessions often paved the way for individuals to successfully take on new technical responsibilities or get involved in Internet activities they had not been able to carry out before. This too suggests that these experiences resulted in learning. Finally, surveys of participants in some of these activities uniformly suggest that NET team members believed participation in such activities did indeed increase their skills, even when the training was relatively brief. To give just one straightforward example, participants in a two-day summer workshop held shortly after their teams had been accepted into NET showed statistically significant gains in self-reported proficiency in Internet use when we compared results from surveys they filled out before the workshop and after it ($F[1,22] = 5.07$, p ($\leq$.05).

Another factor in developing teachers' technical skills was the activities that NET team members offered, ranging from informal consultation with and support of colleagues to formal training activities. Although the amount of such activity and its target (only NET educators or any interested teachers) varied dramatically from school to school, as we indicated in Chapter Five, such activities commonly played an important role in helping teachers increase their knowledge of computing and the Internet. Educators ($N = 290$) responding to the on-line survey we mentioned earlier reported that they had supplied either formal or informal Internet assistance to a median of six colleagues in the district. For example, at one school, NET team members with substantial technical expertise set up and ran a series of lunchtime meetings to pass on some of that knowledge to interested colleagues both inside and outside the team. NET team meetings at this and other schools were also often the occasions for informal assistance that NET teachers reported was very useful in building their Internet-related skills. Finally, a lot of informal assistance occurred in the context of small groups of teachers or even dyads, as exemplified in this excerpt from a request that one team member e-mailed to other NET team colleagues:

> Faye [the librarian and a team member] has shown me how to reset passwords in case of need, but I have yet to get the directions in writing. . . . Faye, could you send me the direction by e-mail, or make a copy of the page you have? Thanks.

Yet another factor contributing to the growth of technical expertise among educators was home computer access. Feeling strongly that home access was important for building expertise, the education staff willingly assisted teachers in learning how to use modems, and they even went so far as to make house calls when necessary and feasible. Indeed, more than 235 teachers and librarians responding to the on-line survey during the project's fourth year ($N = 324$) reported having received personal assistance from NET staff, ranging from brief phone consultations to home visits, to begin or improve their home computer access to the Internet. Further, as we discussed in Chapter Two, many teachers went out and bought computers or modems, spurred at least partly by their involvement in NET. The purchase of a home computer does not in and of itself build technical expertise. However, as with attendance at professional development sessions, there were clear indications that in this case such a connection did exist. First, educators used home computers a substantial amount to access the Internet, as account use data, e-mail messages sent to the NET staff's "trouble" (or help) account, and frequent conversations among NET teachers about such use indicate. Such use alone seems likely to help build skills in a population that, generally speaking, started out with very little technical knowledge and virtually no Internet experience. Furthermore, it was not uncommon for educators to comment that they were able to call on family members, including their children, to teach them how to carry out Internet functions they did not yet know, which also suggests learning. Finally, NET educators also frequently asserted that home computers were good resources for learning because teachers' time at home was not as heavily obligated or as tightly scheduled as it was in school, making home a good place to engage in the time-consuming process of increasing their skills. Thus, home access appeared in many cases to make a significant contribution to the increase that was evident in NET educators' ability to use the Internet. Consistent with this is Becker's finding (1999b) that home Internet access is an important predictor of teachers' professional use of the Internet.

Expansion of Teachers' Roles Outside the Classroom

The core of teachers' work is helping their students learn. But teachers' jobs generally entail at least some other activities, such as building and maintaining community support for the schools through interaction with parents and contributing to the school through committee work. Many educators involved in NET began to assume new and different roles outside the classroom as a result of their Internet use. Although these roles were generally not absolutely unheard of for teachers in the district prior to NET's advent, they were uncommon, and a substantial number of teachers had their first experience in some of these roles in connection with their Internet use. A teacher who engaged in an unusual number of such activities said this in an interview:

> We have, in the United States, approximately [four hundred] physics teaching resource agents, of which I'm one. . . . We'll e-mail back and forth. . . . I am in constant touch with colleagues at the [state] Department of Education on test development. I'm on one of their test development teams. . . . One of the [NET] team members is a very active elementary school science teacher, and she and I are constantly having exchanges over the Web—things that she can do with the kids to get them ready for different activities, suggestions for different activities. . . . I'm making things available to the whole group that I'm working with at the state through a mailing list on things that I come across and that's something that I would not even have any contact with if it hadn't been for Networking for Education. . . . If it depended on me to do it by mail and phone, it would never get done.

As is apparent from this one individual's activities, teachers' professional roles outside the classroom could be quite varied. Generally speaking, the particular role or roles that individual educators assumed seemed to depend on such factors as their specific interests and talents, the time they had available for such new roles, and the needs of the school in which they worked. As we have mentioned, quite a number of teachers became formal peer trainers at times, serving as leaders in professional development sessions for other educators both inside and outside their schools. In this capacity, these teachers engaged in activities such as making decisions about the material to be covered, preparing oral presentations, and constructing written materials to guide their peers' learning. When we consider educators' prevailing norms regarding autonomy and privacy, assuming the role of peer trainer, formally or informally, was quite a break with the past for many teachers. Yet some actively sought out such opportunities. For example, one particularly active Internet user from a school joining NET early on specifically asked a member of the NET education staff if she and some of the others from her team could participate in training teachers just joining NET. (The staff member excitedly said yes.)

Another common role that emerged, mainly because NET was structured in a way that required it, was that of the school-based systems administrator. Individuals serving in this role generally found that they had to learn a substantial amount to perform it adequately. A good number of NET team members were interested enough in the technical aspects of computing that they saw this role as a desirable challenge rather than an insupportable burden. Fortunately for NET, most schools had at least one or two such individuals, perhaps partly because serving in this capacity usually brought a certain amount of respect from colleagues. However, one problem that arose was that these self-selected technical gurus were occasionally more intrigued by the technology itself than by the Internet's potential as an educational tool. As Peter Marcus of the education staff put it: "If anything, [systems administrators] like . . . [the technical aspects] more than they like the part of implementing it into content because the people who gravitate to that like to play with the machines anyway."

Other teachers assumed yet other new roles. Many of these involved becoming an information provider to new constituencies outside the school district. For example, a small number of NET teachers and librarians made presentations on their work at regional or national professional meetings. At least some of these presentations generated enough interest that the NET educators were asked to engage in follow-up activities, such as sharing their acceptable use policies. In addition, other teachers became curriculum developers by posting on Web sites some lessons making use of the Internet that they had developed for their students. Although teachers are quite used to developing plans for classroom activities for their own students, it is very much less common for them to formally present these plans for others to consider adopting. Some of the new information provider roles that emerged among NET educators would have been almost impossible to predict. For example, one educator was inspired by her work on the Internet to begin writing children's books. Another NET team member gained information relevant to solving a debilitating twenty-year-old medical problem on the Internet, an occurrence he termed "a miracle." In fact, he was so grateful for this that he worked in conjunction with a physician to construct a Web page about this illness in the hope that it would help others suffering from the same affliction.

Some teachers became resource providers to their own schools in a new way as a result of NET. For example, one reaction of teachers who had submitted a proposal but were not selected to become part of NET was to try to increase their schools' Internet access by raising funds by other means, such as applying to local foundations or approaching businesses for assistance. These activities were occasionally constrained by the district, which feared that they would interfere with the district's centralized fundraising activities; such limitations, not surprisingly, caused considerable frustration among the educators involved. However, some were able to find ways acceptable to the district to acquire additional computers or to expand Internet access.

Undertaking the new roles we have just described demanded considerable time and energy. Furthermore, release time from teaching in order to carry out such activities was rare, with one exception— those assuming school-based systems administration responsibilities did get release time in numerous schools. Thus, many of the teachers assuming these roles ended up dedicating their own time to them on evenings and weekends because they could not fit this work readily into their schedules during the school day. The fact that NET participants were all volunteers may mean that they were the kind of dedicated and energetic individuals predisposed to taking up such challenges and that such behavior might not be as common among a broader group of teachers. Becker's survey (1999b) of a national sample of teachers suggests that it is teachers who are already predisposed to involvement in leadership activities who are most likely to use the Internet in their work. Nonetheless, for many of the NET teachers, involvement with the Internet through NET led to their assuming these kinds of roles for the very first time.

Increased Professional Pride and Enthusiasm

The outcomes for teachers that we discussed in the first part of this chapter include a substantial amount of new learning and a broadening of their professional networks and work activities. Not surprisingly, then, many of the educators involved with NET felt that their professional capabilities were expanding. One common response to such perceptions was pride in their ability to master new challenges and increased energy and enthusiasm for their work. Indeed, at a conference held in NET's fourth year to showcase the project to individuals from around the country, a participant indicated that the most striking aspect of a workshop run by NET librarians was their pride in their work and their sense of personal growth and development. This sense of pride was also clear in interviews with teachers:

INTERVIEWER: What would you say has been your biggest accomplishment since last spring?

MS. HOFFMAN: To become familiar with the Internet and to get to the point where I was able to find things . . . that I could tie in with the curriculum. I found that very pleasing and very satisfying. . . . I felt as if I was somewhat on a leading edge. . . . Yes, I'm very . . . very proud to be part of that whole [effort].

This teacher mentioned two common themes: technical learning and the ability to use the Internet to function better as a professional. For many educators, the sense of pride came from having proved their ability to learn about cutting-edge technology that had once seemed threatening and difficult. Moreover, despite the initial trepidation many of them had expressed about such learning, generally it did not take them too long to learn enough to feel that they could make at least some productive professional use of the Internet. For example, twenty-one of the twenty-eight participants in a five-day NET summer workshop replied affirmatively to a question on an anonymous follow-up questionnaire about whether they felt ready to incorporate Internet use into their professional activities. Responses such as "Yes, because I've had a really good experience with this once I got on-line. This has given me a new lease on teaching—a new way to do the job that may be fun" were common. Only five individuals qualified their affirmative answers with comments like "Yes, but I'm still unsure of the extent of my knowledge." Not a single one of the twenty-six respondents to the question reported feeling completely unprepared. Although many of these teachers still had relatively rudimentary technical skills, the fact that they were able to learn fairly readily how to accomplish valued ends gave them a sense of pride in themselves and their work.

Educators' enhanced sense of pride and enthusiasm seemed to be related not only to a perception of increased technical competence but also to a sense that Internet use would help them to perform their work in a way that would be beneficial to their students or to themselves. As we discussed in Chapter Six, Internet access helped many teachers take some steps along paths that they wanted to travel in their teaching. It also gave many access to new resources that they believed enlivened and enriched their teaching. And it often improved student-teacher relationships and thus created a more pleasant classroom climate that reinvigorated some teachers.

Not only teachers but principals frequently reported renewed teacher pride and enthusiasm. For example, one principal asserted that Internet access gets teachers "out of the same old rut," and another noted that it refocused teacher conversation from constant complaints about "kids driving [them] crazy" to lively discussions of what the teachers were accomplishing through the Internet and ways to solve the technical problems they were encountering. Thus, this change in emotional tone was apparent not only to the individuals experiencing it but also to others with whom they worked.

STUDENT OUTCOMES

In examining the kinds of outcomes that appeared to occur frequently for students as a result of Internet use, we make no claim that every student with access evidenced all of these outcomes. Clearly, they did not. First, the amount of Internet use by individual students, even when they shared a classroom, often varied substantially. This has obvious implications for the kind and amount of impact likely to result. Second, the kinds of use students made of the Internet and the goals they and their teachers had for such use varied tremendously. Some students used it to communicate with peers and others outside their schools; others used it as an information archive; still others focused on activities such as producing home pages on the World Wide Web. Experiences so different are likely to have quite different outcomes. One NET team member captured this extremely well when she observed that the Internet was like a pencil. Access to a pencil would most likely produce very different outcomes among students using it to draw and among those using it to study algebra or to write poetry. Furthermore, even if one looked at students working in a single subject area, access to a pencil would still be likely to have different consequences for different users, depending on how the teacher channeled the pencil's use. For example, in a language arts class, using a pencil to write poetry would probably have consequences different from the consequences of using it to write critical essays about poems or to mark their meter. Moreover, any one of these uses might also have different outcomes for different students. Some students asked to write poetry might become enthralled with the process; others might find it tedious; still others might use the pencil to doodle, to finish math homework, or to write graffiti on their desks.

Similarly, Internet use is not one thing with narrow, uniform, and readily predictable outcomes. In practice, it is many things with many possible outcomes for different students. Furthermore, even a single category of Internet use, such as its use as an information archive, can produce tremendous variation in likely consequences: using the Internet to see whether a book is in the neighborhood library is very different from using it to access pictures of women's dresses in the 1890s for a history class or to find information on college scholarships. Students involved in NET performed all these activities and more.

In the following sections, we look at six kinds of outcomes of Internet use that NET students experienced: enhanced enjoyment and motivation, a better understanding of both computing and the Internet, a greater ability to produce work of quality, more access to career information and opportunities, exposure to a broader range of perspectives and experiences, and improved reading skills in both English and foreign languages.

Enhanced Enjoyment and Motivation

Rather surprisingly, despite the diversity of activities and thus the possible diversity of results, enhanced enjoyment and increased motivation among students were outcomes linked to Internet use across virtually all Internet activities that we studied.

ENHANCED ENJOYMENT. There is no doubt that the large majority of students in NET elementary, middle, and high school classrooms typically enjoyed using the Internet more than participating in traditional classroom activities. Teachers often noted students' marked enthusiasm for and enjoyment of the Internet. In fact, of the teachers ($N =$ 56) we asked in interviews to characterize the reactions of their students to Internet use, 80 percent reported generally positive responses. In sharp contrast, not a single teacher reported generally negative student responses, although some reported neutral or mixed reactions. Reflecting this perspective, one elementary school teacher reported that involvement in a newsgroup "enhanced tenfold [my students'] enthusiasm for writing." Furthermore, teachers often supported their assertions that students reacted positively with behavioral evidence, as did a high school science teacher whom we interviewed:

> In the class where they are working on Web pages they . . . can't get in the room fast enough. . . . They were killing each other trying to get to the computers. . . . When I unlock the door in the morning the kids are in the room before I can get the key out of the door, because this is one of the rooms [where] I make the equipment available to the kids.

Such reports were hardly surprising. Observers also witnessed many positive reactions, like this one in a high school Spanish class: "Meg . . . was able to get into her account without any problem. When she got into her account, she exclaimed, 'Oh! I got a new [e-mail message]!' and she clapped her hands." Moreover, teachers also frequently reported seeing and hearing evidence of students' disappointment and frustration when Internet use was delayed or postponed, again a reaction quite apparent to our observers.

Interviews with students confirmed teachers' reports that students enjoyed Internet use and were enthusiastic about it. For example, asked what kinds of things he learned from an Internet e-mail exchange with a student from a very different background, one student replied, "Well, writing can be fun." Indeed, in response to a question asking students ($N = 72$) how much fun Internet use was compared to other classroom activities, 83 percent selected one of the two positive options, indicating that the Internet was "more fun" or "much more fun." In striking contrast, only 3 percent selected one of the two negative options, indicating that it was "less fun" or "much less fun." Furthermore, this positive reaction did not appear to be restricted to one age group, because there was no statistically significant difference between the responses of students of elementary, middle, and high school age ($F[2,69] = .99$, ns).

The depth of students' enjoyment of the Internet was made clear by the trade-offs they were willing to make to obtain access. When schools made computers available before and after school, many students voluntarily made use of the Internet during that time instead of spending it at home or with their friends. Furthermore, they often went out of their way to gain access to the Internet during segments of the school day when they could otherwise have been relaxing with friends, such as during their lunchtime or free periods. As a high school student named Carl said when we asked whether Internet access had changed the amount of time he spent "doing independent learning": "If I'm on a free period . . . before . . . I would just talk to friends or something, and now I try to actually find some more things [on the Internet] that I can possibly use later."

Indeed, a number of high school teachers reported that, consistent with research on Internet use that suggests it may strongly motivate students (Neilsen, 1998; Songer, 1996), Internet use actually motivated students to arrive in class on time, to attend classes that they would otherwise have cut, or to start work on assignments well in advance rather than putting them off to the last minute. For example, one teacher mentioned that on the two days a week when Internet use was scheduled he had few problems with tardiness, unlike other days. Another reported: "One of my seniors came in ten minutes late for class, and I said, 'Why were you late?' He said, 'I just came to school. . . . I only come to school for this class.' So they really enjoy [the Internet]." Although some high school teachers saw no such links between Internet use and the way students acted in class, high school students commonly reported such connections when we asked directly about them. For example, one student named Tamika said:

> Before [*laughs*]. . . people . . . would sit outside in the hallway or wherever and walk around. But now . . . more people come to class and

they're like, "Well, can we get on the computer?" So . . . before we had like five people in our class out of . . . twenty. . . . But now they show up.

The students' very positive reactions to Internet use were also made clear by the fact that, as we discussed in Chapter Four, teachers were able to use access as a carrot to shape student behavior. It is also rather ironic that students' eagerness to use the Internet occasionally caused problems. Teachers sometimes had to mediate peer disputes over access or even, as we observed, figure out how to get students to leave the class:

> The bell [signaling the end of class] rings as the girls are just beginning [to read] their [on-line] story. They continue to read and pay no attention to the bell. . . . Ms. Ebert comments, "That was the bell. Was anybody aware of that?" [*The students continue to read for a couple of minutes.*] Ms. Ebert says, "You know what? You really have to go." Robyn says in protest, "We're almost done!" Ms. Ebert replies, "No, I don't think so." Then she comments that [Robyn's regular classroom] teacher is going to kill her. Fiona says, "We'll tell the teacher we lost track of time. We didn't hear the bell." Sarah then says from the other side of the room, "We'll tell her we were all in the bathroom . . . and we couldn't hear the bell."

Such problems serve as clear indicators of students' enjoyment of Internet use.

INCREASED MOTIVATION. Finding that students enjoy using the Internet is not of course the same as finding that it leads to increased learning or motivates them to work. Indeed, Wallace, Kupperman, Krajcik, and Soloway (2000, p. 86) conclude that although sixth-grade science students using the Internet appeared very busy and stayed on task, which one could take as behavioral signs of motivation, their activities "rarely reflected engagement with subject matter." Rather, they were engrossed in Internet searches, which was often not very fruitful in terms of substantive learning. Further, students might enjoy using the Internet before and after school because they could use it then for recreational purposes or because they could learn how to move rapidly and unobtrusively to recreational Web sites during class instead of working. As we mentioned in Chapter Three, unless NET teachers made a determined effort to prevent it, students, especially those in high school, often drifted from academic to recreational sites.

Nonetheless, many other studies have found a variety of types of computer use motivating to students. Schofield (1997, p. 29), for example, concludes that

> the most commonly and consistently found effect of the instructional use of computers . . . appears to be an increase in motivation and closely related constructs such as interest [in] and enjoyment of schoolwork, task involvement, persistence, time on task, and retention in school.

Thus, we now turn to exploring whether access to Internet-connected computers appears to motivate students to engage in learning activities. There is a long history of research on motivation, including achievement motivation, and a broad variety of understandings of the basic construct currently exist (Pittman, 1998). We use the term *motivation* here to refer to high levels of effort and involvement in an activity that persist even in the face of difficulties and to the often accompanying sense of intrinsic interest in engaging in the activity.

In spite of students' tendency to drift to entertainment-oriented Web sites, teachers commonly reported that students found Internet use motivating. As we described in Chapter Six, when teachers taking an on-line survey were asked to select the most important positive impact of Internet use on students, only two of the fourteen options garnered over 20 percent of the responses: "access to better resources" and "motivate students." The belief that students found the Internet motivating was also commonly evident in interviews and conversations with teachers, with statements like the following, from an elementary school teacher, being quite common:

INTERVIEWER: What effect, if any, has the Internet had on your students . . . ?

MS. COOKE: . . . They'll go on the Internet and they'll look at something and they'll be inspired by it and they'll say, "I wanna write about this," or, "I want to do more research" . . . especially in the older students. . . . It's like a springboard for them. They see something, and it makes them want to learn more—want to do more—and I think that's great.

Students themselves quite consistently reported that Internet use was motivating. For example, among the students from all school levels that we interviewed on this topic ($N = 73$), 50 percent said they found it easier or much easier to concentrate while on the Internet as compared to other times in class. Only 5 percent said that it was harder or much harder to concentrate. (Differences between elementary, middle, and high school students were not statistically significant in any of the comparisons in this paragraph.) When we asked middle school and high school students ($N = 25$) about the impact of Internet use on their motivation specifically, 68 percent of them said they felt more motivated, with fewer than 15 percent reporting they were less motivated. This was consistent with the results of a questionnaire completed by another group of middle school students ($N = 39$), 78 percent of whom reported that they paid more or much more attention while on the Internet compared to only 3 percent (one student) who reported paying less attention. When we asked elementary and high school students ($N = 57$) about the impact of the Internet on their own level of effort, over 40 percent reported they worked harder or paid more attention while working on the Internet than while doing other things in school; 25 percent said they worked less hard on the Internet. However, a large majority of these spontaneously went on to indicate that the reason they worked less hard was that they could accomplish what was expected with less effort than they would expend in other situations.

Evidence that students found the Internet motivating emerged not only from answers to closed-ended questions that inquired about specific behaviors related to motivation but also from answers to very general open-ended questions about how the Internet changed students' behavior. When we asked high school students ($N = 44$), "How does use of the Internet affect student actions or feelings in class?" over one-third spontaneously mentioned changes in attention or in the intensity of their participation in ways that indicated increased motivation, more than they gave any other category of response. The comments of an elementary school student in response to a question about whether she felt differently when using the Internet than during other classroom activities succinctly captured the tenor of the responses from students of all ages who reported that "it wakes you up" or "time goes fast" when using the Internet:

SARA: Yes. . . . [O]ne, when we're reading the story [on the Internet], I don't fall asleep. Number two, it's a lot more interesting, and I act more interested because I am more interested. Number three, I'm not bored half to death.

As a middle school student named Bret put it, reflecting on his Internet experience: "Those computers keep your mind working all the time. . . . To get places, you have to think."

A number of possible reasons for this increase in motivation emerged from our analysis of students' and teachers' comments. In discussing this change, students frequently cited reasons similar to those that previous research on motivation and computing has delineated. For example, one frequently cited factor was the increase in the students' perceived level of autonomy and control that accompanied Internet use, which we discussed in some detail in Chapter Six. Consistent with previous research that highlights the importance of feelings of independence in producing motivation (Lepper & Chabay, 1985; Lepper & Malone, 1987; Schofield, 1995), many students reported feeling energized by this change and focusing more on their work because of it. In contrast, when educators structured classes so that students were not able to work with a substantial degree of autonomy but had to do things like listen to a teacher's lecture, students reported much less focus, saying things like, "My mind just drifts off." Second, and again consistent with previous work (Schofield, 1995), students reported that the enjoyment we discussed earlier in this chapter played a big role in increasing their motivation. They were more willing to work hard and to persist because they enjoyed the process of learning in the Internet environment more than they enjoyed learning in other class environments. As one elementary school student named Grace commented:

> I like using the Internet better than doin' regular class work. . . . When I go to that class [in which she uses the Internet] I always try to do really good in it, more than in other classes. . . . I think just because it is fun.

These factors that seemed to contribute importantly to students' feeling motivated are common to many, although not all, computer applications used in schools. In addition, at least two factors appearing to enhance students' motivation were related to particular attributes of the Internet. First, the Internet offers students an extraordinarily wide range of information and communication opportunities, which makes it easier than is typically the case in school for them to connect their schoolwork with personal interests. Second, the Internet gives students the ability to communicate with others and to produce work that others might actually use in some way. We discuss the first of these factors next and the second in the section of this chapter on improvement in students' work.

The wide range of information available over the Internet gives students the potential for more control over the choice of the subject matter on which they will work and enhances the likelihood that they can find some way to meld their existing interests with their schoolwork. (Of course, for students to realize this potential, the teacher must allow students to take advantage of these broader choices.) Previous research clearly suggests that students' ability to personalize work increases motivation (Lepper & Malone, 1987; Schofield, 1995). Our research also suggests such a link, as the following comment from an elementary school teacher illustrates:

> That's the only real accomplishment. . . . I mean, getting kids to write—kids who wouldn't . . . write before . . . who went and used the Internet because they can choose their subject, which is hard to do if you don't have a lot of information. I know this one kid . . . [who] wants to know the daily [sports] stats. . . . [That's his] personal interest. . . . So now he goes and get his stats, which he really . . . just loves. . . . And then to appease me he will write something on the personal interest end of it.

Although a wide range of students found using the Internet quite motivating, NET educators also indicated repeatedly in interviews that they believed Internet access had especially striking motivational effects on a particular subgroup of students. Our data did not allow us to explore the validity of this perception independently, but it is potentially quite important and worthy of further investigation. Specifically, when educators mentioned noticing a differential in the Internet's motivational impact, they virtually always indicated that the impact was strongest among students who were weak academically or who were alienated from the educational system. Educators described students who benefited the most motivationally as "not academically inclined," "slow," and even "proud of not being able to read." (Of course, effort and achievement are interrelated, and the motivation of such students may have grown the most because it was low initially and thus had the most potential for positive change.) The emergence of the unequal access patterns that we described in Chapter Four, in which academically stronger students sometimes received disproportionately more access, is especially noteworthy in light of this suggestion that Internet access can have a very positive impact for at least some initially low-achieving students.

In sum, strong evidence indicates that, in general, students greatly enjoyed using the Internet for both personal and school-related purposes. Furthermore, Internet use was often motivating, creating situations in which students reported feeling more interested in their work, paying more attention to it, and working harder than they would have otherwise. Yet Internet access also offered students a strong temptation to shift their attention from class work to other pursuits, accessing favorite recreational sites with a few clicks of the mouse. In traditional classroom situations, students may daydream, fall asleep, or chat with peers, but they do not have virtually instant access to a huge archive of competing material that many find enthralling. Thus, the same resource that appears to increase work-related motivation also presents an unparalleled temptation and opportunity to turn to material unrelated to work.

Increased Knowledge of Computing and the Internet

As we discussed in Chapters Three and Six, NET set a norm that Internet access should be a tool to enhance academic learning and foster certain kinds of pedagogical practice. Although teachers clearly saw learning Internet skills as likely to be useful to students in their careers or in their later education, as the relatively high proportion of ACP proposals that emphasized the importance of preparing students for a world in which technology is pervasive as a goal evidenced, classes in which the primary goal was to enhance students' knowledge of the Internet and computing were quite rare. One high school did offer a class on building Web pages, in which students learned methods for transferring files and the use of e-mail, hypertext markup language or HTML (which students used in their construction of web pages), and various other Internet-based applications. And students in a high-tech magnet program in another school played a significant part in wiring their high school for Internet access. But such classes were the exception, definitely not the rule.

Despite the fact that students' technical learning was typically not the highest priority for NET teachers, it is worth noting that students who used the Internet often increased their knowledge about computers and about Internet use markedly, even going well beyond the knowledge needed to use the Internet as their teachers intended. For example, Charles, a high school student who gained his first e-mail account through NET and then used his initial rudimentary Internet skills to learn more said:

> I've done a lot of self-teaching and self-learning . . . on computers . . . and . . . on programming in [Perl]. . . . You know, there's not really a class around here that you can take.

Another student reported using internet relay chat (IRC) to get the information he needed for building Web pages.

Such students were unusual in the amount they learned and in the initiative they took to structure new learning opportunities for themselves. But even students who did not show such striking enterprise nonetheless often learned a substantial amount about how to make effective use of their Internet access, sometimes as a result of direct teaching by educators but often as a result of their own exploration in the midst of using the Internet for purposes of work or play. This progress was evident to classroom observers. Students who at first took a long time to perform certain operations, made many mistakes doing so, and frequently had to ask for assistance learned over time to do those and other operations quite smoothly and with much less if any assistance from others. Students were well aware of such learning and mentioned it frequently in interviews, like Eric, a high school student who said, "I've learned a lot about construction technology 'cause that's what I have to look up [for class]. I've learned about computers; I've learned about the Internet itself, all the different systems, how it runs, etc." In addition, when asked to rate on a questionnaire how much they had learned about using computers from using the Internet in school (on a 4-point scale on which 1 was "no learning" and 4 was "a great deal of learning"), small stratified samples of both middle school and high school students ($N = 23$) from NET classrooms ended up with identical mean scores, 3.7, indicating that they believed they had learned quite a bit.

Interestingly, such learning was by no means restricted to older students. Elementary school students too gained a substantial amount of technical knowledge from working on the Internet in the context of academic endeavors. Even students working with teachers who had specifically rated the building of technical knowledge as a very low priority tended to do so. For example, Ms. Ebert, an elementary school NET team member, ranked the building of technical knowledge seventh in a list of ten possible goals for her students' NET activities and characterized it as "a very low priority." Yet her students learned a great deal about working effectively in a multiuser object-oriented (MOO) environment over the course of the year. A MOO environment is an on-line text-based environment, which this educator used with the goal of improving her students' facility with and enjoyment of reading and writing. Sharing a database of virtual rooms, exits, and objects, MOO users interact with each other. Ms. Ebert's third-grade students learned to move though the MOO with ease, to wake interactive storytellers by entering commands, to direct the storytellers to read particular stories, and to leave notes on various MOO bulletin boards. A number of students went well beyond these basic skills, moreover, and learned additional commands that enabled their characters to do such things as hide from others in the MOO (Davidson & Schofield, 2002). Indeed, an observer recorded in a field note that the extent of their knowledge sometimes surprised even their teacher:

> Ms. Ebert helps the girls exit and gets them to the command line in Unix. Robyn, seeing this . . . asks, "Now do we Telnet?" Ms. Ebert looks at the girls and says, "You don't know Telnet." Then Robyn and Fiona say, "Yes, we do! Yes, we do!" and then they recite [the instructions necessary to] Telnet to the MOO.

Even students who were initially anxious about computing and concerned about their ability to do it well gained confidence in their abilities as well as specific skills when working in the supportive environment that Ms. Ebert created. For example, although the students working with her reported initially feeling somewhat anxious and rather worried about whether they could learn all they needed to about computing, these third-grade girls reported significantly decreased anxiety and increased confidence by the end of the school year (Davidson & Schofield, 2002). Although high levels of anxiety about their computing skills did not appear to be widespread among students in NET classrooms, this finding is nonetheless interesting because it parallels the finding we discussed earlier in this chapter that NET teachers tended to learn a great deal about the Internet in spite of the initial anxiety many of them felt.

In closing this section, we should mention that access to the Internet in school was also indirectly conducive to students' technical learning, although we have less detailed information on these indirect paths than on the more direct paths, which we could readily observe. First, a small number of students volunteered in the context of interviews that their Internet experiences in school had interested them to the point where they asked their parents to buy a home computer (or a modem for an existing computer). Educators also reported hearing about this phenomenon from parents and students. We do not know how often such behavior led to the actual purchase of a home computer or modem, but it seems likely that any purchases that did occur would open up considerable potential for student learning. In addition, the relationships that students had with mentors by e-mail occasionally led to additional opportunities for experience with various kinds of computing. In the most striking case, a mentor gave a student an old computer and considerable instruction in its use.

Increased Ability to Produce Quality Work

As we discussed in Chapter Six, the Internet gives students and teachers ready access to more information and the opportunity to contact more individuals who might contribute to students' education than are available in the school. Now, we explore a potentially important consequence of these changes, the increased opportunity for students to produce good work. A great many students in NET classrooms eagerly took advantage of the Internet to locate information pertinent to their schoolwork, often independently of teachers' encouragement to do so. As one high school student put it:

MARCUS: There's so much information out there, it's just . . . it's mind blowing, because you can go to any library in these colleges. . . . You can get information you need. Whenever you have research projects . . . and you need background information, you can get on the Internet and . . . look up science groups. . . . You can talk to science professors. . . .

INTERVIEWER: Do you do these things very often?

MARCUS: Yes, I do. [*He goes on to give numerous specific examples.*]

Although use of Internet sources of information, insight, and expertise may not always have improved students' work, in the eyes of teachers, it frequently appeared to do so. One high school foreign language teacher called her students' use of the Internet "my medicine for good writing skills." And Mr. Rominoff, a high school science teacher, asked about the effect of the Internet on students' "attitudes, or the quality of their work or some other important outcome," stated that "the quality of their work definitely improved because of the additional information."

Students, too, reported a link between Internet access and work quality. For example, Marcus, the student quoted at the beginning of this section had this to say when asked whether he had learned any lessons about himself from his Internet experiences: "Yeah, . . . [I learned that] I can produce some quality work. . . . And actually, I was just surprised. . . . I impressed myself."

Students sometimes reported readily accomplishing things by using the Internet that would have been quite difficult for them to achieve otherwise. For example, Martin, a white high school student who was very skilled at Internet use, reported that

> two months ago, there was a black history contest. . . . They asked fifty question about black history, and I got every single one off of the Internet and got twenty more right than anyone else in the school. And the next month, I won the women's history contest, where I got every single one. . . . So it's a good place for information.

Students conversant with the Internet pointed out a number of ways in which they felt using it improved their work. First, Internet searches allowed them to home in on precise topics more readily than they could with most of the other search techniques available to them, thus supplying them with better information than they would have had otherwise. Two search features were especially important to them. First, they could use the Internet to communicate with specific individuals likely to have the kind of information they needed, rather than relying solely on teachers or school librarians who might lack the necessary expertise. For example, high school students who wanted information on specialized topics in physics for a statewide science competition could look for relevant newsgroups or learn which physicists had published on those topics and then contact them. Another high school student interested in biology used the Internet to become deeply involved in the research of a physician at a nearby medical school, producing work so advanced that her teacher needed her to explain much of it to him. Second, students could use Internet search engines to look for specific combinations of words or topics. This method of searching could save them large amounts of time and energy compared to searching their school library's card catalog, which classified books only by their primary topics. And it left students more time for synthesizing information and producing the work in its final form. In addition, numerous students with home computers emphasized the convenience of being able to carry information on disks from home to school and back, rather than having to lug around heavy books and papers that could get lost or disordered. Some asserted that this convenience led them to do work at home that they would not have done otherwise, and this increased time devoted to work would also be likely to improve it.

Students also contended that the information available on the Internet was often qualitatively better than the information available from most other school resources. They pointed out repeatedly, as we discussed in Chapter Six, that unlike many school resources, the Internet provides up-to-date information. In some cases, the use of such current information had important consequences for the quality of students' projects. For example, one high school student turned to the Internet after discovering that most of the school library's books about the political structure of Germany had been published before its reunification. If he had based his report solely on these outdated and thus inaccurate sources, it would not have been a high-quality product.

Students also used the Internet to communicate with others and to make their work available to a broad audience for use or comment. These practices were also conducive to improving their work. First, students occasionally received feedback from others that was useful to them in making their work better. Second, the knowledge that others outside the school might view their work was quite motivating to many students. As June, a high school student, told us:

> Knowing that other people are going to be exposed to my work, makes me want to do it better . . . you know, work harder on it and . . . you know, check for errors and complete it and make it the best that I can.

It was common for students to assert that they attended more to the quality of their work when they knew it would be placed on-line and read by others outside the school than they did at other times. These reports are consistent with the results of other research. For example, scholars have found that writing produced for outside peers can be better than that done for a teacher (Means et al., 1993; Cohen & Riel, 1989; Sperling, 1996). In addition, research has shown that writing produced for distant peers on an on-line network is often better than that produced for local peers and teachers (Gallini & Helman, 1995).

Students proffered a variety of reasons for attending more to the quality of their work when it had an audience outside the classroom. Some did it because of their desire to make a good impression about themselves, their schools, or their communities on the world outside the school. Students attending a high school populated almost entirely by African Americans, many from lower socioeconomic backgrounds, spoke especially frequently and ardently about the impact of an external audience on the quality of their work, often commenting with words similar to those of their schoolmate Malcolm:

> You put a lot more pride into it, because . . . if you're going to write this for the school mainly, you're going to write it just good enough so your teacher gives you an A. But if you realize that everybody in the world's going to be looking at it, then you get like a sense of pride, like, "Well, this is what everybody in the world's going to perceive of me and perceive of basically my school, my parents, and people who taught me. So basically, if I do a horrible job, people are going to think that my parents didn't teach me, and people are going to think the schools I went to are trash."

In short, some students seemed to view public forms of work as reflecting on not only their own abilities and characters but also on their families and the institutions of which they were a part. This motivated them to work harder than they often did when the audience for their work was more restricted.

Other students indicated that they worked hard to make the materials they posted on the Internet of especially high quality for quite different reasons. One of these was the belief that because others might use materials posted on the Internet in ways that had real consequences it was important to be sure they were accurate and well done. For example, one student who developed a Web page featuring information about careers in medicine explained that he took special care in creating it because others might use it in making career decisions, and hence it was potentially more important than tasks done just for his teacher. Yet another reason students tried especially hard to make the work they posted on the Internet of high quality was that more knowledgeable individuals might encounter it and judge it by higher standards than those that their teachers applied in school. As one high school student explained:

> The Spanish III classes . . . created [a] Spanish home page . . . using HTML, and some of them were really interested in having the best

page they can, and it's a good exercise in writing your whole life story in Spanish. Now if they had to do it on paper, they probably wouldn't have worried that much about having it look right, because they wouldn't have to worry about . . . a real Spanish-speaking person in, say, Venezuela, looking at their page.

We are not, of course, asserting that Internet use makes improvement in students' work inevitable. Students have to decide to use the Internet's information-rich environment productively before it can influence their work in a positive way. Further, improved work is not likely to result when students do not have the requisite skills to use the Internet effectively and to solve problems they encounter. We observed what is likely to happen in such cases in an eighth-grade classroom as a student searched the World Wide Web for material to put in a portfolio she was creating for an assignment on Japan:

> She wasted a good fifteen to twenty minutes spelling *Asia* wrong and searching [the Internet] that way. . . . She did not get a single [relevant] resource. . . . She did not get anything that was useable out of a whole period of working on the computer.

Because training students to use the Internet effectively and efficiently took both knowledge about the Internet, which some teachers did not have in great supply, and time, which was hard for many teachers to find in the already busy school day, many students never got much instruction in Internet skills and were never in a good position to use Internet resources to improve their work.

Finally, a few high school teachers asserted that use of the Internet sometimes actually decreased the quality of students' work by increasing plagiarism. They reported that plagiarism increased with Internet use for a variety of reasons quite apart from the existence of services that sell papers to students. One of these was that teachers could never be familiar with all the sources available on the Internet, whereas they could be familiar with all the resources on a topic available in their school library. When a student copied from the latter, teachers could readily spot and prevent the plagiarism in the early stages of a writing project. These teachers also thought that students were more likely to use large chunks of others' work without integrating it with new material of their own or even rephrasing it when they could easily download this material from the Internet than they were when they had to copy it by hand.

In sum, Internet access provided students with much information and many opportunities for communication that could enhance the work they did as part of their studies. Many teachers and students reported that students often took advantage of these resources. Furthermore, the fact that the Internet provided a potentially broad audience for student work also led some students to take more care with their work than they normally did. However, Internet access actually interfered with the production of quality work in some ways—most notably by wasting students' time when they were not conversant with Internet use or did not have the independent problem-solving skills they needed to work effectively with it. Finally, we should note that improvement of student work due to Internet use was most apparent at the high school level, probably because older students were more likely than younger ones to be doing work that was sufficiently advanced that they could benefit from contact with outside experts or use of the specialized materials available on the Internet.

Enhanced Career Information and Opportunities

Yet another outcome for students in some NET classrooms was increased access to career information and opportunities. Unlike most of the other outcomes we discuss in this chapter, this one appeared to be limited to one age group—high school students. And it appeared among these students even though only one NET team had the stated intention of using the Internet to help high school students learn about the world of work. Further, the one planned curricular activity that did focus on career exploration encountered substantial problems. (In this school in which many students did not pursue higher education, the goal was to connect students with mentors engaged in various trades, but educators had difficulty finding the necessary mentors.) Thus, virtually all the impact in this area came as a result of students' own initiative rather than as a result of educator-planned activities.

Nevertheless, students did find ways to use the Internet to increase their access to career information and opportunities. They used three major categories of Internet activities to help them do so. First, many used the Internet to help select and apply to appropriate colleges or other postsecondary educational institutions or to find help with financing further education. Thus, it was quite common for students to use the Internet to gather information about the colleges they were considering, including college locale, demographic makeup, and majors and courses offered. In addition, they requested application forms on-line and explored tuition costs and scholarship opportunities. Although students could have conducted these information-gathering activities without the Internet, they maintained that using the Internet saved them time and effort. Students also used the Internet to communicate with alumni of colleges they were considering or with graduates of their own high schools currently attending these institutions. Again, students might have carried out these exchanges by telephone or through the postal service, but many would probably not have had them or would have had fewer of them without the convenience of e-mail.

Second, students intending to enter the job market immediately after high school used the Internet to learn more about career paths they might follow. Some students sought information about quite common career paths, such as enlisting in the military. Although similar information was available though other sources, such as local recruiting offices, again the convenience of the Internet led students to prefer it, at least for their initial explorations. Other students searched for on-line information about much more unusual job possibilities, information that would most likely have been more difficult to obtain elsewhere. For example, one student who hoped to earn a living as a professional bike racer found a Web site with a great deal of useful information about the problems and possibilities of pursuing this career path, the equipment and training he would need, and the like.

Third, a substantial number of students used their Internet access to learn about part-time or summer jobs, and some took advantage of Internet access at school to help develop their technical skills to the point that they could obtain jobs doing computer-related work. Using the Internet in one way or another, students from NET schools obtained internships at local universities, consulting work related to home computer use, and positions at local Internet service providers, Internet consulting firms, and nonprofit organizations. Furthermore, the Internet was sometimes the venue that students used to display their skills and let employers know of their availability. For example, one student obtained a position as a result of posting his résumé to a jobs-wanted site. Another, who had developed and posted a home page on the Internet, received an offer of a full-time job in another city as a Web page designer. Many students saw computer-related jobs not only as a way of earning money while still in high school but also as a way of preparing for careers in information technology. As Charles, a high school student who assisted NET educators by serving as a school-based systems administrator in his school, said:

> Careerwise . . . I plan to stick with it—the system administration. I look to go to [a local university] to get a computer science degree. . . . I have done some programming on my own, but I haven't really been . . . exposed in great depth to [it].

Although the vast majority of students who used the Internet in connection with paid employment found jobs related to their Internet and computing skills, there were exceptions. For example, a student who wished to build a career as a musician used the Internet, at home and at school, to communicate with local clubs about bookings for his band.

Overall, a substantial number of high school students did take advantage of Internet access at school to gather information pertinent to continuing their education or finding jobs after graduating high school. Some also used such access to develop marketable technical skills or, less commonly, to find jobs while they were still in school. This occurred in spite of the fact that only one NET team tried specifically to foster such exploration by students. Although students could have carried out many of the activities without Internet access, they often found the Internet their mechanism of choice because of the ease and speed with which they were able to find the information they needed and the ready availability of possibly helpful individuals by way of e-mail.

Exposure to Diverse Perspectives and Experiences

Students in many contemporary U.S. schools, especially European American students, experience marked social isolation because their schools are populated by students all much alike in ethnicity and social class (Kozol, 1991; Orfield & Yun, 1999). Even in schools with heterogeneous student bodies, students with different backgrounds often end up having little contact with each other as a consequence of numerous factors, including the practice of academic tracking (Oakes, 1985; Davidson, 1996; Schofield, 1989, 1995). Therefore, students in general frequently do not interact a great deal in school with those who differ from them in race, ethnicity, national origin, socioeconomic status, or physical abilities (Kozol, 1991; Davidson, 1996; Phelan, Davidson, & Yu, 1998).

One commonly reported classroom use of the Internet is the attempt to decrease this social isolation and to broaden students' horizons by having them interact with people outside the school whose life experiences are different from the students' own (Cummings & Sayers, 1995; Fabos & Young, 1999; Garner & Gillingham, 1996). These outsiders might be individuals in other states or other countries, but they might also be local individuals from backgrounds different than the students'. In Chapter Six, we concluded that Internet access did increase contact between those in classrooms and those outside the school. Here, we address whether such communication was of a kind likely to broaden students' horizons, the extent to which students used the Internet for such communication, and the outcomes for them when they did so.

The frequency with which students used the Internet to gain exposure to individuals and organizations in foreign countries depended heavily on the goals of specific NET team members. The large majority of planned Internet activities did not attempt to put students in touch with those in different nations. The exceptions to this rule occurred mostly in schools whose curricula emphasized international studies. So, for example, students at a middle school with an international studies magnet program exchanged messages with English-speaking peers in other countries about various current events.

When exposure to foreign cultures was an integral part of the teachers' vision of how the Internet should be used, as it was in fewer than 10 percent of the NET curriculum activities, contact with international artifacts or with individuals living in other nations was often substantial. For example, one high school's ACP proposal stated that one of the educators' specific goals was for students to "expand their multicultural, multi-ethnic and global awareness of people and current events." Consistent with this, the foreign language teachers who had submitted this proposal frequently had their classes use informational Web sites originating in different countries. They also had students use the Internet's graphic capabilities to learn about the cultures of these countries. Some students accessed Web sites that let them see these countries' landscapes, for example, or their art. In addition, these students communicated through e-mail or IRC with native (or sometimes nonnative) speakers of the foreign languages they were learning. Although technical and other problems made some of these efforts more problematic than one might imagine (as we discussed in Chapters Three and Four), on the whole teachers felt they were very useful for exposing students to these foreign cultures and thus for broadening students' cultural awareness. Students generally gave similar assessments. The comments of a middle school student, Don, whose social studies class made substantial use of the Internet are illustrative:

> In social studies we learned about the world. . . . [The Internet] took us to different places, and it helped us like picture . . . picture in our minds about . . . places. . . . It helped us picture in our minds . . . how different people live on the earth.

In addition, many individual students, generally of high school age, took the initiative to get in touch with people in other parts of the world even though such contact was not a formal class requirement. For example, when we asked one high school student what he liked best about his experiences with the Internet, he said: "I've been able to talk to a lot of people from around the world. I talk with people from Spain and Brazil, China, Italy, Russia." And a student from another high school finished the sentence, "The thing I like most on the Internet is . . . " with the words, "[to] explore . . . [to] try to . . . talk to different countries and people to learn . . . what they're about . . . different cultures and languages and businesses and things like that." Yet another student, accompanying his family on its first trip to England, amazed his parents when he readily navigated the campus of Oxford University owing to his familiarity with a MOO that resembled it and then took them to meet some English friends he had been corresponding with by e-mail. Although the extent to which such experiences increased the students' knowledge of the world and the range of perspectives students were exposed to is hard to judge, a teacher who felt these experiences were very valuable pointed out that many of the students using the Internet in his classes had previously had very little exposure to any part of the world outside their immediate communities. Therefore, he argued, such Internet contacts were likely to be especially useful in broadening students' horizons.

A small number of NET curricular activities (under 5 percent) were designed to broaden students' perspectives by helping them cross social rather than geographical boundaries, a use others have made of the Internet as well (Cummings & Sayers,1995; Davies, 1995; Brush, 1998). Some of these activities put students in NET classrooms in touch with individuals with different racial or socioeconomic backgrounds with the specific purpose of encouraging students to bridge the gap that such differences often create. For example, an educator in a high school whose student body was virtually 100 percent African American contacted a school in the district that served predominantly European American students to see whether any teachers there would be willing to facilitate an e-mail exchange between the students so they could get to know one another. An English teacher at the second school who decided this would be a useful activity reported that a student of hers who had exchanged a number of e-mail messages with a girl from the first school who happened to have the same first name said with great excitement: "It's amazing. I just can't believe how similar we are . . . how much we have in common." Other studies report parallel findings from e-mail exchanges, with students being struck by unexpected similarities between themselves and those they encounter who inhabit different geographical or social locations (Baugh & Baugh, 1997; McCarty, 1995), although occasional studies also suggest that social differences create barriers that can seriously disrupt communication (Neilsen, 1998).

Some have criticized e-mail exchange efforts that concentrate on helping individuals who differ greatly in social power or affluence to perceive their similarities if they do not at the same time deal with hard questions about why those differences exist and how they affect individuals' lives (Dimitraidis & Kamberelis, 1997; Fabos & Young, 1999). We would argue that enhanced perceptions of similarity among members of groups that have historically been isolated from each other or that have traditionally responded negatively to each other can be a useful first step in thinking deeply about the causes of such differences. Enhanced perceptions of similarity undermine a common explanation for such differences that has historically been all too readily accepted by those fortunate enough to experience greater degrees of power and prosperity—that there is something in the nature of the other person, group, or nation that makes these differences right and natural.

A particularly interesting case of communication across social boundaries, and one that resulted in a considerable change in students' perspectives, was a yearlong e-mail interchange between a small group of sighted third-grade girls and a blind adult male, whom they knew by the initials TCC. Like other potentially broadening e-mail exchanges between children and adults reported in the literature

(Goldman, Chaiklin, & McDermott, 1994), this one developed fortuitously rather than as part of a curriculum planned to help students cross the existing social barriers between the blind and the sighted.

At first, the third graders were hesitant to correspond with TCC because he was blind. As one student put it: "Well, when I first met TCC [on-line] I wasn't too sure I was going to enjoy . . . a blind person. . . . My impression of him was he was a blind person; he didn't know how to do most things." However, over the course of the year's correspondence, the students' attitudes and understandings changed dramatically (Murphy, Naples, Schofield, Davidson, & Stocks, 1997). Initially anxious, reticent, and rather uninterested, the students over time began to correspond eagerly with TCC, bombarding him with questions about what it was like to be blind, how he managed a variety of everyday activities, and how he felt about many things. Initially viewing him (and other blind people) as rather helpless, they discovered he was capable of doing many of the same things they did even though his methods were different from their own. They discovered, for example, that although he could not read handwritten letters he could read Braille and that although he could not see cars he could clearly hear traffic and that this allowed him to walk independently along city streets.

As time passed, the interaction between the students and TCC evolved into more than an opportunity for the students to learn about blindness. The correspondence became an opportunity to build a reciprocal relationship, a friendship in which the writers shared a wide variety of thoughts and concerns. Furthermore, the participants found ways to supplement their on-line communication; they exchanged audiotapes and other artifacts from their lives. At the end of the school year, the same child who voiced her initial hesitation to correspond with TCC said, "But now my impressions have changed greatly. . . . I didn't think that he would become my friend and I would write to him a lot, but he has become my friend—one of my best friends." Another child reported that when one of her friends who had not participated in the e-mail interchange made a mocking comment about TCC's blindness, she defended TCC, saying, "Don't laugh at him because he's blind. . . . You're just the same way except you're not blind." The experience was meaningful enough to TCC that toward the end of the year he visited the school and met with the students even though he had to travel over two thousand miles to do it.

Ms. Ebert, who supervised this e-mail exchange, and the students felt the experience changed the students' attitudes not only about their specific correspondent but about blind individuals as a group and even perhaps about accepting others more generally. Indeed, when asked a very general question about what she had learned from her correspondence with TCC, one of the third graders responded that she had learned, "That it doesn't matter what you look like on the outside, it's just what you are inside," and she went on to discuss how personal characteristics such as generosity of spirit are more important than external characteristics such as the appearance of one's hair or face. Yet another student responded to the same question by saying, "I've learned that people with disabilities aren't really different except for their disability. . . . It's only that [they] can't see or . . . [can't] hear."

Finally, students could experience a broadening of perspectives within disciplines. High school students who used the Internet in science classes spoke of their exposure to a wider variety of scientific viewpoints than they had had before on the issues that interested them. Thus, students using the Internet can gain not only new facts relevant to a discipline they are studying but increased awareness of disciplines as fields with contending voices and viewpoints. However, we did not study the evolution of such new understandings closely enough to do more than briefly mention this possible outcome of Internet access.

Although experiences such as those mentioned in this section often appeared to broaden students' perspectives in clear and valuable ways, we are not arguing that students using the Internet to contact people different from themselves automatically bridge social divides or understand the perspectives of these others. In fact, one of the most striking aspects of the interaction between the sighted elementary school students and their blind correspondent was the extremely important role Ms. Ebert played. She initially encouraged the students to respond to TCC in spite of their somewhat negative images of him. She carefully discussed with them the kinds of questions they might profitably and appropriately ask. She provided an environment in which the students could engage in a variety of off-line activities that supplemented their on-line experience, such as beginning to learn Braille or trying to understand the experience of blindness through identifying toys and eating lunch while blindfolded. Thus, she created an environment conducive to change. In addition, TCC was a remarkably patient, responsive, and reflective correspondent whose e-mails also enhanced the potential for student change.

Reinforcing the point that mere communication with those who are in some way different does not automatically enlarge students' understanding and bridge social divides is the fact that some e-mail activities designed with this goal in mind seemed to have little if any of the desired impact. For example, educators designed an Internet activity to put African American elementary school students living in a very poor area of the school district in touch with college students in the hope that such interchanges would expand the elementary students' horizons and sense of possibility. (Apparently, no one thought about the educative potential of this experience for the college students, most of whom came from much more privileged backgrounds. However, to be fair, the individuals who organized this activity were responsible only for the education of the elementary school students.) In contrast to the teacher who organized the e-mail exchange with TCC, the teacher whose students engaged in this e-mail activity played very little role in structuring the interactions or in creating classroom activities to reinforce constructive lessons to learn from them. The resulting interchanges were not only sporadic but also often superficial. For example, during interviews we conducted at the end of this e-mail exchange to assess its impact, it became apparent that at least one of the elementary students involved thought that his correspondent resided in a penitentiary rather than at a college because of a coincidental similarity in the names of the two institutions and the fact that in this student's experience the penitentiary was a more salient institution than the college.

In short, although it appears that e-mail exchanges have the potential to greatly expand students' horizons, it would be a mistake to assume that the mere opportunity to interact with those whose situation is quite different from students' own will necessarily enhance students' understanding of such individuals, their perspectives, or the groups to which they belong. Rather, the lesson emerging from a comparison of the different e-mail activities in NET schools is that the teacher plays a crucial role in shaping the kinds of experiences students have in such exchanges and in influencing if and how they will broaden students' perspectives.

Enhanced Reading Skills in English and Foreign Languages

Even if Internet use does increase student motivation and improve the quality of their work, as the evidence seems to suggest, such changes are not the same thing as a demonstrable change in academic achievement as it is usually measured. It seems reasonable to expect that greater interest, attention, and effort would lead to more learning, and some studies support this contention (Anderson, Shirey, Wilson, & Fielding, 1987; Asher, 1980). Other work suggests that the more time students spend working on a topic the more they are likely to learn (Caldwell, Huitt, & Graeber, 1982; Carroll, 1963; Egbert & Kluender, 1984; Fredrick & Walberg, 1980; Sjogren, 1967), which also suggests that increased motivation is likely to lead to enhanced learning. Further, students and teachers believed that students' enhanced motivation often influenced the quality of their work. However, even when changes in motivation or the quality of specific work products linked to Internet use are apparent to teachers or students, such changes in and of themselves do not constitute clear evidence that Internet use influences academic achievement.

For the numerous reasons discussed earlier, we did not focus any major research effort on assessing the impact of Internet use on subject matter outcomes, in spite of their obvious importance. However, many teachers frequently mentioned change in one particular academic skill: reading. Therefore, we briefly discuss this outcome. Educators in elementary schools most commonly reported improvements in reading, which is hardly surprising because that is the educational level at which teachers first introduce students to reading and at which they teach it specifically as a subject to all students.

The Internet activity designed to increase reading skills that we studied most closely took place in a third-grade classroom. Students used the Internet to access a MOO designed primarily to improve reading skills through practice as the students read the stories posted there. Ms. Ebert, who organized this activity and taught the students as they participated in it, asserted that students' participation definitely enhanced their reading skills. She also reported that other Internet activities, such as e-mail interchanges outside the MOO, also led to improvement in students' reading.

Reports of this sort from other elementary school NET team members were common. For example, a teacher in another elementary school discussed a difficult student whose reading she felt had benefited greatly from an e-mail activity:

> He was a nonreader, and now he's a . . . solid grade-two reader. He's a behavior problem too, but . . . somebody wrote him a letter, and I said, "Let's write [back to] him on the computer," and he . . . liked it.

Yet another elementary school teacher, Ms. Dalton, in yet a third school, reported considerable progress in her lower-achieving students' ability to read, which she attributed to Internet use:

> We have children who are not really readers, but it's amazing, you put them in front of the screen and they're reading the information on the screen. There is just something about that technology that's more interesting to them. So we've been able to capture low-level readers and actually increase their reading ability via . . . the Internet.

Comments about Internet use improving reading were much less common from teachers at the middle school and high school level, although they were not unknown. The secondary teachers most likely to attribute improvement in reading to Internet use were members of a group of foreign language teachers participating in NET whose students used the Internet both for accessing foreign language materials on the World Wide Web and for e-mail exchanges. In discussing the consequences of such activities, one of the teachers said:

> On the research side, they've definitely improved their skills. . . . The reading has also improved. . . . A lot of text that we use . . . [is] from newspapers, and that's not something they're used to seeing. They're usually used to seeing just regular textbook Spanish. So it's . . . created a bit more work for them, but at the same time they've managed to expand their vocabulary.

Secondary students themselves occasionally reported improving their reading in a foreign language through Internet use. However, the limited data we have on the topic suggest that most older students, like their teachers, did not report much improvement in their reading as a result of Internet use. In fact, when asked to indicate how much they had learned in a variety of areas (research skills, reading, writing, problem-solving skills, computer skills, and the like) as a result of Internet use, a small sample of middle and high school students ($N =$ 29) ranked reading as the area in which they gained the least from Internet use, with the mean response falling close to the answer option "a little bit."

We have little systematic evidence to suggest why Internet use might have increased reading skills for elementary school students, assuming the teachers were correct in their observations that it did so. However, two factors seem pertinent here. Reading is a skill that improves with practice. Although Internet use in elementary schools often entailed a significant amount of reading, the work may have given students an arena for more concentrated practice of this skill than they would have had otherwise. Further, it is possible that Internet use changed not only the amount they read but the focus they brought to their reading. As we discussed earlier, Internet use was motivating to many students. To the extent that elementary students were more motivated when reading on the Internet than they were when reading in other contexts, they might well have learned more. This idea is certainly consistent with Potter's conclusion (1992) that involvement in a telecommunications project was very motivating to middle school students and for that reason significantly improved their reading.

In sum, there is some reason to think that Internet use may have improved reading skills for elementary school students just learning to read and for high school students learning foreign languages. However, evidence for this outcome is sketchy. We mention it more to suggest a possibility for further exploration than to assert a clear finding.

CONCLUSIONS

A number of potentially important outcomes for teachers and students appeared to flow from Internet use within the context of NET. For teachers, such access appeared, first, to increase work-related communication with other professionals. Although some of the teachers' increased contact with others was with individuals outside their schools as one might expect, a substantial increase in contact with colleagues within their school was also common. Much of this communication occurred in the context of teachers' increased involvement in an expanded set of professional development opportunities. Second, teachers, many of whom began as novice computer and Internet users, acquired a substantial amount of knowledge about how to use Internet technology in their work. Third, some teachers began to play new professional roles outside the classroom. Finally, a strong sense of enhanced pride in and enthusiasm for their work was evident in many educators as a result of their involvement with Internet use.

For students, the clearest and most consistent outcome connected to Internet use was an increase in their enjoyment of their time in school and in their motivation. Increased knowledge of computing and the Internet also resulted for many students, due either to direct instruction or their own exploration. In addition, many teachers and students reported that Internet access often enhanced student work, although we have no strong independent evidence that this was the case. A small proportion of the Internet activities that NET stimulated were intended to broaden students' perspectives and social experiences by putting them in touch with individuals with backgrounds different from their own. Some of these efforts appeared to accomplish this goal with striking success, but others were less effective. Finally, we had reports from a substantial number of elementary school educators that involvement with Internet activities improved students' reading ability, a claim that we could not fully explore.

Of course, Internet use was not the only possible source of these outcomes. Consider the influence of NET itself. It is not only possible but likely that specific characteristics of NET played a role in fostering many of these outcomes. For example, NET required that educators apply for Internet access as members of a team. That requirement most likely accounted for some of the increase in communication among NET educators, especially within their own schools. Similarly, the considerable support and technical assistance NET supplied undoubtedly helped to account for many educators' impressive gains in Internet-related skills. NET's use of volunteer educators, resulting in some self-selection of individuals who were particularly motivated and energetic, may also have set the scene for the marked expansion in teachers' roles outside the classroom. Thus, it is not Internet access in and of itself but access occurring in a particular context that yielded the outcomes we have described here.

Further, the extent to which many of these outcomes occurred varied with the age of students. In addition, it varied from school to school and even from classroom to classroom within a school. In Chapter Five, for example, we highlighted differences in the extent to which the NET team members at various schools formed cohesive groups and collaborated among themselves. These differences have obvious implications for the extent to which Internet access was associated with increased communication among teachers in a given school. The case is the same for many of the student outcomes we have discussed. The amount that students learned about the Internet, the extent to which reported improvements in work occurred, and the extent to which communication with individuals of other backgrounds had the intended impact on students varied markedly from situation to situation. Thus, even when factors at the project and district level were fairly uniform, there were many variations at the school and classroom level that influenced the extent to which the outcomes discussed occurred. Therefore, none of the outcomes we discuss here is guaranteed or certain; rather, all are the consequences of a complex set of interacting factors.

In this and the previous chapter, we have focused on changes occurring within NET classrooms and on the impact of use for educators and students. However, recall that NET hoped not only to affect changes within the schools, but also to encourage district change as well. Specifically, NET hoped to institutionalize Internet use in WPS and to influence the district's overall technology planning. In the chapter that follows, we consider the extent to which NET achieved this goal as well as factors that shaped the institutionalization process.

CHAPTER EIGHT

Achieving Institutionalization

～〜〜 Numerous studies have documented the challenges that those who attempt to bring about change in classroom practice must face. But even when teachers and schools initially embrace a given change, further challenges remain. A critical question about any externally funded innovation is whether and in what form it continues to exist after the external funding is gone. Yet studies of change in educational institutions have generally paid more attention to the implementation of change projects than to the continuation of such change once outside funding has ceased (Miles, 1983; Miles & Ekholm, 1991; Miles & Louis, 1987).

The results of large-scale studies of federally sponsored school change efforts and the findings of smaller investigations both suggest that research into the process of successful institutionalization is warranted. It appears that relatively few change projects have been institutionalized even when participants perceive them as successes. This is true even when project objectives have been met (Berman & McLaughlin, 1977, 1978; Reed & Williams, 1993). Grassroots efforts are particularly unlikely to be institutionalized. Although they often generate a substantial amount of support from individuals, they frequently have a hard time mustering the internal district support necessary for their long-term continuation (Berman & McLaughlin, 1978).

In this chapter, we discuss the Networking for Education Testbed (NET) as a case of institutionalized but attenuated grassroots change. Previous studies indicate that school districts and the programs they institutionalize tend to mutually adapt (Berman & McLaughlin, 1978). The NET case is consistent with this pattern. However, it is also somewhat unusual: first, because the initial change effort was grassroots rather than top-down in nature and, second, because substantial institutionalization occurred in spite of the fact that many of the variables that the existing literature suggests improve the chances for institutionalization were not present. Nor was the school district that undertook NET known for embracing change from outside. As one individual with decades of experience as an administrator in the Waterford Public Schools (WPS) district put it toward the end of NET, change projects

> rarely stay. There isn't a project still in existence that ever lived beyond—this [NET] probably, I think, will be the first project that has ever introduced a change with the kind of impact that this project has [had]—where it will live on.

This assessment is especially striking given that this administrator was initially quite critical of NET.

To provide a context for considering what NET achieved, we next present a brief picture of the factors that ordinarily support institutionalization, the relative unavailability of these supports for NET, and the ways that the district initially greeted NET. We then describe the degree of institutionalization that NET actually achieved and consider some of the means by which it was achieved. We focus especially on the intriguing question of how NET staff were able to muster the power, visibility, and support necessary to influence district administrators. Finally, we discuss trade-offs and compromises made during the institutionalization, describing the aspects of NET that were not institutionalized. Consistent with a Web model approach to understanding how organizations are influenced by computing technology (Kling & Scacchi, 1982; Kling, 1991, 1992), we conclude that the history and evolution of social arrangements and relationships among key NET participants and district officials and the preexisting district context, especially ongoing district concerns, substantially shaped institutionalization. In particular, NET education staff's understanding of the district's broad political and social features and its computing history played a critical role in achieving institutionalization of key aspects of NET, including many infrastructure elements. At the same time, aspects of the NET approach that exacerbated major ongoing district concerns tended not to be institutionalized.

Our discussion addresses the extent to which institutionalization occurred during the five years of NET's life and in the three years after NET's external funding ended in 1998. We cannot say whether and to what extent in the long term the district will support the technical infrastructure and training associated with NET's approach to providing Internet access to schools. The answers to these questions are still being played out at the time of this writing. For example, the district has trained and prepared hundreds of teachers for Internet-based classroom instruction since the official conclusion of NET, and it has placed Internet-ready computers in all the district's non-NET schools. Yet, three years after NET officially ended, the file servers at these schools were not being used to create student accounts, both because teachers had not been trained to support this basic function and because there was debate in the district about whether students at non-NET schools should have individual accounts at all. Whether and when the district will resolve this issue is an open question.

Thus, this chapter's principal intent is not to assess how successful institutionalization will be in the long run. Rather, we seek here to contribute to knowledge about ways of achieving initial commitment to institutionalization. NET presents an especially interesting case in that it illustrates how an effort that many in the district bureaucracy initially criticized and discounted came to achieve sufficient district acceptance and support to set the institutionalization process in motion.

NET'S INITIAL POOR PROSPECTS FOR INSTITUTIONALIZATION

Research on the institutionalization of change in schools is not nearly as extensive as that on education reform more generally. However, what research there is suggests that certain factors are frequently associated with successful efforts to institutionalize new approaches to education. First, the degree of stability or variability in the environment affects this process (Fullan & Stiegelbauer, 1991; Goodman &

Dean, 1984). When districts are in a state of turmoil and flux, it is virtually impossible to establish an effective institutionalization process (Fullan & Stiegelbauer, 1991). Frequent changes in a district's top administrators, for example, make it difficult to muster the internal support necessary to encourage and maintain other changes. Second, when many changes are being championed or are occurring at the district level, it is difficult to promote any particular innovation because top administrators' attention and effort is divided. So chances for institutionalization of a given change improve when a change is introduced in a district that has few other change efforts competing for the attention of a stable cadre of key leaders.

Third, an internal press for a particular reform can substantially improve that reform's chances of institutionalization. Studies show that, not surprisingly, a district's chief executive officer and other central administrators often play a major role in sustaining a change when they show specific forms of support for putting that change into practice (Fullan & Stiegelbauer, 1991). Typically, change is sustained when district officials mobilize broad-based support for the innovation early in the process and remain involved (Berman & McLaughlin, 1978). Further, having officials' commitment from the outset is important; mobilizing their support once a project is under way is not usually possible (Berman & McLaughlin, 1978). Because middle- or lower-level managers ignored or threatened by a change may employ strategies to effectively subvert its institutionalization (Goodman & Dean, 1984), the commitment of these managers is also vital. In short, if key internal players in a district champion a given project from the beginning, its chances for longevity improve markedly.

Finally, the community can play a critical role in promoting and maintaining change. A strong and active community can either exert pressure for district change (Lewis, Baca, Bansford, & Commins, 1985; Post, 1992; Spuck & Shipman, 1989) or divert or derail a change agenda (Detwiler, 1994; Fullan & Stiegelbauer, 1991; Post, 1992; Spuck & Shipman, 1989). Thus, another factor conducive to institutionalization is active community support for the change effort. In fact, prominent scholars have argued that schools as institutions are particularly oriented toward conforming to community understandings about what schools are and do, maintaining high levels of community support, and striving to be seen as legitimate by the community (Meyer, Scott, & Deal, 1981; Morris, 1996). This suggests that community pressure for institutionalization may be important.

NET began with none of these factors. First, there was little stability in district leadership. Throughout NET's life span, the district was in the midst of transitions in leadership as well as significant internal organizational reform. This situation affected NET in various ways. For example, during NET's life, the district hired a superintendent of schools, near retirement age who was expected to have a relatively short term in office, to run the WPS. A new superintendent came to the district at roughly the same time that NET ended and the district adopted a new districtwide technology plan. So during NET's life it was never entirely clear how Internet access would fit into the long-term evolution that the new superintendent would set.

Complicating this situation, the superintendent who presided during NET's tenure focused largely on establishing site-based management in the district, and in so doing dismantled much of the district's long-established, centralized support structure for teachers in favor of school-level control. During this process, it was unclear which of the staff charged with supporting teachers in curriculum development and other ways would continue to have a job and what those jobs would entail. Even the name of the division charged with supporting such activities changed multiple times, along with its responsibilities. For a time, the district instructed division staff, who had traditionally approached schools and given assistance, not to go to schools unless the school and its teachers specifically requested their services. Rumors circulated that the district would lay off 75 to 80 percent of these individuals, as well as a group of midlevel district administrators and teachers on special assignment. Though these massive layoffs did not occur, the district did fail to renew the contracts of many employees (such as classroom aides) who were not tenured, reassigned some employees to new positions, and froze staffing levels. Understandably, morale was low in the division supplying teacher support services. It did not improve when the support staff were moved from a space in the central administration building to a distant and much less physically attractive location. These events, which diverted the attention of central support staff and depressed morale, hampered the establishment and maintenance of effective working relationships between these district staff, NET staff, and NET team members.

Furthermore, at the same time that NET staff were struggling to bring about institutionalization of their approach to Internet use, the school board faced two significant problems—a decline in the district's enrollment (especially of children with affluent parents) and gaps in achievement between African American and European American students. In short, during NET's life, district leaders, policymakers, and central staff were distracted from attending to educational technology issues by many things: the future leadership of the district was in question; the district was making substantive organizational changes; and it had to promptly address difficult and controversial problems.

Second, there was no major press from within the district's central administration for the specific changes that NET advanced. No top administrator consistently lobbied in a highly visible or vocal way on behalf of Internet use and NET's approach to it. A major report that the superintendent made to the community during NET's life, for example, focuses on school restructuring, redistricting, and finances, with almost no mention of technology. Further, just as NET began, a high-ranking district administrator and NET champion left to assume a position in another district. It was unclear for a substantial period thereafter who in the district would take responsibility for NET. Eventually, the district assigned another relatively high-level administrator to supervise NET. After a while, the district transferred the responsibility to yet another individual, an assistant superintendent. Although this individual thought Internet use had great educational potential, he generally did not make strong public statements about the importance of continuing such use after NET ceased to exist. And even NET's initial proponent in the central administration was not as supportive as he could have been. For example, soon after NET was funded, this individual mentioned in a meeting that numerous other district employees attended that he had not even read the NET proposal, suggesting less than total involvement with it. Also, no top district administrator was a heavy user of the kind of computer technology that NET was trying to bring to the schools, which meant that none of these individuals was having the kind of personal experience with the Internet that might lead him or her to envision educational uses for it. In fact, some of our interviewees theorized that because many of these individuals had typically had secretarial assistance throughout their careers, they lacked typing skills and thus did not even envision themselves as ever becoming computer users.

Compounding this unfavorable situation, relationships between NET, high-level district bureaucrats, and some district support staff who might have been NET's logical proponents began very poorly. For example, members of the district's division of technical affairs (part of the department of business operations) might logically have aligned themselves with NET. Staff in this division managed the district's mainframe computer system and repaired existing computers in the schools and thus might have valued NET because it brought in new computer resources and up-to-date technology. A high-level manager charged with implementing an administrative computer network for the district's teachers and principals was a second potential ally. A third set of individuals who might have supported NET were district staff who had in the past trained district teachers in the use of technology. They might all have associated Internet availability with the need for services they provided and with a rationale for training staff during a time of uncertainty and retrenchment.

Yet, for a variety of reasons we discuss later in this chapter, relationships with these individuals did not begin well, and, consistent with the literature, many of these individuals employed strategies that appeared counter to institutionalization (Goodman & Dean, 1984). For example, early in NET's life, representatives from the division of technical affairs and other district staff expressed serious concerns about NET and its operations at school board meetings, key public and political forums. They were also not quiet about their lack of enthusiasm for NET when interacting with NET staff. For example, a technical affairs manager told one NET staff member "that he felt that Networking for Education was yet another technology boondoggle, and in a couple of years it would go away and things would be back to normal, like every other educational fad that comes and goes."

Third, although NET had substantial support from teachers, principals, and students, members of the community at large never came forward in force to lobby for (or against) continued instructional use of the Internet after NET's external funding expired. Generally, principals reported and district officials believed that parents wanted more access to technology for their children. Moreover, the city of Waterford has a goal of attracting software firms to the region and has been relatively successful at doing so. Presumably, schools' investment in technology would better enable students to succeed in the local job market. However, neither political leaders nor a broad segment of the community strongly pressured school board members to make increased student use of networking technology a high priority. Further, owing to the continuing budget crisis that we discussed in Chapter One, the district had no surplus money readily available to support the purchase, use, or maintenance of educational technology, which meant that a major commitment to the use of the Internet in district schools could continue only if the board either approved a tax increase or agreed to issue bonds in support of that commitment. However, because the local tax base included an unusually high proportion of individuals without school-age children, board members were worried that raising taxes to support educational technology would lead to their defeat in future elections. In short, even if NET's Internet initiative had begun in a stable district, with strong support from the district hierarchy and the community, its continued existence would have been far from guaranteed due to strong fiscal constraints.

In sum, because of the district's lack of stable leadership, the ongoing organizational changes, the difficulties that NET staff experienced developing positive relationships with key district members, the lack of vocal and visible community pressure for instructional use of the Internet, and the district's financial problems, it did not appear likely at the outset that NET would achieve any significant degree of institutionalization. Few key political figures championed NET's existence, and it faced large structural constraints to its continuation—factors that suggest that at NET's conclusion Internet resources might have come to be seen as an undesirable social object (Kling, 1992). After giving an overview of the level and degree of institutionalization achieved, we consider how NET managed to turn the tide and garner support for continuing Internet use.

THE LEVEL AND DEGREE OF NET'S INSTITUTIONALIZATION

Scholars define *institutionalization* in various ways. At its most basic, "Institutionalization is the point at which an innovative practice, having been implemented, loses its 'special project' status and becomes part of the routinized behavior of the institutional system" (Berman & McLaughlin, 1974, p. 16). Further, institutionalization implies "stabilization of the change, and its continuation" (Miles & Ekholm, 1991, p. 2). In practice, because institutionalization is a complex process, these results occur to varying degrees and on a variety of levels (Curry, 1992; Goodman & Dean, 1984). Curry describes three levels useful for conceptualizing what happened in NET's case. First, a program can achieve structural institutionalization, which means that the innovation is represented in multiple concrete ways throughout the organization and that individuals in the organization know about and are able to perform the new behaviors. Second, a program might achieve procedural institutionalization, so that policies and behaviors associated with the innovation become standard operating procedure. Third, a program might achieve incorporation, which means that the host organization accepts the values and norms associated with the innovation and builds them into its culture. NET achieved partial institutionalization on all three of these levels.

The financial support for much of this institutionalization arrived through the WPS school board's unanimous and enthusiastic passage of a $25 million technology plan during NET's final year. Funded by a public bond issue, the plan provided every school in the district with access to the Internet in library- or classroom-based labs over a three-year period. In addition, the plan gave each classroom teacher a computer and access to three kinds of software: instructional software, which teachers selected from a list of options; administrative software, for managing grade and attendance data, for example; and word processing software. The plan did not guarantee participating schools access to the Internet from all classrooms, but it did provide every classroom with a computer equipped for Internet access. So if schools could find their own funds to install wiring earlier than planned, they had computers ready to be used on-line. Funds from the bond issue paid for wiring all classrooms in schools gaining Internet access during the technology plan's third year. In the following paragraphs, we consider the extent to which various aspects of NET were institutionalized with implementation of this plan.

Structural Institutionalization

The structural institutionalization of NET was represented in multiple, concrete ways throughout the Waterford school district even after the project ended. Most basically, all the hardware that NET brought to the district to control and distribute access to the Internet continued to reside in the NET schools and classrooms where it had been originally placed. In addition, NET's education staff continued to guide implementation of and provide support for Internet-based curricular activities. Specifically, under the auspices of the technology plan, the district created an instructional technology unit and hired the director of NET's education staff to oversee it. This structural change was further solidified when the district superintendent agreed with the teachers' bargaining unit to create two new job categories appropriate for this unit for teachers interested in supporting and managing staff development efforts associated with technology. The district hired the remaining members of NET's education staff to fill these positions. Thus, the district integrated NET's education staff into its core budget and the bureaucracy's organizational chart. This organizational replication of NET staffing is especially noteworthy given the interim superintendent's focus on eliminating central administrative office personnel and distributing control of and power over instructional support activities to individual schools. The district's budget-related resistance to hiring new staff was so apparent that one manager commented during a meeting that "saying the word *employee* is like saying the word *cancer* or *leprosy* to the board."

Other aspects of NET were also folded into the school district's structure. In particular, control over wide-area networking and responsibility for Internet access was transferred from NET to the division of technical affairs. Individuals from this office, previously rather negative about NET, began willingly to maintain and control the district's wide-area network, an event we will discuss later in this chapter.

Procedural Institutionalization

A number of NET practices and policies also became standard on the procedural level. First, during the three years after NET ended, the instructional technology unit staffed by former NET members continued to train teams of teachers from various schools in a manner intended to foster teacher leadership and collaboration in Internet use and to guard against the emergence of courses focused on technical features of computer use with no reference to the broader curriculum. The technology plan called only for each school to select a single designated technology teacher, with the intent that this individual would provide professional development and support services to other teachers. However, the instructional technology staff applied successfully for external funds and lobbied successfully to have state grant monies dedicated to support training for school teams made up of seven teachers, an approach to Internet use clearly reminiscent of NET's. Each team included English and language arts teachers, who under the aegis of the technology plan were expected to incorporate technology use into the third-, fifth-, seventh-, and tenth-grade English and language arts courses. The teams also included the school librarian, a business teacher, and two teachers responsible for managing the school's basic technical needs. As of fall 2000, roughly seven hundred of the district's approximately 2,900 teachers from a wide variety of schools had each participated in sixty to eighty hours of computer-related professional development activities that, although more extensive than NET's training, were quite similar in spirit and approach to what NET teachers had experienced.

Second, the district also retained a number of NET Internet access policies and procedures. Most apparent were the library computer laboratories with Internet access established in each district school. As we discussed in Chapter Five, NET had strongly promoted library-based access and librarian involvement. Students were also given direct access to the Internet in computer laboratories in many district schools. Again, this was consistent with NET's emphasis on giving students direct contact with the on-line world. Furthermore, the district continued to provide teachers with free home access to the Internet by means of the modem pool initially established for this purpose in conjunction with NET. (Recall that the modem pool allowed educators to connect to the Internet from their homes by using their own modems and telephone lines.) This practice no doubt encouraged teachers' home use of the internet, which NET strongly promoted.

Incorporation

We note, with regard to incorporation (the extent to which the district embraced values and norms associated with NET), first, that in adopting some of the procedures just described the district signaled its support of certain core NET norms, values, and beliefs. For example, NET education staff believed intensely in the importance of teacher empowerment. As we discussed in Chapter Two, one way NET worked to achieve this goal was by asking teachers to write their own curriculum units; it did not dictate how teachers and students should use the Internet. The instructional technology unit staff tried to retain the spirit of this approach by having English and language arts teachers develop curriculum units incorporating Internet use that they and other district language arts teachers could use. Although this approach is less individualized than the original NET approach, it does retain the core concept of teacher involvement.

Further, many aspects of the official district philosophy on technology embedded in the technology plan adopted near NET's end are similar to the philosophy that NET promoted. Most basically, the district promotes wide-area networking and the Internet in particular as valuable instructional resources, and it conceptualizes technology use as a tool for learning rather than as an end in and of itself. For example, the executive summary of the district's technology plan asserts that technology should be infused into the core content areas of the WPS. It asserts also that students should be provided with the opportunity to become proficient at using technology as a tool for learning. In addition, the technology plan did not promote the integrated learning systems that many in the district favored early in NET's life, but instead provided a significant amount of Internet access and promoted content-centered Internet uses similar to those NET embraced.

As we will show later, although certain aspects of NET were institutionalized, others were not. Furthermore, we are not asserting that NET in and of itself caused the district to adopt a technology plan nor that it single-handedly shaped the form of that plan. The district would likely have adopted some sort of extensive new technology plan even if NET had not existed. However, NET did influence the plan that was eventually adopted and substantially influenced its implementation. Further, the presence of NET appears to have encouraged the district to move more quickly to adopt a technology plan than it otherwise would have. The impact of NET on the technology plan that the district adopted was generally agreed to be substantial. As one district official commented:

> [NET] put the technology vision in front of us. And so I think to the degree that there is a plan and that there was the recognition of a plan . . . [and of] the importance of the Internet as an information source . . . I think is . . . to be credited to the Networking for Education Testbed project.

EXPLAINING INSTITUTIONALIZATION
Factors and Strategies Fostering Change

In addition to establishing that NET did achieve some degree of institutionalization in a climate not initially conducive to it, we also identified factors and strategies that led to this outcome. Further, we have identified some more basic factors, those that underlie the success of many of the strategies that we describe in the following pages.

The first of these foundational factors was the high and sustained level of effort that NET education and technical staff devoted to furthering institutionalization throughout NET's life. Staff not only developed an infrastructure for supporting classroom use of the Internet but also devised strategies to encourage district employees' long-term interest in the Internet as a school and classroom resource. As one NET staff member noted with some humor, they were willing to try almost anything that might help them to achieve this goal:

> I spent four years developing strategies! I've had review committees that co-opt people! I've tried to find advocates in this organization. I have trained the wife and the daughter of one of those advocates. . . . We . . . hosted a dinner . . . for all the board members in the WPS. . . . We spent a thousand bucks on that dinner! I mean, there are seventeen hundred things that we have attempted to do to force institutionalization in the district!

Similarly, various individuals near the top of the district hierarchy referred to the NET staff's tenacity and their willingness to "weather the storm of adversity" that they encountered at various points. As one put it, "The one thing about NET is that when those guys are invited to be part of something, they give all they got. . . . [T]hey have a passion." Although we do not deal with persistence specifically in the upcoming discussion of factors and strategies fostering institutionalization, this characteristic of the NET staffs' behavior appeared to be extremely important.

A second factor basic to the effectiveness of the strategies we will discuss was that NET staff worked on institutionalization almost from NET's outset. This gave them ample time to figure out both the types of knowledge that others in the district would need in order for institutionalization to go smoothly and how to help them develop this knowledge. It also gave them time to build relationships and trust with various district employees, to address some important individuals' initial associations of negative social meanings with NET, and to publicize NET's efforts and successes. As one district administrator noted, all too often the "university kind of people don't know what to do when they're successful." In other words, although researchers often carefully plan how to implement change projects and how to collect their data, they typically do not devote an equivalent amount of effort to figuring out how to leave those changes intact in the setting where they have worked, perhaps because they lack knowledge about how to do so effectively or because this is not a high priority for them. The NET experience points to the importance of making institutionalization a goal pursued in day-to-day activities over a long period.

Third, during the course of NET, the National Science Foundation (NSF) required the district to contribute matching funds to grants it gave to the project. In addition, other funding sources were aware of these matching funds and the commitment they implied. This put some pressure on the district to institutionalize at least some NET components. If it did not do so, observers might raise questions about having spent district money on an effort not worth continuing. Further, the requirement for matching funds set a precedent for spending district money on Internet access. Because inertia often shapes bureaucratic behavior, this fact too was important.

In addition to bearing these foundational factors in mind, readers should note that the following discussion does not describe every strategy that NET used to foster institutionalization but concentrates on strategies that appeared to pay off. For example, NET staff worked quite hard to win a positive national reputation. They presented papers about NET at national events and conferences, and they posted information about NET and its accomplishments on a frequently visited Web site. Comments from a member of the WPS office of planning and development about three years into NET's life suggest that NET succeeded in attaining national recognition:

> [In] going to conferences especially or workshops dealing with technology, I've not been in one where Waterford Public Schools have not been used as an example of good things that are happening in terms of systemic change involving technology. . . . I'm the one who usually goes to those from our office, and we just hear people talking about [us]—Waterford is mentioned and the whole room starts to buzz. Everybody knows that Waterford is doing something good—something wonderful. . . . Program officers brag about what's going on. They . . . seem to feel as though they made a really good investment in Waterford.

However, the board of education did not exhibit any great appreciation for this national approval, and in some instances appeared quite unaware of it, as indicated by this field note from a board meeting held within a year of the time the comment just quoted was made:

> Ms. Jackson [a board member] asked whether or not there was anywhere where she could go or any classroom that she could visit where

she could see a technology plan like . . . [the one under discussion] in action. Mark Schneider [head of NET's education staff] jumped in and said that people from "around the world" were coming to see how they were using technology in this district. He said that they come to see Networking for Education . . . [as well as other technology projects]. He indicated that "the world believes that we are state of the art." He said that . . . [board members] should visit their own schools.

Because schools as institutions are notably concerned with how their communities perceive them and because district failure to support and enhance an activity with a positive national reputation could prove publicly embarrassing, it might appear that NET's national reputation would have exerted some pressure on the district to institutionalize NET innovations. However, NET staff commented frequently that they were better known nationally than locally. Thus, in the long run, their efforts at achieving a national reputation did not appear to contribute directly to the process of institutionalization. Members of the school board, who faced elections every few years, appeared more impressed by evidence of local approbation.

We turn now to consider five factors and strategies that appeared to exert strong joint pressure on the district to institutionalize many aspects of NET: highlighting and amplifying a recognized district problem, offering and promoting a tried solution to that problem, coming to be perceived as indispensable, building viable relationships in the bureaucracy, and helping district personnel develop the knowledge necessary for institutionalization.

Highlighting and Amplifying a Recognized Problem

As we mentioned in Chapter One, the WPS district had put a freeze on the purchase of new instructional technology in the period preceding NET. However, since the 1980s, when the district purchased a large number of Tandy computers, computer technology has moved ever more strongly into the mainstream of U.S. life and work. It has also greatly expanded its capabilities. Such developments made the district's antiquated technology an increasing problem. The ubiquitous presence of the Internet, Web addresses, and consumer on-line services have made the general public aware of the vast array of possibilities available through technology and have also made powerful computers linked to the Internet ever more attractive to the household user. District employees and officials were well aware that Waterford lagged behind many other school districts in terms of the technology it provided for its students and staff, and they were beginning to explore ways to address this situation through a technology plan at roughly the same time that NET started. In short, quite apart from any influence that NET's presence exerted, it was clear that the district had a problem—what to do about technology, an expensive item, during an era when it also faced a major budget crisis and enrollment and redistricting issues that were splitting the community and draining public support from the schools.

The feeling that something had to be done about the district's technology and that the solution was not likely to be easy heightened over the course of NET, as district officials and board members became aware that other districts were making substantial financial commitments in this area. For example, during public meetings, some school board members reminded less enthusiastic colleagues that by delaying or failing to fund technology the district was falling further behind its suburban counterparts. This, some argued, could only impede the district's efforts to compete with private schools or suburban public schools for students. At the same time, no ready solution was apparent because neither the district's first technology plan, developed through a protracted process led by external consultants during NET's first year, nor the second, developed internally roughly a year after that, were deemed acceptable by the school board.

Even though the school board recognized the dearth of up-to-date technology as a problem, district matters like internal reorganization, consideration of a candidate to replace the current superintendent, controversy over redistricting for neighborhood-based schools, new core curriculum frameworks, and proposals for charter schools often pushed decisions about technology to the back burner. As one school board member put it:

> I think we're so messed up in politics. . . . Redistricting and everything . . . keeps taking the place of . . . [discussions about the technology plan]. All of a sudden it looks like . . . [technology is] important, and then all of a sudden boom! Here comes redistricting again.

An assistant superintendent added:

> We have so many initiatives that we're working on constantly, and [there are] so many programs that we're trying to make sure are

working for our kids. . . . I don't think [failure to focus on technology in the district] stems from a lack of interest. I think it may be a lack of prioritization.

In this environment, NET furthered institutionalization by making the matter of technology more salient and creating pressure for Internet use in the district. First, the staff did all they could to amplify and strengthen the belief that the district was woefully in need of a drastic technological upgrade. For example, they talked in public forums (such as school board meetings) about the increasing social and educational role being played by the Internet. And, prior to the explosion of Internet use among the public in the middle of NET's life, the education staff made sure to give each district official and board member an Internet account, met privately with many of these individuals to train them in Internet use, and in some cases even visited their homes to facilitate Internet access. Later, one member of the education staff again met privately with each school board member to discuss in detail how technology such as the Internet might benefit the district, why technology was useful, and why a technology plan was necessary. These efforts were so ardent that at one point an individual high in the district hierarchy, who saw such meetings as a ploy by the NET education staff to curry favor and secure jobs for themselves in the future, chastised NET education staff for them. Such activities did not lead for the most part to substantial Internet use by board members or district officials. Nevertheless, such efforts were likely important because a number of district officials and board members had little or no personal knowledge of advanced technology and meetings like this educated them to some extent about resources available on-line. As one district official put it, "[NET education staff] keep me informed of what's available and the potential that's there on the Information Superhighway and everything dealing with technology."

In addition, NET staff heightened the sense of pressure that district officials were experiencing due to awareness that the schools' computers were antiquated by creating a groundswell of demand for technology in the schools. Demand from teachers, students, and principals for technology increased over the course of NET, and NET education staff explicitly viewed fostering this grassroots demand as a tool to influence those in power, believing that evidence of such demand put pressure on the school board and administration to institutionalize Internet use. For example, when discussing the district's hesitancy to commit some matching funds it had promised to NET, one member of the education staff commented, "Assuming that the board is not willing to move, we need to bring another thousand teachers on . . . get people itching." Thus, NET staff used a variety of strategies to make sure that district officials and board members knew not only about resources available through the Internet but also about demand for Internet access by schools and teachers.

Another strategy that NET staff used to make demand for Internet access salient involved inviting board members, high-level district administrators (such as members of the office of planning and development and of the divisions of professional development and technical affairs), and even district officials' family members to participate in the annual competitive process (ACP) to select NET schools. Because the number of proposals received each year substantially outnumbered the number that NET could fund, this strategy dramatized the unmet demands for Internet use in the district. Using newsletters and other mechanisms, NET education staff also repeatedly reminded district officials and board members of statistics demonstrating local educators' support and demand for Internet connections. Indeed, at a school board meeting one week prior to the board's vote on the third and final technology plan, a member of the education staff reminded participants that during NET's fifth year forty-one schools had responded to the ACP, which made for thirty-two losers because only nine schools could be accepted that year. Similarly, NET staff reminded board members that certain schools were so eager for technology that they had sought and successfully obtained grants to fund that technology after failing to win resources through the ACP.

NET also increased pressure on decision makers by promoting the idea that moving quickly to embrace technology might solve another aspect of the district's technology problem—lack of funds. First, by authoring a variety of successful grant proposals, individuals connected to NET demonstrated that funds were available to support many different aspects of technology use in schools. Second, NET staff encouraged the idea that the dollars available to support many different aspects of technology would likely go to those districts savvy enough to establish themselves early on as pioneers in the educational technology arena. In meetings at which board members discussed adopting the technology plan, for example, NET education staff and district officials with whom they worked closely alluded to the potential availability of these funds. At the same time, they suggested that a board failure to act decisively and promptly would jeopardize opportunities to apply successfully for this money as well as drastically slow the technical implementation process:

> [At a board meeting,] Mr. Leo [a high ranking WPS administrator] then mentioned that there were some grants available that could help with the funding, but he said that the deadlines for the applications were really soon . . . and that in order to even apply for them, [the board] really had to have a plan, and that plan had to be accepted and in place in order [for the district] to be considered in any real sense for that grant money. . . . Mark Schneider also added that in his work with NET, they've noticed that there was typically a one-year lag time between the start of a grant once you win it and actually getting computers to the classrooms. . . . At that point . . . a board member . . . said, "I think this really looks like a commonsense plan." Then she added, "I think we need a plan if we want to get money, and I think that now is the time."

NET increased pressure on the school board to do something quickly in the technology arena in yet another important way. Because addressing inequity was one of the district's goals, the fact that some but not all schools received valuable equipment and support from NET created a new area in which the district was vulnerable to criticism. NET education staff members repeatedly emphasized that the district must do what NET could not do: it must provide equivalent technology access to all schools if it wanted to fulfill its agenda of providing equal learning experiences for all WPS students. For example, when the board discussed redistricting, individuals affiliated with NET argued that the district should adopt a technology plan concurrently in order to ensure that all students in all schools, no matter what the neighborhood, had access to comparably rich technological resources for instruction.

In sum, although the existence of NET was not the cause of the district's technology concerns, the behavior of those associated with NET increased the salience of these concerns so that it became harder for district officials and board members to push them to the back burner as they had again and again for many years. Moreover, NET did not stop there. As we will discuss in the next section, it presented the district with a tested approach to the use of advanced technology in classrooms and a vision of how it could deal with the newly highlighted and exacerbated problem of antiquated technology.

Offering and Promoting a Tried Solution to a Recognized Problem

Although NET activities highlighted the fact that the district's existing instructional technology was outdated, this by itself did not seem to be enough to spur major expenditures in an era fraught with large and recurring budget deficits. Many policymakers and administrators in the district were initially somewhat skeptical about the likely educational value of computers and applications such as Internet use. For example, one school board member observed that the computers purchased for the district during the 1980s were "collecting dust somewhere, and kids even throw their lunches around the room around these computers." Essentially, the board and district at large were faced not only with the recognition that WPS technology was sparse and old but also with the fact that new instructional technology expenditures would go to waste if they did not lead to productive technology use by teachers and students.

NET contributed to institutionalization of Internet use in the district because it gave many educators the opportunity to use the Internet in their work and to use it in ways they and others judged to be educationally valuable. As we described in Chapter Two, NET staff worked closely with teachers in order to garner their support for Internet use in the schools, and teachers' enthusiasm for NET was widely interpreted as evidence of the Internet's educational value. Although many in the central administration viewed NET education staff as politically naive and even insensitive at times, they nonetheless came to see the staff as practical, hardworking, and very knowledgeable about getting Internet access and helping teachers use technology effectively in classrooms. Comments like the following from a board member and district administrator illustrate this view:

> I think what works . . . what type of technology should actually be going into these schools and where should we be focusing that energy—I think that's the type of knowledge Networking for Education brings [to] our tech plan.

> When you talk with school staff, they're very excited about the [NET] project. Every school wants to be a Networking for Education site. That

speaks well for the project. I think they are getting people involved in it—teachers—they're getting in there and they're helping to spread the gospel, and . . . I think that's good.

Such positive images of NET-facilitated activities and educators' reactions to them are especially noteworthy in that, in the beginning, many district staff viewed NET as an outside project promoted by university-based individuals unaware and unappreciative of the constraints in public schools. It was far from a foregone conclusion that anyone would come to perceive NET-sponsored activities as successes. Yet because the district did come to perceive NET as successful at the classroom level from early in its life, many in the district turned to its education staff for ideas about implementing technology more broadly. This phenomenon contributed directly to the institutionalization of Internet access. For example, the district invited both NET's director and members of the education staff to participate in authoring the district's second technology plan. Though it eventually rejected this plan, the district incorporated many of its ideas in the plan it eventually adopted.

NET's success with teachers helped it gain support from highly placed individuals in the central administration, support that in turn influenced the destiny of the education staff and Internet use in the district. Even the individual in charge of developing a wide-area network for the district's administrators and teachers eventually proposed to his superiors that the director of the division of technical affairs, the director of the NET education staff, and he work together to create the district's third technology plan, the one that it eventually adopted. Notably, this district official, himself a former teacher, had a close relative teaching at a NET school. Initially, he criticized NET harshly. However, after hearing reports from this relative and other teachers, he concluded that NET staff could and did work successfully with teachers to produce desirable results in the classroom, a result that clearly contributed to the respect he developed for NET and for the potential of Internet use in schools. As he eventually remarked:

We're dealing with a generation that has not been exposed to computers at all. It's the majority of our teaching population. So just to get them acquainted or familiar or comfortable with technology is a major task in itself. . . . I deal a lot with teachers, a lot of my friends are teachers, relatives are teachers, so I see the excitement . . . or the use of the Internet by those people. And . . . that's the level that I think NET has hit and hit well.

NET did all that it could to make sure that decision makers became aware of how the Internet could be used in the classroom and to highlight ways the Internet could be useful to students, including those in schools serving disadvantaged young people. For example, NET staff arranged for policymakers, top administrators, and district staff to hear teacher and student testimonials about how access to the Internet had affected them. A field note describes a dinner meeting of top WPS administrators and members of the board of education at which a student gave this type of testimonial:

LaToya, [a] . . . student from Brayburn [a school located in a relatively poor section of the city and whose student body is roughly 99 percent African American], spoke about her collaboration with physicians at Waterford Hospital using the Internet. She made the point that it was very difficult for her to get to Waterford Hospital on the bus, which took a lot of time and effort, and that using the Internet she was able to interact almost daily with her physician mentor at Waterford Hospital to continue the work she had started this summer.

Similarly, the education staff published glowing student and teacher testimonials in NET informational newsletters. They posted these newsletters on-line and sent them directly to various individuals in the district administration and school board. The concrete and emotionally compelling illustrations of how technology can work productively in students' lives not only showed the results of Internet use for individuals but also illustrated that technology could work for many types of students who attend Waterford schools, including students from homes where access to computers or the Internet was not likely to be available.

Also, rather creatively, NET education staff took advantage of opportunities to work with individuals who had indirect access to power through their influence with those in positions of authority. The goal of such activities was to create positive attitudes about NET and about the Internet's educational usefulness. Specifically, NET staff provided Internet training to family members and staff of a number of influential decision makers at both the school and district level. For example, NET staff trained the wife, daughter, and secretary of one high official, Jim Harrison, in Internet use because he himself was not a regular user. This strategy was apparently successful, as during an interview he spoke with striking enthusiasm about the consequences of both his secretary's and his daughter's Internet use. The payoff of this strategy was also apparent when he spoke to NET funders and school board members:

> Jim Harrison spoke for about fifteen minutes. The only times that he seemed to be speaking from his heart with genuine commitment and enthusiasm, from my perspective, [were] . . . when he spoke of the way the Internet changed students' attitudes toward themselves and toward school work. As he had in an interview with me, he made specific reference to the fact that he was basing his comments here on his daughter's reactions. He said he thought use of the Internet gave students a sense of competence and confidence, of increased self-esteem, and the like. He said again and again that he felt that technology was a vital component in helping to raise academic achievement.

Although districts do not necessarily institutionalize change efforts because they have gained student and teacher support, the perception that a project has been successful is, reasonably enough, one of four principal factors that superintendents weigh when considering whether they will continue supporting such efforts (Berman & McLaughlin, 1976). It is clear that many school board members and high-ranking district officials viewed NET's ability to interest and excite students and teachers as one important indication of success at the classroom level. Further, local administrators often do not search outside the district for better solutions to their problems because they feel that the success of an innovation depends on local conditions (Berman & McLaughlin, 1976). Thus, NET's ability to build interest and use at the classroom level and to call the positive response to such use to the attention of decision makers contributed substantially to the district's institutionalization of Internet use and many aspects of NET's approach to the use of this technology.

Becoming Perceived as Indispensable

NET's education staff were, in effect, institutionalized when they became the core of the district's new instructional technology group. Of course, one factor that undoubtedly contributed to their employment in this unit was their positive reputation at the school level. However, over its life, NET did transfer many technical responsibilities to the district's technical staff, working with that staff to help it develop the skills necessary to assume such responsibilities. Because the school district possessed a group of individuals assigned to support professional development in a wide variety of areas, including two people who specialized in training teachers in the use of technology, the education staff might also have focused some energy on inculcating in these individuals the willingness and ability to replicate NET's approach to teacher training and support. This, in effect, would have provided replacements for themselves. Yet, in the end, the district hired the director of NET's education staff to head the newly created unit of instructional technology, and it hired the remaining NET staff to fill other positions in that office. This institutionalization of key NET staff markedly influenced the extent to which NET's philosophy was institutionalized. In this section, we describe important factors that encouraged others in the district to conclude that NET education staff were if not indispensable then at least too valuable to lose.

One thing that NET demonstrated over the course of its existence was that those associated with it knew not only how to work well with teachers and students but also how to go about garnering external funding to support educational technology initiatives. During NET's life, in addition to receiving the two NSF grants that made up NET's core funding, those affiliated with NET won a major grant from the U.S. Department of Commerce as well as sizable grants from two local foundations. Although NET's university-based director took the lead in winning the large initial grants, over the years some of the education staff participated increasingly in fundraising efforts, even writing some grant proposals themselves. The fact that NET staff had a positive track record with major granting agencies and foundations undoubtedly contributed to their aura of indispensability. Key district officials also came to believe that not institutionalizing NET at some level might hinder the district's chances for receiving major grants. Specifically, an employee of the NSF whom those in the district perceived to play an important role in funding decisions reportedly told the district assistant superintendent that NET was one of the foundation's outstanding programs and that failure to pass a technology plan that would ensure continuation of Internet access would reduce the district's chances of receiving this individual's support for technology-related projects in the future.

District officials were well aware of the education staff's access to external funders, because the staff sent the funding sources quarterly, annual, and other reports about NET's progress. Because the school board hoped to find outside funds to bolster and support the district's technology plan, these connections were important. During NET's life span, the NSF had granted about $15 million worth of funding to educational projects in the district, including NET. Reflecting concern about the NSF's possible reaction if the district failed to follow up on NET, a local newspaper story that ran just prior to adoption of the third technology plan stated that board members and district staff "said that without a technology plan, it would appear as if the National Science Foundation had wasted the $5 million it invested in the district five years ago as part of a pilot program [NET]."

It was also important that, as NET's local reputation grew, no individuals or group stepped forward to challenge the belief that those working for NET had the most creative, clear-cut, and effective ideas for implementing instructional technology in the district at the classroom level. At one point during NET's life, for example, the district's office of planning and development approached a variety of individuals not connected with NET for ideas about launching new technology initiatives. However, according to a number of individuals, these efforts did not lead to many viable ideas. At least partly as a result of this experience, staff in this office reverted to using ideas that NET staff had initially championed. In short, NET staff tended to be more familiar than their district peers with ways to implement up-to-date technology in the classroom, and they were often, as one informant expressed it, able to "grab the discussion." Moreover, because of the district's state of transition and even turmoil at times, it is not surprising that no one else worked to seize clear leadership in the instructional technology arena. The resulting power vacuum contributed to the NET staff's ability to step forward, be influential, and be noticed. For example, one board member remarked:

> It seems to me before long folks who are much more innovative [than others in the district] in the work that they do, like Mark and Peter and Nellie [all members of the NET education staff], may more likely be the people who continue on doing the training [in instructional technology].

Finally, the value of NET education staff knowledge about teacher professional development and support with regard to Internet use was enhanced because they did not share their knowledge and experience with district support staff, who might then have assumed such responsibilities. In fact, members of the district's division of professional development were generally very removed from NET. Indeed, two and a half years into NET, one individual in this division stated that in all the meetings she had attended about various curricular projects in the schools no one had ever brought up NET.

NET staff did approach district professional development personnel to discuss setting up meetings to work out support for educators interested in using the Internet in their work. However, these meetings never occurred, for a variety of reasons. First, the division of professional development was in a state of flux and even disarray throughout much of NET's existence. Second, NET's education staff and the staff in the division of professional development had very different philosophies about teacher training, with the district support staff preferring a more directive approach than NET's. Thus, NET education staff doubted meetings would be productive in furthering their goals. Third, near NET's beginning, the high ranking district official who initially championed NET and served as its district liaison appointed an individual from the division of professional development to become the new NET liaison when this official left the district to work elsewhere. However, NET's director, Don Quick, backed vigorously by the head of the education staff, argued successfully to have someone with a higher position in the district assume that responsibility, behavior that not surprisingly created considerable resentment on the part of the individual that NET staff would not accept as liaison. NET set up an education advisory group, intended to provide a place for district curriculum and training specialists including those from the division of professional development, to discuss training and curriculum issues with NET education staff, but this group met only sporadically.

Given the above, education staff were able to make it clear to key district administrators that if they were not kept on after NET was officially over, key functions necessary to maintain effective classroom Internet use would be left unperformed. NET staff also further highlighted their usefulness and knowledge as they described the activities they conducted, and they challenged district officials to think about who would carry out such activities in their absence. For example, during one of their meetings, education staff drafted the following document, a version of which NET delivered to various individuals in the district hierarchy:

Networking for Education Testbed has installed network LANs [local area networks] with wide-area connectivity at twenty schools in the district. In addition, NET provides support for over [three thousand] staff users who access the Internet from school and home. NET funding ends on approximately January 30, 1998. After that date, either the district will support the activities created by NET or the project will not continue. This creates obvious questions as to (1) Whether the district will choose to continue the activity [and] (2) If it chooses to continue the activity, who will be responsible for support? In order to contemplate the scope and scale of transferring from an NSF-funded research activity to a district activity, NET has put together a rough draft of issues that pertain to supporting this effort. This document is being created one year in advance so that adequate time occurs for discussion and resolution of these issues.

Accompanying this document was a list to show what each group in NET provided and which aspects of these activities it had transferred to district personnel by then. The list contained numerous education staff activities, including monitoring newsgroups, monitoring NET's "trouble" account (an e-mail help account to address users' technical problems), publishing and maintaining the district's home page, and providing a variety of other support and in-service professional development activities. However, the transfer side of the list was left conspicuously blank, indicating that services provided by the education staff had not been transferred to other district employees and that it was not clear to whom these responsibilities should be transferred. Education staff also took advantage of other opportunities to remind district officials of what they did for the district and what would occur at the end of NET. For example, one member of the NET education staff remarked:

> I think I've done it three times now—say to Jim Harrison, "A year from now, . . . I will be handing you the keys to the car. The car has about [ten thousand] users; it'll have twenty-nine servers; it'll have about [five hundred] computers; it'll have a group of people that are powerfully using the technology, and they expect support. Here's the car." And that seems to have an effect on him.

In short, the NET education staff made it quite clear that they carried out myriad support activities for the district and that no one was ready and waiting in the wings to assume these duties. Moreover, the school board was leery of turning to outsiders for help in this area because, as one board member noted, it is difficult for a district to know when and whether it should trust the advice it gets:

> You have people like the Board and like the superintendent who don't have the factual or the knowledge base [about technology] having to be dependent on other people to inform you to make [technology] . . . decisions, and it's very difficult to sort of know who to trust and who to listen to.

This feeling was reinforced very early in NET's life when a group of principals decided to invest a substantial amount of Title 1 money in a technology product that an outside vendor offered and promoted. This product and the services provided with it proved quite disappointing to many, and that made NET's education staff look more knowledgeable, competent, and trustworthy in comparison.

Improving Relationships with the Bureaucracy

In virtually any change project, it is important to establish positive relationships with individuals who can help implement, extend, and sustain the effort. In the context of a bureaucracy, these relationships are especially important. However, NET director Don Quick and the NET staff initially lacked strong ties to powerful figures in most arms of the bureaucracy. Furthermore, NET education staff, who thought of themselves as teachers more than administrators, were not initially fully aware of bureaucratic intricacies such as the difference between specific individuals' formal titles and their actual power and the fact that individuals with impressive titles and substantial power over some things might be quite powerless in relation to other things. This situation caused a variety of difficulties, especially during NET's early years. For example, wiring buildings for Internet access took far longer than NET staff anticipated, partly because of the numerous steps required to install wiring in aging schools but also because NET education staff did not understand enough about how the bureaucracy actually functioned to achieve their goals as expeditiously as they wished.

For NET, one particularly important section of the district bureaucracy was the department of business operations, especially its division of technical affairs. Relations with staff in this department were crucial for institutionalization because these staff members were the logical people to assume technical responsibility for Internet access when NET was over. Furthermore, because NET's technical staff were employed by collaborating research-oriented institutions rather than by the district and expressed no interest in becoming WPS employees, it was essential to successful institutionalization to find people within the district who could take on the time-consuming job of managing and working to expand the technical infrastructure that NET established. Unfortunately, as we mentioned previously, NET staff's relations with certain key individuals in this part of the central administration were initially quite poor. Complicating the situation even further was the fact that NET was using cutting-edge technology quite unlike the technology used previously in the district. If individuals in the division of technical affairs were to take over a significant amount of the work previously performed by NET technical staff, NET would have to supply these individuals with extensive training.

Thus, relationships with staff in the department of business operations had substantial import for institutionalization, and that is one reason we will discuss those relationships in some depth here. Two additional reasons are that the issues that led to the initial conflicts are quite likely to arise in similar change efforts and that even though conflict with department staff, as well as with other individuals in the district, continued at some level throughout NET's existence, virtually all the individuals we interviewed in the department of business operations agreed that the relationships between them and NET staff improved significantly over NET's life. Indicative of this improvement were the positive comments made at a school board meeting by Max Schwartz, from the department's division of technical affairs, who had criticized NET quite vehemently in earlier years:

> Max said that he gets lots of calls and there are lots of schools who would like to be brought on with two or three computers. . . . He said that thanks to Networking for Education they will have the resources to bring these sites on-line because of the equipment he'll have to bring people through the central site. He said that by the end of the Networking for Education process, that WPS will have the ability to do it all.

It is worth considering how NET was able to overcome major impediments to good collaborative relationships with the existing bureaucracy. In addition, it is worthwhile to consider why relationships improved with relevant individuals in the department of business operations even though they did not evolve substantially with most relevant individuals in the division of professional development during NET's life.

The initial conflicts with the department of business operations, and especially with its division of technical affairs, had several important sources. First, people in NET did not attempt to elicit broad support or input from individuals with technical skills and responsibilities in this department until NET was actually under way and in some senses a fait accompli. For example, members of this department criticized NET for failing to include representatives of the department who had technical responsibilities in developing the proposal NET submitted to NSF to fund the project and in early key decisions about Internet access for NET schools. As one powerful individual from this department put it, "They perceive this as some kind of research project, and we're the test tube, and the experimental animals never get to [*laughs*] dictate the experiment." Thus, numerous members of this department initially felt that NET did not adequately recognize or exhibit respect for their responsibilities and expertise, as this e-mail message from one such individual to the NET director during NET's first year illustrates:

> NET staff has not recognized that there are two offices, Computers in the Classroom [where professional development personnel were located] and the division of technical affairs, at the Board who already deal with technology. To date, they have been largely ignored. It is difficult to imagine how one "institutionalizes" something by ignoring those parts of the institution who hold that responsibility.

Even a school board member who lobbied heavily for institutionalizing Internet use in the district was concerned about the impression that NET education staff sometimes conveyed:

> I can remember sitting in one presentation and almost [getting] . . . the feeling that . . . those who were in charge of Networking for Education viewed themselves as just a little bit above everybody else. . . . "You guys don't really understand that this is really cool," and . . . you know, "You'll want to do this."

NET's close association with two major local universities also contributed to tensions between individuals. Although school district and university personnel sometimes collaborated productively, relations between the district's central administration and university faculty during NET's life were not routinely highly collaborative or collegial. For example, many of the faculty associated with a major education research institute at one of the universities often conducted their research in suburban school districts, parochial schools, or even in distant cities rather than in the WPS. And during NET's life, individuals associated with the same institute applied for major grants involving district-university partnerships but looked elsewhere for their partners, as did the school district. Indeed, as NET began, individuals from the department of business operations asserted that university professors often collected their data and then left districts with little in return. They also alleged that university employees connected to NET were straying beyond the confines of their research and inappropriately involving themselves in district technology policy. Finally, they lashed out against what they felt were exorbitant overhead charges that the university took from NET grant monies, pointing out that the school district was taking the lower of its two rates of indirect costs in order to maximize program dollars for teachers and students and asking why the university did not show a similar concern for maximizing NET's potential impact. (Indirect costs are funds given by funding agencies to universities and other institutions that employ researchers obtaining grants from these agencies. These funds cover overhead costs associated with the conduct of the research, such as library and administrative services.)

Battles for power and organizational turmoil in the district were a third factor that appeared to contribute to negativity toward NET among members of the department of business operations. During much of NET's life, it was unclear who would remain in what positions and whether departmental divisions might be reorganized in the course of the project. When NET staff assumed some kinds of technical responsibilities that had traditionally been split between the divisions of technical affairs and of professional development, they cut into others' domains of responsibility. Thus, surmised some, district employees resisted NET because they feared that it might make them look less worthwhile or needed. As one district administrator told us, "The central office is just so scared of losing their little power base—which is absolutely no power whatsoever, but in their minds it's some power—that they can't see beyond that."

Consideration of these conflicts suggests that there are effective ways to address them and thus foster institutionalization. First, to address concerns about project ownership and to convey respect for district expertise, a school district can be given some control by the granting agency over how monies gained from external sources are spent, and it can be involved in decision making. Both these strategies eventually contributed markedly to improving NET staff's working relationships with district staff generally and especially with relevant individuals in the department of business operations. For example, during the last three years of NET, NSF funding went directly to the school district. The district then subcontracted with the universities for technical and research services. In contrast, during the first two years of the grant, NSF funding had gone initially to the universities. The change came about principally because the NSF insisted on it in order to further project institutionalization through increased district involvement. Commenting on the message this funding shift conveyed, Tony Leo, an individual near the top of the district's administrative hierarchy, asserted it was key to institutionalization because

> We have more control of this, so there is a chance for us to integrate this and institutionalize it, because you don't get that unless you've got key players in the institution you want to integrate it into doing that— building a base of understanding for it in the organization and getting people behind it. . . . I think, when the money moved, people in there realized that they could have more of a say over what happened, and that it was, indeed, ours. . . . [I]t wasn't them out there with their program. . . . And if it had stayed that way, I'm sure in the fifth year now people would be rooting for the program to go away . . . "because we're tired of them coming in here telling us what to do."

A district administrator initially strongly critical of NET also observed that this move helped lessen the feeling that NET was doing something to the district and its employees rather than working with those employees to implement a change effort.

In addition to giving central administrative staff an increased sense of ownership, this shift in financial control also gave WPS employees more input into the organization and implementation of NET activities. For example, once the district gained more control over the budget, individuals in the department of business operations insisted on purchasing a new server to be centrally located in their office so they could, among other things, give Internet accounts to teachers and other individuals not participating in NET. NET had wanted this money to go toward funding a new technical staff person to assist at NET schools and with other technical work. Despite severe short-term conflict over this issue, in the long run, the district's ability to accomplish some of its own goals through control of the money contributed to a sense of district ownership and improved district personnel's working relationships with NET staff. This particular decision may have also have been beneficial in that giving accounts to individuals from schools not participating in NET increased the level of technical expertise and involvement in Internet activities among teachers in general, making it more likely that institutionalization of Internet activities would ultimately be successful. Individuals responsible for technical activities in the district were very pleased that they could provide these valued services to schools and said this turn of events contributed substantially to their increasingly positive feelings toward NET.

NET staff worked to respond to district administrators' complaints about exclusion and to increase positive relations with district staff by inviting individuals from the department of business operations (as well as other district offices) to participate in NET activities and processes. For example, they invited some technical staff from this department to participate in the ACP. More significantly, several of the district technical staff (as well as one individual from the division of professional development) were involved in ongoing technical advisory group meetings. During these meetings, which occurred regularly for years, NET staff and district technical personnel discussed such topics as options and preferences for connecting to the Internet, the merits and drawbacks of various operating systems and server platforms, how the current skills and work roles of technical personnel in the district meshed with those of NET staff, how to develop an action plan to address gaps in technical knowledge, what it would take to keep Internet use running in the district after NET, how to institutionalize technical research as well as production, and procedures for handling Internet connections at non-NET schools. Efforts like this drew the attention of school board members, causing one to remark that NET staff had "done a great deal to invite those people [in]."

NET and district personnel also found ways to address the second source of the tensions between them: the concerns arising from NET's association with local universities. Clearly, NET could not disclaim its association with these institutions because it was firmly rooted in them. However, to address worries that NET might implement Internet access and then retreat to an ivory tower, leaving the district and its teachers in the lurch, NET's director and its staff proclaimed the project's commitment to institutionalization early on. Further, NET backed this verbal commitment with visible efforts to help district personnel develop the knowledge necessary to support Internet access and ultimately to embed control of many parts of its activities firmly in the district.

Also, rather than take a proprietary stance toward ideas (as university personnel sometimes do, because generating ideas affects tenure and promotion), NET generally allowed the district to claim ideas emerging from NET activities as its own. The text of the district's technology plan is indicative of this strategy. Even though NET personnel were significantly involved in the planning process, the plan makes no formal acknowledgment of the ideas that emanated from the district's experience with NET. Similarly, on some occasions, NET education staff participated in grant-writing activities but agreed to leave their names off the submission in order to minimize the potential for conflict with individuals in the district who might question their influence. As one NET education staff member explained, "You have to be able to swallow your pride. . . . That was also very important because the bureaucracy then didn't feel like we were out there to get a position for ourselves." Such behavior led one individual located in the district central office to comment that bad feelings between district and NET personnel "were quickly dispelled by the, amazing, to me, ability and willingness of the university people to say, 'We'll let it go.' [NET's director] gave a cutting-edge idea to the school district of Waterford."

The sense of distance that district staff initially felt from NET was also reduced because NET's education staff, and not NET's university-based participants, were responsible for working closely with district policymakers and lobbying the school board for institutionalization. NET education staff had demonstrated their commitment and allegiance to the Waterford schools through years of service as teachers and support staff. In short, they were not outside change agents going from district to district bringing a predefined program to a variety of school systems, nor were they university-based personnel linked more closely to their project than to the district.

Finally, NET staff found ways to reduce the tensions aroused by district staff's concerns that NET posed a threat to the long-term employment or power of those with technical responsibilities in the district. To address such worries about turf, NET made it very clear that critical technical personnel working for NET would depart when NET ended, because they wanted to return to their regular work lives rather than become employees of the WPS. The message was that NET would not in the long run threaten the job security of individuals in the district's division of technical affairs, and that indeed these individuals would become even more essential if the district did make a long-term commitment to giving its students and teachers Internet access.

Relationships between NET staff and the staff of the division of professional development and its organizational successors, which generally did not improve over time, did not benefit from most of the factors that improved relationships with district technical staff and their colleagues in the department of business operations. For example, this division did not gain the same sorts of material resources as the department did after NSF transferred control of some grant resources to the district. Nor did professional development staff have the same opportunities for input into NET, because the education advisory meetings that members of this staff would logically attend were held only sporadically. In contrast, technical advisory meetings were much more frequent. Furthermore, NET education staff were long-term employees of the WPS and had no desire to leave the district when NET was over, so turf issues between these individuals and members of the division of professional development remained. As one member of the education staff described relations between his group and those in the division of professional development, "There could very well be that real fear . . . [the fear] that 'these people are out after my job.'" And indeed NET education staff felt no great compulsion to ensure that those in the division of professional development would be able to handle Internet training in the long run, saying things like, "There's not as much of a need for us to get those people to do it; whereas the technical people have to do it if the project is going to survive within the school district. So the immediacy hasn't been there." In short, the education staff pursued relationships with this group less ardently than it did with the district's technical staff because building good working relations was not essential to the survival of the NET approach to technology use within the district and might even have been counterproductive.

Building Technical Knowledge in the District

Once a school district has committed itself to institutionalization of a change, it must build sufficient knowledge and expertise in the district to institutionalize and sustain the change. This is particularly important when the individuals who initially implemented the intended change will no longer be present when the external funding for the change effort ends. No matter whether a change effort involves new curricula, new assessment methods, Internet use, or something else, individuals in the district must have the expertise to continue the innovation if institutionalization is to have a chance of success. In the case of NET's change effort, the development of the technical knowledge of pertinent district staff was essential because district technical staff did not initially have the requisite knowledge to effectively support Internet access in the district. Because the NET education staff hoped to continue training and guiding the district's teachers in Internet use after NET's end, development of the knowledge necessary for these tasks within the district was given low priority even before the district decided to continue employing the NET education staff in this capacity. In this section, we consider factors that facilitated the building of technical knowledge among the district's technical staff.

Although accustomed to and expert in the support of the district's mainframe computer system, the district's technical staff had little knowledge of or experience with systems supporting Internet use. Perhaps most challenging, these individuals had not worked with Unix, the programming language that NET selected to support its servers and networking systems. As one district employee described it, with laughter in his tone, "We were . . . at ground zero, I suppose, as far as Unix knowledge when we started this." Just as important, district staff needed to adopt a new mind-set, one that saw experimentation and tinkering as routine, because, as one NET staffer commented:

> In a mainframe sort of environment, if you touch something you're not supposed to touch, you get in trouble, and so it's almost a culture sort of thing where everything has to be checked through management to make sure they can do it first. . . . [T]he sorts of technologies we're working with, the only way you can really learn them is to break them, because only by breaking them do you see the consequences. And it's seeing the consequences of something breaking that give you the epiphany of, "Oh! That's how all this stuff fits together."

Finally, both NET and district technical staff observed that the district's technical staff already had sufficient work to keep busy aside from shouldering responsibilities for Internet access support or even for learning how to provide such support. Understandably, then, both groups were concerned about whether and to what extent district technical staff were acquiring the knowledge necessary to maintain NET's technical architecture and to support the expanded infrastructure that the technology plan envisioned.

Yet by the time NET ended, the division of technical affairs could and did support many aspects of the district's access to Internet resources. Its staff were able to maintain the district's central servers, which provided access to the Internet for district employees who did not have access through a school server, in spite of the fact that doing so required them to use the Unix programming language. In addition, they operated a central modem pool, a responsibility that NET had initially placed elsewhere. They were also able to help set up and maintain networking systems at individual schools. Although many involved with NET felt that the district technical staff should have learned still more about supporting Internet use, these were nevertheless notable accomplishments.

One basic and critical factor that facilitated building this knowledge was having a substantial amount of time in which to do so, a factor that also emphasizes the importance of a long-term commitment to institutionalization. Staff members developed the knowledge necessary to support NET's technical infrastructure over a period of years. Further, rather than transferring responsibility from NET to the district for the various systems all at once at the end of NET, transfer of responsibility occurred in stages. This strategy gave district staff excellent opportunities for ongoing learning because they could continue to seek assistance from NET staff when necessary after the formal transfer of specific technical responsibilities. For example, recall that the district's technical staff began to voluntarily grant and administer individual Internet accounts for educators at non-NET schools after purchasing a server in NET's third year and later took responsibility for operating a modem pool. During NET's fourth year, district staff were also responsible for the technical work required to set up three NET schools selected through the ACP. Later, they began to maintain the server that was the main point of Internet access for district administrators and others.

In addition to helping district technical staff build their knowledge gradually, NET staff also established deadlines for transferring technical responsibilities and adhered to them even when district employees did not appear entirely ready to assume the new tasks. This practice made it clear that no one's lackadaisical approach to learning or lack of time would keep the transfer of responsibility from taking place. In essence, NET staff created a situation that forced learning in the context of real problems, for once the deadline for transfer of responsibility for a task occurred district staff found themselves needing to be able to perform that activity effectively in order to avoid phone calls from frustrated teachers or administrators. NET technical staff soon discovered that district technical staff sometimes learned best when forced to fix real problems. As one NET staffer told us:

> We've had things where I've gone over and explained it, and it's asked again and I've gone over and explained it, and it's asked again and I've gone over and explained it, and then it's asked again and I don't explain it and it breaks. And then after it breaks I don't get asked it anymore because now they understand.

The district technical staff too found some merit in learning in the crises that failures in their knowledge created, in spite of the extra pressure this put on them. As a member of the district staff noted, it is difficult to know exactly what you do not know until you apply knowledge:

> I think before a crisis, it's really . . . I don't even know that I don't have the knowledge. [*Laughs.*] . . . But I think that's when the issue comes up, . . . when something goes wrong, then there's a transfer of knowledge.

Another district staff member asserted that outside of the context of a crisis it can be difficult to make knowledge acquisition a priority:

> Mark [Schneider, a director of the NET education staff], is, like, "*I'm turning* [the NET server] *off* [which meant that district technical personnel would have to operate the server] *on such and such a date and that's the end of that!!*" . . . I mean, sometimes he's a little insensitive to what the other people actually have to do in order to do this, but his persistence is a big deal. [Otherwise] it wouldn't happen because we're all too busy with other stuff.

Although there was substantial debate about the degree to which NET staff should spend time working actively with district staff to build their Internet-related technical knowledge and to help when crises occurred, staff in both groups generally agreed that crises sparked effective knowledge development. When coupled with transferring responsibility gradually and the availability of expert support from NET, crises enabled district staff to identify necessary additional training and to arrange opportunities to get that training.

NET staff also arranged a great many routine training sessions, and these too were essential to preparing district technical staff for their new duties. The most effective approach to these sessions, according to all concerned, placed NET and district personnel together to work collaboratively toward achieving a specific goal in a real-world setting such as a school. It was also useful, said district personnel, to work in situations similar to apprenticeships, in which district personnel assisted knowledgeable NET staff in solving technical problems. District personnel consistently emphasized that they learned best when they attempted to implement technical procedures themselves and had access to face-to-face assistance from NET staff when they ran into difficulties. NET staff supplemented such training experiences with written information on technical procedures and policies that they made available on-line. Finally, by joining the "trouble" account mailing list, district technical staff could also monitor the messages that teachers and others sent about technical difficulties and the NET staff responses to these inquiries. District staff generally praised the written information that was available and suggested that the more of this was available the better.

In sum, NET gave high priority to helping the district's existing technical staff members learn the things they needed to know in order to support Internet use in district schools. Development of such knowledge was not easy because those individuals already had a wide range of time-consuming duties. However, the two staffs used numerous mechanisms—including joint problem solving, apprenticeship-like relations, formal transfer of responsibility, and ongoing support—to create a learning environment in which district technical staff could expand their expertise and be ready to replace NET technical staff when external funding for NET ceased.

TRADE-OFFS AND COMPROMISES
What the District Did Not Institutionalize and Why

The WPS district institutionalized a number of NET's components, and the factors that led to this outcome are important. However, the district did not retain other NET components—in particular the emphasis on voluntary and self-directed teacher participation, teacher control over student access, and research and experimentation, and the factors behind this outcome are also of considerable interest. In particular, we will argue here that the district tended not to institutionalize aspects of the NET approach that exacerbated its ongoing problems or concerns. Consistent with findings reported in the literature on schools as institutions (Meyer et al., 1981), the district also tended to reject practices and policies that might make it appear that the district was drifting from community understandings about how a public school should operate.

Voluntary and Self-Directed Teacher Participation Versus Mandated Use for the Good of the System

As we discussed in Chapter Two, one hallmark of NET was its emphasis on voluntary and self-directed teacher participation in Internet activities. NET staff believed strongly that teacher commitment and creativity were best fostered through voluntary participation. Teachers decided whether they would participate, defined how they would use the Internet, and determined where and how often they would do so. Recall, for example, that NET teachers decided whether they wanted Internet access concentrated in computer labs or distributed across individual classrooms; they also developed their own Internet-supported curricula.

With the institutionalization of Internet access, the district dramatically curtailed the emphasis on educators' voluntary and self-directed participation. The technology plan as implemented placed Internet-connected computers in laboratories and mandated that English and language arts teachers at four predetermined grade levels guide students in their use. Thus, the district expected all English and language arts teachers at these grade levels to implement technology-enriched curricular activities, whether that was their preference or not. As one member of NET's education staff noted, centralized decisions that defined clearly how and when teachers would use technology "go kind of counter to what we believe here in Networking for Education." The reasoning behind this decision to locate technology use in English and language arts classrooms, however, was that it would encourage continuation of another key NET component, content-centered uses of technology, because the district saw access to the Internet as especially useful in teaching English and language arts. NET staff therefore viewed this decision as neither a failure to institutionalize nor as a prime instance of institutionalization of NET's approach but as a compromise.

Also consistent with reduced emphasis on voluntary teacher participation was the demise of the ACP described in Chapter Two. When the district institutionalized Internet use, it abandoned this process in favor of giving all schools Internet access and having the district define which schools would receive access first during a three-year rollout. (It is also of interest that the district considered variants of this decision. For example, the technology plan that preceded the one the district eventually adopted allowed individuals from schools slated to receive technology later in the planned rollout process to apply for early access through a proposal.)

Because many in the district regarded NET's ability to foster productive Internet use by educators as exemplary, it is worth considering what led the district to abandon these elements of NET's approach that were believed to have contributed to that productive use. The heart of the matter was that NET's goals and the district's goals for educational technology differed in a fundamental way. NET was oriented toward the empowerment of teachers and the creation of exemplary and innovative curricular uses of the Internet. Employing a competitive process for selection into NET and asking teachers to define when and how they would participate were program features highly compatible with these goals. In contrast, public schools have increasingly been expected to effectively address inequalities in resources and outcomes for different social and in particular ethnic groups. Consistent with this expectation, during the long process of devising an acceptable technology plan, various school board members asserted that it was critical to design a plan that guaranteed each and every child in the WPS the opportunity to make use of modern computer technology in some significant way. School board members also wanted a plan that ensured that these experiences would be standardized, so that students transferring from school to school would not miss such experiences and be behind their new classmates in technical skills. Access for all and standardized experiences had a particular appeal to policymakers in Waterford because the school district had grappled for years with marked inequalities in outcomes between its European American and African American students. Because of this situation, differences between schools in resources or basic curriculum were potentially very controversial.

Thus, any technology plan that allowed all teachers to decide when and under what conditions they would use computers for instructional purposes was unpalatable in light of existing district concerns.

First, such a plan would virtually guarantee that some students would have the opportunity to use computers, whereas others would not have or at the least would have much less access than others. Second, as WPS board members observed early in NET's life, competitive processes like the ACP can easily exacerbate inequities that already exist. They complained, for example, that WPS teachers from schools with relatively more affluent and more European American students were more likely to author winning NET proposals than were other teachers at least in part because they were more likely to have had the experience of writing proposals for other purposes or a history of participating in special programs. Moreover, even if all schools had equivalent technological resources, there would always be the possibility that the technology use selected by proposal would be focused in a niche serving nonrepresentative groups of students within the selected schools. This sometimes did occur at NET schools, and when it did the students served generally had a stronger academic record than their peers. Further, differences in the socioeconomic background of European American and African American students and the corresponding differences in their average levels of academic achievement meant that European American students sometimes had more Internet access than their African American schoolmates (Schofield and Davidson, in press-a).

Even if the district could have designed a method that both ensured voluntary participation and gave students of all types equal access to teachers who wished to use the Internet in instruction, voluntary participation poses an additional problem: it may create predictable inefficiencies in student learning. For example, students who did not use the Internet in class one year might find themselves mixed the following year with students from classes that had used it. The current teachers would have to let the untrained students catch up with the others on their own, waste some students' time by repeating basic Internet training, or try to devise a schedule to get the untrained students trained without wasting the others' time.

Student Internet Access

Teacher Control Versus District Policies

As we described in Chapter Two, NET gave teachers a great deal of control not only over whether and how they would participate but also over whether and how their students would access the Internet and its resources. So, for example, NET educators could create student Internet accounts as they wished. Students could use such accounts for a variety of purposes, including e-mail exchange, Web page construction, access to newsgroups, and somewhat more controversial uses such as Internet Relay Chat. Perhaps even more notably, NET staff did not try to put in place severe access limitations or software that filters out certain kinds of Internet material, although, as we described in Chapter Three, they did block some newsgroups early on. Rather, they encouraged teachers and other educators to develop policies and practices at the school level that would guard students against exposure to content or experiences that these educators deemed inappropriate.

With institutionalization of Internet use, however, the district implemented policies to ensure centralized control over students working on-line and to try to forestall student access to objectionable materials. First, the district put a concept-filtering policy into place, which resulted in the installation of a content filter designed to prevent certain sorts of materials—most notably those pertaining to sex and violence—from entering the district at all by way of the Internet. Second, although the district placed servers at non-NET schools, it did not train the teachers there who are in charge of performing basic technical functions in how to make student accounts, at least partly because of ongoing concerns in the central administration about the problems such accounts might create. Therefore, students at non-NET schools cannot use district-provided Internet access to create Web pages or to communicate through personal e-mail accounts with individuals in other places in the way students can at former NET schools. Although some students at non-NET schools have reportedly taken advantage of the free e-mail accounts and Web page space that some commercial Internet service providers offer, the policy of not promoting student accounts will inevitably limit and shape students' Internet use. In general, those with whom we spoke about student Internet use at non-NET schools reported that it consists predominantly of Web-based searches. Although resource constraints prevented us from independently investigating use at non-NET schools in the years following NET, this reported trend raises the possibility that some of the uses we describe in this book and the outcomes associated with them may be less prevalent in schools gaining Internet access through the district's technology plan than in those that gained access through NET.

For example, some of the outcomes we described in Chapter Seven, including exposure to a more diverse range of perspectives and experiences and an increased ability to produce quality work, are related to students' ability to interact with others on-line.

The district's concern about its reputation in the community and its desire to avoid unfavorable publicity, particularly in light of its long-standing problem with declining enrollment, certainly strengthened the hand of those who were hesitant to give students Internet accounts. The opportunities for communication that these accounts offer are controversial because, as we discussed in Chapter Three, they might bring students to the attention of those who might wish to harm or exploit them and because educators might lose control over the ways in which students present themselves and represent their schools and communities. As one individual explained, when NET was responsible for providing Internet access, the district tolerated its looser, less centralized control and its provision of student accounts because responsibility for the consequences of Internet access did not fall so squarely on the district itself. Furthermore, in the early days of NET, it is quite likely that at least some district policymakers did not fully recognize the range of the problems that might arise as a result of student Internet use because most of them were not themselves familiar with the Internet and because public discussion of such issues was not yet widespread. However, once the district assumed full responsibility for providing Internet access, it wished to be sure its policies would withstand scrutiny if problems did arise. As one NET staff member who had access to district discussions regarding this matter stated straightforwardly, "Once a district is responsible [for Internet access], it is a district issue and filtering is necessary."

A second reason that district administrators were concerned about student accounts was that they saw the specter of security breaches. The district now stores many student records on computers, and district officials responsible for record keeping expressed worry that students might find ways to access these records by way of their Internet accounts. In short, the district's desire to prevent incidents that might lead to internal problems or to questions from the public about its decision to provide students with access to the Internet led it to exercise much tighter control than NET staff did over the ways in which students work on-line. Although some degree of student Internet account use may eventually evolve in non-NET schools, tensions between this type of use and the district's public relations and security concerns will likely shape the extent to which this occurs and the ways it occurs.

Embarking on Uncertain Explorations Versus Implementing Known Practices

Ongoing research and evaluation were integral components of NET in both the educational and the technical arenas. The authors of this book and other members of the research staff, for example, received funding to consider the process and outcomes of Internet use in the schools. Further, the technical staff experimented with new practices by installing different server platforms in different schools, using different router configurations, trying out different means of supplying connectivity, and employing new versions of the Unix operating system. From the outset, there was essentially no effort to institutionalize the research evaluation components of NET. Among the reasons for this decision was the fact that the district had discontinued many of its own evaluation activities in light of budget constraints and personnel changes. Indeed, the extremely low priority the district gave to such activities was made evident when a high-ranking official tried to commandeer for other purposes money that NSF had earmarked explicitly for research and only backed off when those connected to NET made it clear they would not tolerate this. District staff also showed little interest in evaluating the technology plan, which may reflect not only a tight budget but also the high degree of public support for technology use that generally exists throughout the nation, so that the district saw little need to invest funds in such an evaluation. As one scholar of institutionalization notes, in public schools, it is often the case that "effectiveness is defined in terms of conformity to norms of the wider society about proper ways to organize, regardless of whether these can be shown to have any link to the quality of output" (Morris, 1996, p. 432). In other words, schools look effective in part if they conform to people's beliefs about how they should operate and appear, even if this has little or nothing to do with how well students and teachers perform.

However, because the district does have a division of technical affairs, NET personnel hoped that the district would commit itself to continued technical experimentation and innovation. In the end, however, the district did not institutionalize this component of NET either.

The district's ongoing budget committed no money to technical experimentation. Moreover, district staff chose not to use Unix, the operating system that NET had specifically chosen to use because it allows system administrators to experiment and because it is constantly evolving. NET technical staff had rejected suggestions to adopt various commercial alternatives, arguing that these were too likely to be static and to become outdated. In contrast, while NET schools retained their original UNIX-based operating systems, the district decided to employ one of these alternative commercial operating systems in all schools receiving Internet access through the technology plan.

Again, the decision not to institutionalize the technical experimentation that was integral to NET reflects the belief that continuation of such work would likely have exacerbated various ongoing district concerns. First, and perhaps most basic, operating system experimentation would likely not only have led to equipment expenditures above and beyond those needed to provide basic Internet access but also to higher expenditures on salaries. For example, hiring an experienced Unix programmer for the district proved to be essentially impossible because of the district's salary constraints for technical positions. Although it might well have been feasible to justify hiring an expensive programmer in terms of likely future cost savings relative to hiring outside vendors or consultants to keep up with technology changes, the district shied away from this step in light of pressing financial concerns.

It is also relevant that engaging in technical experimentation is not necessarily congruent with public images of what a school district should be doing. Indeed, throughout NET's life, staff in the division of technical affairs expressed ambivalence about institutionalizing technical experimentation, asserting that such experimentation is not appropriate in the context of a public school environment. Some members of division staff argued, for example, that a district's computer division should provide a dependable dial tone for computer network users rather than do things like experiment with different router configurations in the hope of eventually improving service or decreasing costs. One problem with technical experimentation is that one cannot guarantee that it will pay off. Moreover, it might well disrupt use of the network in the interim. Individuals in the division of technical affairs ultimately deemed commercial alternatives more practical than NET's approach, both because the district could purchase external support, requiring less time from district technical staff who might otherwise have to track developments in Unix or address major technical problems themselves, and because district staff believed that exploration and further development were more appropriately conducted by others. In short, members of this division ultimately chose to pursue reliability and efficiency rather than to risk the uncertainty and costs that can accompany experimentation.

CONCLUSIONS

Five factors played an especially significant role in helping NET achieve partial institutionalization: highlighting and amplifying a recognized district problem, offering and promoting a tried solution to that problem, becoming perceived as indispensable, building viable relationships with relevant parts of the bureaucracy, and helping individuals within the district develop the knowledge necessary to support institutionalization of Internet use. At the same time that the district institutionalized many aspects of NET, it did not institutionalize other aspects of NET that exacerbated or had the potential to exacerbate major ongoing concerns or problems in the district. Moreover, once NET ended, the district tended to modify or reject NET practices that might have raised public questions about whether the school district was operating as a school district should. In short, in accord with Web models that conceptualize computer systems and their use as complex social objects, we find that NET's organizational and historical context and the degree to which NET staff attended to and were able to respond to contextual factors heavily shaped NET's ultimate outcome.

Looking closely at the factors that promoted NET's partial institutionalization, we found that when NET highlighted a recognized problem in the district it also situated itself carefully within the district's broader organizational context, making itself look more like a potential ally and collaborator in the district's struggle to address its dearth of a modern technological infrastructure for its students and teachers rather than like a project promoting an innovation that did not meet existing needs. That is, NET's goal of institutionalizing Internet use in the district was consistent with the district's self-assessment that it needed to improve in the realm of technology, and NET staff and team members worked to keep this problem in the forefront of policymakers' minds. Of course, the explosion in technology use that occurred during NET's life also helped very significantly in this regard. Nevertheless, NET staff's ardent efforts to familiarize policymakers with contemporary technology and to remind them that funding for such technology was likely to go to those who acted quickly worked quite effectively to keep the need for a technology plan salient even in the context of other pressing problems in the district.

Further, although NET in some ways exacerbated the district's problem of antiquated technology by creating a groundswell of demand for Internet access and the relatively powerful computers necessary to support such access, it suggested solutions at the same time. Specifically, the district came to see NET as offering a tried and reliable approach that teachers and students would use enthusiastically and productively. As an individual high in the district hierarchy put it:

> At least we could [with NET]—point to practice and say "This stuff really works," and "Here's how it works" and so forth. So I think that it . . . helped bring practical application to the table . . . and sort of helped us think through guiding principles and so forth.

Moreover, because teachers are often reluctant to participate in externally based change efforts, their great interest and enthusiasm for NET was especially striking. NET staff made sure they did all that was possible to make policymakers aware of NET's positive reputation at the classroom level, a critical strategy that contributed importantly to institutionalization.

We have also emphasized that NET's institutionalization was multifaceted. That is, in addition to NET's technology and methods being adapted, NET personnel—specifically its education staff—were hired by the district, despite the fact that the district faced a significant and ongoing deficit and that new hiring was at a standstill. The hiring of the education staff in turn greatly increased opportunities to institutionalize less tangible aspects of NET—namely its general philosophy and procedures. The education staff members integrated their roles into the district by making themselves essentially indispensable on a variety of fronts and by demonstrating tremendous energy, the willingness to work very hard, and a diverse array of talents. They had the ability to bring in external funding, to work effectively with classroom teachers, and to carry out a wide variety of technical and professional development tasks. The NET education staff made sure that policymakers knew of the many different activities they carried out and challenged district staff to identify other individuals who might assume these duties in the future. Moreover, no group or individual stepped forward to challenge the assertion that NET staff had the most creative and clear-cut ideas for implementing instructional technology as well as the practical skills for carrying out the implementation.

Finally, in order for Internet use to continue among teachers and students in the district after NET ended, it was critical to help the district's technical staff develop knowledge—in particular technical expertise and troubleshooting capabilities related to wide-area networking—that would not otherwise be available in the district at that time. That is, NET staff needed not only to convince district staff of the educational worth of Internet use but also to prepare some of those staff to carry out critical technical activities. Further, because the technical knowledge that district staff needed was diverse and complex, NET staff had to form positive working relationships and set up training with key individuals long before NET's end. Owing to the initially tense and at times even adversarial relationships between NET and district staff and the numerous existing responsibilities of district technical staff, this was no small task.

Several things helped NET staff improve relationships with NET critics in the district bureaucracy, including those with technical responsibilities. First, NET staff implemented strategies designed to involve district employees in making decisions about Internet use, and ultimately the district rather than the universities became the institution to which the external funds supporting Internet use flowed. These factors increased the sense of district ownership markedly, with a consequent positive change in attitudes toward NET. Second, NET shared ideas with various district staff and learned to invite their input as well as hiring district insiders (namely, former teachers and support staff). This helped to further the spirit of collaboration and to develop increased trust. Third, NET staff highlighted the fact that if the district were to institutionalize Internet use, district employees who assumed responsibility for former NET activities would become even more important to the district's functioning because so many individuals were clamoring for Internet access. This likely motivated individuals concerned about their job status in a district that was downsizing. Such strategies might well be of use in fostering institutionalization in the context of other change efforts or districts.

Finally, there is something to be learned from considering the nuts and bolts of how NET helped individuals in the district develop the technical knowledge they needed. One factor that supported this learning was gradually moving control of and responsibility for some

NET activities to appropriate district personnel. This staggered transfer of responsibility occurred over a period of years. NET also established and generally adhered to deadlines for the transfer of responsibility, but its staff were available to assist if necessary even after the transfer of responsibility took place. This allowed district staff to take responsibility with the knowledge that help would still be available if an unsolvable problem occurred. NET staff also conducted formal and informal training sessions designed to expand the district technical staff's knowledge. The most effective of these sessions arranged for NET and district personnel to work collaboratively toward achieving tangible technical accomplishments.

In sum, it appears that schools can achieve substantial institutionalization of an innovation even when the odds against it initially appear high. Nevertheless, it is also critical to bear in mind that the district did not institutionalize many potentially important aspects of NET even though they appeared to be successful in many ways. When aspects of a change effort threaten to make a district's existing difficulties worse, the district may well reject them unless someone finds a way to remove whatever threat they contain. For example, laboring under financial constraints, the WPS district did not budget for teacher professional development, a vital component of NET, in the technology plan it eventually adopted. But when former NET staff raised the money from foundation sources to support this activity, the district did not oppose it. Although every school district presents a unique social and political context, we believe that those concerned with achieving institutionalized change can learn from considering both the strategies that NET employed successfully and the factors that worked against the institutionalization of some aspects of NET.

CHAPTER NINE

Conclusion

⟿

In Chapter One, we pointed out that although schools in the United States and around the world have spent billions of dollars to connect students and teachers to the Internet a number of fundamental questions about Internet use in schools remain unanswered. Specifically, little solid evidence exists about the impact of Internet use on teachers and students. Further, scholars know relatively little about the challenges that schools will have to meet in order to maximize the potential of Internet use to improve education. In this concluding chapter, we try to draw lessons from our study of NET that will be helpful to others interested in the theory and practice of attempting to enhance students' education through Internet tools and resources.

Two issues arise immediately. The first is the extent to which it is reasonable to distill general lessons from the study of one attempt to bring the Internet into the classrooms of a particular school district. The second is the rapid pace of technological change, which makes any book about the Internet likely to be at least somewhat dated by the time it is in readers' hands.

Three factors should contribute to making the lessons emerging from NET broadly useful. First, although NET occurred in the context of a single district and a particular time frame, the schools we studied were highly varied in terms of their size, their students' ages and backgrounds, and the kinds of Internet activities they undertook. Second, in selecting lessons to emphasize, we have drawn not only on our experiences studying NET but also on broader knowledge about Internet use in schools that we gathered from eight years of involvement with this topic through activities such as reading what other researchers have written, talking with educators from the United States and elsewhere, participating on advisory committees for other major efforts to bring the Internet to schools, and serving on a pertinent committee at the National Academy of Sciences. We have elected to discuss here only those lessons from NET that our broader knowledge suggests are likely to be relevant to other situations. Third, we have supplied extensive information about NET and the school district in which it was located because the extent to which lessons emerging from NET are likely to be applicable in other settings depends heavily on the extent to which those settings and the Internet uses undertaken there are similar to NET's settings and uses. Readers of this book can use this information to make informed judgments about the extent to which the lessons we draw from NET are likely to apply to their own situations.

To address the issue of technological change, we argue that although rapid technological change is undeniable and important to keep in mind, its existence does not vitiate the usefulness of understanding NET or of drawing lessons from our study of it. Of course, the Internet and associated technology have developed drastically since NET was started, and they are likely to continue to change at a rapid pace. Some of these changes, such as the emergence of the World Wide Web and its readily used search tools, the potential increases in the speed of connection that schools are likely to be able to purchase, and the increasing power and decreasing price of laptop computers, have potentially major implications for the Internet's use and likely impact in education. For example, increased bandwidth makes it much more feasible for students to access graphic materials on the Internet than it was when NET began. Further, some school districts have begun to supply their students with Internet-ready laptop computers, a strategy highly likely to increase students' Internet use. Where we believe that changes in technology or in the nature of the Internet are particularly likely to influence the applicability of the lessons we draw here, we explore that influence.

However, as we discussed in Chapter Three, schools and the teachers and students within them change much less rapidly than technology. Most of the factors we and others have found important in shaping teachers' and students' reactions to Internet use are longstanding characteristics of our educational system and seem unlikely to change dramatically in the near future. To take just one example, it seems unlikely that the factors we discussed in Chapter Four, such as teachers' conceptualization of the classroom as a private domain for independent professional action, the tendency toward batch processing of students, and the fact that teachers' time is a scarce resource, will change markedly in the foreseeable future because of their deep roots in our current educational system and the myriad forces reinforcing them. Instead, it seems likely that such factors will continue to have an impact on how schools use the Internet even as technology becomes cheaper, faster, and more ubiquitous, although it is also true that the implications of such factors could change as technology changes. Thus, in thinking about the extent to which the lessons emerging from NET apply to other situations, it is important to weigh the extent to which the Internet technology in the two situations differs and to identify the implications of this variation. Being aware of this fact and wishing to make our conclusions as useful as possible, we have made a point of focusing on those lessons from NET that we believe to be of broad applicability across a range of technical setups.

THE INTERNET'S IMPACT IS VARIABLE, OFTEN POSITIVE, AND STRONGEST ON DIMENSIONS OTHER THAN ACADEMIC ACHIEVEMENT

There is little reason to believe that Internet access will fundamentally transform education or its outcomes as some expect it will. Indeed, one lesson readers should learn is that the outcomes of Internet access are likely to be extremely variable. First, of course, levels of Internet use varied greatly from school to school, in spite of the fact that NET educators had volunteered, indeed even competed, to obtain Internet access. Use was quite low at numerous schools, and without use Internet access is extremely unlikely to have any significant impact on education. In addition, as we discussed in Chapter Five, the kind of use also varied markedly. For example, some teachers tended to use the Internet primarily as an archive, and others tended to use it mostly for communication. Furthermore, some Internet uses were much more central to the curriculum than others. Thus, once again, variation in outcomes seems to be related to the ways that educators use the Internet and the extent to which Internet activities focus on topics integral to the curriculum. Finally, as we discussed in Chapter Four, students in the same school, and even in the same classroom, sometimes ended up with different levels of Internet access, a situation that also presumably increases variation in outcomes.

In spite of the great variation in the amount and kind of Internet use apparent in NET schools and the disparities between students' levels of access, certain generally positive changes did accompany Internet use frequently enough to appear to be likely consequences of such use. For instance, as we discussed in Chapters Six and Seven, Internet use appeared to increase teachers' and students' use of up-to-date and extensive educational resources, including the expertise of others with whom they communicated. It also gave students new opportunities to learn in the context of meaningful experiences embedded in real-world situations. Furthermore, it often increased students' motivation, their acquisition of technical skills, and their ability both to share their work with those outside the school and to work cooperatively with such others.

In addition to such changes, which were generally consistent with teachers' goals for Internet activities, Internet use also frequently fostered classroom changes that educators had neither anticipated nor designed. These included more positive student-teacher relations, the emergence of new and constructive student roles, and increased student independence. These and many other outcomes of Internet use discussed earlier in this book are potentially significant positive changes in the context in which students and teachers function. However, such outcomes are not inevitable. Indeed, we saw cases in which Internet use was structured so that it seemed unlikely to result in many of the outcomes just mentioned. However, in conditions similar to those prevailing in NET, a significant subset of teachers, classrooms, and students are likely, we believe, to achieve such outcomes.

Because of the generally positive changes that often accompanied Internet use, it is hardly surprising that NET team members were typically very favorable about the Internet as an educational resource. For example, of the NET team members ($N = 36$) who experienced Internet access in their classes and whom we then interviewed about the trade-offs they would be willing to make to have such access in the future, 97 percent reported that they would prefer having Internet access to reducing class size by one student. Furthermore, 86 percent said they would prefer it to receiving $500 a year for instructional resources of their choice, and 66 percent even indicated a willingness to teach one additional class period a week in order to free up the time for a teacher to provide Internet technical support to their schools. Thus, NET educators valued Internet access very strongly, in spite of all the problems and difficulties associated with it (see Chapters Three and Four). Indeed, when teachers and librarians using NET Internet accounts ($N = 321$) judged in an on-line survey how the effort they put into education-related Internet activities compared with the overall worth of these activities to themselves and their students, the most popular response was the most positive option available, that the Internet's "value far outweighs effort" (42 percent). Only about 7 percent selected either of the two options that indicated that the effort put into using the Internet was greater than the Internet's value. Finally, the strength of educators' positive reaction to the Internet was made clear when they completed this sentence fragment: "If I heard that next year they were going to take Internet access away at [my school], I would . . ." NET team members completing this sentence ($N = 35$) typically indicated that they would respond with negative emotions such as sadness, disappointment, or anger (48 percent), or with attempts to retain access or find other means of access (28 percent). The emotion in their reactions was palpable; responses like "fight" or "cry" were very common. Some teachers even responded, no doubt with hyperbole, "kill myself" or "consider quitting." Readers should keep in mind that NET educators had volunteered to participate in NET and thus might well be more positive than their peers about Internet use. However, Becker's work (1999b) suggests that other teachers feel the same. For example, almost half of the teachers responding to a national survey regarding Internet use characterized access to the World Wide Web as "essential" to their teaching, and almost 90 percent saw it as either "valuable" or "essential."

Elementary and high school students' ($N = 24$) responses to questions about their reactions to not having Internet access were similar to those of their teachers'. For example, students reported that they would "fight it and protest," "be sad," and "be highly upset" if they learned their schools would no longer have Internet access. Consistent with such positive sentiments were the reactions of high school students ($N = 23$) who were asked whether they would prefer "a class where the Internet is used or the same class where it is not used." Almost 90 percent of these students chose the former, commonly citing both their enjoyment of Internet use and its usefulness in their work.

Nevertheless, in spite of the strong positive reactions from teachers and students, we have little reason to believe that Internet use can be expected to have a strong effect on students' performance on the kinds of standardized tests typically used to measure achievement in school subjects. Although, for the reasons we discussed in Chapter Seven, we did not set out to study changes in academic achievement flowing from Internet use, our work does provide numerous reasons to question whether policymakers, parents, and educators can realistically expect such use to routinely foster significant amounts of such change in the relatively near future. First, with a few exceptions, such as the elementary school teachers who felt that using the Internet improved their students' reading ability, teachers were unlikely to report improved academic achievement as a consequence of Internet use. For example, only two of twenty-three teachers, when asked a general question about the impact of the Internet on student outcomes, mentioned changes in subject matter skill (specifically, improvements in foreign language reading or writing skills), although all mentioned one or another kind of change they valued. Consistent with this, when middle and high school students ($N = 29$) were asked to indicate how much having the Internet available had contributed to their learning in several areas, they were more than twice as likely to say that they had learned a lot of computer (72 percent) or research (72 percent) skills than to say they had learned a great deal of subject matter material (34 percent).

Perhaps one reason that NET teachers and students did not see increased academic achievement as a strong, clear outcome of Internet use was that such improvement was often not teachers' primary goal for Internet activities. Although teachers were free to pursue whatever goals they wished when developing Internet activities, only about one-third of the groups submitting proposals to the annual competitive process even mentioned increased achievement in subject matter areas. A larger or roughly equal proportion of proposals mentioned other goals, such as preparing students to live in a world in which technology plays an important role (43 percent), expanding students' global awareness (37 percent), and supporting interdisciplinary curriculum efforts (35 percent). Although increased academic achievement might be a by-product of Internet use in the service of other goals, such an outcome does not seem too likely unless teachers specifically seek it, and even then a linkage is not inevitable. Indeed, as we discussed in Chapter One, one of the few extensive studies of the impact of the Internet on the learning of science concluded after four years of research that the Internet was less promising as a tool to improve learning than researchers expected and that face-to-face communication plays a central role in learning (Feldman et al., 2000). Similarly, another study (Songer, 1996) concluded that the learning of students using the Internet was very similar to that of students in similar classes without Internet access.

In short, on-line activities are not currently a panacea for poor test scores. Further, measuring the Internet's value to students' education by this metric may well be inappropriate. As we discussed in Chapter Seven, the fact that the Internet is a flexible tool that different individuals can use for a wide variety of purposes makes precise assessment of its impact much more complex and problematic than assessment of the impact of technological tools that have more bounded and focused uses, such as artificially intelligent tutors designed to teach specific subject matter. At a minimum, attempts to assess the utility of the Internet for education need to start with a careful assessment of the goals that Internet use is intended to serve. Assessors should not assume that standardized test scores are the appropriate metric.

Many resources designed to help educators use the Internet to increase subject matter knowledge are now available that were not available or widely known during the NET years. Other developments, such as the trend toward relatively inexpensive handheld wireless devices that can connect to the Internet, are giving educators many practical options for Internet use that were not typically available in NET classrooms. Thus, it would be premature to conclude that Internet use in the future will not increase academic achievement as it is most commonly measured.

However, to make increased academic achievement a realistic goal, educators must give serious thought to the specific kinds of added value the Internet brings to the educational process in various subjects. Bransford, Brown, and Cocking (1999) suggest that there are several ways in which the Internet can be particularly useful in schools. First, it can create new opportunities for learning by bringing real-world problems into the classroom, by letting students find problems to study as well as solving problems that educators set for them, and by letting students interact with experts in a variety of ways. Second, it can facilitate students' work with and provision of feedback to each other. Third, it can create closer connections between the school and the community as well as help teachers overcome their sense of isolation by linking them to peers around the nation. NET schools made use of virtually all of these uses of the Internet, and some seemed more likely to lead directly to measurable gains in student achievement than others. However, the important point here is that it is not access to the Internet itself that holds promise for increasing academic achievement but thoughtful use of that access in a manner designed to take advantage of the particular ways in which the Internet can improve the learning environment of a school or classroom. For example, the Internet holds clear potential for improving foreign language learning because it opens up the possibility that students can readily access a wide variety of material in the language they are studying and can communicate with native speakers of a foreign language. Communication with such individuals is unlikely to be available in the students' classroom and is likely to be educative if well structured. Certainly, it seems likely to add more academic value than communication with individuals who are not substantially more expert in the language than students' classmates are, an activity that occurred in some NET classrooms. Similarly, students' use of the Internet to consult dictionaries or other materials that may well be readily available in the classroom in books seems unlikely to improve their learning substantially, whereas their use of the Internet to access age-appropriate focused resources pertinent to the curriculum but unavailable to them otherwise would seem likely to have a much higher payoff. In sum, there is no guarantee that Internet access will have a measurable impact on students' scores on many of the standardized tests that drive so much of our educational system. Those wishing to use the Internet to this end will need to carefully determine the curriculum areas in which Internet access may add the greatest value, rather than assuming that this technology will automatically yield improved test scores.

INTERNET USE HAS THE POTENTIAL TO EMPOWER STUDENTS IN NEW AND USEFUL WAYS

Students in U.S. schools, especially secondary schools, often play rather passive roles. In fact, Goodlad's massive study (1984, p. 109) of schools in the United States concluded:

> The intellectual terrain is laid out by the teacher. The paths for walking though it are largely predetermined by the teacher. For the most part, the teachers controlled rather firmly the central role of deciding what, where, when, and how their students were to learn. . . . The picture that emerges . . . is one of students increasingly conforming, not assuming an increasingly independent decision-making role in their own education.

This occurs in spite of the fact that "teachers verbalize the importance of students increasingly becoming independent learners" (p. 109). Yet there is reason to believe that students' perception that they have some control contributes to increased motivation (Ames, 1990) and that feeling in control is related to students' positive attitudes toward school (Henderson & Dweck, 1990). Furthermore, recent reform efforts have emphasized the crucial importance of students' active involvement in authentic, challenging tasks (Means, 1994).

Our study suggests, as do others, that Internet use brings with it the possibility of creating active, empowering roles for students, especially at the middle and high school levels (Neilsen, 1998; Peck, Cuban, & Kirkpatrick, 2000). As we mentioned in Chapter Six, students often felt more independent when using the Internet than they did at other times, and Internet access fostered the emergence of new and active student roles ranging from student assistant to tutor to technical expert. Involvement in such roles seemed useful to both the students involved and to others. Students assuming such roles often expanded their existing technical knowledge substantially in the context of situations in which they had to solve actual problems rather than the less compelling problems that educators constructed just for teaching purposes that are typical of classrooms. The knowledge thus gained was undoubtedly of use to many students in preparing for the job market or for further education in technical areas. In addition, many of these students found the experience of having others, especially their teachers, recognize their expertise by calling on them for help highly gratifying, because it made them feel more valued and mature.

The emergence of these new student roles typically seemed not only beneficial for the students involved but extremely helpful to peers, teachers, and others in the broader school community. For example, students at one NET school in a technically oriented program took major responsibility for planning and installing the wiring necessary to bring Internet access to many of their school's classrooms. They also prepared computers for Internet access and took responsibility for a wide variety of related tasks including installing computer hardware and updating software, tasks that gave their peers and teachers resources they would not have had otherwise.

Internet access also empowered students by making it easier for them to pursue their own interests within school contexts. For example, using the Internet, high school students conducted research projects on topics of special interest to them under the guidance of mentors expert in those subjects. Other students posted materials on the Internet in order to receive feedback from others with relevant specialized knowledge when no one with equivalent knowledge of the topic was available within their school.

However, the Internet's potential to enhance students' independence and their active involvement in their own education will be fully realized only if schools adopt such empowerment as a goal and carefully plan to make it happen. If policymakers and teachers do not value empowerment, they are unlikely to create conditions that foster it, and students will exhibit only those modest increases in it that may occur as by-products of some teachers' needs for student assistance with Internet use in the classroom or of the extra demands that the incorporation of Internet activities into their classrooms makes on teachers. Creating conditions that foster student empowerment requires both attention and resources. For example, one NET school found that its plans to have elementary students serve as peer and parent trainers foundered over the difficulty of finding a time during the school day to train students to fulfill those roles. Teachers in other NET schools found not only that it took considerable time and effort to locate mentors who could assist students with special projects but that sometimes they simply could not find such mentors. They also found that unless they had made advance arrangements to get feedback from knowledgeable sources, student work posted on the Internet sometimes stimulated few or no constructive responses. In addition, not all students were well equipped to pursue their own interests effectively on the Internet. Some did not have the required Internet skills; many others tended to drift off to recreational sites if educators did not structure their work sufficiently well and monitor them. In addition, students often did not have the research and critical thinking skills to make wise judgments about the balance and accuracy of the materials they encountered on the Internet.

Schools hoping to foster students' independence and active involvement through their Internet use will have to deal constructively with such issues. For example, they will have to make time in teachers' schedules for developing and coordinating Internet activities that facilitate students' pursuit of their own interests within a subject area and simultaneously ensure that students learn the core material in that area. Schools will have to recognize that setting up many Internet activities is likely to be more time-consuming and complicated than making plans that do not require coordination with others and that educators may well have to reformulate Internet activities annually due to the ever-changing availability of mentors and opportunities, the changing circumstances of collaborators, and the varying interests of individual students.

Furthermore, schools will need to recognize that making efficient and constructive use of the Internet requires skills that not all students have. The increasingly wide availability of home Internet access and school laptops seems likely to reduce this problem over time. However, the continued existence of the *digital divide,* the gap in computer access and skills between those with more and those with less privileged backgrounds, makes it important to deliberately train students in these skills. Moreover, educators must teach students effective search strategies and ways to distinguish between information that is likely to be reliable and that which is not, a skill that one NET teacher felt she needed to develop in her students but that she characterized as "a problem" because it involved "turning away from the teaching" of her subject matter. Although more and better resources than were available to NET teachers for dealing with such issues have recently emerged (see, for example, Burbules & Callister, 2000), the practical question of where such information fits in the school curriculum is far from solved. Moreover, it is not likely that educators will find a single solution to this problem, since students can vary so markedly in terms of such critical factors as prior Internet experience, prior research and analysis experience, age, and so on.

Finally, schools must recognize that empowering students through Internet use is likely to entail some risks. Students may hack (or tamper with) the systems they are supposed to be administering, harm others by spreading rumors by e-mail or posting doctored visual images, or seek out or be inadvertently exposed to various materials that teachers and parents alike would agree are inappropriate for children and youths. This last risk brings us to consideration of another important lesson emerging from NET: schools need to carefully and creatively foster responsible Internet behavior.

SCHOOLS NEED TO FOSTER
RESPONSIBLE INTERNET BEHAVIOR

The Internet connects schools and those in them to the world outside, perhaps the Internet's biggest advantage. Yet this also poses one of the Internet's biggest problems. Once logged onto the Internet, individuals can access all manner of materials that educators and most parents are likely to deem inappropriate or objectionable. Whether or not such material is actually harmful to students—an outcome that depends both on the exact content of the material and various characteristics of the student viewing it—access to it from school may pose a major public relations problem. Furthermore, the Internet may be used as a channel of communication between students and adults outside the school who may wish to exploit or harm them. Although we are aware of no such problems arising in NET, such individuals do exist, and some use the Internet to contact children.

Many school districts have responded to concerns about student access to objectionable material by installing filtering or blocking software designed to keep such material out of the school, as the Waterford district did when it institutionalized Internet activities. It is likely that most schools will have no practical choice but to adopt such software, because current legislation mandates the use of filters by schools receiving subsidies through the very popular E-rate program.

Nevertheless, even schools that have filters in place must find effective ways to teach responsible Internet behavior (COPA, 2000; Computer Science and Telecommunications Board, National Research Council, 2001). This is a pressing need for many reasons. First, filters are far from foolproof. A study in *Consumer Reports* (2001) finds that they let through a substantial amount of objectionable material (which the article defines as material that has explicit sexual content or that promotes crime, bigotry, violence, tobacco use, or drug use) and that their effectiveness has not increased notably in the last four years. Second, filters are relatively easily circumvented by individuals with technical skills, and there are even Web sites that provide instructions for this task, so "There is no way to prevent determined youth from finding their way to 'inappropriate' material if they are motivated to do so, especially when they are pooling their skills and sharing things that they find with one another" (Burbules & Callister, 2000, p. 110). Third, although filters may prevent students from accessing certain Web sites, many do not prevent students from receiving e-mail from those who might wish to take advantage of them or from participating in Internet Relay Chat sessions, which are notorious for their unrestrained and highly sexualized interchanges. Fourth, filters do not prevent students from engaging in behaviors potentially harmful to themselves or others, including posting material about themselves that others could use to harm them, posting false and hurtful information about others, and hacking into others' accounts. Finally, although the filters that schools use reduce students' exposure to certain kinds of material at school, they do nothing to foster responsible Internet use outside the school, a critical omission in an era when Internet access is becoming ubiquitous. The proliferation of school-provided laptop computers makes this issue even more pressing, because such equipment gives students the potential to access the Internet by way of a service provider that does not employ filtering software.

As we discussed in Chapter Three, NET used two main approaches to foster responsible Internet behavior. The first was an acceptable use policy (AUP). Like most AUPs, NET's policy made Internet access contingent on students' and parents' signing an agreement that outlined appropriate and inappropriate kinds of Internet use and stated that students' access to the Internet could be revoked for policy violations. Such policies are very common; roughly 90 percent of the school districts in the United States have them (Willard, 2000). The second approach was to have NET teachers set up their own policies and procedures regarding students' appropriate use of the Internet, thus encouraging teachers to supervise their Internet-using students to the degree they felt was necessary given the students' ages, computer skills, and the like.

These approaches have much to recommend them, although each has its downside. The AUP involved a considerable amount of paperwork. Also, it raised the possibility (rarely realized in reality) that certain students would not be allowed to use the Internet, which would clearly complicate efforts to integrate Internet use fully with the curriculum. The downside of expecting close teacher supervision of Internet use, in addition to putting yet one more demand on teachers' time and attention, was that teachers might strongly limit potentially useful student access in order to avoid the possibility of problems.

These two approaches, along with NET's extremely limited attempts to block certain kinds of material early in its life, appeared quite successful; the number of serious incidents arising from inappropriate use was extremely small. However, in our view, NET would have better served students' interests had it found additional ways to actively support and encourage responsible Internet use. Of the secondary school students we interviewed in our research on this topic ($N = 54$), one-third reported being aware of specific infractions of the AUP. About half of the reported infractions involved visits to sexually explicit sites like Playboy and PornHall. The others ranged from printing out of bomb-making instructions to hacking into others' files to using teachers' or other students' accounts. Whether or not one considers such behaviors as actively harmful to students or others, it does seem clear that when students spend school time on such activities they are distracted from more responsible uses of their time and their school's resources.

Interviews we conducted with high school students ($N = 48$) in the spring of the school year suggested that many students in NET classrooms had only the vaguest notion of the behavior they had agreed to in signing NET's AUP the preceding fall, and some did not even remember having signed it. Interchanges like the following were common:

INTERVIEWER: Did your teacher tell you any rules for behavior [while using the Internet]?

HANNAH: No.

INTERVIEWER: Do you remember signing an Ethics Policy [the name used for the AUP in Hannah's school]?

HANNAH: Yeah.

INTERVIEWER: Do you remember any specific rules from that?

HANNAH: No, I don't.

Like Hannah, many students reported that their teachers had not laid down any rules or guidelines about Internet use. When students did remember specific guidelines or rules, they tended to say that they recalled comments of this sort their teacher had made in class rather than provisions of the written AUP. Our findings suggest that although NET's AUP protected the school district by stating the conditions under which students could be deprived of Internet access, it was not particularly effective at educating students about the choices they were likely to have to make. Thus, it seems reasonable to suggest that schools should make a place in the curriculum to deal seriously with such issues. Although explicitly covering such material in the classroom does not guarantee that all students will profit from it, devoting school time to acceptable use issues does signal their importance as well as provide a clear opportunity for learning.

Finally, one occurrence during the NET years suggests that students are not the only denizens of schools who need to be encouraged to make responsible use of the Internet. This was the admittedly unusual case of a teacher who used a NET computer to access and download pornographic materials, which a student then discovered on the computer. Interestingly, this teacher seemed to feel quite put upon when the school principal questioned such behavior. Similar behavior has been reported in other workplaces as well, suggesting that as Internet access becomes more widespread in schools, districts should consider developing and adopting AUPs for adults as well as students.

MEASURES OF EQUALITY OF ACCESS TO TECHNOLOGICAL RESOURCES NEED TO BE EXPANDED

Both NET and Watertown Public Schools (WPS) staff were sensitive to the issue of equality of access to technology for students with different backgrounds. Indeed, the original NET grant listed "achieving equality" as one of its four basic goals. The facts that for much of NET's life the WPS school board president and the head of the board's technology subcommittee were African American and that WPS faced a long-standing and troublesome achievement gap between its European American and African American students contributed to a political and policy environment in which equity and equality were salient issues. Yet, as we discussed in Chapter Four, in NET classes with a heterogeneous student body, a variety of factors frequently produced circumstances in which students who were advantaged in comparison to their peers received more Internet access. Further, as we have discussed elsewhere (Schofield & Davidson, in press-a), access tended to be located in particular niches in NET schools that served relatively advantaged students. So, for example, a full 25 percent of the 99 Internet curriculum activities described by NET teachers responding to a survey about their Internet use occurred in classes serving exclusively or primarily academically advanced students, whereas fewer than 5 percent of these activities were focused on lower-achieving students.

The fact that such phenomena occurred in NET, which had enhancing equality as one of its major goals, presents something of a paradox. We believe the best explanation for these outcomes is the fact that NET staff and WPS policymakers and staff tended to think about equality of access in a way currently quite common in the United States—in terms of equality in the amount of technology available in schools serving students of different backgrounds. Thus, for example, after some WPS school board members complained heatedly that not enough schools serving predominantly African American communities had been selected as early NET schools, individuals associated with NET made special efforts to bring the Internet to a set of these schools to redress the situation. However, to our knowledge, issues within schools, such as the tendency for Internet access to be more common in classes populated with relatively advanced students and the tendency toward unequal student Internet access within heterogeneous classrooms, never became issues. Neither NET nor district staff appeared to notice these inequalities.

The way that individuals connected with NET and the WPS think about equality mirrors the way that others think of and measure equality. For example, the National Center for Education Statistics produces frequently updated information about computer and Internet access in U.S. schools [http://nces.ed.gov/pubsearch/pubsinfo.asp?pubid=1999017]. This information compares computer and Internet access in schools with varying proportions of minority students and with varying proportions of students eligible for free or reduced-price lunch. It also compares the percentages of rooms with Internet access in schools serving different populations. However, it gives no statistics that show which students within a school or a classroom typically get the use of the technology resources there. Other major studies take a similar approach (Anderson & Ronnkvist, 1999). The information that such sources provide, which currently suggests continuing though narrowing disparities in Internet access between schools serving students from minority and majority group backgrounds, is undeniably very useful. However, a focus on such data alone could lead one to the false conclusion that students from disparate backgrounds have access to the same level of technological resources when this is not the case, owing to the kinds of within-school processes we describe in this book.

GIVING A HIGH PRIORITY TO HUMAN INFRASTRUCTURE

When anyone mentions bringing the Internet to schools, the image that comes to mind is one of physical changes such as the laying of wires and the arrival of file servers, network cards, and classroom computers. Indeed, such events were crucial to NET, as they have been to other efforts to bring the Internet to schools around the country. However, our study of NET suggests that just as crucial to constructive Internet use but more easily overlooked is the provision of a social and organizational environment that will foster such use. Such an environment has numerous components, as we discussed in Chapter Five and elsewhere in this book. Here, we highlight some of the components that seemed to be especially important.

First, it is crucial that adequate technical training be available to teachers. It is reasonable to predict that more and more teachers will bring computer and Internet skills to their jobs as Internet use becomes part of daily life and that access to the Internet's resources will become increasingly easy, and these events might seem to make such training unnecessary. However, because of the rapid pace of technical change, the large number of teachers who lack even basic computer and Internet skills, and the fact that schools of education have been slow to make the development of computer and Internet skills a high priority, it seems reasonable to expect that training will remain an important need for years to come. Despite the obviousness of this point and the existence of federal initiatives designed to help school districts pay for this training, the districts, hard pressed for money, still often neglect to supply the resources necessary for effective training. For example, although professional development for teachers was a highly salient and valued part of NET, the WPS technology plan that the district adopted toward the end of NET's life did not set aside a substantial amount of money for such efforts. Rather, the district relied primarily on external funding that former NET staff in the district's unit of instructional technology garnered from foundations to support technical training for WPS educators.

Educators need not only an opportunity to build their skills in using technology but also readily available technical support for times when problems develop. As we discussed in Chapter Three, teachers depend on tried and true practices and often have to work within constraints set by the class schedule in their schools, so things like technical glitches that disrupt their plans for a class discourage Internet use. NET was well aware of this issue and in response worked hard to develop school-level expertise so that a great deal of problem solving could be done at the school level, thus expediting the solution of technical problems. However, considerable outside support was also necessary. For example, in one nine-month period, NET's centralized, on-line troubleshooting service dealt with over seven hundred e-mailed requests from district educators for assistance with general computing, networking software, hardware, and so on. Handling many of these problems required multiple e-mail exchanges, phone calls, and school visits by NET staff, all in addition to the ongoing training and routine support that NET supplied on its own initiative. Thus, school districts must not think of technical training as a one-time effort; technical training and support are ongoing needs that only increase with the constant changes in the technical world. Indeed, recent survey research has underlined the importance of technical support by demonstrating a connection between the quality of the support provided (it should offer such things as one-on-one assistance, for instance) and the frequency of teachers' computer use with students (Ronnkvist, Dexter, & Anderson, 2000). Yet the same survey found that fewer than one-quarter of U.S. schools have a full-time technology coordinator.

To achieve the most productive use of technology such as the Internet, educators also need support in learning how to integrate technology use into their pedagogical practice and their curricular materials. Without such support, technology like the Internet is likely to be only an expensive and little-used add-on, relegated to the periphery of teaching and learning in schools (Ronnkvist et al., 2000). This additional support is necessary for a variety of reasons. First, even teachers who have received technical training frequently lack the deep familiarity with technology that would help them design the most productive ways to use it in teaching. Second, many teachers have not had a substantial amount of experience with curriculum development activities, let alone the development of curricula employing computer technology. Third, teachers may not have a great deal of time or energy to devote to curriculum development. Finally, teachers may want and need the flexibility to adapt promising curriculum ideas involving technology use to their own circumstances. However, without some support in integrating technology into their teaching, they are unlikely to make as much progress in this direction as both they and their students might desire. Today, many Internet resources can assist teachers in enhancing their curricula through use of computer technology. However, such resources alone are not likely to be sufficient. Teachers are also likely to need to interact with others who can bring them ideas directly and help them develop approaches that work in their classrooms.

The support provided needs not only to help teachers understand how they can use the Internet or other kinds of technology in their work, it must also deal with the fit between educators' visions of education and the opportunities that new technology provides. As others who have studied change in schools have pointed out (Fullan & Stiegelbauer, 1991), even when other conditions for change are favorable, fundamental change is not likely to occur unless educators believe that change is likely to be valuable. Thus, helping teachers see how the Internet can assist them in accomplishing what they want to accomplish or helping teachers develop new visions of education that capitalize on the potential of technology for improving education is crucial. Classroom teachers are the ones who ultimately determine how often and how well students use available technology and the intended goals for such use. As we discussed in Chapter Six, NET educators who were generally satisfied with their current approach and saw Internet use primarily as an opportunity to enrich that approach and their students' education used the Internet in ways that resulted in quite modest and often unanticipated changes in their classrooms. Nonetheless, they were typically very happy with the results of their Internet use and spoke enthusiastically about them. They often did not consider the possibility that they could have used the Internet to facilitate more fundamental changes in their teaching.

Experience with NET and other attempts to use technology in education (Schofield, 1995) suggests that successful professional development efforts are not only thorough but also well coordinated and organized. For example, technical training supplied before teachers have access to their own computers is likely to be relatively ineffective, because without the opportunity to build promptly on what they have learned people tend to forget much of that learning. Similarly, training on computers or with software that differ in any substantial way from the resources teachers will be using is also likely to be ineffective, because computer novices are unlikely to be able to transfer their new skills readily from one set of equipment or applications to others. Although such caveats may seem obvious, our experience with NET as well as prior research suggests that there are many forces in schools that lead to such suboptimal learning situations for teachers. For example, if technical training has been scheduled for a given in-service day but the equipment's arrival is unexpectedly delayed, the training is likely to proceed anyway because teachers' available time is so restricted. And when a district has different kinds of computers and software in different schools or classrooms, transfers of teachers may well reduce the effectiveness of any previous technical training those teachers have received.

Finally, the support and professional development infrastructure for educators, crucial as it is, is unlikely to be all that teachers need to make optimal educational use of the Internet. Businesses have discovered that in order to make the best use of technology they often have to redesign their traditional ways of doing things. The same is likely to be true in schools. The traditions that need to be addressed will depend, of course, on the current situation in any given district, school, or classroom and on the particular uses of technology desired. However, planning to deal with such matters is so crucial to success that it should be part of any technology initiative. Issues that did not to our knowledge arise in NET schools but that educators might expect to arise when schools move to use the Internet's capabilities in major ways include what role outside mentors or project partners should have in grading students and whether older students should be able to design courses of their own choosing using the Internet and other resources. Because of the extent to which the Internet allows ready communication between distant places, there may be possibilities as yet hardly envisioned for enriching students' educational experiences. For example, programs could be set up that would allow high school students interested in the language, history, and culture of another country to live in that country for a semester and simultaneously enroll in some courses at their usual school by way of the Internet so that they could pursue these courses in their native tongue. Similarly, advanced high school students with strong interests in a particular subject, such as biology or environmental science, might join practicing researchers in the field and at the same time complete curriculum requirements in other areas at their schools by way of the Internet.

NET began in the early days of the use of the Internet in education, so Internet activities in NET schools involved less striking revisions of traditional ways of doing things than are inherent in some of the possibilities we have just discussed. However, even NET educators' often modest uses of the Internet highlighted the importance of institutional flexibility and willingness to change if teachers are to use the Internet productively. For example, issues that arose in NET schools included the need for additional time for educators to develop skills and plan Internet activities; the need to build into the already crowded curriculum enough room to teach all students Internet skills, including keyboarding; and the need to find time when staff could train corps of student assistants to assist teachers in training other students and handling minor technical problems that developed in the classroom. Furthermore, numerous scheduling issues arose, ranging from such relatively minor ones as the need to coordinate the schedules of teachers planning interdisciplinary Internet activities and the need for more flexible student scheduling to such major ones as the need to revamp the schedules of juniors and seniors in one high school so that they could work together on Internet-assisted research projects. Thus, on a range of issues from the fairly minor ones of logistics to the more fundamental ones of who evaluates a student's performance and whether students must be physically present in their usual school to gain credit for courses offered there, school districts will have to be open to change in order to realize the full educational potential of the Internet.

A FINAL NOTE

In this concluding chapter, we have outlined what we believe to be the major lessons emerging for other schools from the NET experience. On the one hand, we argue that Internet use in the schools has the potential to change education in highly valuable ways; on the other hand, we suggest that Internet use is far from a surefire cure for low test scores. Furthermore, schools will have to meet myriad conditions before they can take full advantage of all that the Internet can contribute to education. Satisfying these conditions will often require substantial expenditures or institutional change. Will Internet access in classrooms be worth its generally considerable cost in funds, time, and effort? That will depend on the goals that educators and members of the broader community have for their schools and on the care and wisdom with which those implementing Internet access and use approach their task.

—⁓— Appendix

Designers of every research project face choices about methodological issues that have tremendous implications for what they will learn.
In designing our study of NET, three considerations were paramount.
First, we were studying a phenomenon, Internet use in the schools,
about which little was known. Second, as we discussed in Chapter
One, we believed it important to understand the organizational context in which technology use occurs, the social processes surrounding
technology use, and participants' understandings of and reactions to
the specific technology in question. Third, Networking for Education
Testbed (NET) was large and relatively complex. NET ultimately
involved nearly thirty schools and several thousand Internet account
holders, and it extended over five years.

In this Appendix, we describe the particulars of the research on
which this book is based, including how these factors influenced the
approach we took to studying NET, how we selected the schools we
would study most closely, and what data we gathered. Because
researchers are never entirely separable from their research, we also
describe factors in our backgrounds that may have influenced our
choices.

THE USE OF BOTH QUALITATIVE
AND QUANTITATIVE METHODS

Qualitative methods, because of their great flexibility, are especially
well suited for exploring phenomena about which little is known
(Heyink & Tymstra, 1993). Qualitative methods are also especially
suitable for understanding the kinds of issues we believed would be
important in this research. For example, qualitative methods are
widely acknowledged to be very useful for understanding social
processes (Babbie, 1998; Bogdan & Biklen, 1982). Further, they are
commonly acknowledged to be an excellent way to explore the

perspectives of individuals and their understandings of the meaning of their experiences (Bogdan & Biklen, 1982; Taylor & Bogdan, 1998). Thus, qualitative methods seemed quite appropriate for the study of NET.

On the other hand, the size and complexity of NET made quantitative methods seem attractive and appropriate. Quantitative methods tend to be significantly less labor intensive than qualitative ones. Thus, because of their efficiency, they are well suited for the study of an activity like NET. They are also readily used across large numbers of different cases, whereas qualitative methods, being more labor intensive, are particularly well suited for the close scrutiny of one or a relatively small number of cases. Because the schools participating in NET as well as the specific Internet activities in them varied tremendously, it seemed prudent, even essential, to develop a research strategy that was responsive to this variation and not too narrowly focused on a small number of cases.

Weighing these considerations and their conflicting implications led us to evolve an eclectic research strategy. First, we undertook detailed, primarily qualitative case studies of NET as it was implemented in five very different schools in order to study closely the organizational context in which the Internet was used, the social processes that shaped Internet use, and participants' attitudes toward and practical uses of the Internet. Second, once we identified specific issues of special interest or importance through our research in these five schools, we investigated them in a much broader array of milieus, using either qualitative or quantitative methods depending on what was most appropriate and feasible for each issue.

In addition, we used primarily qualitative methods to systematically study two aspects of the broader social and organizational context within which the NET schools implemented their Internet activities. The first of these was NET itself, including the philosophy and modus operandi of the NET staff and the nature of their interactions with district educators. The second was the Waterford Public Schools (WPS) district, especially aspects of the district pertinent to the use of instructional technology.

We selected this eclectic strategy because it took advantage of the strengths of qualitative methods but also mitigated their two primary weaknesses in the context of our research: they are extremely labor intensive, and they encourage a focus on a very small number of cases, a focus that we expected to be productive but that could also result in a failure to understand phenomena of interest as they occurred in a larger number of schools.

THE FIVE CASE STUDIES OF NET SCHOOLS

The core of our research was the detailed study of five schools participating in NET. This was the largest number of case studies of NET teams and their activities that we could carry out and still reserve the resources necessary for the other important research activities. However, as will become apparent later, we did conduct additional case studies, focused around specific, much more narrowly drawn themes, at additional NET schools.

Selecting the Case Study Schools

In selecting the five case study schools, two factors were paramount: the time at which each school joined NET and the age of the students it served.

Recall that NET grew from three schools with instructionally oriented Internet activities in its first year, to ten in its second year, and to thirteen in its third year, adding new schools annually for a total of twenty-nine by its fifth year. (A fourth first-year school housed the professional development center for NET and did not have a formal NET team. Because it did not function in the same way as the other NET schools, we did not consider it as a potential site for one of our NET school case studies.) We considered only schools joining NET in its first and second years. There were three reasons for this decision. First, prior research suggests that it often takes from two to five years for educators to build their computer skills and to discover through trial and error how they can best make use of various computer applications in their work (Hadley & Sheingold, 1993; McKinsey and Company, 1995). Thus, in order to gain a fuller picture of the Internet's possibilities, we decided to study closely only schools that we could follow for a number of years. Because funding for our research was concurrent with funding for NET implementation, this goal meant that research had to focus on schools joining NET fairly early in its history.

Second, once a school was selected to participate in NET, it took a considerable period of time, often up to a year, to get the school set up with the amount and kind of Internet access called for in its NET team's proposal: wiring had to be installed, and computers had to be ordered, configured for use, and put in place. A school's designation as, for example, a second- or third-year school based on the time at which it was selected to join NET is therefore potentially misleading. There was less time to study Internet use in schools joining NET after the first two years than one might assume.

Third, in qualitative research, it is important to begin data analysis during the course of the data gathering so that ideas that emerge from analysis can inform subsequent data collection. Furthermore, a considerable amount of time is needed after data analysis for writing. Thus, it did not seem wise to focus our most intensive work on schools joining NET in the second half of its life because we would then have faced inadequate time for these crucial parts of the research process.

In selecting case study schools, we also weighed the age of the students enrolled. Developmental differences in students of different ages and structural differences in the schools that serve these different students appeared potentially important. So we needed to study Internet use in elementary, middle, and high schools in order to capture possible differences between such schools. Ultimately, we found that many of the issues discussed in this book played out quite similarly across age levels; therefore, the differences between these schools did not become a primary focus in our writing even though it was an important factor in selecting the case study schools.

We chose the five schools selected for study in the following straightforward way. First, we selected all three schools joining NET in its first year, one elementary school and two high schools. Then, we selected two more schools from the seven that joined NET in its second year, a middle school and an elementary school. We selected the middle school because it was the only middle school participating in NET in its first two years; we selected an elementary school in order to provide a second elementary school in the set of five case studies. We selected this particular elementary school over three others partly because its location was convenient for the research team and partly because the Internet curriculum projects planned there were quite different from those planned in the schools we were already studying.

Data Gathering in the Case Study Schools

Data gathering in these five schools, consisting primarily of interviews and nonparticipant observation, was systematic, sustained, and intensive. For example, we were careful to be systematic in deciding which individuals should participate in interviews. When the number of individuals in a given role was relatively small or when a particular role was central to NET functioning, we interviewed all individuals in the role who were willing to be interviewed. (We audiotaped interviews with the participants' permission.) Thus, we interviewed principals in all five schools. In addition, we interviewed eight *whiz kids*, students with advanced technical skills who played an important role in supporting Internet use in their schools. (We did not receive parental permission to interview the ninth and only other student who played such a role in NET.)

Also, we typically interviewed educators who were members of the NET teams at these five schools annually for at least three successive years, a total of 128 interviews. Generally speaking, the response rate for these and similar interviews was very good. For example, we were able to interview thirty-nine of the forty-one teachers and librarians who were members of the NET team at these schools. This high response rate was most likely due to a combination of factors. First, NET team members knew that research was an integral part of the project. Second, the research team members were extremely flexible about scheduling. Third, research team members got to know NET educators through activities such as observing classrooms and attending NET team meetings before requesting the initial interviews, and this acquaintance was a basis for rapport and trust.

The number of times we interviewed a given NET team member depended on two factors. First, we typically interviewed NET team leaders in these schools more frequently than others on their team. Second, we interviewed educators at schools in which Internet use was relatively pervasive somewhat more often than those in schools in which it was essentially nonexistent because many of the questions (for example, What do students like most or least about Internet use?) were irrelevant in the latter situation. We were careful, however, to interview NET team members from all these schools with regard to most topics, in order not to skew the data.

When it was not reasonable to interview virtually all occupants of a NET-related role in these schools, we systematically selected a subsample in a way that reflected our research purposes. For example, in order to get a relatively representative picture of students' experiences with the Internet in these five schools, we randomly selected seventy-six students to interview, stratifying by race and gender within each school, from the large number of students in classes in which teachers used the Internet. Student response rates varied somewhat from school to school but did not fall below 72 percent and generally were somewhat higher than that. When we were unable to get permission to interview a selected student, we randomly selected another student of the same race and sex from the same class as a substitute.

Finally, to get a sense of the context in which the NET teams at the case study schools operated, we decided to interview six additional faculty members at each school, three nominated by the NET team leader in each school as non-NET team members who were making use of the Internet in their work and three nominated as individuals who had not made professional use of the Internet and who were unlikely to change in this regard. We were able to interview three nonusers in each school. However, in a few schools, the NET team leader could not name three individuals who used the Internet in their work but who were not NET team members, and we had to settle for interviewing fewer of these educators. (We did also check with other team members and the NET education staff to see whether any such person at the school was being overlooked.) When the team leader nominated more than three individuals from a school in either category, we randomly selected three to interview from that group.

For the nonparticipant observation in these five schools, observers used the *full field note* method of data collection (Olson, 1976), which requires observers to take extensive handwritten notes during the events they are observing. Shortly thereafter, the same observers audiotaped these notes for later transcription and analysis. When deciding where to conduct observations, our general rule was to observe in a way that would provide the broadest and most complete information about what was occurring related to Internet use. This led to the practice of observing in the classrooms of all the NET team educators involved in using the Internet, rather than observing only in the classrooms of those who were the most enthusiastic, the most skilled in Internet use, or the most comfortable being observed. Fortunately, no team educator denied us permission for this observational work in his or her classroom. However, for reasons relating to efficiency and veridicality, we did not undertake repeated observations in the classrooms of NET team members who rarely used the Internet or in the very small number of classes in which it became apparent that students were using the Internet primarily because of a researcher's presence. Using this approach, we gathered data from over 230 class sessions in more than thirty-five different classrooms in which the Internet was in use in these five schools. We also attempted to observe all NET team meetings at the case study schools over a three-year period; we observed 108 such meetings. However, in one school, we conducted NET team observations for only two years, because the team rarely met.

In many classrooms, especially those with a small number of Internet-connected computers and in which the teacher used the whole class method of instruction, it was possible to observe Internet use without making formal decisions about what to sample in that classroom. However, sometimes the nature, extent, or organization of the Internet activity made this approach likely to create unacceptable biases in the data. For example, in one school, about thirty-five students worked in pairs on individual research projects on thirteen Internet-connected computers in conjunction with a group of five teachers during a set class period. Complicating matters further, these computers were spread out among different classrooms. Initial observations suggested we could not realistically expect to systematically capture the essential occurrences in these classes without specific decision rules. For example, if a student in the classroom being observed went into a different classroom, the observer had to decide whether to follow that individual or to stay with the class. Thus, in this setting, we decided to focus each classroom observation on a specific, randomly selected pair of students in a rotating order. Although such variation in observational procedures across schools created some issues in data analysis, it seemed warranted. We decided we could get the clearest idea of what was occurring at individual schools by accepting some degree of variation in observational procedures when circumstances warranted it.

We also collected a wide variety of archival materials at these five schools. Because we gathered more such materials in a larger set of schools, we will discuss them in the following section.

ADDITIONAL RESEARCH IN
SUPPLEMENTAL SCHOOLS

Our five case studies allowed us to get a rich and detailed sense of what was happening in five varied schools. However, because conclusions about NET based on this handful of schools might nevertheless be misleading, we gathered a subset of the same information in a much broader set of schools as well.

Selecting Supplemental Schools and Setting Goals

In the study's second year, we gathered a subset of the information gathered at the five case study schools in all five of the additional schools participating in NET at that time that were not the focus of intensive study. (We did not generally carry out similar activities at the one remaining NET school that served primarily as the NET professional development center.) We also extended this supplemental data gathering to include all three schools joining NET in its third year. For the reasons discussed earlier in this Appendix, data-gathering efforts were much more restricted in schools joining NET in its last two years, although when it was possible to gather relevant data there we did so. So, for example, teachers at the fourth-year schools participated in an on-line survey that we conducted. (The fifth-year schools were not yet fully on-line at that point.) And we collected archival materials, such as the proposals educators wrote for the annual competitive process (ACP), from all NET schools regardless of the year they joined NET.

Our goal in the five case study schools was to get a broad array of information that would sensitize us to as many issues as possible, including unanticipated ones, and provide a detailed sense of the dynamics and contexts of Internet use in those schools. Our goals for data gathering in the supplemental schools devolved from that first goal. This data gathering was designed to provide information on how the issues emerging in our initial analysis of the five case study schools played out elsewhere in NET and how we might need to extend, refine, or modify our initial analysis. For this reason, the data gathering in the supplemental schools was more narrowly focused than that in the case study schools. We carefully tailored our research in the supplemental schools to cover the topics that emerged as important in the five case studies and explored the ways in which what occurred in the supplemental schools was similar to or different from what occurred in the case study schools.

Data Gathering in Supplemental Schools

Our primary supplemental qualitative data-gathering effort was a set of extended open-ended interviews with the NET team leaders at all the supplemental schools, designed to explore the issues raised by our study of the five case study schools and to highlight any inconsistencies between the way we were beginning to understand Internet use and the supplemental schools' experiences. In addition, we interviewed a subsample of NET team members at second-year supplemental schools who were not team leaders, bringing the total number of educator interviews at the supplemental schools to thirty-two. A modest number of students ($N = 15$) at these schools completed both open-ended interviews and the accompanying questionnaires. We chose interviewees by using the same kind of carefully thought-out strategies that we had used at case study schools. We also took advantage of an opportunity that arose to administer only the questionnaires to an additional sample of students at two middle schools.

In addition, because we were learning about a relatively large number of schools, we also turned to other quantitative methods. First, starting toward the end of NET's first year, NET set up an automated system to collect information on Internet account usage in NET schools. For the next three years, this system allowed us to gather information separately on both teacher and student account use, including information such as the number of educators from each school who logged on to their accounts each month. Thus, we collected at least one year's worth of information on account usage at all schools joining NET in its first three years, with schools joining NET earlier being followed for longer periods of time and those joining it later being followed for shorter periods.

Second, at the end of NET's second and fourth years, we conducted on-line surveys designed to reach the educators who had Internet accounts through NET. Account holders were presented with the first of these surveys automatically when they logged into their accounts. This survey reappeared on successive logins until either the account holder completed the survey or the survey period of roughly three months had passed. We presented the second survey at a Web site to which we directed account holders in an e-mail message. All survey responses were sent in anonymously.

Establishing a precise response rate for these surveys is very complicated. In the three months the second-year survey was on-line, 220, 228, and 146 educators, respectively, used their accounts. However, it was clear from our data gathering at NET schools that we could not sum these three numbers and assume they represented 594 different account users. Some individuals used their accounts frequently. These individuals were almost certain to be counted two and three times if the monthly numbers of users were summed to get the size of the Internet user population. However, because we received 318 responses to this survey, it is safe to say that our response rate was at least 53 percent of those educators using their Internet accounts at least once in that three-month period (318 of 594). Because most of the questions on the survey dealt with issues pertaining to topics of most relevance to Internet users, we decided that it was best to think of educators who used their Internet accounts, rather than all educators who held accounts, as the population we were surveying.

However, this figure most likely seriously underestimates the actual response rate from account users. Indeed, although the survey was not put on-line until the last week of May, in that one week of the month it was posted, more than 150 of the 220 educators using their accounts that month (68 percent) responded. And the surprisingly high figure for one week of Internet use again suggests that they formed a core of heavy users, because one would not expect such a high proportion of a given month's users to be on-line in one week unless many of them were on-line week after week. Thus, although it would be inappropriate to claim an overall response rate of nearly 70 percent, because that figure derives from just the first week during which we gathered data, this relatively high rate is worth noting.

The difficulties in estimating a response rate for the second on-line survey (administered in NET's fourth year) are even greater. As in the case of the first survey (administered in NET's second year), we decided to consider the population of interest to be educators using Internet accounts gained through NET rather than all account holders. In addition, because servers were located at each school, as NET expanded, collecting and analyzing account use data became more and more cumbersome and time-consuming, and finally NET halted this activity due both to resource constraints and to the fact that educators were making increasing use of Internet applications that did not require an account. Thus, we do not have data on the number of educators using their accounts in the time period that the second survey was on-line. However, we do have data from the period immediately preceding it. Although this makes calculation of a precise response rate impossible, our knowledge of NET from other sources suggests that these data should not be seriously misleading. For instance, even though the number of NET account holders was continually increasing, there was a countervailing trend in that educators were also increasingly using nonaccount-based Internet resources such as the World Wide Web and were using their NET accounts less.

The second survey stayed on-line for roughly two months at the end of the spring semester of NET's fourth year, and 325 teachers and librarians responded. The average number of individual educators using their accounts during each month in the semester immediately preceding the one in which we administered the survey was 159. However, in preceding years, account use in the spring semester had been greater than in the fall semester, with use in the spring being roughly 132 percent of use in the latter (that is, 148 percent, 156 percent, and 116 percent in the three succeeding years). Thus, total use during the survey semester might be estimated at roughly 210 individuals per month. This suggests an estimated response rate around 75 percent (325 respondents of 420 possible account users), although the likelihood of double-counting again suggests that the number of apparent users is inflated and that the response rate may thus be higher. However, we must acknowledge that there is no fully satisfactory way to obtain a clear response rate for this survey. In any event, in the absence of any dramatic increase in account use, which other data suggest was highly unlikely, the response rate for the second survey was not likely to be below that estimated for the first survey.

The results of these surveys must be interpreted carefully, given the major uncertainties surrounding the response rates and the fact that we surveyed only individuals using their accounts rather than all those participating in NET or all account holders. Thus, for example, it would clearly be inappropriate to use these data to generalize about all teachers or all NET team members. However, we found these surveys, as one set of information in a much larger set of triangulated data, quite useful for some purposes. Specifically, although one would never use these data to estimate the average expenditures of NET educators on home computer equipment intended to facilitate Internet use, they provide reasonable evidence regarding the amount of money spent by the subset of individuals responding to the survey. Thus, they provide a rough estimate of the minimum amount of personal money NET educators spent for this purpose. Similarly, we were able to see whether the responses from those in the case study schools were drastically different from the responses of those in the other NET schools, even though we needed to draw such inferences cautiously. (For example, if the response rate in one set of schools were different from that in another, incorrect conclusions might be drawn.)

Finally, in addition to the account usage data and the on-line surveys, we also collected a significant amount of archival material relating to the supplemental schools and in some cases to other NET schools as well. As always, we made decisions about what material to gather with specific research goals in mind. So, for example, we obtained copies of all ninety-two proposals submitted to the ACP, in order to see whether the Internet activities planned at the case study schools differed in striking ways from those planned elsewhere. Further, we obtained copies of each NET school's improvement plan, a document in which the staff at each school set out its goals for the future and its plans for meeting those goals, to see whether NET teams at the case study schools were in environments that were likely to give more or less administrative support to technology-related initiatives than were the schools of other teams.

Focusing on Specific Issues in Appropriate Supplemental Schools

Because an important purpose of this supplemental data gathering was to illuminate particular issues emerging from research at the five case study schools, there were occasions when it seemed important to study some of the supplemental schools in more detail than others because they were especially well suited to shed light on one of these issues. In deciding where to gather such data, consistent with Glaser and Strauss's call (1967) for theoretical sampling in qualitative research, the primary consideration was always the extent to which different locations could shed light on the topic under investigation.

To clarify this process, we present an extended example. It became clear early in our work that the amount of Internet use at the five case study schools varied tremendously. Understanding this phenomenon was clearly important for our research goals. Comparison of the five case study schools yielded some interesting ideas about this variation and its origins, but it did not seem appropriate to rest our conclusions too heavily on these schools, for a number of reasons. First, there were just five of them. Moreover, in the analysis of this issue, the research team had to think of them as two smaller sets whose differences we had to explain: high-use schools and low-use schools. Thus, it seemed wise to explore this issue in depth in additional schools. Even more important was the possibility that the case study schools were not the highest- and lowest-use schools. It would not make sense to examine the issue of high and low Internet use and its causes in schools that might be in the middle of the continuum of use when other NET schools were also considered.

Therefore, we set up the following process to select the schools to be included in a study of the antecedents of high and low levels of Internet use (we discuss the results of this work in Chapter Five). First, we asked members of the NET education staff to nominate high- and low-use schools from among the ten first- and second-year schools. They made these nominations before the fourth- and fifth-year schools had time to fully implement their Internet activities and when the third-year activities were still in their infancy. In frequent touch with the schools as they supported curricular activities, the education staff were in a good position to be aware of Internet usage levels.

NET staff nominated three schools, all of which were case study schools, as clear examples of high use: Bogart High, Brayburn High, and Southland Elementary. In addition, staff mentioned a substantial amount of networking activity at Clark Elementary and Avery High, two schools that were not case study schools, bringing the total number of schools nominated as high-use schools to five.

Staff nominated two schools as clear examples of low use: the first, Riverdale Elementary, was a case study school; the second, Meadowlark Elementary, was not. In addition, the education staff suggested that Regent Middle School, also a case study school, might be considered a low-use school as well because team members were struggling to implement educational activities but had not made progress of the kind staff had seen at many other schools.

Following the principle of triangulation, we examined account use, survey, and interview data from all first- and second-year schools in order to select the set of high- and low-use schools for further study. At four of the five nominated high-use schools—Bogart, Brayburn, Southland, and Clark—we documented a wide variety of sustained curricular activities through questionnaires and extensive educator interviews. In addition, combined teacher and student account use during school hours at each of these schools was higher than use at any of the other schools participating in NET during the third year that we collected account use data. We used these data because they were the last full year of pertinent data available at the time we had to designate the high- and low-use schools and because earlier account use (or lack of it) was more likely to be influenced by technical limitations or project start-up problems.

Because the length of time that a school has been wired for access might affect Internet account use, we also compared teacher and student account use during school hours across the first-year schools and across the second-year schools. The first-year schools that staff suggested to us as high-use schools, Bogart and Brayburn, averaged 145 and 114 hours per month, respectively, compared to 0.1 hours per month at the other first-year school. At the second-year schools that staff nominated as high-use schools, Southland and Clark, use averaged 159 and 63 hours per month, respectively, compared to an average of 36 hours per month at the remaining second-year schools. Thus, the data on four of the schools nominated as examples of high use triangulated well. We then selected these schools as our high-use schools.

We did not select Avery High, the fifth school that the education staff nominated as a potential high-use school, because account use there was just 21 hours per month, well below the average for all first- and second-year schools, let alone the ones designated as high-use schools. Education staff reported a high rate of nonaccount-based usage such as searching of the World Wide Web at Avery, which might help to explain the discrepancy between the nomination and the account use data. Indeed, when responding to questionnaires, educators at Avery did report a variety of curricular activities using the Internet. However, we could not verify this high Web use independently. Further, the team leader at that school reported that the team had experienced difficulty sustaining widespread high levels of Internet activity. Because of the questions that the lack of triangulation between our different sources of data raised, we decided not to study Avery as high-use school.

We ultimately studied as low-use schools all three of the schools that the education staff suggested as such after inspection of account use, interview, and questionnaire data confirmed the accuracy of this designation. In fact, both Meadowlark and Riverdale Elementary

Schools had many months in which educators made virtually no account-based use of the Internet during school time (a total of five hours or less for all educators with accounts). Regent Middle School attained higher and more consistent account use, but use was still modest. Account use data also suggested that we might consider one other elementary school a low-use school because use there was very similar to use at Regent (between 36 and 42 hours per month during school hours). Interviews with the team leaders and other team members at both Regent and the additional elementary school confirmed that educators there had not attained the levels of use they had originally envisioned. In addition, the NET team leader at Regent confirmed that relatively few team members were participating regularly in NET activities. For example, in an e-mail message, this NET team leader wrote:

> I have an overwhelming workload this year, and I have had to let some things slide. Unfortunately, Networking for Education Testbed is one of those things that has shifted to the back burner. Likewise, a number of my colleagues here who are on the NET team have been too busy to get very involved, so I felt there wasn't much to tell.

Resource constraints meant we had to choose either Regent Middle School or the elementary school for supplemental data gathering. We selected Regent for a number of reasons including the clear evidence of limited team involvement there, its more convenient physical location, and the fact that the two low-use schools already selected were elementary schools so that studying a middle school added diversity to the study.

Thus, in exploring the antecedents of high and low levels of Internet use we carefully selected specific supplemental schools that were well suited to shedding light on this question and carried out data gathering there and in the five case study schools in a manner designed to probe this issue in depth. For example, we interviewed NET team members at all of these schools in detail about the functioning of their teams. Furthermore, team members at these schools described each of their Internet activities in detail on specially designed questionnaires so that we could explore whether the kind of uses made of the Internet differed at high- and low-use schools. We undertook intensive follow-up activities, including telephone interviews when necessary, in some situations to gather supplemental information about NET activities from team members at all these schools.

When it was warranted, we carried out similar intensive, focused data gathering at additional schools on other topics as well. For example, analysis of Internet activities at the case study schools suggested that student e-mail interchanges set up between individuals who are quite different in some regard (physical condition and ability, geographical location, native language, and so forth) may play a constructive role in broadening students' perspectives. To enhance our study of this topic, we conducted parallel extensive data gathering in an additional school where students were working on a set of Internet activities designed for a very similar purpose but spanning two other potentially important differences: differences in racial makeup and in socioeconomic background. We conducted over sixty interviews with students from this school and from the partner school in the e-mail exchange. In addition, we interviewed the educators most closely involved with these activities.

GATHERING CONTEXTUAL DATA

We focused the majority of our data-gathering efforts on the five case study schools and the broader set of eight supplemental schools as just described. However, a Web model approach to understanding computer use and implementation suggests the importance of understanding the larger context in which use occurs. In addition, some of our research questions, such as whether schools would institutionalize NET activities and what might account for the failure or success of NET's efforts to become institutionalized, pertained to the broader organizational unit of the district. Thus, we also undertook a substantial set of data-gathering activities that focused on two important contexts beyond the schools in which the NET teams functioned: NET itself and the WPS district.

In order to get a clear picture of NET, we routinely observed NET education and technical staff meetings, attending a total of roughly 180 such meetings over the course of our research. In addition, we interviewed individuals with major responsibilities in NET formally and repeatedly. Thus, we interviewed all education staff members, the head of the NET technical staff, and NET's director at least three times each. We interviewed other NET staff with technical responsibilities once or twice. Furthermore, we set up numerous channels of informal communication with NET staff, including e-mail and phone contacts.

In addition, we systematically observed NET staff as they inter-acted with the numerous individuals and entities in the district. So, for example, we routinely observed meetings ($N = 17$) of the NET staff with various district advisory committees. In addition, we observed dozens of professional development sessions ($N = 66$) dur-ing which NET staff (and later district teachers working in coopera-tion with NET staff) interacted with educators who were either actual or prospective members of NET teams in the schools or with district technical staff who needed to learn network-related skills.

Finally, we gathered a broad array of archival materials. These ranged from products intended for public consumption, such as the newsletters produced by NET staff and the materials posted on NET's home page, to planning documents intended for internal use.

Although these data-gathering activities were designed primarily to provide information about NET, they often yielded rich data about what was occurring at a wide range of NET schools and within the district bureaucracy, allowing additional triangulation as we exam-ined data gathered directly in those latter milieus.

In order to get a fully rounded picture of the NET staff's function-ing, we routinely followed up the kinds of data-gathering activities just described with parallel efforts targeted at those interacting with the staff. So, for example, participants in a training session offered by NET staff members in NET's first, second, and third years completed questionnaires both before and after that experience. Response rates on such questionnaires were generally adequate to excellent, usually ranging between roughly 70 percent and 90 percent, although one had a response rate of only 56 percent and was accordingly interpreted very cautiously. Although schedule conflicts occasionally made it impossible for research staff to attend training sessions, we did rou-tinely observe them, rather than selecting for observation only a sub-set likely to have been biased in some foreseeable way. Furthermore, when we conducted extended interviews with district technical staff and administrators, we asked them about their perceptions of the NET staff and staff activities.

All these research activities provided one important window into the context in which the NET schools functioned. However, we also undertook another set of activities designed to fill out our under-standing of pertinent aspects of the district and its functioning. The most important of these was a series of interviews conducted with individuals in district policy and administrative positions who had the potential to influence the district's support for Internet use. Specifically, we conducted forty-seven interviews with twenty-three individuals whom we selected on the basis of district roles (superintendent, school board member, heads of WPS departments, and so forth). Those individuals whose responsibilities brought them into the greatest amount of contact with NET staff we interviewed up to five times, whereas those with less contact we interviewed less frequently, generally only once or twice.

We also observed a variety of district activities related to NET, such as school board meetings dealing with technology ($N = 16$) and meetings of the district committees and subcommittees set up to select NET schools through the ACP ($N = 16$). As in our other observational work, we were systematic in deciding what to attend, in order to get as balanced a picture as possible of what was occurring in the district with regard to NET. Finally, we collected a large set of archival materials pertinent to understanding the district's functioning. These included annual reports to the community prepared by district officials, the three technology plans developed during NET's life, statistics on the composition of the student bodies at various district schools, and newspaper reports about the district.

THE RESEARCH TEAM
Background and Role in NET

The last three decades have witnessed an increasing acceptance of the idea that the personal characteristics of researchers are likely to influence both the data that a research project generates and the conclusions drawn from the data. This is expected to be true even when researchers make attempts to minimize this impact (Altheide & Johnson, 1994; Harding, 1987; Phillips, 1990; Ratcliffe, 1983; Reinharz, 1992). Thus, readers may wish to know the background of those conducting the inquiry on which this book is based.

Janet Schofield, a social psychologist, has studied computer use in schools for almost two decades. Initially, the goal of her work was to understand how computer use shapes schools, classrooms, teachers, and students. However, the results of early work led to her conviction that addressing this topic effectively requires an understanding of the social structure and functioning of schools and classrooms, because these two factors have an important influence on the nature and amount of computer use, which in turn shapes the impact of that use (Schofield, 1995). She also has a long-standing interest in issues relating to educational equity and equality. In particular, she has spent many years studying both school desegregation and gender issues arising in school computer use.

Ann Locke Davidson is an educational anthropologist with a long-standing interest in how individuals, particularly those in schools, respond to situations involving cultural and other sorts of social change. Her work has also focused on the implications of social difference and on the interactions of individuals from different social worlds, an interest that Chapter Three of this book reflects. Finally, she has looked at tools, actions, and policies that enable individuals to address social divides. Beyond these areas of interest, she has worked as a teacher in a variety of settings and as a supervisor of prospective high school teachers. Thus, she has extensive experience in U.S. classrooms and educational settings.

The research team included many others and had an intentionally broad range of expertise. Important here were several postdoctoral fellows with backgrounds in fields ranging from social psychology to engineering and public policy to sociology. Similarly, the graduate students involved with this research had backgrounds in fields as diverse as social psychology, sociology, anthropology, public policy, educational policy, and educational technology. In addition, a number of undergraduate students from various fields assisted in a variety of ways.

Because Janet Schofield served as one of the principal investigators on the initial NET grant, as well as on most of the subsequent related grants, it is important to discuss her relationship to those responsible for implementing NET. Professor Schofield initially learned about NET when she was approached by NET's prime mover, Don Quick, who indicated that he and Peter Marcus had laid the groundwork for an attempt to bring the Internet to the WPS but that the National Science Foundation (NSF), the primary funding agency, required a strong research component focused on understanding the implementation process and the consequences of Internet use. Because none of the individuals initially associated with planning NET had either the time or the training to undertake such an enterprise, they were in need of someone to do so. Being close to completing the writing of *Computers and Classroom Culture*, Schofield was interested in further pursuing her study of educational technology. However, at that point, she had little or no experience with the Internet and no clearly formed attitude about the potential of the Internet for education. Indeed, at that time, in 1992, the Internet was not the part of everyday life it is now, and she had not yet made use of it for personal or professional purposes.

Professor Schofield decided to participate in writing the grant and to head NET's research staff on two conditions: that she have access to needed information and that she be able to conduct the research in a manner not subject to revision by other principal investigators or by NET staff, although she would welcome their comments. So, for example, she would make the final decisions about the topics the research team would study, the methods they would use, and the conclusions they would draw. (Because the other principal investigators' professional expertise was in entirely different areas and Don Quick was convinced that the outcomes of NET would be positive, these conditions were not controversial.) Further, she would need the cooperation of the other principal investigators, the NET staff, and the NET team members in carrying out this work. In exchange, Schofield agreed to supply NET with information that would give it useful feedback on its functioning. In addition, she agreed that she would be sensitive to the fact that both NET staff and educators already had heavy demands on their time.

This agreement held up remarkably well in practice. For example, NET staff greatly facilitated the research by letting participating educators know that it was an important part of NET's obligation to the NSF. In return, the research team provided NET with such useful information as feedback from surveys of those participating in training efforts. Further, when it became apparent that account use data that the research team desired would be very helpful to the NET education staff as well and that both groups felt that on-line surveys were likely to be useful, research and education staff worked with NET's technical staff to produce data in a form that both groups felt would be useful. Some results of this work were placed on-line for the use of the larger NET community.

Over NET's course, the distinction between researcher and implementer was not always easy to maintain. However, strong efforts were made to maintain this distinction because of Schofield's belief that it would be difficult for the research team to report fairly and credibly on NET if researchers were significantly involved in NET's implementation. For example, during NET's first year, a small group including NET's director and the heads of NET's education, technical, and research staffs met frequently to make a wide variety of decisions concerning NET's implementation. Although Schofield made her role as researcher explicit in these meetings by getting permission from the other participants to take copious field notes for research purposes, it was not uncommon for the others to solicit her opinion on various matters. (Later, these meetings came to include many more members of NET's education and technical staffs, making it somewhat easier for her to maintain the role of researcher.) Furthermore, educators and students frequently asked research team members observing in classrooms to provide information about the Internet or to provide technical assistance when problems arose in using the Internet. In general, research team members contributed what they were asked for to the extent they were able. However, owing to role conflict concerns, they did not volunteer to become more deeply enmeshed in implementation.

Some who advocate forms of research in which the distinction between researchers and those whom they study is less clear (for example, Richardson, Stewart, & Simmonds, 1978) may not care for the approach we took. We acknowledge that greater collaboration with NET participants in producing our analyses would have been useful in many respects. Yet all research design decisions involve trade-offs. It seemed to us that the potential loss in credibility if we gave others in NET a formal role in determining our focus or our conclusions was greater than the potential gains. Furthermore, we consistently and actively solicited reactions to our developing understanding of the issues surrounding Internet use from individuals involved with NET, for the purpose of enhancing accuracy and enriching our analyses. These individuals included NET staff and team members, especially when we had reason to believe they had access to information or perspectives that we did not. Further, we were open about the papers and conference presentations we were producing, and we carefully considered any comments NET participants gave us about our ideas as we developed those ideas further in this book and elsewhere.

PROCEDURES TO MINIMIZE ERROR AND BIAS IN DATA GATHERING

As we indicated earlier, the two major methods of data gathering used in this study were intensive qualitative observation and repeated semi-structured interviews. We have discussed both the amount of data collected using these techniques and how we decided when and where to gather data. Now, we turn to discussing other aspects of conducting this work, with special attention to procedures that we put in place in recognition of the fact that some degree of subjectivity influences virtually every step of the research process. Although it is clear that the theoretical assumptions, methodological predilections, and even the life experiences of researchers are likely to play a role in shaping issue focus, issue conceptualization, and data interpretation, we believe it is eminently desirable to try to ensure that data gathering and analysis are as balanced, accurate, and open to new possibilities as possible. Thus, we adopted numerous specific procedures to foster the attainment of this goal.

Field Note Procedures

One major potential problem with qualitative observational methods is what Smith and Geoffrey have termed (1968, p. 255) the "two-realities problem": the fact that field notes cannot possibly capture everything that has transpired in the environment being observed. They capture occurrences that are only a part of the fuller set of behaviors that the researcher is trying to document and understand. Furthermore, there is the possibility that selective recording of certain types of events means that the field notes are not only partial but systematically biased.

Although the two-realities problem is impossible to surmount completely, we took various steps to minimize its effects. First, we made a serious effort to have more than one research team member studying each of the schools we researched in depth. Although this did not ensure lack of bias, it did give us a minimum of two perspectives on each situation. Further, our overall focus on the social processes related to Internet use and the consequences of such use gave us a starting point for winnowing out occurrences likely to be irrelevant to our work.

Even with such a focus, we had to make decisions about which aspects of a situation should get the closest attention. As one way of responding promptly to this need, we began data analysis in the first year of data gathering, trying to determine the issues, or themes, that seemed most important. This work led to the development of a constantly growing set of codes for analysis of the observational data, as we describe in more detail below. This work also helped guide data gathering, as observers became aware of more and more topics that were of interest to the research and thus aware that they must give information pertinent to these topics priority when they had to make observation choices. However, we took great care not to let this turn into a situation in which hastily constructed understandings were confirmed through data gathering skewed toward confirmation. Instead, we began to isolate issues about which we wanted information to be as full as possible. To give just one example, early on in the research, we developed a code we called *access.* It referred to teachers' willingness or unwillingness to allow students access to the Internet outside of formal class settings. Because codes like *access* referred both to evidence of a phenomenon and to evidence of its opposite, observers gathered information on the desired topics whether it supported one view of what was occurring or an alternate view. Furthermore, we made a point of searching for data that could undercut our developing understanding of the situations we studied.

Unwarranted observer inferences can also be a potentially serious source of inaccuracy and bias. To mitigate this problem, we took care to make the field notes as factual and as concretely descriptive as possible. For example, instead of or in addition to saying that a student appeared to like using the Internet, the observer recorded the behavior that led to the inference, such as a request to be allowed to use the Internet during free time or stalling tactics and complaints when the teacher indicated that a period of Internet use was over. Further, rather than paraphrasing comments and conversation, we made a point of attempting to capture individuals' actual words and accompanying nonverbal behaviors related to Internet use. For example, if a teacher asserted in a loud tone, "These technical glitches are driving me crazy," the observer noted those words and the manner in which they were spoken rather than merely recording in the field notes that the teacher was frustrated by technical problems. We monitored transcribed field notes so that we could remind observers of the importance of such procedures when necessary.

Another source of potential error in observational research stems from researchers' failure to take account of the fact that people who are being observed will often, because of that observation, act differently than they otherwise would. We made conscious efforts to minimize observers' impact on the situations they observed and to recognize when the influence was substantial. For example, we took great pains not to be seen by either students or teachers as members of the school's or district's authority structure or as implementers of NET, because we felt that this would inhibit individuals' openness and spontaneity. In order to minimize our impact on the situations we observed, we made it a rule not to interfere with students' behaviors unless they posed an obvious and immediate danger to the student or others. Similarly, we scrupulously avoided public comments evaluating students', teachers', or others' actions. We also observed many settings routinely so that our presence became less and less a novelty. As we became an accepted part of these settings, our presence appeared to have a diminishing impact. In addition, although we responded in socially normative ways to greetings, questions, and the like, we generally focused on research activities such as observing and taking notes rather than getting actively involved in ongoing interactions in a way intended to shape them. Finally, we made strong efforts to resist being drawn into controversies and political maneuvering and even to resist validating another individual's perceptions of a situation by explicitly reinforcing particular views, as the following field note illustrates:

> A couple of times Dick [a NET team member] seemed to be asking for me to confirm his view of things by saying, "Didn't you read that?" or, "You saw what he was doing." And I . . . said that I did not understand a lot of the subtext; that I'm more or less like a sponge right now. I'm just taking in all the information, and I'm not trying to make value [judgments] about it. . . . And he said that he understood that. . . . I tried to be very careful not to make Dick think that I was on his side against anyone else. At the same time, I didn't want him to think I was discounting what he was saying.

These behaviors created a role for us in the district that typically did not appear to disturb behavior markedly. For example, in the presence of a research team member visibly engaged in taking notes, one individual delivered a verbal message to another after stating that the message was too sensitive to be sent over e-mail. He would have been very unlikely to speak this openly if a strong level of trust with the observers had not been established. On another occasion, a teacher printed out copyrighted information in an observer's presence, simultaneously making a joke about "demonstrating poor moral behavior," which indicated that although he felt this behavior did not reflect well on him, the observer's presence did not inhibit him from engaging in it.

In spite of the apparent success of our efforts to minimize our influence on the environments we studied, there were times, especially when observers were relatively new in a setting, when it was clear that their presence disrupted the normal flow of events in some significant way. (The most obvious and common event of this type was a teacher's attempt to use an observer's presence to foster desired behavior in students by explicitly reminding the students that they were being observed.) Thus, from the very first, research staff were trained to look for and record such an impact. In addition, as part of the very first set of codes developed for data analysis, we created a code for information related to others' reactions to the research staff and for behavior that appeared to be influenced by an observer's presence. We paid careful attention to such situations for three reasons. First, noting such situations often helped us find ways to be less disruptive of normal classroom behavior patterns. Second, such occasions suggested topics about which individuals or groups were especially sensitive and thus were clues to issues that we needed to approach with special care and reassurances about confidentiality. Finally, noting that specific behaviors appeared to occur because of an observer's presence lessened the likelihood that such behaviors would be confused later in data analysis with behaviors likely to have occurred in any event.

Interviews

To get the most out of the formal and informal interviews used extensively in this research, we made concerted efforts to build rapport with respondents to encourage them to share their thoughts frankly and freely. Several factors seemed crucial to achieving this goal, including noninterference in the events we were privy to, a nonjudgmental and sympathetic attitude, and careful guarding of the confidentiality of information we gathered. Perhaps the success of these efforts is best attested to by the kind of information made available to members of the research team. It was not unusual for individuals to say things in interviews that could clearly have created difficulties for them or others they cared about had interviewers not treated the information confidentially. For example, one teacher spoke openly in an interview about accessing pornographic Internet sites from school. Another teacher said about the information divulged in an interview, "I'm baring my soul here."

One goal of special concern, given that the research team was associated with NET, was making it clear that our role was not to bolster or defend NET or to get involved in its internal politics but to understand what was occurring. Although we have no way of knowing with certainty how successful we were in this endeavor, the following excerpts, first from a field note regarding a conversation with an individual holding a responsible position in the WPS and then from an interview with Peter Marcus of NET's education staff, suggest that our efforts were not without effect:

> Ms. Jenkins said that she had never told anybody in NET about this because she felt like she did not need to fuel any fires, but . . . that there were several people in the administration who were negative about NET who were trying to hold up things and make things more difficult for NET.

> What I like best about the [research] people is that fact that they've been collecting information. . . . They can watch us go through those hoops and look at it from the outside and say, "Here's what seems to be happening." That part I like a lot. I also like the fact that to me it's not aligned with one group or another. It's not with the supercomputing center; it's not with the WPS; it's not with Fairfield University. I like the fact that there seems to be this neutral group that is looking at it.

In constructing and conducting interviews, we made additional strong efforts to minimize error and bias. For example, we routinely audiotaped and transcribed formal interviews to get as complete and accurate a record as possible of respondents' comments. In addition, interviewers avoided asking leading questions and, as we mentioned, assured individuals that responses would be confidential, to encourage frankness. Although interviewers worked from carefully designed sets of open-ended questions, they were encouraged to probe respondents' replies extensively and to follow up on topics that interviewees suggested were important even when they were not addressed in the prepared questions. Also, we made a practice of asking at least two kinds of questions about issues of major interest. First, we asked very broad questions that helped us understand the situation from the participants' perspective. This let us see whether the issues we were currently highlighting in our work were salient to participants and to revise our thinking and data gathering if they were not. For example, we asked students, "What effect, if any, has the Internet had on the way you act in class?" to learn whether the issues we were exploring pertaining to student change were the ones salient to students. Later, we asked students targeted questions about specific changes we had reason to think might be occurring, such as, "Do you feel more or less motivated to do your schoolwork when the Internet is used in a class compared to when the Internet is not used in that class?"

Informal interviews ranged from extended conversations with individuals, which occurred between classes, while waiting for a meeting to start, and in other similar contexts, to very brief interchanges that occurred in similar settings. Notes on such conversations were recorded immediately after the conversations occurred to minimize errors in recall. However, because we did not audiotape these informal interchanges as they occurred as we had the interviews, we treated these records as field notes rather than as interviews in the ensuing data analysis.

Archival Material

In collecting the large amounts of archival material we used, we took care again to procure data that were as representative and valid as possible and to be cognizant of unavoidable biases. For example, with participants' permission, the research team's e-mail address was added to the NET teams' distribution lists in the case study and supplemental schools. Thus, we had access to a much broader and less selective set of e-mail interchanges than we would have had we relied on individuals to supply us with copies of interchanges they thought were particularly revealing or important. Of course, such efforts did not yield perfectly complete or representative data sets. For example, the set of interchanges that NET team members sent to the distribution lists was clearly not identical to the full set of e-mail flowing between them, because individuals often corresponded by e-mail with particular colleagues on their team as well as with the entire group. Nonetheless, becoming part of the distribution list did provide us with a fuller and more representative set of information than would have been available otherwise.

DATA ANALYSIS

Data analysis procedures in qualitative research are complex and iterative and thus are hard to describe succinctly. They were even more complex than usual in this study, owing to the massive and varied set of data gathered. Nonetheless, we summarize our approach to data analysis here because it is likely to be of considerable interest to many readers.

First, we can note a few general points. We took seriously the idea that data analysis should be an ongoing and iterative process. Thus, as we indicated earlier, we began work on data analysis early in our research because we were deeply committed to using the flexibility of the qualitative approach to shift the focus of our data gathering in directions that the ongoing analysis suggested would be fruitful. As the field notes and other data accumulated, members of the research team indexed, read, and reread them. The large size of the database we generated created a very real danger that we might get bogged down in a morass of detail. Thus, we emphasized also generating working memos about emerging ideas and themes so that we could seek data relevant to these themes in planned and systematic ways. We took care to explore ways in which we could disconfirm or refine as well as support emerging ideas.

Field Notes

As is apparent from the preceding discussion, qualitative field notes were a cornerstone of our work. The research produced over seven hundred separate sets of field notes based on the observations in classrooms, meetings, and other milieus. After transcription, research team members carefully read and indexed these notes using coding categories of several types. The goal of this coding was to create files of information pertinent to specific topics that we could examine in detail when we covered these topics in our analytic work.

We derived the initial coding system from the rather general questions that guided the research at its inception. However, this system expanded markedly over time as experiences with NET and the initial analysis suggested new and potentially important topics for investigation. Over time, we commonly adopted subcodes as experience suggested conceptual distinctions that had not been salient initially. In such cases, we used both the subcode and full code files in subsequent analysis.

Many of our codes were relatively straightforward. For example, the code *Title 1* referred to WPS district or individual school expenditures of Title 1 money, especially on technology. However, other codes involved considerably more inference. An example of such a code is *outcomes,* which we defined as goals for, and intended or unintended consequences of Internet use (positive or negative) for teachers, students or others.

Coders were carefully trained and closely supervised by Ann Locke Davidson, who routinely examined samples of their work to catch and correct any problems. Coders were individuals deeply involved in the research whose responsibilities also included data gathering. The reason for this dual role was twofold. First, we thought that coders who also served as data gatherers would be more aware of the way the data they generated were used and that this might improve data quality. That is, the coders would note any deficiencies in the data gathering that made it hard to code certain protocols, and this would most likely have a feedback effect on subsequent data gathering. Second, broad knowledge of NET sometimes made apparent the connections between field note material and codes that someone with less knowledge might not note. For example, a coder might read about an interaction in which an education staff member encouraged a teacher to approach her principal directly about a NET-related issue rather than use the education staff as an intermediary (or an interaction in which the education staff member did the reverse). Knowing that the NET education staff strongly endorsed a teacher-oriented grassroots philosophy of change might lead the coder to assign the code *NET staff change model* to this material. A coder lacking this type of background knowledge might not as readily see the relevance of such information to that code.

After research team members entered the codes into electronic files, using Ethnograph software, they printed out all coded segments of the protocols and filed them under the appropriate code. (Material pertinent to two or more codes was printed and filed multiple times so that it was present in the file for each code to which it was pertinent.) For efficiency's sake, we organized protocols within Ethnograph in catalogs of similar kinds of materials. (For example, we made catalogs for education staff meetings, for the various classrooms observed, and so forth.) Thus, when exploring a given code, we could easily pull out all materials pertinent to it or only the materials stemming from a specific milieu. This was very helpful in organizing the massive amount of material that our research generated. For example, it made it convenient to compare the field notes relevant to a code according to whether they stemmed from a case study school, NET team meetings, or supplementary schools.

Interviews

The results of formal interviews were also a crucial part of our data set. Because we developed numerous and varied sets of questions to use in our interviews with students, educators, administrators, NET personnel, and others, analysis of the data was complex because the interviews touched on many and highly varied topics. Moreover, the sheer amount of data to consider was substantial, since we conducted over four hundred interviews during the course of NET. These interviews ranged in length from roughly twenty minutes to over two-and-a-half hours, typically generating texts ranging from six to more than twenty single-spaced pages when they were transcribed.

We typically analyzed the interviews in two ways. First, we printed out and coded complete transcripts of all interviews as described for the field notes so that we could place all material relevant to the various codes in the appropriate files, along with related material from the coded field notes. We designed this practice to ensure that anything said in interviews pertinent to topics for which there were codes would become part of the data file for that code.

Then, we also analyzed a large subset of the interview materials in a second, somewhat more quantitative way, using an approach similar to Kvale's meaning categorization (1996), in which codes and subcodes based both on relevant preexisting literature in the field and on individuals' responses to the questions are developed.

More specifically, we began by printing out all responses to a given question from the interview transcripts and filed them together. (We defined a response as all the respondent's words from the point at which he or she first began to answer that question to the point at which the interviewer asked the next question on the interview guide.) As readers may have noted earlier in this book, the number of educators we queried about different topics varied. This was due to the fact that some questions were asked in only one year's round of interviews, whereas others, on particularly important topics, remained part of the interviewing for a number of years. Because new NET teams were formed each year, the latter kind of question was asked of many more team members than the former. Then Ann Locke Davidson, or another interview analyst working closely with Janet Schofield, read and reread all the responses to each question. Next, the interview analyst constructed coding categories reflecting the kinds of responses given by the interviewees, carefully defined them, and then refined them on the basis of the results of preliminary efforts to use them in coding the data.

An interview analyst, typically a graduate student, then went through all responses to each question, usually assigning one code to each response. Multiple codes were allowed when the question made them appropriate. For example, a broad question about the kinds of changes that Internet use had sparked might lead individuals to mention several distinct changes. This coding was reviewed by Dr. Davidson, and she and the other coder resolved discrepancies between her coding and that of the other coder through discussion. In the small subset of cases in which these two individuals could not agree, Professor Schofield made a coding decision in discussion with them.

After completing this coding, we constructed tables to graphically display distinctions of pertinence to the research, as long as the number of individuals in a relevant category was large enough to warrant the category's inclusion. So, for example, we routinely grouped responses from educators by the year during which their team had joined NET and by the school level in which they worked (elementary, middle, or high school). Although we did not perform formal statistical tests on these data, we visually inspected the tables to see whether the data suggested patterns that we should more formally explore through further data gathering and analysis. We completed this laborious process for almost one hundred questions.

Two factors weighed heavily in deciding which questions to analyze this second way. First, we carried out this process only when a substantial number of individuals had responded to the same question. For example, some of the questions we asked of the WPS superintendent reflected that individual's unique position in the district and were not asked of others. In this and similar cases, there appeared to be little to gain by going through the summarizing process just described. Second, because the summarizing process was extremely labor intensive, we used it only to analyze questions that seemed especially pertinent to themes that ultimately emerged as central to this book. For example, we summarized answers to large numbers of questions dealing with the impact of the Internet on classroom functioning and with individuals' perceptions of outcomes of Internet use, topics we discussed at length in Chapters Six and Seven. However, we did not analyze in this fashion themes that at one point had seemed important enough to ask questions about but that ultimately did not seem worthy of detailed attention in this book. For example, although we asked educators questions about parent and community attitudes toward Internet use, we saw little evidence in the schools we studied that these attitudes played a strong role in shaping such use. Thus, although we carefully reviewed the responses to such questions during the initial interview coding process, we did not go through the formal summarizing process with questions on this topic.

Archival Material

We also formally coded and analyzed some archival material. For example, we carefully examined all proposals submitted to the ACP, coding them for such things as the number of members on each proposed NET team and whether the proposal called for lab- or classroom-based access, in order to let us calculate the total number of individuals formally involved with aspiring NET teams and the percentage of proposals envisioning classroom-based access. We also performed more complex coding tasks, such as categorizing the proposed goals for Internet use, laying the basis for the discussion of these goals presented in Chapter Two. We developed the coding categories we used on the basis of careful examination of the goals mentioned in the proposals. The actual coding of the proposals themselves was carried out in a manner similar to the process that Kvale (1996) calls meaning categorization. We coded e-mail received from all sources using the same codes as we used for field notes, and we placed copies of e-mail messages in the appropriate files.

However, many archival materials were merely consulted as needed, and we took material from them directly (for example, we used WPS publications to obtain information about the backgrounds of students within the system and in given schools).

Questionnaires and Surveys

Finally, we produced descriptive and inferential statistics as appropriate on quantitative data sets from questionnaires and surveys. For example, we conducted repeated measures analysis of variance on the responses that educators participating in the NET training workshops gave to Likert scales on questionnaires completed before and after this experience, to see whether participation led to changes in such things as their sense of competence and comfort with Internet use. Similarly, we performed analyses of variance to investigate possible differences related to school level and gender in students' responses to questionnaires about the ways in which Internet use changed classroom functioning. (For these analyses, we combined data from both the case study schools and the supplemental schools. The number of respondents varied from question to question because some questions appeared on all questionnaires, whereas others did not, due to time constraints.) We found few statistically significant school level or gender differences, which accounts for the fact that our description of changes in classroom functioning in Chapter Six does not focus much attention on these variables.) In addition, we produced descriptive statistics, such as frequency distributions and means, for the data collected from the on-line surveys.

Drawing Conclusions and Writing This Book

The organization and analysis described so far in this Appendix did not lead automatically to the conclusions we present in this book. We still had to integrate the information provided by the various data sets in order to produce the understanding of the process of introducing the Internet into schools that we present here.

This task entailed two different kinds of integration of materials. First, we took triangulating data from a variety of sources very seriously (Webb, Campbell, Schwartz, & Sechrest, 1966). In drawing conclusions, we took care to look at the varying sources of information to see whether they all led to similar conclusions. When they did not, we undertook further data gathering or analysis efforts to try to learn the reason for the discrepancy.

Second, because each data source also typically made unique contributions to the analysis, providing information that other sources did not, we combined relevant material from various sources to construct our analysis of a situation. Well before writing on any specific topic started, the authors created lists of the code word files to be consulted as well as lists of the pertinent archival materials and the relevant interview and survey questions. Although these lists often expanded in the course of thinking and writing as new connections were made or new ideas emerged, they served three important purposes. First, they helped us make sure that we used all pertinent information in the analysis. This was very important given the size and complexity of the database and the fact that we gathered information over such a long period of time. Second, these lists helped us set priorities for data analysis because they made it easy to see, for example, which interview questions needed to be summarized before analysis on a given question could start. Third, constructing these lists frequently helped us isolate areas in which we needed more data, and this allowed us to plan additional systematic data collection.

The final step in the analysis was the actual writing of this book. As part of this process, we worked through ideas that had emerged earlier in discussions, outlines, and memos in more complete and refined ways. We discarded some lines of thought as evidence for them seemed lacking or incomplete. We added others as the process of discussion and writing itself suggested new ways of thinking about what we had learned. The draft of each chapter or section produced by one of the authors was carefully read by the other, who then produced a detailed written critique of it. This critique led to extensive revisions and additional written responses from the chapter or section author. This process played a critical role in shaping the evolution and final form of this book.

⟶ References

Altheide, D. L., & Johnson, J. M. (1994). Criteria for assessing interpretive validity in qualitative research. In N. K. Denzin & Y. S. Lincoln (Eds.), *Handbook of qualitative research* (pp. 485–499). Thousand Oaks, CA: Sage.

American Association of University Women. (1993). *Hostile hallways: The AAUW survey on sexual harassment in America's schools.* Washington, DC: Author.

Ames, C. A. (1990, Spring). Motivation: What teachers need to know. *Teachers College Record, 91*(3), 410–414.

Anderson, R. C., Shirey, L. L., Wilson, P. T., & Fielding, L. G. (1987). Interestingness of children's reading material. In R. E. Snow & M. C. Farr (Eds.), *Aptitude, learning, and instruction: Vol. 3. Cognitive and affective process analyses* (pp. 297–337). Hillsdale, NJ: Erlbaum.

Anderson, R. E. (1993). *Summary of computers in American schools, 1992: An overview.* IEA Computers in Education Study [On-line]. Available: http://www.soc.umn.edu/~iea/synopsis.htm

Anderson, R. E., & Ronnkvist, A. (1999). *The presence of computers in American schools.* (Teaching, Learning, and Computing: 1998 National Survey Report No. 2). University of California, Irvine, and University of Minnesota, Center for Research on Information Technology and Organizations [On-line]. Available: http://www.crito.uci.edu/TLC/findings/Internet-Use/startpage.htm

Apple, M. (1998). Teaching and technology: The hidden effects of computers on teachers and students. In L. E. Beyer & M. W. Apple (Eds.), *The curriculum: Problems, politics, and possibilities* (pp. 289–311). Albany: State University of New York Press.

Applebee, A. N., Auden, A., & Lear, F. (1981). *Writing in the secondary school: English and the content areas.* Urbana, IL: National Council of Teachers of English.

Asher, S. R. (1980). Topic interest and children's reading comprehension. In

R. J. Spiro, B. C. Bruce, & W. F. Brewer (Eds.), *Theoretical issues in reading comprehension* (pp. 525–534). Hillsdale, NJ: Erlbaum.

Attewell, P. (1994). Information technology and the productivity paradox. In D. H. Harris (Ed.), *Organizational linkages: Understanding the productivity paradox.* Washington, DC: National Academy Press.

Attewell, P., & Battle, J. (1999). Home computers and school performance. *Information Society, 15,* 1–10.

Babbie, E. (1998). *The basics of social research.* Belmont, CA: Wadsworth.

Bacharach, S. B., Bauer, S. C., & Conley, S. C. (1986). Organizational analysis of stress: The case of secondary and elementary schools. *Journal of Work and Occupations, 13,* 7–32.

Bacharach, S. B., Bauer, S. C., & Shedd, J. B. (1986). Education and reform. *Teachers College Record, 88,* 241–256.

Bangert-Drowns, R. L., Kulik, J. A., & Kulik, C. C. (1985). Effectiveness of computer-based education in secondary schools. *Journal of Computer-Based Instruction, 12*(3), 59–68.

Banks, J. A., & Banks, C. A. (1995). *Handbook of research on multicultural education.* New York: Macmillan.

Baugh, I. W., & Baugh, J. G. (1997). E-mail learning communities. *Learning and Leading with Technology, 25*(3), 38–41.

Baym, N. K. (1997). Interpreting soap operas and creating community: Inside an electronic fan culture. In S. Kiesler (Ed.), *Culture of the Internet* (pp. 103–120). Hillsdale, NJ: Erlbaum.

Becker, H. J. (1985). How schools use microcomputers: Results from a national survey. In M. Chen & W. Paisley (Eds.), *Children and microcomputers: Research on the newest medium* (pp. 87–108). Thousand Oaks, CA: Sage.

Becker, H. J. (1990). *When powerful tools meet conventional beliefs and institutional constraints: National survey findings on computer use by American teachers* (Report No. 49). Baltimore, MD: Center for Research on Elementary and Middle Schools, John Hopkins University. (ERIC Document Reproduction Service No. ED 337142)

Becker, H. J. (1999a, April). *Changing teachers' pedagogical practices through the use of the World Wide Web.* Paper presented at the annual meeting of the American Educational Research Association, Montreal, Canada.

Becker, H. J. (1999b, February). *Internet use by teachers: Conditions of professional use and teacher-directed student use.* (Report No. 1). University of California, Irvine, and University of Minnesota [On-line].

Available: http://www.crito.uci.edu/TLC/findings/Internet-Use/
startpage.htm

Becker, H., & Ravitz, J. (1997, August). *The equity threat of promising
innovations: The Internet in schools.* Paper presented at the
annual meeting of the American Psychological Association,
Chicago, IL.

Becker, H., Ravitz, J., & Wong, Y. T. (1999, November). *Teacher and teacher-
directed student use of computers and software.* (Report No. 3). University of California, Irvine, and University of Minnesota [On-line].
Available: http://www.crito.uci.edu/tlc/findings/ComputerUse/
html/startpage.htm

Becker, H., & Sterling, C. (1987). Equity in school computer use: National
data and neglected considerations. *Journal of Educational Computing
Research, 3,* 289–311.

Benne, K. D. (1970). Authority in education. *Harvard Educational Review,
40,* 385–410.

Bereiter, C., & Scardamalia, M. (1987). *The psychology of written communication.* Hillsdale, NJ: Erlbaum.

Berenfeld, B. (1996). Linking students to the infosphere. *T.H.E. Journal,
23*(8), 76–83.

Berman, P., & McLaughlin, M. (1974). *Federal programs supporting educational change: Vol. 1. A model of educational change.* Santa Monica,
CA: Rand Corporation.

Berman, P., & McLaughlin, M. (1976). Implementation of educational
innovation. *Educational Forum, 40,* 345–370.

Berman, P., & McLaughlin, M. (1977). *Federal programs supporting
educational change: Vol. 7. Factors affecting implementation and
continuation.* Santa Monica, CA: Rand Corporation.

Berman, P., & McLaughlin, M. (1978). *Federal programs supporting educational change: Vol. 8. Implementing and sustaining innovations.* Santa
Monica, CA: Rand Corporation.

Bettencourt, B., Dillman, G., & Wollman, N. (1996). The intragroup
dynamics of maintaining a successful grassroots organization: A case
study. *Journal of Social Issues, 52*(1), 169–186.

Bierstedt, R. (1970). *The social order.* New York: McGraw-Hill.

Bishop, A. P. (1991, December). *The National Research and Education Network (NREN) Update 1991.* (Report No. IR053929). Syracuse, NY:
Syracuse University. (ERIC Document Reproduction Service No. ED
34090)

Bogdan, R. C., & Biklen, S. (1982). *Qualitative research for education: An introduction to theory and methods.* Needham Heights, MA: Allyn & Bacon.

Bosco, J. (1986, Fall). The organization of schools and the use of computers to improve schooling. *Peabody Journal of Education, 64*(1), 111–129.

Bowers, C. A. (1988). *The cultural dimensions of educational computing: Understanding the non-neutrality of technology.* New York: Teachers College Press.

Bransford, J. D., Brown, A. L., & Cocking, R. R. (1999). *How people learn.* Washington, DC: National Academy Press.

Brush, T. (1998). Using CMC to bring real-world experiences into the classroom: The electronic "pen- pal" project. In Z. L. Berge & M. Collins (Eds.), *Wired together: The online classroom in K–12* (pp. 101–109). Creskill, NJ: Hampton Press.

Burbules, N. C., & Callister, T. A., Jr. (2000). *Watch it: The risks and promises of information technologies for education.* Boulder, CO: Westview Press.

Cahall, L. (1994, February). The urban child and the AT&T learning network: Online interactions open up the inner city to the world. *Computing Teacher, 27*(5), 19–20.

Caldwell, J. H., Huitt, W. G., & Graeber, A. O. (1982). Time spent in learning: Implications from research. *Elementary School Journal, 82*(5), 471–480.

Campbell, L. P. (1984). On the horizon: A computer in every classroom. *Education, 104*(3), 332–334.

Carlitz, R. (1991, Summer). Common knowledge: Networks for kindergarten through college. *Educom Review, 26*, 25–28.

Carroll, J. B. (1963). A model of school learning. *Teachers College Record, 64*(8), 723–733.

Cattagni, A., & Farris Westat, E. (2001). *Internet access in U.S. public schools and classrooms: 1994–2000* (NCES 2001–071). U.S. Department of Education: Office of Educational Research and Improvement [On-line]. Available: http://nces.ed.gov/pubs

Christy, A. (1998). Key pals: The goodwill ambassadors of the 1990s. In Z. L. Berge & M. Collins (Eds.), *Wired together: The online classroom in K–12* (pp. 93–99). Creskill, NJ: Hampton Press.

Clinton, W. J. (1996, November 4). Remarks by the President to the People of the Sioux Falls Area [On-line]. Available: http://library.whitehouse.gov/search/query-pressreleases.html

Cognition and Technology Group at Vanderbilt. (1997). *The Jasper project:*

Lessons in curriculum, instruction, assessment, and professional development. Hillsdale, NJ: Erlbaum.

Cohen, D. (1987). Educational technology, policy and practice. *Educational Evaluation and Policy Analysis, 9*, 153–170.

Cohen, D. (1988). Educational technology and school organization. In R. S. Nickerson & P. P. Zodhiates (Eds.), *Technology in education: Looking toward 2020* (pp. 231–264). Hillsdale, NJ: Erlbaum.

Cohen, M., & Riel, M. (1989). The effect of distant audiences on students' writing. *American Educational Research Journal, 26* (2), 143–159.

Collins, A. (1990). The role of computer technology in restructuring schools. In K. Sheingold & M. Tucker (Eds.), *Restructuring for learning with technology.* New York: CTE, Bank Street College.

Collins, A., Brown, J. S., & Newman, S. E. (1989). Cognitive apprenticeship: Teaching the crafts of reading, writing, and mathematics. In L. B. Resnick (Ed.), *Knowing, learning, and instruction: Essays in honor of Robert Glaser* (pp. 453–494). Hillsdale, NJ: Erlbaum.

Computer Science and Telecommunications Board, National Research Council. (2001). Youth, pornography, and the Internet: Can we provide sound choices for a safe environment? Washington, DC: National Academy Press.

Consumer Reports Online. (2001, March). *Digital chaperones for kids: Which Internet filters protect the best, which get in the way?* [On-line]. Available: http://www.consumerreports.org/Special/ ConsumerInterest/Reports/0103fil0.html

COPA. (2000, October). Final report of the (COPA) Commission presented to Congress [On-line]. Available: http://copacommission.org/report

Corcoran, T. B. (1990). Schoolwork: Perspectives on workplace reform in public schools. In M. W. McLaughlin, J. E. Talbert, & N. Bascia (Eds.), *The contexts of teaching in secondary schools: Teachers' realities* (pp. 142–166). New York: Teachers College Press.

Crandall, D. P., & Associates. (1983). *People, policies, and practices: Examining the chain of school improvement: Vols. 1–4, 10.* Andover, MA: Network.

Cremin, L. A. (1964). *The transformation of the school: Progressivism in American education, 1876–1957.* New York: Vintage Books.

Cuban, L. (1986). *Teachers and machines: The classroom use of technology since 1920.* New York: Teachers College Press.

Cuban, L. (1990). Reforming again, again, and again. *Educational Researcher, 19*(1), 3–13.

Cummings, J., & Sayers, D. (1995). *Brave new schools: Challenging cultural illiteracy through global learning networks.* New York: St. Martin's Press.

Curry, B. (1992). *Instituting enduring innovations: Achieving continuity of change of higher education.* (ASHE-ERIC Higher Education Report No. 7). Washington, DC: George Washington University, School of Education and Human Development.

Curtis, P. (1997). Mudding: Social phenomena in text-based virtual realities. In S. Kiesler (Ed.), *Culture of the Internet* (pp. 121–142). Hillsdale, NJ: Erlbaum.

Curtiss, P. M., & Curtiss, K. E. (1995). What second graders taught college students and vice versa. *Education Leadership, 53*(2), 60–63.

Daft, R., & Becker, S. (1978). *Innovation in organizations.* New York: Elsevier.

Davidson, A. L. (1996). *Making and molding identity in schools: Student narratives on race, gender and academic engagement.* Albany: State University of New York Press.

Davidson, A. L. (1999). Negotiating social differences: Youths' assessments of educators' strategies. *Urban Education, 34*(3), 338–369.

Davidson, A. L., & Schofield, J. W. (2002). Female voices in virtual reality: Drawing young girls into an on-line world. In A. Renninger & W. Shumar (Eds.), *Building virtual communities: Learning and change in cyberspace.* New York: Cambridge University Press.

Davidson, A. L., Schofield, J. W., & Stocks, J. E. (2001). Professional cultures and collaborative efforts: A case study of technologists and educators working for change. *Information Society, 17,* 21–32.

Davies, M. S. (1995). "Virtually integrated classrooms:" Using the Internet to eliminate the effects of unconstitutional racial segregation in the public schools. *Journal of Law and Education, 24*(4), 567–599.

Dawson, J. A. (1985). *School improvement programs in thirteen urban schools: A report of a four-year documentation study.* Philadelphia: Research for Better Schools.

Detwiler, F. (1994). A tale of two districts. *Educational Leadership, 51*(4), 24–28.

Dimitraidis, G., & Kamberelis, G. (1997, May). Shifting terrains: Mapping education within a global landscape. *Annals of the American Academy of Political and Social Science, 551,* 137–150.

Donath, R. (1995, September). The AT&T learning network: How English teaching can change in the days of the data highway. *Educational Media International, 32*(3), 140–145.

Doyle, W., & Ponder, G. A. (1978). The practicality ethic in teacher decision-making. *Interchange, 8*(3), 1–12.

Education Commission of the States. (1983, November). *A summary of major reports on education.* Denver, CO: Author.

Egbert, R. L., & Kluender, M. M. (1984). Time as an element of school success. In R. L. Egbert & M. M. Kluender (Eds.), *Using research to improve teacher education: The Nebraska consortium* (Teacher Education Monograph No. 1) (pp. 89–107). Washington, DC: Clearinghouse on Teacher Education.

Ellsworth, J. H. (1994). *Education on the Internet.* Indianapolis: Sams.

Erickson, F. D. (1993). Transformation and school success: The politics and culture of educational achievement. In E. Jacob & C. Jordan (Eds.), *Minority education: Anthropological perspectives* (pp. 27–52). Norwood, NJ: Ablex.

Evans-Andris, M. (1996). *An apple for the teacher: Computers and work in elementary schools.* Thousand Oaks, CA: Corwin Press.

Fabos, B., & Young, M. (1999). Telecommunication in the classroom: Rhetoric versus reality. *Review of Educational Research, 69*(3), 217–259.

Feldman, A. (1999, April). *Network science: An assessment.* Paper presented to Planning for Second Information Technology in Education Study (P-SITES), Menlo Park, CA.

Feldman, A., Konold, C., & Coulter, B. (2000). *Network science a decade later: The Internet and classroom learning.* Hillsdale, NJ: Erlbaum.

Fine, M. (1993). Sexuality, schooling, and adolescent females: The missing discourse of desire. In L. Weis & M. Fine (Eds.), *Beyond silenced voices: Class, race and gender in United States schools* (pp. 75–99). Albany: State University of New York Press.

Flinders, D. J. (1989). *Voices from the classroom: Educational policy can inform practice.* Eugene, OR: Eric Clearinghouse on Educational Management, University of Oregon.

Frederick, R. (1986). A later elementary school group: 20–30 children—ages 8–10. In J. Moyer (Ed.), *Selecting educational equipment and materials for school and home* (pp. 63–70). Wheaton, MD: Association for Childhood Education International.

Fredrick, W. C., & Walberg, H. J. (1980). Learning as a function of time. *Journal of Educational Research, 73,* 183–194.

Fullan, M. (1993). Change processes in secondary schools: Toward a more fundamental agenda. In M. McLaughlin, J. Talbert, & N. Bascia (Eds.), *The contexts of teaching in secondary school: Teachers' realities* (pp. 224–255). New York: Teachers College Press.

Fullan, M., & Newton, E. (1988). School principals and change processes in the secondary school. *Canadian Journal of Education, 13*, 404–422.

Fullan, M. G., & Stiegelbauer, S. (1991). *The new meaning of educational change.* (2nd ed.). New York: Teachers College Press.

Futoran, G. C., Schofield, J. W., & Eurich-Fulcer, R. (1995). The Internet as a K–12 educational resource: Emerging issues of information access and freedom. *Computers and Education, 24*, 229–236.

Gallini, J., & Helman, K. (1995). Audience awareness in technology-mediated environments. *Journal of Educational Computing Research, 13*(3), 245–261.

Garner, R., & Gillingham, M. (1996). *Internet communication in six classrooms: Conversations across time, space, and culture.* Hillsdale, NJ: Erlbaum.

Glaser, B., & Strauss, A. (1967). *The discovery of grounded theory.* Chicago: Aldine.

Goldman, S., Chaiklin, S., & McDermott, R. (1994). Crossing borders electronically. In G. Spindler & L. Spindler (Eds.), *Pathways to cultural awareness* (pp. 247–283). Thousand Oaks, CA: Corwin Press.

Goodlad, J. I. (1984). *A place called school: Prospects for the future.* New York: McGraw-Hill.

Goodman, P. S., & Dean, J. W. (1984). Creating long-term organizational change. In P. S. Goodman and Associates (Eds.), *Change in Organizations* (pp. 226–279). San Francisco: Jossey-Bass.

Grant, G. (1988). *The world we created at Hamilton High.* Cambridge, MA: Harvard University Press.

Green, K. C., & Gilbert, S. W. (1995, March/April). Great expectations: Content, communications, productivity, and role of information technology in higher education. *Change, 27*(2), 8–18.

Grey, D. (1999). *The Internet in school.* New York: Cassell Academic.

Gross, N., Giaquinta, J., & Bernstein, M. (1971). *Implementing organizational innovations: A sociological analysis of planned educational change.* New York: Basic Books.

Hadley, M., & Sheingold, K. (1993). Commonalities and distinctive patterns in teachers' integration of computers. *American Journal of Education, 101*(3), 261–315.

Harding, S. (Ed.). (1987). *Feminism and methodology.* Bloomington: Indiana University Press.

Hargreaves, A. (1993). Individualism and individuality: Reinterpreting the teacher culture. In J. W. Little & M. W. McLaughlin (Eds.), *Teachers' work: Individuals, colleagues, and contexts* (pp. 51–76). New York: Teachers College Press.

Hart, A. (1985). Case study prepared for the Utah State Office of Education. Salt Lake City: University of Utah.

Hativa, N. (1994). What you design is not what you get (WYDINWYG): Cognitive, affective, and social impacts of learning with an ILS—An integration of findings from six years of qualitative and quantitative studies. *International Journal of Educational Research, 21*(1), 81–112.

Heaviside, S., Farris, E., Malitz, G., & Carpenter, J. (1995). *Advanced telecommunications in U.S. public schools, K–12.* (Publication No. NCES 95–731). Washington, DC: U.S. Printing Office.

Henderson, V. L., & Dweck, C. S. (1990). Motivation and achievement. In S. S. Feldman & G. R. Elliott (Eds.), *At the threshold: The developing adolescent* (pp. 308–329). Cambridge, MA: Harvard University Press.

Heyink, J. W., & Tymstra, T. J. (1993). The function of qualitative research. *Social Indicators Research, 29,* 291–305.

Hodas, S. (1996). Technology refusal and the organizational culture of schools. In R. Kling (Ed.), *Computerization and controversy: Value conflicts and social choices* (pp. 197–218). New York: Academic Press.

Hof, R. (1997, February 10). Netspeed at Netscape. *Business Week* [Online]. Available: http://www.businessweek.com/search/97browsi/htm

Hoffman, D. L., & Novak, T. P. (1999). *The evolution of the digital divide: Examining the relationship of race to Internet access and usage over time.* Paper prepared for the public conference Understanding the Digital Economy: Data, Tools and Research, Vanderbilt University: Owen School of Management [On-line]. Available: http://www2000.ogsm.vanderbilt.edu

Honey, M. (1994). NII roadblocks: Why do so few educators use the Internet? *Electronic Learning, 14*(4), 12–13.

Honey, M., & Henriquez, A. (1993). *Telecommunications and K–12 educators: Findings from a national survey.* New York: Center for Technology in Education. (ERIC Document Reproduction Service No. 359 923)

Honey, M., & Moeller, B. (1990). *Teachers' beliefs and technology integration: Different values, different understandings* (Tech. Rep. No. 6). New York: CTE, Bank Street College.

Huberman, M. (1993). The model of the independent artisan in teachers' professional relations. In J. W. Little & M. W. McLaughlin (Eds.), *Teachers' work: Individuals, colleagues, and contexts* (pp. 11–50). New York: Teachers College Press.

Huberman, M., & Miles, M. (1984). *Innovation up close: How school improvement works.* New York: Plenum.

Hunter, B. (1992). Linking for learning: Computer-and-communications network support for nationwide innovation in education. *Journal of Science Education and Technology, 1*(1), 23–34.

Kantrowitz, B., Rosenberg, D., & King, P. (1994, May 16). Men, women, & computers. *Newsweek* [On-line]. Available: http://archives8.newsbank.com

Kerr, S. (1996). Visions of sugarplums, the future of technology, education and the schools. In S. T. Kerr (Ed.), *Technology and the future of schooling* (pp. 1–27). Chicago: University of Chicago Press.

King, J., Grinter, R. E., & Pickering, J. M. (1997). The rise and fall of Netville: The saga of a cyberspace construction boomtown in the great divide. In S. Kiesler (Ed.), *Culture of the Internet* (pp. 3–33). Hillsdale, NJ: Erlbaum.

Kling, R. (1991). Computerization and social transformations. *Science, technology, and human values, 16*(3), 342–367.

Kling, R. (1992). Behind the terminal: The critical role of computing infrastructure in effective information systems' development and use. In W. Cotterman & J. Senn (Eds.), *Challenges and strategies for research in systems development* (pp. 327–373). New York: Wiley.

Kling, R., & Scacchi, W. (1982). The web of computing: Computer technology as social organization. In M. C. Yovits (Ed.), *Advances in computers: Vol. 21* (pp. 1–90). New York: Academic Press.

Kozol, J. (1991). *Savage inequalities: Children in America's schools.* New York: Harper Perennial.

Krantz, M. (1997, August 11). Censor's sensibility. *Time,* [On-line]. Available: http://www.cnn.com/ALLPOLITICS/1997/08/04/time/internet.html

Kulik, C., & Kulik, J. (1991). Effectiveness of computer-based instruction in secondary schools. *Computers in Human Behavior, 7,* 75–94.

Kulik, J. A., Bangert-Drowns, R. L., & Williams, G. W. (1983). Effects of computer-based teaching on secondary school students. *Journal of Educational Psychology, 75,* 19–26.

Kvale, S. (1996). *InterViews: An introduction to qualitative research interviewing.* Thousand Oaks, CA: Sage.

Lagemann, E. C., & Shulman, L. S. (1999). *Issues in education research: Problems and possibilities.* San Francisco: Jossey-Bass.

Lepper, M. R., & Chabay, R. W. (1985). Intrinsic motivation and instruction: Conflicting views on the role of motivational processes in computer-based education. *Educational Psychology, 20*(4), 217–230.

Lepper, M. R., & Malone, T. W. (1987). Intrinsic motivation and instructional effectiveness in computer-based education. In R. E. Snow & M. J. Farr (Eds.), *Aptitude, learning, and instruction: Vol.3. Conative and affective process analyses* (pp. 255–296). Hillsdale, NJ: Erlbaum.

Lewis, G., Baca, L., Bansford, J., & Commins, N. (1985). Factors influencing Title VII bilingual program institutionalization. *Journal of Educational Equity and Leadership, 5(4)*, 309–319.

Lewis, L., Parsad, B., Carey, N., Bartfai, N., Farris, E., & Smerdon, B. (1999). *Teacher quality: A report on the preparation and qualifications of public school teachers.* U.S. Department of Education, National Center for Education Statistics. Washington, DC: U.S. Government Printing Office. Available: http://nces.ed.gov/pubs99/1999080.htm

Lieberman, A., & Miller, L. (1990). The social realities of teaching. In A. Lieberman (Ed.), *Schools as collaborative cultures: Creating the future now* (pp. 165–193). Bristol, PA: Falmer Press.

Little, J. W. (1982). Norms of collegiality and experimentation: Workplace conditions of school success. *American Educational Research Journal, 19(3)*, 325–340.

Little, J. W. (1990a). Conditions of professional development in secondary schools. In M. W. McLaughlin, J. E. Talbert, & N. Bascia (Eds.), *The contexts of teaching in secondary schools: Teachers' realities* (pp. 187–223). New York: Teachers College Press.

Little, J. W. (1990b). Teachers as colleagues. In A. Lieberman (Ed.), *Schools as collaborative cultures: Creating the future now* (pp. 165–193). Bristol, PA: Falmer Press.

Lortie, D. C. (1975). *School teacher: A sociological study.* Chicago: University of Chicago Press.

Loveless, T. (1996). Why aren't computers used more in schools? *Educational policy, 10(4)*, 448–467.

Martin, D. (1991). New findings from qualitative data using hypermedia: Microcomputers, control, and equity. *Computers and Education, 16*, 219–227.

McCarty, P. J. (1995, October). Four days that changed the world (and other amazing Internet stories). *Educational Leadership, 53(2)*, 48–50.

McConnaughey, J. W., & Lader, W. (1999). *Falling through the net: Defining the digital divide.* NTIA Project [On-line]. Available: http://www.ntia.doc.gov.ntiahome/fttn99/contents.html

McConnaughey, J. W., Lader, W., Chin, R., & Everette, D. (1998). *Falling through the net II: New data on the digital divide.* NTIA Project. [On-line]. Available: http://www.ntia.doc.gov/ntiahome/net2/falling.html.

McDonald, J. P. (1996). Below the surface of school reform: Vision and its foes. In L. Schauble & R. Glaser (Eds.), *Innovations in learning: New environments for education* (pp. 353–368). Hillsdale, NJ: Erlbaum.

McKee, S. (1999, November). Do wired schools mean better learning? [Letter to the editor]. *PC World, 17(11)*, 23.

McKinsey & Company, Inc. (1995). *Connecting K–12 schools to the information superhighway.* National Information Infrastructure Advisory Council (NIIAC). Palo Alto, CA: Author.

McLaughlin, M. W. (1993). What matters most in teachers' workplace context? In J. W. Little & M. W. McLaughlin (Eds.), *Teachers' work: Individuals, colleagues, and contexts* (pp. 79–103). New York: Teachers College Press.

McPherson, G. (1972). *Small town teacher.* Cambridge, MA: Harvard University Press.

Means, B. (1994). Introduction: Using technology to advance educational goals. In B. Means (Ed.), *Technology and education reform* (pp. 1–21). San Francisco: Jossey-Bass.

Means, B., Blando, J., Olson, K., Middleton, T., Morocco, C., Remz, A., & Zorfass, J. (1993). *Using technology to support education reform.* U.S. Department of Education and Office of Educational Research. Washington, DC: U.S. Government Printing Office.

Mehta, M. D., & Plaza, D. E. (1997). Pornography in cyberspace: An exploration of what's in USENET. In S. Kiesler (Ed.), *Culture of the Internet* (pp. 53–67). Hillsdale, NJ: Erlbaum.

Mendels, P. (1999, September 8). Survey finds teachers unprepared for computer use. In *New York Times* [On-line]. Available: http://www.nytimes.com/library/tech/99/09/cyber/education/08education.html

Mendels, P. (2000, February 23). Crumbling schools have trouble getting online. In *New York Times* [On-line]. Available: http://www.nytimes.com/library/tech/00/02/cyber/education/23education.html

Meyer, J. W., Scott, W. R., & Deal, T. E. (1981). Institutional and technical sources of organizational structure: Explaining the structure of educational organizations. In J. W. Meyer & W. R. Scott (Eds.), *Organizational environments: Ritual and rationality* (pp. 45–67). Thousand Oaks, CA: Sage.

Mickelson, K. D. (1997). Seeking social support: Parents in electronic support groups. In S. Kiesler (Ed.), *Culture of the Internet* (pp. 157–178). Hillsdale, NJ: Erlbaum.

Midgley, C., Feldlauger, H., & Eccles, J. (1989). Student/teacher relations and attitudes towards mathematics before and after the transition to junior high school. *Child Development, 90,* 981–992.

Miles, M. (1983). Unraveling the mystery of institutionalization. *Educational Leadership, 41*(3), 14–19.

Miles, M., & Ekholm, M. (1991, April). *Will new structures stay restructured?* Paper presented at the annual meeting of the American Educational Research Association, Chicago, IL.

Miles, M., & Louis, K. S. (1987). Research on institutionalization: A reflective review. In M. B. Miles, M. Ekholm, & R. Vandenberghe (Eds.), *Lasting school improvement: Exploring the process of institutionalization* (pp. 25–44). Leuven, Belgium: Acco.

Morris, D. E. (1996). Institutionalization and the reform process: A system dynamics perspective. *Educational Policy, 10*(4), 427–445.

Mostow, J., Aist, G., Huang, C., Junker, B., Kennedy, R., Lan, H., Latimer, D., IV, O'Connor, R., Tassone, R., & Wierman, A. (2000). *Controlled evaluation of a reading tutor that listens* [On-line]. Available: http://www.cs.cmu.edu/~listen

Murphy, K., Naples, L., Schofield, J. W., Davidson, A., & Stocks, J. E. (1997, March). Difference blindness/blindness difference: Student explorations of "disability" over the Internet. In P. Phelan (Chair), *Transcending borders: Exploring relationships among programs, practices, and students' ability to challenge social divisions.* Symposium conducted at the meeting of the American Educational Research Association, Chicago, IL.

National Commission on Educational Excellence. (1983). *A nation at risk: The imperative for educational reform.* Washington, DC: U.S. Government Printing Office.

Neilsen, L. (1998). Coding the light: Rethinking generational authority in a rural high school telecommunications project. In D. Reinking, M. C. McKenna, L. D. Labbo, & R. D. Kieffer (Eds.), *Handbook of literacy and technology: Transformations in a post-typographic world* (pp. 129–143). Hillsdale, NJ: Erlbaum.

Newman, D. (1992). Technology as support for school structure and school restructuring. *Phi Delta Kappan, 74,* 308–315.

Niemiec, R. P., & Walberg, H. J. (1985). Computers and achievement in the elementary schools. *Journal of Educational Computing Research, 1*(4), 435–440.

Oakes, J. (1985). *Keeping track: How schools structure inequality.* New Haven, CT: Yale University Press.

Oettinger, A. G. (1969). *Run computer run: The mythology of educational innovation.* New York: Collier Books.

Olson, J. (1988). *Schoolworlds/microworlds: Computers and the culture of the classroom.* Oxford: Pergamon Press.

Olson, S. (1976). *Ideas and data: Process and practice of social research.* Homewood, IL: Dorsey Press.

O'Neill, K., & Gomez, L. (1998, November). Online mentors: Experimenting in science class. *Educational Leadership, 54,* 39–42.

Orfield, G., & Yun, J. (1999). *Resegregation in American schools.* Cambridge, MA: Harvard University, Civil Rights Project [On-line]. Available: http://mirror.shnet.edu.cn/harvard/www.law.harvard.edu/groups/ci vilrights/publications/resegregation99.html

Organization for Economic Co-Operation and Development. (1999). *Education policy analysis 1999.* (Report No. 50921 1999). Paris, France: The Centre for Educational Research and Innovation [On-line]. Available: http://www.oecd.org

Owston, R. D. (1997). The World Wide Web: A technology to enhance teaching and learning? *Educational Researcher, 26*(2), 27–33.

Papert, S. (1980). *Mindstorms: Children, computers, and powerful ideas.* New York: Basic Books.

Papert, S. (1993). *The children's machine: Rethinking school in the age of the computer.* New York: Basic Books.

Pate, P. E. (1986). A middle school group: 20–30 children—ages 11–14. In P. Moyer (Ed.), *Selecting educational equipment and materials for school and home* (pp. 71–73). Wheaton, MD: Association for Childhood Education International.

Peck, C., Cuban, L., & Kirkpatrick, H. (2000). *Techno-promoter dreams, student realities.* Unpublished manuscript, Stanford University, Department of Education.

Pelgrum, W. J., & Plomp, T. (1991). *The use of computers in education worldwide: Results from the IEA "Computers in education" survey in nineteen educational systems.* Oxford: Pergamon Press.

Perkins, D. N. (1985). The fingertip effect: How information processing technology shapes thinking. *Educational Researcher, 14*(7), 11–17.

Perlman, L. J. (1992). *School's out: Hyperlearning, the new technology, and the end of education.* New York: William Morrow.

Phelan, P., Davidson, A. L., & Yu, H. T. (1998). *Adolescents' worlds: Negotiating family, peers, and school.* New York: Teachers College Press.

Phillips, D. C. (1990). Subjectivity and objectivity: An objective inquiry. In E. W. Eisner & A. Peshkin (Eds.), *Qualitative inquiry in education* (pp. 19–37). New York: Teachers College Press.

Piller, C. (1992, September). Separate realities: The creation of the technological underclass in America's public schools. *MacWorld, 9,* 218–230.

Pittman, T. S. (1998). Motivation. In D. T. Gilbert, S. T. Fiske, & G. Lindzey (Eds.), *The Handbook of Social Psychology* (pp. 549–590). New York: McGraw-Hill.

Post, D. (1992). Through Joshua Gap: Curricular control and the constructed community. *Teachers College Record, 93*(4), 673–696.

Potter, R. L. (1992). *Using telecommunications in middle school reading.* Bloomington, IN: Phi Delta Kappa Educational Foundation.

Powell, A. F., Farrar, E., & Cohen, D. K. (1985). *The shopping mall high school: Winners and losers in the educational marketplace.* Boston: Houghton Mifflin.

Ratcliffe, J. (1983). Notions of validity in qualitative research methodology. *Knowledge Creation, Diffusion, Utilization, 5*(2), 147–167.

Ravitz, J. L., Becker, H. J., & Wong, Y. T. (2000). *Constructivist-compatible beliefs and practices among U.S. teachers.* (Teaching, Learning, and Computing: 1998 National Survey Report No. 4). Irvine, CA: University of California, Irvine, and University of Minnesota, Center for Research on Information Technology and Organizations. [On-line]. Available: http://www.crito.uci.edu/TLC/findings/Internet-Use/startpage.html

Reed, C., & Williams, R. (1993). Institutionalizing action research in the Puget Sound educational consortium member districts. (ERIC Document Reproduction Service No. EA025251) [On-line]. Available: http://ericae.net/ericdb/ED361872.htm

Reinharz, S. (1992). *Feminist methods in social research.* New York: Oxford University Press.

Rezabeck. L. L. (1993). Computers and copyright concerns. In R. Muffoletto and N. N. Knupfer (Eds.), *Computers in Education: Social, political, and historical perspectives.* Cresskill, NJ: Hampton Press.

Richardson, J. T., Stewart, M. W., & Simmonds, R. B. (1978). Researching a fundamentalist commune. In J. Needleman & G. Baker (Eds.), *Understanding the new religions.* New York: Seabury Press.

Riel, M. (1992). Making connections from urban schools. *Education and Urban Society, 24*(4), 477-488.

Roberts, N., Blakeslee, G., Brown, M., & Lenk, C. (1990). *Integrating telecommunications into education.* Upper Saddle River, NJ: Prentice Hall.

Roeser, R. W., Midgley, C., & Urdan, T. (1996). Perceptions of the school psychological environment and early adolescents' psychological and behavioral functioning in school: The mediating role of goals and belonging. *Journal of Educational Psychology, 88*(3), 408–422.

Ronnkvist, A. M., Dexter, S. L., & Anderson, R. E. (2000). *Technology support: Its depth, breadth, and impact in America's schools.* (Teaching, Learning, and Computing: 1998 National Survey Report No. 5). Irvine, CA: University of California, Irvine, and University of Minnesota, Center for Research Information Technology and Organizations [On-line]. Available: http://www.crito.uci.edu/TLC/findings/Internet-Use/startpage.html

Rosenholtz, S. J. (1987). Education reform strategies: Will they increase teacher commitment? *American Journal of Education, 95,* 534–562.

Samson, G. E., Niemiec, R., Weinstein, T., & Walberg, H. J. (1986, Summer). Effects of computer-based instruction on secondary school achievement: A quantitative synthesis. *AEDS Journal, 20,* 312–326.

Sandholtz, J. H., & Ringstaff, C. (1996). Teacher change in technology-rich classrooms. In C. Fisher, D. Dwyer, & K. Yocam (Eds.), *Education and technology: Reflections on computing in classrooms* (pp. 281–299). San Francisco: Apple Press.

Sandholtz, J. H., Ringstaff, C., & Dwyer, D. C. (1997). *Teaching with technology: Creating student-centered classrooms.* New York: Teachers College Press.

Sarason, S. B. (1971). *The culture of the school and the problem of change.* Needham Heights, MA: Allyn & Bacon.

Sarason, S. B. (1990). *The predictable failure of educational reform: Can we change course before it's too late?* San Francisco: Jossey-Bass.

Schofield, J. W. (1982). *Black and white in school: Trust, tension, or tolerance?* New York: Praeger.

Schofield, J. W. (1989). *Black and white in school: Trust, tension, or tolerance?* (Rev. ed.). New York: Teachers College Press.

Schofield, J. W. (1994). Barriers to computer usage in secondary school. In C. Huff & T. Finholt (Eds.), *Social issues in computing: Putting computing in its place* (pp. 547–578). New York: McGraw-Hill.

Schofield, J. W. (1995). *Computers and classroom culture.* New York: Cambridge University Press.

Schofield, J. W. (1997). Computers and classroom social processes: A review of the literature. *Social Science Computer Review, 15*(1), 27–39.

Schofield, J. W., & Davidson, A. L. (1997). The Internet in school: The shaping of use by organizational, structural, and cultural factors. In S. Lobodzinski & I. Tomek (Chairs), *Proceedings of WebNet 97—World Conference of the WWW, Internet, and Intranet* (pp. 485–489).

Charlottesville, VA: Association for the Advancement of Computing in Education.

Schofield, J. W., & Davidson, A. L. (in press-a). Achieving equality of student Internet access within schools. In A. Eagly, R. Baron, & L. Hamilton (Eds.), *The social psychology of group identity and social conflict.* Washington, DC: APA Books.

Schofield, J. W., & Davidson, A. L. (in press-b). The impact of Internet use on the fourth R—Relationship between teachers and students. *Mind, Culture, and Activity.*

Schofield, J. W., Eurich-Fulcer, R., & Britt, C. L. (1994). Teachers, computer tutors, and teaching: The artificially intelligent tutor as an agent for classroom change. *American Educational Research Journal, 31*(3), 579–607.

Shade, L. R. (1999). Net gains: Does access equal equity? *Journal of Information Technology Impact, 1*(1), 25–42.

Sheingold, K. (1990, December). Restructuring for learning with technology: The potential for synergy. In K. Sheingold & M. S. Tucker (Eds.), *Restructuring for learning with technology* (pp. 9–27). New York: CTE, Bank Street College; and Rochester, NY: National Center on Education and the Economy.

Singleton, R. A., Jr., Straits, B. C., & Straits, M. M. (1993). *Approaches to social research.* (2nd ed.). New York: Oxford University Press.

Sizer, T. R. (1985). *Horace's compromise: The dilemma of the American high school.* Boston: Houghton Mifflin.

Sjogren, D. D. (1967). Achievement as a function of study time. *American Educational Research Journal, 4,* 337–343.

Smith, C., Snir, J., & Grosslight, L. (1992). Using conceptual models to facilitate conceptual change: The case of weight/density differentiation. *Cognition and Instruction, 9*(3), 221–283.

Smith, L. M., & Geoffrey, W. (1968). *The complexities of an urban classroom.* Austin, TX: Holt, Rinehart and Winston.

Smith L. M., & Keith, P. (1971). *The anatomy of educational innovation.* New York: Wiley.

Songer, N. B. (1996). Exploring learning opportunities in coordinated network-enhanced classrooms: A case of kids as global scientists. *Journal of Learning Sciences, 5,* 297–328.

Sperling, M. (1996). Revisiting the writing-speaking connection: Challenges for research on writing and speaking instruction. *Review of Educational Research, 66*(1), 53–86.

Sproull, L., & Faraj, S. (1997). Atheism, sex, and databases: The net as a social technology. In S. Kiesler (Ed.), *Culture of the Internet* (pp. 35–51). Hillsdale, NJ: Erlbaum.

Sproull, L., & Kiesler, S. (1991). *Connections: New ways of working in the networked organization.* Cambridge, MA: MIT Press.

Spuck, D., & Shipman, K. (1989). The establishment of a new school district: A study of power and conflict. *Planning and Changing, 20*(3), 180–189.

Stearns, M. S., David, J. L., Hanson, S. G., Ringstaff, C., & Schneider, S. A. (1991, January). *Cupertino-Fremont model technology schools project research findings: Executive summary (Teacher-centered model of technology integration: End of year 3).* Menlo Park, CA: SRI International.

Stevenson, H. W., & Nerison-Low, R. (1999). *To sum it up: Case studies of education in Germany, Japan, and the United States.* Office of Educational Research and Improvement. U.S. Department of Education [On-line]. Available: http://www.ed.gov/offices/OERI/SAI

Sussman, L. (1977). *Tales out of school: Implementing organizational change in the elementary grades.* Philadelphia: Temple University Press.

Talab, R. S. (1986). *Commonsense copyright: A guide to the new technologies.* Jefferson, NC: McFarland.

Talbert, J., & McLaughlin, M. (1993). Understanding teaching in context. In D. K. Cohen, M. W. McLaughlin, & J. Talbert (Eds.), *Teaching for understanding: Challenges for policy and practice* (pp. 167–206). San Francisco: Jossey-Bass.

Tapscott, D. (1998). *Growing up digital: The rise of the Net generation.* New York: McGraw-Hill.

Taylor, S. J., & Bogdan, R. (1998). *Introduction to qualitative research methods: A guidebook and resource.* (3rd ed.). New York: Wiley.

Teachers feel computer gap with students. (1989, August 29). *Pittsburgh Post Gazette,* p. 11.

Thomas, K. (2000, February 17). Online schoolkids search, play all day: Educational sites given short shrift by students. *USA Today,* p. 3D [On-line]. Available: http://pqasb.pqarchiver.com/USAToday/main/doc/

Turkle, S. (1984). *The second self: Computers and the human spirit.* New York: Simon & Schuster.

Turkle, S. (1995). *Life on screen: Identity in the age of the Internet.* New York: Simon & Schuster.

Tyack, D., & Tobin, W. (1994). The "grammar" of schooling: Why has it been so hard to change? *American Educational Research Journal, 31*(3), 453–479.

U.S. Congress, Office of Technology Assessment. (1988). *Power on! New tools for teaching and learning.* (OTA-SET-379). Washington, DC: U.S. Government Printing Office.

U.S. Congress, Office of Technology Assessment. (1995). *Teachers and technology: Making the connection.* (OTA-EHR-616). Washington, DC: U.S. Government Printing Office.

U.S. Department of Education. (1993). *Digest of Educational Statistics.* Washington, DC: Author.

U.S. Department of Education. (1999). *The educational system in the United States: Case study findings.* Washington, DC: U.S. Government Printing Office [On-line]. Available: http://www.ed.gov

U.S. Department of Labor. (1991). *What work requires of schools: A SCANS report for America 2000.* Washington, DC: Secretary's Commission on Achieving Necessary Skills, U.S. Department of Labor.

Van den Berg, W., Van Velzen, W. G., Miles, M. B., Ekholm, M., & Hameyer, U. (1986). *Making school improvement work.* Heverlee, Belgium: Acco.

Viadero, D. (1997). A tool for learning. *Education Week, 17*(11), 12–18.

Walker, D. (1984). Promise, potential, and pragmatism: Computers in high school. *Institute for Research in Educational Finance and Government Policy Notes, 5*(3), 3–4.

Walker, D. (1996). Toward an ACOT of tomorrow. In C. Fisher, D. Dwyer, & K. Yocam (Eds.), *Education and technology: Reflections on computing in classrooms* (pp. 91–106). San Francisco: Apple Press.

Wallace, R., Kupperman, J., Krajcik, J., & Soloway, E. (2000). Students online in a sixth-grade classroom. *Journal of the Learning Sciences, 9*(1), 75–104.

Webb, E., Campbell, D., Schwartz, R., & Sechrest, L. (1966). *Unobtrusive measures: Nonreactive research in the social sciences.* Skokie, IL: Rand McNally.

Wehlage, G. G., & Rutter, R. A. (1986). Dropping out: How much do schools contribute to the problem? *Teachers College Record, 87,* 374–392.

Wentzel, K. R. (1998). Social relationships and motivation in middle school: The role of parents, teachers, and peers. *Journal of Educational Psychology, 90*(2), 202–209.

Wentzel, K. R., & Wigfield, A. (1998). Academic and social motivational influences on students' academic performance. *Educational Psychology Review, 10*(2), 155–175.

Wertheimer, R. (1990). The geometry proof tutor: An "intelligent" computer-based tutor in the classroom. *Mathematics Teacher, 83,* 308–317.

Willard, N. (2000). Choosing not to go down the not-so-good cyberstreets [On-line]. Available: http://netizen.uoregon.edu/documents/nwnas.html

Willis, J., & Mehlinger, H. (1996). Information technology and teacher education. In J. Sikula (Ed.), *Handbook of research on teacher education* (pp. 978–1029). (2nd ed.). New York: Macmillan.

Wilson, B., & Corcoran, T. (1988). *Successful secondary schools: Visions of excellence in American public schools.* East Sussex, England: Falmer Press.

Windschitl, M. (1998). The WWW and classroom research: What path should we take? *Educational Researcher, 27*(1), 28–33.

Wright, W., Jr. (1992). Breaking down barriers: High schools and computer conferencing. In G. Hawisher & P. LeBlanc (Eds.), *Re-imagining computers and composition: Teaching and research in the virtual age* (pp. 102–114). Portsmouth, NH: Boynton/Cook.

Young, V., Haertel, G., Ringstaff, C., & Means, B. (1998). *Evaluating global lab curriculum: Impacts and issues of implementing a project-based science curriculum.* Menlo Park, CA: SRI International.

Zehr, M. A. (1997). Partnering with the Public. *Education Week, 17*(11), 36–39.

Zuboff, S. (1988). *In the age of the smart machine.* New York: Basic Books.

Name Index

∼∼ Subject Index